Unlocking the Groove

Profiles in Popular Music

Glenn Gass and Jeffrey Magee, editors

WITHDRAWN
Ohio University Libraries

Unlocking
the
Groove

Music
GV
1796
.E44
B88
2006
c.2

Rhythm, Meter, and
Musical Design
in Electronic Dance Music

Mark J. Butler

Indiana University Press | Bloomington and Indianapolis

OHIO UNIVERSITY
MUSIC/DANCE LIBRARY

This book is a publication of

Indiana University Press
601 North Morton Street
Bloomington, IN 47404-3797 USA

http://iupress.indiana.edu

Telephone orders   800-842-6796
Fax orders   812-855-7931
Orders by e-mail   iuporder@indiana.edu

© 2006 by Mark J. Butler

All rights reserved

No part of this book may be reproduced or
utilized in any form or by any means, electronic
or mechanical, including photocopying and
recording, or by any information storage and
retrieval system, without permission in writing
from the publisher. The Association of American
University Presses' Resolution on Permissions
constitutes the only exception to this
prohibition.

The paper used in this publication meets the
minimum requirements of American National
Standard for Information Sciences—Permanence
of Paper for Printed Library Materials, ANSI
Z39.48-1984.

Manufactured in the United States of America

Library of Congress Cataloging-in-Publication Data

Butler, Mark J. (Mark Jonathan), date
        Unlocking the groove : rhythm, meter, and musical design in electronic
dance music / Mark J. Butler.
              p. cm. — (Profiles in popular music)
        Includes bibliographical references (p.   ), discography, and index.
        ISBN 0-253-34662-2 (cloth : alk. paper) — ISBN 0-253-21804-7 (pbk.
    : alk. paper)   1. Techno music—Analysis, appreciation.   2. Techno music—History
and criticism.   3. Musical meter and rhythm.   I. Title.   II. Series.
      MT146.B88   2005
      786.7'164—dc22   2005020156

                        1   2   3   4   5   11   10   09   08   07   06

WITHDRAWN
Ohio University Libraries

For Richard

WITHDRAWN
Ohio University Libraries

CONTENTS

Acknowledgments

Throughout the course of this project, DJs, producers, and fans of electronic dance music have shared their time and knowledge with me, and I would like to thank them first. Your insights and perspectives have enriched this study in essential ways. In Indiana, where this project began, I learned much from those within the dance music community, who have cultivated their scene with great energy and devotion. For interviews, conversations, and other feedback, I thank DJ Shiva, Adam Jay, DJ Impact, Don Dresser, Jimmi Journey, Micah, Mystik, Neal Blue, Stanley, and Vixen Swift. The Disc Jockeys and Electronic Musicians Association at Indiana University and the IU-Ravers discussion board also provided valuable contexts for my research. In Detroit, Tim Steward was very helpful, as were many other members of the 313-list based around the world. Most recently, in the summer of 2004, I had the privilege of speaking with a number of producers whose music is discussed in this book; my gratitude goes out to Graham Massey of 808 State, Rick Smith of Underworld, and Carl Craig for their willingness to be interviewed. For their assistance in arranging these interviews, thanks also are due to Markus Arnold of 808state.com, Yannick Joubert of dirty.org, Mike Gillespie of The Sunday Club, and Danielle Short at Tomato.

Many people within the music industry were instrumental in facilitating the multimedia components of this project. For their assistance and willingness to help, I would like to express my thanks to Shari Wied at Hal Leonard, Tim Price and Vicki Rees at Minus Inc./Plus 8, Reggie at Planet E, Carola Stoiber at Tresor, Toby Silver at V2, Bobby Robertson and Jillian Tribble at Warner-Chappell, and Pete Gardiner at ZTT. Moreover, I am deeply appreciative to the many musicians who graciously agreed to share their music, including Carl Craig, 808 State, James Ruskin, Jeff Mills, Kenny Larkin, Mario Più, Richie Hawtin (Plastikman), and Underworld. And finally, I thank Stacy Dominguez at Roland, Nick Hahn at Pioneer, Pablo La Rosa at Stanton, Sruthi Pinnamaneni at Renegade Marketing, Jay Starr at Akai, and Martha Whiteley at Technics for their help with the photographs of electronic dance music equipment that appear in chapter 1.

The research for this book was carried out at two institutions: first at Indiana University, and subsequently at the University of Pennsylvania. Marianne Kielian-

Gilbert, my advisor at Indiana, played a crucial role in shepherding my project through to completion, always taking what I had to say seriously and spending many hours tirelessly poring over my ideas. Robert Hatten, Gretchen Horlacher, and Sue Tuohy each provided distinctive and essential contributions as well. In addition, a writing group consisting of Judy Barger, J. Peter Burkholder, David Griffioen, Luiz Lopes, and Felicia Miyakawa provided key intellectual and emotional support. The IU School of Music provided essential financial backing during the 2001–2002 academic year in the form of a Dissertation-Year Fellowship, and subsequently recognized my work with a Dean's Dissertation Award. Finally, I am also very grateful to the Society for American Music for honoring my research with the Wiley Housewright Award.

Since coming to Penn in the fall of 2003, my colleagues in the Department of Music have continually encouraged my work, asking thoughtful and provocative questions and providing an environment conducive to the completion of my book. Thanks are due in particular to Tim Rommen, who offered valuable feedback on drafts of each chapter during the summer of 2004. In addition, I would like to express my appreciation to Roger Grant and Michael Masci for their assistance with the preparation of the index. I am also very grateful to department staff members Maryellen Malek, Laura Chen, Alfreda Frazier, and Margie Smith, who have helped with countless faxes, mailings, and other matters, and to Eugene Lew, who advised me on the production of musical and audio examples.

My editors at Indiana University Press have been very helpful, and I thank them for their support and assistance. They include Gayle Sherwood, music editor during the first year of work on my book; Suzanne Ryan, who has guided me through the subsequent stages of the project; and assistant music editor Donna Wilson.

Friends in the academic community have been especially important sources of support throughout my work on this project. For many stimulating conversations, feedback on ideas, encouragement, and advice, special thanks are due to Nina Fales, Mark Katz, Fred Maus, Felicia Miyakawa, and Martin Scherzinger. To my friends from Chapel Hill, thanks for driving me all over the state of North Carolina; my interest in this topic began with those clubbing experiences. Thanks also to Brent Talbot for accompanying me to many dance events in Indiana, Detroit, and New York. And to all those who have enlivened my trips to annual conferences through excursions to clubs, thanks for being such great dancing compatriots.

To my parents, I extend my profound gratitude for the love, encouragement, and support they have provided throughout my education and career. And finally, to my partner, Richard Herendeen, who has aided this project in countless ways,

I offer my heartfelt appreciation. Without his support, the completion of this project would not have been possible.

Photograph of Technics SL-1200 MK2 turntable used by permission of Technics USA.

Photographs of Pioneer DJM-600 and Pioneer CDJ-1000 used by permission of Pioneer Electronics (USA), Inc.

Photograph of Final Scratch used by permission of Stanton Magnetics.

Photographs of Roland TR-808 and Roland TB-303 used by permission of Roland Corporation U.S.

Photograph of Akai MPC-2000 used by permission of Akai Professional America.

808 State, "Cubik (Kings County Perspective)," used by permission of ZTT Music.

Carl Craig, "Televised Green Smoke," used by permission of Planet E Communications, Inc.

James Ruskin, "Connected." Written and produced by James Ruskin, Mikrofisch/ BMG Music Publishing Company. Taken from Tresor 145, *Point 2.* Licensed from Tresor Records, Berlin. http://www.tresorberlin.de.

Jeff Mills, "Jerical," used by permission of Tresor Records.

Kenny Larkin, "Track," used by permission of Kenny Larkin.

Mario Più, "Communication (Mas Mix)," used by permission of Warner-Chappell Music.

Plastikman, "Panikattack," used by permission of Plus 8 Records, Ltd.

Underworld, "Cups" (V2/JBO 63881-27042-2), used by courtesy of V2 Records, Inc., and Hal Leonard Corporation.

Getting into the Groove: Approaching the Study of Electronic Dance Music

Introduction

It's the evening of May 27, 2001, and the Detroit Electronic Music Festival is in full swing. Near the waterfront, people are packed in tight, dancing to the rhythms of DJ Stacey Pullen. The scene is full of contrasts: on the one side, the Detroit River flows gently by; on the other, the steel and glass cylinders of the General Motors headquarters rise into the sky. On a surface of unforgiving concrete, sweaty bodies shake loose limbs. The presence of technology is almost overwhelming: the music blasts out of huge speaker stacks, and traditional instruments are nowhere in sight. Instead, the DJ manipulates two turntables and a mixing board, selecting sounds from a variety of vinyl records. And yet the human element is everywhere to be found. It is visible in the joy written across Pullen's face, in the spontaneous creativity of the dancing audience, and in the funk of the bass lines that emerge from the midst of the seemingly endless machine-generated beats.

The crowd is unusually diverse as well. Teenagers from downtown Detroit mingle with suburban kids from across the Midwest. A young raver in a wheelchair, her arms covered from wrist to shoulder with plastic beads, spins about near a group of gay men. A middle-aged African-American woman in a jogging suit listens intently to the music, her eyes closed, while a tour group from Amsterdam takes in the scene. People of all stripes, from all walks of life, have come here to hear this music, yet they respond as a group. The beat can not only be heard, it can be *seen* in their movements, and felt in their bodies.

Sometimes Pullen cuts the bass drum out. The audience turns to him expectantly, awaiting its return. For one measure, and then another, he builds their anticipation, using the mixing board to distort the sounds that remain. As the energy level increases, he gauges their response. A third measure passes by, and a fourth, and then—with an instantaneous flick of the wrist—he brings the beat back in all of its forceful glory. As one the crowd raises their fists into the air and screams with joy, dancing even more energetically than before.

3

In spite of the ubiquitous presence of technology, Pullen is clearly in control. The music that he plays is *thick*—layer upon layer of percussion interspersed with repetitive synthesizer patterns and fragmentary bass lines. Pullen keeps the configuration constantly changing as he brings patterns in and out with the mixing board. Although the texture is dense, each layer offers a distinctive sound, a thread one can follow through the fabric of the music. Some patterns align, while others seem to float independently. Removing certain sounds brings others to the fore. Remarkably, however, the flow never ceases. For a full two hours, Pullen leads the audience through one soundscape after another. Although he constructs his performance from individual records, he shapes it into a continuous musical journey. Rather than separate compositions played one after the other, we hear a single musical tapestry that is constantly transforming.

The common motif running through this cloth, however, is rhythm. Rhythm is evident everywhere: in the motions of the dancers, in the constantly shifting array of patterns coming from the speakers, and in the ways Pullen changes and combines records. The most obvious rhythmic force is the bass-drum beat: loud and insistent, it sounds out the same basic quarter-note pattern throughout most of the performance, and Pullen keeps it at a more or less constant tempo. In many ways, the beat *is* the music. Fans often describe the music simply as "beats" (as in, "let's go to the club and hear some beats"), and from this performance it is clear that the beat also defines the music as dance music. When Pullen removes the beat, the audience's dancing changes dramatically. Some people stop dancing altogether, whereas others continue, albeit hesitantly, as if awaiting the beat's return. In some of these passages there is no reason why the crowd cannot continue to dance, as the sounds that remain continue to present a steady pulse. Yet without the emblematic beat the audience's dancing begins to dissipate. Because the beat commands such stature, removing it and bringing it back is one of the most powerful things a DJ can do.

At the same time, there is an astonishing array of rhythmic diversity beyond the beat. For the most part, the rhythm pattern of each sound within the texture is unique, creating a distinctive set of expectations both individually and in each new textural combination. The patterns themselves are relatively simple, a characteristic that allows them to be interpreted in a variety of ways. Musicians seem to delight in this possibility, presenting each sound in many different contexts and sometimes creating dramatic reinterpretations. They also use technology to create novel rhythmic experiences. For instance, they might explore the tension between mechanically precise patterns and those that bear a more "natural" rhythmic profile, or create combinations of layers that seem to repeat indefinitely without aligning. Rhythm, therefore, is the *raison d'être* of electronic dance music—one of its most prominent and interesting characteristics, and the force that inspires audiences to move with such fervor.

In this book I explore the beats and rhythms that make electronic dance music so rich. Throughout the work I emphasize principles of design that permeate this music from the shortest rhythm pattern to the lengthiest DJ performance. I aim to highlight what is alluring about the various ways in which electronic dance music, or "EDM," shapes time. I am motivated by my own fascination with this repertory, as well as by an apparent paradox underlying a great deal of discussion about EDM. On the one hand, fans, musicians, and critics speak of the rhythmic attributes of EDM more than any other quality; their descriptions of what they love about the music are full of references to "beats," "rhythm," and "time." On the other hand, they often describe these features in surprisingly reductive terms, claiming, for instance, that *all* of the myriad genres of dance music have the same meter (4/4), which they tend to link, through implicit or explicit comparisons, to perceived notions of simplicity.

Without valorizing "complexity" in the structural domain, I wish to complicate this picture by showing how electronic dance music supports experiences of time that are both rich and diverse. I reference this releasing of temporal possibility most succinctly through the metaphor of "unlocking the groove." This phrase takes as its point of departure the term "locked groove," which electronic dance musicians use to describe short patterns etched into records in a way that allows them to repeat continuously. Locked grooves are DJ tools, sold on specially made records whose actual physical grooves are perfect circles rather than the usual spiral. Rarely lasting more than a few measures, they boil the notion of "groove" down to its purest musical essence: a short configuration of bass line and percussion that unfolds in continuously repeating cycles. In performance, DJs combine these tools with full-length tracks to create "groove" on a much larger scale. It is this broader sense of the phenomenon—groove as the way in which the rhythmic essence of music flows or unfolds—that I evoke in the title of this book.[1] Enjoined with this notion is the idea of "unlocking," a usage that at first glance might seem to simply play off the meaning of a term from EDM culture. Yet this punning has a theoretical underpinning. More than a

---

1. "Groove" is a complex construct that suggests multiple meanings within both musical and scholarly discourse. In a discussion of an "analytic musicology of rock," Allan Moore concisely expresses each of the two senses I have referenced here. He offers a specific definition of groove as "the pattern laid down by the bass and drum kit" while also noting that "in conversation among fans, music with a good groove tends to be music users can relate to easily" (2001b: 34). For extended discussion of groove from a music-theoretical perspective, see T. Hughes 2003. For views on groove from popular music studies, see Keil and Feld 1994.

simple poetic conceit, it expresses a fundamental argument. As I explore the rhythmic dimensions of EDM, I will consistently contend that its groove—far from being locked in to a single, restricted type—promotes multiple interpretations and flexible interactions, an *unlocking* of temporal experience into many possible directions.

Building the Groove

An exploration of electronic dance music might proceed in a multitude of directions. Consider, for instance, the scene I have just described. The details I have provided suggest a number of topics and subtopics that might be explored fruitfully: these include DJing (the DJ's cultural and musical roles, DJ-audience interaction, technical aspects), musical intersections between humans and technology, the use of pre-existing materials in musical creation (sampling, the use of records in DJ performances), dance (relationships between dance and music, individual vs. collective behavior), texture, repetition, form, rhythmic and metrical aspects (the musical and cultural significance of "the beat," metrical dissonance, temporality in a broad sense), place (the role of urban locales in the delineation of EDM genres, relationships between the local and the global), and identity (age, place of origin, class, physical ability, sexuality, ethnicity, gender). And these are only a few potential starting points. Other possible areas of investigation not emphasized in my description include genre (how genres are defined, musical characteristics of various genres, their histories), relationships to other musical traditions (such as African music), improvisation, virtuosity, timbre, the body (how the music invites embodiment and is embodied, musical "gestures"), multimodality (interaction of dance, music, visuals, etc.), spiritual and religious dimensions, drugs and psychedelic experience in relation to music, authenticity, group dynamics and boundaries, youth culture and "resistance," beliefs about the future, and relationships between EDM and postmodern society.

Most of these themes have been at least touched on in existing research on electronic dance music, although relatively few have been addressed in significant detail. Not surprisingly, a number of studies focus on the DJ—EDM's most public figure—from historical, cultural, and social perspectives (Austin 1994, Brewster and Broughton 2000, Fikentscher 2000, Langlois 1992, Rietveld 1998). The role of technology in producing and consuming music has also been a site of recent interest; in this vein, EDM is often discussed as one of several techno-centric musical styles (see, for instance, Katz 2004, Taylor 2001, and Théberge 1997). Within this broad domain, the specific subtopic of sampling and other types of musical borrowing has been frequently invoked (Katz 2004, Schloss 2004[2]), although often in a general sense in which the practice is portrayed as an indicator of postmodernism (Loubet 2000, Loza 1996). Receiving the greatest amount of attention, however, have been various aspects of identity in relation to musical experience: in particular, sexuality (Amico 2001, Buckland 2002, Currid 1995, Fikentscher 2000, W. Hughes 1994, Loza 2001), gender (Bradby 1993, Pini 2001, Rietveld 1998), and ethnicity (Hesmondhalgh 2000, Maira 2002 and 2003, and Noys 1995, as well as many of the other sources previously listed). Other topics that have been begun to be addressed include authenticity and issues of prestige (Thornton 1996, the first published monograph on electronic dance music) and genre (McLeod 2001).

Alongside the works listed in the previous paragraph, almost all of which were written by authors affiliated with academic institutions, stand a number of sources by journalists and music critics. For the most part, these works are histories that trace the development of particular genres of electronic dance music. Some books focus on a single genre, often in association with a particular geographic location—for instance, Sicko 1999 focuses on Detroit techno[3]—whereas others aim to be comprehensive, tracing the development of multiple genres through individual chapters or essays (Brewster and Broughton 2000, Reynolds 1999, Shapiro 2000). As scholarly sources, these works are not without problems. Although most contain bibliographies, references to specific sources and page numbers are few and far between, making it difficult to trace recurring statements to any printed source and to ascertain the origin of certain widespread claims made about some of the now legendary founding figures of dance music. Furthermore, there is a great deal of redundancy in their accounts, and little citation of the others' work; one often has the sense that these authors, in their efforts to tell "the story" of electronic dance music, are, on an individual level, reinventing the wheel through uncritical repetitions of the same stories about its genesis.[4]

2. Although hip-hop music differs in important ways from electronic dance music—most notably in its emphasis on orality through rap—the two styles have much in common, especially in the realms of musical style and production (the details of which will be addressed further in the following chapter). For this reason I invoke research on these aspects of hip hop at various points throughout this study.

3. Complementing this work are the monographs by Fikentscher (2000) and Rietveld (1998), which focus on New York "garage" and Chicago house, respectively.

4. A typical example is a statement famously ascribed to Detroit techno musician Derrick May, in which he characterizes techno as "like George Clinton and Kraftwerk stuck in an elevator together." Some versions of the statement appear with the added phrase "with only a sequencer to keep them

In sum, although research on electronic dance music has sprouted from an almost barren landscape in the early 1990s to a blossoming growth in the new millennium, its development remains scattered. Some of its fields of inquiry have received significant attention, but most are still in an early stage, and others have been neglected altogether. And the resources that *are* available are not without problems. Although popular-press works can function as important sources of historical and stylistic information—indeed, they often serve as the *only* such sources, as the frequency of their citation in academic works suggests—their lack of rigor suggests the need for critical reappraisal by historically oriented scholars. Existing academic texts, meanwhile, tend to trade too much in generalizations: we read about the social spaces of "youth" (Thornton 1996: 14–25) or about how house music lost its "African-American sensibilities" after being imported to Europe (Rietveld 1998: 26).[5]

Although these tendencies have been balanced to a certain extent by an increasing emphasis on ethnography in popular music studies,[6] there is still one area in which generalizations are invoked freely—namely, the domain of musical sound. In fact, discussion of EDM as music remains at such a general level that one could easily discover most of the characteristics mentioned in currently published accounts of its sound after a few minutes' casual observation of any DJ performance. In essence, we know that this music has a "4/4 beat," which DJs keep at a constant tempo somewhere in the range of 120–180 beats per minute (depending on the genre involved); that it is repetitive; that it is played at very high volumes, emphasizing low (bass and sub-bass) frequencies; and that it is formed from combinations of diverse sound sources (records, samples, etc.). Other sources provide a few additional details: for instance, Fikentscher, in addition to articulating the points listed above, notes the importance of timbre to DJ mixing (2000: 87–88) and the fact that "larger musical phrases" tend to occur in four-measure multiples (2000: 83).

Accounts that do invoke the musical qualities of EDM, meanwhile, tend to speak of the music only in a broad sense: it is referenced simply as a general category, with specific examples barely mentioned if at all. Fikentscher, who

---

company." The quote is ultimately traceable to Cosgrove 1988, where it appears amid a sort of pastiche of description by the author intermingled with statements attributed to "Derrik [*sic*] May."

5. For similar critiques of homogenizing references, see Pini's comments on the postmodern "loss of the subject" approach espoused by Redhead (1993) and Rietveld (1998) [Pini 2001: 46–48] and Amico's comments on Fikentscher's (2000) use of terms such as "gay sensibilities" [Amico 2003: 257].

6. In particular see Buckland (2002), Malbon (1999), and Pini (2001), all of which show a pervasive interweaving of broad theoretical concerns with the specific perspectives of individual participants in EDM cultures.

devotes ten pages to EDM's sonic organization (more than any other currently published source), begins to buck this trend by discussing four exemplary EDM tracks; nevertheless, he devotes but a single paragraph to each.[7] In fact, the most specific descriptions of individual tracks are often found in popular-press sources. Although these accounts can be highly evocative, they are also problematic in their own way. Consider, for instance, the following excerpt from Simon Reynolds's *Generation Ecstasy:*

> On tracks like Hyper-On Experience's "Thunder Grip" and DJ Trax's "We Rock the Most," breakbeats swerve and skid, melody shrapnel whizzes hither and thither, and every cranny of the mix is infested with hiccupping vocal shards and rap chants sped up to sound like pixies. The vibe is sheer Hanna-Barbera zany-mania, but beneath the smiley-faced "hyper-ness" the breaks and bass lines are ruff B-Boy bizness. (Reynolds 1999: 256)

For the music-lover, this account offers many resonances. It references specific elements of the sound (breakbeats, melodies, vocal elements), their perceived behavior (swerving, whizzing, hiccupping), and certain broad aesthetic qualities (the "vibe," a sense of "hyper-ness"). Nevertheless, it does little to help us understand *how* the music creates these effects (for instance, the reasons why breakbeats seem to "skid"). In general, this sort of description seems to function mainly as a way of enhancing impressions gained from listening—producing a kind of head-nodding affirmation in those who know the music, but leaving the uninitiated with only a vague sense of musical particularities.[8] Furthermore, although the titles of specific tracks are given, along with the recording artists responsible for them, they are invoked only as tokens of a type; their unique qualities are not addressed individually. Thus, we are left to wonder why, for instance, fans and musicians might have preferred the particular pleasures of Hyper-On Experience's "Thunder Grip" to the countless other breakbeat-based tracks released around the same time.

At the same time, many descriptions that employ more conventional language are plagued by remarkably imprecise usage of even rudimentary musical terminology. Consider, for instance, the following passage:

7. In electronic dance music, a "track" is the equivalent of a song or composition. (See the glossary for definitions of this and other terms that are used throughout this study.) I exclude my own work on EDM from the trends described in this paragraph because it can be viewed as part of the larger project in which this book is involved.

8. One also wonders about the long-term ramifications of descriptions constructed almost entirely from *other* contemporary cultural references. While this issue has the potential to emerge in any sort of writing, the very pop-cultural cachet that makes Reynolds's prose appealing intensifies its effect in this regard.

> Trance techno house matured in an exciting direction, which had a recognizable North West European texture and structure, like Jark Prango's *Complete Control* (Fresh Fruit, 1993) which built layer after layer of sound to a catargic [*sic*] crescendo or Paragliders's *Paraglide; Blue Sky Mix* which gave the listener a sensation of flying at breakneck speed at more than 140 bpm. Trance is a particular language of electronic dance music making which takes to a logical conclusion the notion of letting "the self" go and "dissolve" in a sensory overload of repetitive sounds [DJ White Delight, 1994]. Hereby song structures are determined by its effectiveness to take the dancer "out of this world." (Rietveld 1998: 95)

Left unspecified in this description are, among other things, the characteristics of a "North West European texture," as well as the way in which the "song structures" of trance are determined by an ability to "take the dancer 'out of this world'." Elsewhere in the text, musical terms are used even more approximately. For instance, Rietveld's explanation of the role that pitch plays in DJ mixing points out that "since songs and tracks are made to overlap, a sense of harmony may be achieved if the melody scales of the different songs fit" (Rietveld 1998: 131). What sort of phenomenon is being described here? A listener familiar with EDM might infer that the author is referring to the way in which DJs sometimes match *keys* between overlapping records, thus preserving a sense of *consonance*—but references to "melody scales" do little to make this clear. Meanwhile, an excerpt by Buckland that *does* invoke the phenomenon of key involves other problematic references:

> David Morales' remix of "Goldeneye" by Tina Turner exemplifies the cues DJs served up for the dancers. After building up layers of rhythms, which acquainted dancers with the tempo and timbre of the track, and after repetition had made it familiar, the explicit rhythm track was pulled away, leaving the unembellished key signature chords of the harmony chiming out. A key chord sustained itself under the second repeated cycle of these chords to create a dramatic tension of expectation. (Buckland 2002: 79)

What exactly are "key signature chords" (or "key chords")? Tonic chords? "Primary" chords (tonic, subdominant, dominant)? Chords belonging to a particular key? Although most of Buckland's musical descriptions are relatively clear (and her work is noteworthy as the first to devote detailed attention to the relationships between music and dance in EDM), this use of terminology is curious given the absence of notational symbols such as key signatures in this music.

The difficulty of speaking about musical sound with precision is a well-documented phenomenon, of course. Music is often portrayed as the most abstract of the arts, resistant to linguistic and visual representation. And within this overall category, popular music presents its own set of problems. Its proximity to contemporary culture can cause it to seem transparent, as if there is no meaning within it to be revealed. Furthermore, although theories of its musical organization (and corresponding analytical methodologies) have begun to emerge, this particular area of inquiry is still relatively new, and individual approaches have not yet emerged as definitive. This situation is complicated by the absence of visual traces, since the majority of contemporary popular music is created without the aid of scores (which have been central to the practices of musicology and music theory).

Electronic dance music intensifies these difficulties. Although scholars of other types of popular music have often found grounding in the concreteness of song lyrics, EDM allows no such comforts, for most of its genres contain no consistent verbal component. Lacking any text in which meaning might reside, created by synthesizers and drum machines rather than "real" instruments, and "performed" through the playback of recordings by DJs, electronic dance music can seem like the *ne plus ultra* of music's abstractness, the epitome of Hanslick's arabesques.

Clearly, then, there are many reasons why most published accounts of EDM have neglected its sound, and why those who *have* spoken about its musical construction have not always been successful. Of course, some of these reasons are positive ones. It is logical that scholars have concentrated on areas of investigation (e.g., social and cultural arenas) for which clearly established theoretical frameworks exist. Furthermore, most of the scholars who have researched EDM come from disciplines other than music. It is understandable that they have focused on concerns central to their fields; I do not mean to suggest that choosing to investigate parameters other than sound represents a failure on their part. Indeed, at least some of the responsibility for this lacuna in EDM research must lie with those for whom detailed accounts of musical organization *are* a primary concern—namely, theorists and musicologists, who came to the study of popular music somewhat late, and who have until recently focused on a relatively limited range of repertoire (in particular, "classic" and "progressive" rock from the 1960s and '70s).

In spite of these observations, it is not my aim to criticize music scholars, who have had to overcome many ideological and methodological obstacles in order to study popular music, or scholars working in other areas, who have produced a number of excellent studies that shed light on important dimensions of EDM culture. Instead, my principal objectives are to create a space in which EDM *can* be discussed as music, and to explain why it is important that it be discussed in this way.

The Sound (and Its Surrounds)

The sound of electronic dance music matters. The people involved in EDM culture—fans, DJs, and producers—care deeply about sound. The sound is the force that drives people to dance—indeed, causes them to feel that they *have* to dance. The sound is what producers spend their time crafting, leading fans to collect their records obsessively.[9] The sound motivates DJs to play *this particular record* at *this particular moment*. Furthermore, sound affects the ways in which DJs alter and combine records, as well as producers' decisions during the compositional process. Therefore, studying the sonic dimensions of electronic dance music can help us understand the specific choices and behaviors that go into its creation and appreciation. As an essential part of the cultural complex in which EDM is embedded, sound deserves scholarly investigation.[10]

As the emphases of the previous paragraph should suggest, an important goal of this book is to promote and enhance understanding of an aspect of electronic dance music that people value. I hope to highlight some characteristics of EDM that will help those who are unfamiliar with it to appreciate it, to enable more precise and nuanced discussions of its musical qualities, and to enrich the musical experiences of those for whom it is already a familiar style. I have deliberately chosen to focus on an element of EDM that is central to accounts of its power: rhythm. I often take rhythmic concepts used by participants in EDM culture (e.g., "the beat," "phrasing") as specific points of departure for my explorations, but I am also motivated by my own sense of what is, or what might be, important in the music (for instance, rhythmic surprise, or gradually unfolding metrical processes). Naturally, I will not be able to address *everything* that people value about EDM's sound; to treat its musical organization comprehensively would require several additional volumes addressing other broad categories (e.g., timbre; the ways in which dance embodies and is shaped by music) as well as the development of new methodologies to enable the study of these topics. Although I recognize the importance of these other dimensions of musical experience, I must leave them for future studies, while hoping that the ideas put forth here will be helpful in developing such work.

9. Fans and musicians in this culture use the term "producer" to refer to a person who creates and records EDM compositions. I will describe the creative activities of the producer in detail in chapter 1.

10. The caption I have chosen for this section references the name of an important early electronic dance music track by Detroit techno producers Kevin Saunderson and Santonio Echols ("The Sound," released in 1987 under the recording name Reese & Santonio). In subsequent chapters I will discuss the track from the B side of this record, entitled "How to Play Our Music," in detail.

Making a case for studying EDM as music is important, not only because I wish to justify this particular undertaking, but also because the significance of EDM's musical aspects has been argued *against*. This tactic of downplaying is generally aimed at highlighting the centrality of "context" to the electronic dance music experience. Rietveld, for instance, goes so far as to state that "without being submerged in its physical presence, house music is quite meaningless" (Rietveld 1998: 150). She reiterates this theme in various ways throughout her book, at one point writing that:

> It is only when played to and interacted with a dancing crowd, that house music, as a medium, is complete. In addition, a dance record is also pretty meaningless when it is separated from other dance records. One should look at dance singles as words which are looking for a sentence; they need to be combined to create a soundscape. (Rietveld 1998: 107)

It is true that most EDM tracks are made with the expectation that, in live performance, they will be combined with other tracks and danced to; as a result, several key potentials of this music are only realized fully within a live dance context. At the same time, it is absurd to assert that EDM records—or words, for that matter—are meaningless in isolation. Even though they usually function within a larger context, their individual meaning (or range of potential meanings) has much to do with how they can be combined, as well as with how they *are* combined. Because individual records have meaning, one record (or word) will often seem perfect for a particular context, whereas another will seem completely wrong.

In fact, this particular emphasis, which seems to suggest that functionality is one of the distinguishing characteristics of electronic dance music, plays into a long-standing stereotype about dance music in general. On the contrary, all music fulfills various functions, and musical meaning is always created within particular contexts. Hence, the position of this study is much closer to that articulated by Ben Malbon, who writes that "the clubbing experience is primarily about music and the clubbers' understandings of that music" (1999: 79). Drawing upon the work of ethnomusicologist John Blacking (1973), Malbon argues further that "performed music means nothing without a musically adept audience; that is, without an audience who respond to, and distinguish between, different sounds and sequences of music, the performance of that music would be pointless" (1999: 82). In short, although sound is imbricated in culture, and culture shapes the ways in which it is created and experienced, this particular culture would not exist without "the sound" that distinguishes it.

In referencing the relationship between sound and its cultural context, I invoke a methodological specter that has haunted popular music studies since its inception. At a broader level, this issue—or, more specifically, this *opposition* of sound and context—has played a pivotal role in dividing and containing the various subdisciplines of musical study. A typical music-theoretical strategy at this juncture in my argument—one that appears in many justifications of analytical approaches to popular music—would be to stake a claim in favor of studying "the music itself." The motivation behind this position is understandable: since the earliest days of academic popular-music study (well before the emergence of any significant music-theoretical activity in this area), the very act of analysis has been called into question.[11] Music theorists have found themselves having to defend what they do; to frame the situation in emotional terms, the way of interacting with music that feels most comfortable to them has been labeled suspect. Appeals to "the music itself," however, create at least two difficulties. First—and this is the more familiar objection—they rely on a formulation of musical autonomy that has been problematized in countless accounts, a historically specific formulation that conceals its own origins. Second, they do nothing to break down the dichotomy between music and context but, instead, simply shift the emphasis from one side of the binary to the other. For this reason, I wish to take a somewhat different tack.

Before I proceed further, let me be clear: I am in favor of close readings. In fact, the majority of this text will consist of detailed analyses of specific electronic dance music tracks. I will be concerned with how the musical attributes of these tracks should be conceptualized, and in conceptualizing them I will sometimes make use of theories developed to study Western art music (although the ramifications of such applications will always be at the forefront of my discussion). I will use musical notation, both "traditional" and newly developed, as well as terminology from a wide variety of sources. But to view this work as a study of musical "objects," and to imagine that my concern with musical detail isolates this work from some larger cultural context, is to misread it (and, indeed, a variety of other analytical texts) in a fundamental way.

What I wish to challenge about this view of analysis is its artificial separation

11. For instance, John Shepherd, writing in the second issue of *Popular Music,* argues that "while it is true that historical musicology has developed a formidable range of analytic techniques and terms for coming to grips with the internal parameters of 'music,' such techniques and terms have a very limited application" (Shepherd 1982: 146), while Philip Tagg, writing in the same issue, specifies that "popular music cannot be analysed using only the traditional tools of musicology" (Tagg 1982: 41). To be fair, both authors are clearly in favor of an engagement with musical sound via modes of analysis that take cultural meaning into account. Nevertheless, it is remarkable to note how readily "traditional tools" were assumed to be problematic before they had been applied with any breadth. See Covach 1997b: 83, for a similar critique.

of music and context, and, by extension, its separation of analytical approaches that focus on "music" from those that focus on "context."[12] The regulatory effects of this discourse have constrained not only the musical possibilities of sociocultural analysis but also the sociocultural dimensions of musical analysis.[13] To claim that the analyst is not part of the social world is false. Even when only one person is involved in its creation, music emerges within the enabling framework of society. Another dimension is added as listeners hear and try to make sense of the results. And if some of these efforts result in an analysis, musical discourse enters the world in another way. Hence I, the analyst, in dialogue with the music's creator(s) as well as with those who read my work, am part of the "social context" of this music. A composition is an invitation to participate in a particular musical experience, and my analysis is an invitation to the reader to participate in my way of hearing and thinking about the piece, as well as in a dialogue about my interpretations. Ultimately, the effectiveness of my analysis depends on whether the experience of "hearing it as I do" proves useful or thought-provoking in some way to other people. Analysis, therefore, is a social practice.

Making this assertion involves a refutation of claims of authenticity for any particular social context. Such claims are implicit in the argument that analysis separates music from its social contexts: if in fact analysis *does* perform this separation, then it separates music only from *certain* contexts, which are perceived to be the important ones. In other words, it involves a claim that "this is where the music *really* happens" or "this is what it *really* means." In contrast, I wish to argue, as Maria Pini has, that

> We have to resist the kind of totalitarianism which very clearly underlies much existing club cultural criticism. By totalitarian I am referring to the assumption that club cultures *can* be reduced to, or read in terms of, a singular meaning structure. Hence, it is common to read of rave being ultimately, or at very least centrally, about one thing. (Pini 2001: 54)

In the case of electronic dance music, the dance floor has consistently been treated as the authentic locus of musical experience; recall, for instance, the

---

12. In arguing against this separation I am inspired by the work of Kevin Korsyn, who, in a critique of disciplinary divisions within the study of music, reveals a "deep complicity between those who advocate study of 'the music itself' and those who believe priority should be given to the study of context" (Korsyn 2003: 47–48). Korsyn highlights the way in which each approach employs "a certain Moebius-strip logic through which inside and outside, content and frame, mutually determine each other" (124) and argues instead for a "postdisciplinary" approach to music scholarship (40).

13. This argument is developed in greater length in Scherzinger 2001, a critique of ethnomusicological accounts of African music.

above quotation from Rietveld (p. 13). And although the significance of this site cannot be denied, it could also be argued that other important aspects of EDM have been neglected because of a tendency to focus on this most immediate and obvious of social contexts. For instance, the role of the producer—the figure who creates the records played on the dance floor—has hardly been addressed in current literature. One cannot help but wonder to what extent this situation derives from the producer's relative anonymity within EDM scenes, his or her literal physical absence from the social contexts that *have* received attention.

In this study I approach electronic dance music in terms of a number of different ways in which one might interact with it. These possible subject positions include those of the analyst, the DJ, the producer, and the clubber. Although I focus on the musical choices and experiences associated with these figures, it should be clear from my arguments that I view these *musical* behaviors as no less social than, say, the interaction between a DJ and a clubbing crowd. Furthermore, I do not believe that any of these perspectives should be privileged within the larger realm of scholarly discourse; rather, each should be thought of as a possible vantage point, a lens through which EDM may be experienced. My own interaction with these roles is social in a variety of ways: as an analyst (in the broadly social sense defined above), as a long-time clubber, and as an ethnographer (in a more traditionally "social" sense). I will detail the position of ethnography within this study later in this chapter (see the "Methodology II" section, pp. 26–29). For now, however, I want to continue to focus on analysis.

I have argued that analysis is a social practice. Within my own analyses, therefore, I want to allow these social dimensions to emerge rather than effacing them. Throughout this study, my own voice forms a clear part of my analytical arguments. I seek to identify my position with respect to the music and the other people who participate in it. Furthermore, I do not claim any singular authority to speak about this music. This does not mean that I do not claim *any* authority but, rather, that I bring particular strengths, weaknesses, and perspectives to my interactions with it.

The explicit positioning of the analyst *within* the analysis is part of what I believe to be a larger trend within music theory. Other characteristics of this trend include explicit attention to the goals of analysis, demonstrated sensitivity to the regulative effects of methodology (instead of assuming that an analytical "tool" is neutral, innocent, or transparent), an emphasis on musical experience over structure, and a tendency to allow for the possibility of multiple interpretations or hearings. Although no one has, to my knowledge, identified this development in writing or given it a name, I would like to portray it as a "reflexive turn" within the discipline.[14] Within ethnomusicology and other anthropologically oriented fields, this term has been used to characterize a broad critique of the discipline's methods, a movement aimed at uncovering the (often implicit) regulating effects of these practices and the power relations in which they are involved. In particular, "reflexive" approaches have sought to respond to the problematic role of the ethnographer within a social context. Instead of writing about culture from an omniscient point of view, as if one is outside of it—what Donna Haraway (1991: 189) calls "the god-trick of seeing everything from nowhere"—an increasing number of authors have sought to identify their position (political and otherwise) within a given culture as specifically as possible.[15] Revealing tendencies that are analogous in certain respects, music theorists have begun to highlight the political implications of theory and analysis (Maus 1993, Krims 2000, Scherzinger 2001), call attention to the rhetoric by which analysis operates (Guck 1994, Lewin 1993), dismantle certain pervasive conceptual frameworks (Hasty 1997), and foreground the analyst's voice, in sometimes quite radical ways (Hirata 1996).[16] Like the ethnomusicological sources that I have invoked in comparison, these works respond to methodological tendencies that are often left unspoken: in particular, a preference for singular, controlling readings; silence regarding the goals and possible outcomes (intentional and otherwise) of analysis; treatment of the music as "data" that is "run through" a method; and a style of presentation in which the analysis emerges, fully formed, in the pages of the theory journal, with any fissures and discontinuities that might have disrupted its formation having been discarded prior to its presentation.[17]

Another characteristic of the reflexive turn within anthropology is an emphasis on "radical specificity." Countering the tendencies of many ethnographies

14. Korsyn (2003: 21–23) also uses this term to describe developments in scholarship, although in a broader way and with somewhat different emphases. He highlights an increasingly explicit focus among scholarly institutions (professional societies, journals) on their own standards and practices. Drawing on the work of social theorists such as Ulrich Beck, he initially emphasizes the regulatory effects of this reflexivity; however, he eventually comes to note the potential for critique that reflection can offer and positions his own work within this trend.

15. See, for instance, Kisliuk 1998 and Barz and Cooley 1997.

16. I have only listed a handful of writers whom I consider most exemplary of this trend; undoubtedly more could be named, depending on the strictness with which one applies the "reflexive" analogy. Furthermore, since I wish to focus on music theory, I have completely omitted discussion of the "New Musicology," which would certainly be relevant to a broader treatment.

17. A characteristic example of this focus on a singular, finished analysis is Allen Forte's analysis of Schoenberg's Klavierstück op. 11, no. 1. At the outset of his description of Schoenberg's "harmonic vocabulary," for instance, Forte states directly that "it consists of six hexachords and their complements, six pentachords and their complements, and two tetrachords and their complements" (Forte 1981: 133); he does not explain how this information was discovered or note alternative possibilities.

(especially older ones) to generalize about cultural beliefs and practices,[18] reflexive accounts focus instead on describing the particular experiences of specific people at historically situated moments. Analysis, likewise, has the potential to create a kind of radical specificity with regard to pieces of music. As I explained above, existing accounts of EDM—even those that take care to emphasize the importance of sound to its meaning (such as Malbon 1999)—either completely ignore its musical qualities or reference them only in a general sense. Given the instantiation that cultural critiques of music demand in other arenas, it is surprising that they are so willing to forego this particular specificity. Moreover, as with other kinds of generalizations, abstractions about music carry risks. Invoking "music" only in a general sense can allow various political agendas to be mapped onto it. Music can be said to express the "resistance" of youth or the cultural characteristics of various ethnic groups.[19] Although specific instances of these claims may be apropos, there is always the danger that the music will be made to say what the writer wants it to say. This act of ventriloquism can also occur when the music *is* discussed in detail, of course, but the radical specificity that analysis fosters works against this tendency. Furthermore, ignoring music has the potential to reinforce beliefs about its abstractness, its "absoluteness": if we cannot speak with precision about music, but only about that which is seen as surrounding it, then perhaps it is ineffable after all. In contrast, I wish to argue for a kind of "thick description" of musical sound,[20] a practice that can counterbalance the tendency of particular musical configurations to disappear within accounts of cultural meaning.

Having argued for the importance of studying EDM as music and for a dissolution of artificial divisions between methods that study sound and those that study context, I would like to return to the musical event I detailed at the beginning of this chapter. In describing this scene, I deliberately highlighted a number of different social roles, including those of the DJ and various members of the audience. But there is one role that I have omitted: my own. Where am I within this event?

The answer is that I am there, in the middle of the crowd, dancing. As the DJ plays I am listening to the music, thinking about it. I notice the people around me, how they communicate with and respond to the DJ, how they move in

18. For instance, Evans-Pritchard's account of Nuer religion includes many broad ascriptions such as "Nuer take nature for granted and are passive and resigned towards it" (1956: 200).

19. See previous comments on generalizations in EDM research beginning on p. 8.

20. Here I reference the work of Clifford Geertz (1973), who espoused "thick description" as a model for ethnography.

relation to the music, the expressions on their faces. I watch the DJ as well, the way he uses the turntables and mixing board, his reactions to the music and the crowd. At times I take a break and direct all my attention toward observing the scene, but mostly I am focused on experiencing it in a state of awareness, taking it all in. Afterward, my friends and I talk about it. It's interesting to hear their responses. It's not just that I'm gathering ethnographic "data" about their perceptions; their reactions, even when they differ from my own, enrich my sense of what took place.

A few days later, I am in my car, driving back from Detroit to my home in Indiana. I am listening to a recently purchased Underworld album, nodding my head along with the beat. Suddenly the location of the beat changes, leaving me surprised, and extremely curious about how the music created this effect. After that, I'm at my desk, with headphones on, listening to the same short passage over and over, experimenting with different ways of writing it down. And from there I take the recording to a friend who is a DJ, play it for her, ask her to talk about its effects.

All of these are ways in which I have interacted with electronic dance music. As I have argued above, none should be thought of as more "authentic" than another, for all involve differently shaded engagements with the music. On the one hand, my desire to pay close attention to musical sound undoubtedly stems in part from my training as a music theorist: at an intuitive level, detailed readings make sense to me as a way of interacting with music, a fact that was certainly a factor behind my choice of field. On the other hand, my personal history as a clubber and follower of EDM since my late teen years and my secondary training as an ethnomusicologist (Ph.D. minor) motivate a broader interest in the flow of behaviors and practices into and out of EDM's musical aspects.

For this reason, my relationship with EDM is not the only one that informs this study; crucial to its development have been the vantage points of DJs, producers, and fans, which are presented throughout the text. My methodology is principally twofold: on the one hand, I have analyzed specific EDM tracks, exploring their rhythmic characteristics and developing conceptual approaches for understanding their internal organization; on the other, I have engaged in field research in the form of interviews and other modes of cultural interaction. I present overviews of these methods in the following two sections; technical concerns related to analysis and field research (e.g., issues related to transcription, lists of interview questions) are detailed in appendices A and B, respectively.

Methodology I: Musical Analysis

My interaction with electronic dance music started with and has continually returned to its sound. In order to engage with this sound in detail, I have employed musical analysis throughout this book. Specifically, I have analyzed and transcribed many short excerpts from EDM tracks as well as nine complete tracks. Transcriptions of the latter, which form the basis of most of the analyses in chapters 5 and 6, appear in appendix C. I also have listened to a much larger number of tracks with an ear toward their distinctive features without necessarily analyzing them methodically.

The production and performance traditions of EDM complicate efforts to specify a "track" as the object of analysis. A track can be experienced in a variety of ways, which divide into two general categories:[21] either it will be heard in its original, studio-produced form, prior to any alteration and recontextualization by a DJ; or it will be encountered in combination with other records in a DJ mix. In this study, detailed analyses involving references to specific passages in the music or transcriptions are based primarily on unmixed tracks, whereas comments on the ways in which records are combined come from interviewing DJs, observing live performances, and listening to recordings of DJ mixes (both live and studio-produced). In this way, I am able to balance in-depth musical analysis with an awareness of how tracks are realized in performance contexts, and I will frequently point out connections between the characteristics of individual tracks and the ways in which DJs transform them.

I favor unmixed tracks as an analytical point of departure primarily for practical reasons. The ways in which DJs overlap records with similar rhythmic and timbral qualities in live performance makes it impossible to say with certitude which sounds are proper to a given track in its original recorded form (as opposed to sounds introduced through modifications to that record or through the addition of another record), as well as to specify with precision where any given track begins and ends (which also makes it impossible, from the standpoint of rhythmic analysis, to identify the exact duration of a track). Given the preliminary state of

---

21. After being created and recorded by a producer, tracks are sold to fans for personal listening or to DJs. DJs most commonly mix tracks in live performance, but some also record mixes in studios, resulting in tapes or CDs that fans can purchase as a sort of home-listening analogue to the live dance-music experience. Live performances can be recorded and sold for home listening too, of course, while recordings of individual tracks can re-enter the studio to be "remixed" and released in versions that differ from the initial one. I will discuss the specific practices involved in DJing, production, and remixing further in chapter 1.

knowledge about EDM's musical characteristics, it seems desirable to begin with the clearest possible point of focus, thus allowing a basic level of understanding to be developed before factors that might complicate and obscure the situation are introduced. It is my hope that these factors *will* be dealt with in greater detail as the study of EDM as music develops and that the ideas put forth here will prove useful in this regard.

In broader terms, however, individual unmixed tracks are important, in both musical and social ways. In addition to being the locus of activity for the producer, unmixed tracks are always the starting points for DJ performances, or "sets." Consequently, to understand how and why DJs choose particular records, alter their sound, and combine them with other records to create a larger musical whole, we must become thoroughly acquainted with the characteristics of individual tracks; in short, we cannot understand the building unless we also understand the blocks. In fact, cultivating this sort of knowledge is an important part of the craft of DJing, as many DJs whom I interviewed pointed out; Jimmi Journey, for instance, notes that

> You want to memorize your records: not only their beats and their measures and their times, but all the instruments involved, because sometimes there's another DJ going on before you. Who knows what record you're going to be stuck with when it's your time to go up to mix into, so you've always got to be listening and [ready to] say, "OK"—instantaneously—"I've got a record that'll go with that. And that'll be my foundation and I'll build from there." (Interview with the author, 4 November 2001)

Many EDM fans also spend time listening to records on their own, apart from DJ sets, as the frequency of conversations about individual tracks on internet bulletin boards attests. Therefore, although the emphasis of previous research on the dance floor as the principal context of EDM also might lead analysts to privilege music as it is heard in that location, the inclusion of other perspectives shows that unmixed tracks are equally relevant to EDM's social contexts. Once again, we must be wary of allowing the most common context of the *researcher*—in this case, that of an audience member listening to a set, without access to precise information about its constituents—to influence the direction of research.

The visual representation of sound presents another area of concern for the analyst. As a general rule, electronic dance music is not notated. This is equally true both before and after its creation: most producers do not compose tracks on paper, and no one transcribes works for sale to other performers (as occurs, for instance, with other types of popular music). Although the "oral" aspects of EDM creation should not be overemphasized, it is unclear how typical familiarity with and/or use of notation is within EDM as a whole.[22] To facilitate the close engagement with musical sound that is an essential part of music-theoretical research, however, it is desirable to transcribe all or part of the tracks that I will consider in detail. I present transcriptions with the understanding that they are not prescriptive (they are not "scores," and they could not be used to realize an EDM work), nor are they solely descriptive (they are more than simply records of "what happens" in a track).[23] Although they tend more toward the latter than the former (especially in the transcriptions of complete tracks presented in appendix C), their primary function is *analytical;* each transcription should be understood as one interpretation of what happens in a passage, viewed from a particular theoretical perspective.

As with any notational system, the transcriptions included in this book represent some features more effectively than others. For instance, they do not show the tremendous array of timbral variation within EDM—although instrumental names do connote certain broad characteristics, and the timbres of sounds with less specific names are usually described in prose.[24] In addition, these transcriptions do not show the tiny variations that can occur when "swing" and other aspects of expressive timing are employed. These limitations should not be taken as reasons to reject transcription altogether, for any system of representation will favor certain types of information over others. The bias of a particular notational system is often cited as a reason that one type of transcription is better than another, or that verbal description is preferable to transcription. However, this tendency works the other way as well: certain types of transcription convey particular kinds of information better than others, and transcription in general conveys certain types of information more effectively than verbal description. Hence, transcription can aid in the creation of radically specific accounts of electronic dance music—although it must always be practiced with awareness of the tensions between oral and written forms of expression and of the interpretive power of particular notational techniques.

22. Many sequencing programs do represent music graphically, the most common format being a kind of textural graph often described as "piano roll" notation. Although different from conventional staff notation, this feature still allows the producer to work closely with a visual representation of sound. Of the producers whom I interviewed, a few (such as Rick Smith of Underworld) described occasionally using traditional notation during the process of musical creation, but most said they did not.

23. This distinction between "prescriptive" and "descriptive" notation is drawn from Seeger 1958.

24. This deficiency with respect to timbre is hardly unique to my transcriptions, however; timbre is underrepresented in many different notational systems. It would certainly be very useful to have a system of transcription capable of representing the timbral nuances of EDM, but that difficult task must be left for a future work.

I approach the pieces I analyze from a variety of conceptual standpoints. At a broad level, I view musical and social experience as both enabling and realizing each other's possibilities; in a more specifically music-theoretical sense, I draw on concepts and categories used by EDM fans and musicians, approaches that I have developed especially for the study of this repertory, and published approaches to rhythm and meter by other music theorists. In so doing, I want to address certain holes and misportrayals in discourse on rhythm and meter. The first of these is the generally insufficient theorization of these parameters as they occur in popular music. EDM is not alone in foregrounding rhythmic and metrical qualities; scholars of other popular repertories continually mention their salience. Yet detailed considerations of rhythm in popular music are still quite rare. They have thus far occurred mostly in sources that make stylistic comparisons or that focus on explicating a particular work; little attention has been given to the development of broader conceptual frameworks. As a result, many phenomena crucial to popular music's distinctive sonic attributes, such as syncopation, "the beat," and "groove," have only just begun to be addressed in scholarly discourse.[25]

In the field of music theory, however, rhythm and meter *have* received a great deal of attention, especially within the last twenty years. Nevertheless, research has focused almost exclusively on classical music. Therefore, if I wish to make use of the sophisticated approaches that theorists have developed, I must draw on research that uses classical works as its analytical bases. This will immediately raise alarm bells for scholars of popular music, who have spilled a great deal of ink decrying the application of theories to repertoires for which they might not be "appropriate." Richard Middleton, for instance, cites a number of problems with "old-style musicological pop text," including "a tendency to use inappropriate or loaded terminology," "a skewed focus" (in his view, an emphasis on pitch and harmony over rhythm and timbre), an overemphasis on "features that can be notated easily," an aesthetic of "abstractionism," and a monologic approach to listening that ignores "the possibility of variable aural readings" (Middleton 1990: 4). As Tim Hughes has noted, however, problems such as loaded terminology, skewed perspectives, and a preference for singular readings are potential risks of any scholarly approach (T. Hughes 2000: 200); moreover, to cite a caveat articulated by Martin Scherzinger with reference to African music, but applicable to any style, "the imposition of some idealizing

25. Examples of popular-music analyses involving rhythmic qualities include Covach 1997a, Headlam 1997, and Neal 1998, while stylistic comparison is a particular concern in Krims 2000 and Stewart 2000. Treatments of broader theoretical issues related to rhythm appear in Temperley 2001, Stephenson 2002, and Hughes 2003.

inscriptions (or formalisms) on any scholarly account of African music is un-avoidable and thus not limited to those analyses that currently go by the name of musical 'formalism' " (Scherzinger 2001: 7).

Furthermore, denials of the appropriateness of a given term often are based on the assumption, mentioned above, of a particular social context as authentic: that is, terms seen as foreign to that context are labeled "inappropriate." This premise is in turn intertwined in a curious way with the intentional fallacy: in sociocultural accounts of music, the pronouncement of suitability often depends not so much upon whether the person who created the music thought about it in this way, but whether it is thought about in this way in the music-culture in which it was created. Applied consistently, this measure would rule out the key theoretical concepts of many a scholarly apparatus: to provide just two examples, I have never heard a raver describe his or her experience in terms of a "botched body without organs" (Jordan 1995, citing Deleuze and Guattari) or "subcultural capital" (Thornton 1996, citing and extending Bourdieu).

Hence, although I do not dispute the value of theorizing concepts originating within a particular culture, and I will often employ this technique myself, I believe that the opposite approach can also be productive. Applying music-theoretical concepts developed in association with Western classical music to electronic dance music, and comparing these two largely unrelated repertories, can benefit not only popular music, but also the larger field of music theory in general. Classical music still functions as the unmarked category in music theory: it is assumed, often unconsciously, to be normative. This situation applies even though some theorists do take pains to note that their comments apply only to Western classical music. Such a result is in part due to the generalizing nature of theory (even when it is explicitly claimed that a particular theory speaks only for Western art music, that theory is very often assumed to be about music more generally); it is also a consequence of the fact that other types of music are, for the most part, still not analyzed in music-theoretical ways. As a result, much of what we as music theorists know about "music" is actually based on what we know about Western art music. Even though we are more aware now than in the past that our knowledge of music is incomplete, the power of a theory of Western classical music to speak for music more generally still holds within the discipline. Were this not true, the incompleteness of our knowledge would be a great cause for concern—a matter requiring immediate remediation. Paradoxi-cally, applying current theories to other repertories has the power to call attention to this incompleteness. Provided that the analyst remains sensitive of the rami-fications of his or her actions and addresses these concerns explicitly, working across the disjuncture between *music* and *theory* can highlight assumptions within current theories of "music" and also reveal some of the distinctive aspects of the music in question. As this book proceeds, I will illustrate some ways in which this can occur.

Although the book as a whole focuses on electronic dance music in a broad sense, detailed analysis focuses on techno—a term that I use to refer to a specific subcategory of EDM, as I will explain further in chapter 1. In effect, this means that the majority of notated examples are drawn from the work of techno producers and DJs.[26] I made this decision in recognition of the substantial differences that exist among the many varieties of electronic dance music: to provide a thorough account of every genre would generate an unwieldy length, while always speaking only of "electronic dance music" runs the risk of neglecting important stylistic differences. Nevertheless, listening to and thinking about works in other styles has been essential to this study, and field research involved a multiplicity of genres. The performances I attended involved many different styles, and interviews were not limited to techno musicians and fans. Hence, I am able to draw cross-genre conclusions in addition to making points that are most relevant to a particular style.[27] In general, my most expansive claims extend to electronic dance music as a whole, while more specific, detailed points focus on techno. I make this distinction clear by using "electronic dance music" when proposing broad points and "techno" in situations where my scope is more narrow. In the context of this project, therefore, techno functions as a kind of case study: it exemplifies certain distinctive characteristics of a larger style, while also presenting its own unique constellation of features.

Having addressed these general concerns, I refer the reader to appendix A, where I provide a detailed account of specific transcription techniques and the rationale behind them.

26. Three specific exceptions involve tracks by The Chemical Brothers, Azzido Da Bass, and Mario Più. These works were chosen as clear examples of particular rhythmic and metrical phenomena.

27. Another question concerns the terms "genre" and "style," which have been assigned a huge range of (often quite contradictory) meanings in musical scholarship. In general, I use "genre" to refer to the musical classifications employed by fans, musicians, and journalists, who use the term extensively in association with labels such as techno, house, trance, and so on. This usage emphasizes the social construction of these categories. I use "style" as a more general term referring to the characteristic features of various musical domains: of individual compositions, of the output of a particular artist, of genres, and at the broadest level, of entire musical categories (e.g., EDM). Moore (2001a) provides a useful survey of the many meanings applied to these terms within humanities discourse, while McLeod (2001) theorizes the function of "genre" within electronic dance music.

Methodology II: Field Research

Field research for this study consisted of interviews with DJs, producers, and fans of electronic dance music; attendance at various types of EDM events; and other activities such as reading and posting to electronic discussion boards. Most of the interview phase of the project took place in fall 2001 and spring 2002, as part of the research for a doctoral dissertation completed at Indiana University in May 2003. The majority of interviewees were based in Indiana at the time of the interview, either in Bloomington (home of Indiana University), Indianapolis, or West Lafayette (home of Purdue University).[28] The reader should understand their comments, therefore, as situated within a particular geographical and historical location, although my experiences with dance music in other locations lead me to believe that many of their remarks are more broadly applicable. During the summer of 2004, interviews by telephone with three internationally active producers whose work is analyzed in subsequent chapters (Carl Craig, Graham Massey of 808 State, and Rick Smith of Underworld) strengthened this conviction.

In addition to scheduled interviews, I have had numerous informal conversations about EDM with interviewees and other fans and musicians. Participation in various electronic mailing lists provided another important source for discourse on the music. I was also active in the Disc Jockeys and Electronic Musicians Association (DJEMA), an official Indiana University student group, during the 2001–02 academic year. I explain more specific details of my approach—such as where interviews occurred, how they were transcribed, and the types of questions asked—in appendix B.

I have emphasized the variety of contexts in which EDM functions, and an important part of my research agenda has been to attend to the music in these diverse contexts: not only on my own, but also at clubs, raves, DJ tours, and music festivals.[29] My own history with these environments predates this project; I first became enthralled with club music and culture as a college freshman and

28. In conversation, many people have expressed surprise to me over the existence of EDM culture within a largely rural state such as Indiana. However, dance music has been alive and well throughout the Midwest (and in many other nonurban parts of North America) throughout much of the past decade (since the early to mid-1990s); before that, as I will explain in the following chapter, the region gave birth to both Chicago house and Detroit techno.

29. A particularly important event for me has been the Detroit Electronic Music Festival, which I have attended annually since 2001. Held in open-air Hart Plaza in downtown Detroit, this free festival presents four simultaneous stages of electronic music for twelve hours per day over a three-day Memorial Day weekend. Musicians working in a variety of genres have performed, but techno is featured most prominently. Attendance over the course of the festival has consistently been extremely large, with official estimates exceeding one million in most years. Since 2003, this event has been known as the Movement Festival.

have followed its development since that time. However, I began to think about my experiences more analytically when, during the early years of a Ph.D. program in music theory, I became interested in EDM as a research subject. My relationship to the music as a fan persisted (and it would be disingenuous to claim that I think about this music only "objectively," that I do not love it in a personal way), but I also began to attend to my experiences more self-consciously, learning to refine and capture my perceptions by writing them down, and highlighting their relationships to larger discourses by discussing the music with others and considering it in relation to a variety of theoretical frameworks.

Field research is a common method in the humanities, but it is still virtually unheard of in music theory, which has tended to emphasize individual analytical engagements with single pieces of music.[30] Yet several reasons make field research a valuable activity for theorists in particular. First, music theorists often expend considerable energy trying to determine how the composer worked—how he or she put the music together. Likewise, musicologists attempt to reconstruct the ways in which audiences responded to musical works during the time of their inception. For scholars studying contemporary styles, much of this information is available directly from the source, and in many cases it is available *only* in this way; with EDM, most of the information that DJs, producers, and fans can share is simply not available in print. Second, theorists studying popular music in particular have generally not received substantial institutional training in this repertoire, even though they may have spent many years performing and/ or listening to it. Field research is one way of compensating for this deficiency, providing a broad perspective that might otherwise be lacking.

The use of cross-disciplinary methodology also can work against the fragmentation that has characterized scholarship on popular music throughout its history. Within this general field, scholars are spread across a wide range of disciplines (music theory, musicology, ethnomusicology, communication studies, cultural studies, sociology), and interaction among different fields is often scarce or nonexistent. There has been a particularly pronounced division between disciplines that are associated with Western classical music and those that are not, with the former decrying the lack of close analysis in popular music studies and the latter critiquing theory and musicology for neglecting social context. Having attempted to problematize this division in my arguments on the relationship of music and context, I wish to work across (and against) these disciplinary boundaries; in methodological terms, this involves the combination of approaches traditionally associated with music theory and ethnomusicology. I believe that the

30. For an exception, see Krims 2000.

tensions that inevitably arise between the (sometimes quite different) perspectives of these two fields can be productive rather than destructive: ethnomusicology's insistence on specific, local meanings can counter theory's tendency toward abstraction, for example, whereas theory can reveal trends and commonalities among the vast array of individual musical experiences.

Like most theorists, I first came to music as a performer (specifically, as a classical pianist), but thinking about what I did in "the field" as focus of research was a new experience for me. Although I was perfectly comfortable going to clubs, so long as I functioned as just another body on the dance floor, the thought of initiating contacts with individual musicians filled me with apprehension. Once those contacts developed, however, I felt a new kind of personal involvement with the music, a more broadly social engagement that complemented the intensely personal interaction of analyst and piece with which I was already familiar. Most surprising to me, I came to feel politicized by this engagement. During the period that I was researching and writing my dissertation, the EDM scenes that thrived in many American cities were targeted by a government "crackdown." Because of a perceived relationship between dance music culture and drug use, and as a result of the actions of government agencies, politicians, and the news media, EDM events and clubs were forcibly shut down across the country. In Indianapolis, this crackdown was officially declared by the mayor in a press conference on June 10, 2001, the morning after the shutdown of a dance music event by the police. Subsequent efforts involved the enforcement of curfew laws and statutes from the Prohibition Era requiring "dance hall permits" for the operation of musical establishments. The future of "the scene" became a major topic of discussion among locals. As a researcher, I was troubled by the way in which the government and the media colluded in disseminating a grossly oversimplified and often inaccurate portrayal of EDM culture; by the moral panic that emerged in response to the perceived threat of youth music (strongly evoking earlier reactions to rock 'n' roll and rap); and by the very real concern that the focus of my research might be forced into oblivion.[31] As a theorist, I was unac-

31. For the text of the press release issued by Indianapolis mayor Bart Peterson at the outset of these events, see http://www6.indygov.org/mayor/press/2001/June/01-06-10b.htm. Its depiction of rave is generally both factually incorrect and stereotypical, involving extremely improbable and sensationalistic claims of activities such as "unprotected sex involving multiple partners" as well as the misleading suggestion that the event was held in a hidden and dangerous location (this particular event occurred at The Sport Zone, an indoor sports facility where events such as youth camps are held). Contemporary news reports (Schwartz 2001) record five drug-related arrests among approximately 1100 people in attendance.

For an opinion piece critiquing the shutdown of an event in Missouri around the same time, see http://www.riverfronttimes.com/issues/2001-07-25/radarstation.html. An article about legal accustomed to feeling such a direct involvement between current events and the music I studied.

Perhaps more surprisingly, my experiences also challenged some of the perspectives that I brought to the field as an ethnomusicologist. Because of my concern with musical specificity, most interviews centered on detailed discussion of musical characteristics, although issues of cultural meaning were also discussed as they emerged. This approach has become uncommon in ethnomusicology, which has come to focus more and more on the cultural functions of music and much less on the details of its construction.[32] Hence, at the start of my field research I was concerned about its prospects for success. My ethnomusicological training had led me to expect that people would be most interested in the cultural meanings associated with their musical activities and that they would find in-depth discussion of musical features to be obscure and irrelevant. In contrast, participants were eager to discuss both the technical *and* the cultural realms of music-making. Those who were musicians seemed to have a particular hunger to talk about musical details; many interviews lasted significantly longer than I had expected and ended with comments about how rarely they had the chance to discuss these kinds of features. These experiences lend support to the claim that divisions between social "context" and musical "structure" are products of academic disciplines, having much less relevance within specific music-cultures.

Track Listing

Like most of the rhythmic structures found in electronic dance music, this book is presented as a cycle: it begins with broad concerns, moves toward increasingly detailed musical discussion, and then returns to larger issues as it approaches

---

tions taken in Texas (http://www.dallasobserver.com/issues/2001-06-28/feature2.html/page1.html) provides a well-balanced and comprehensive account of the events occurring around this time and the issues involved. Reactions to the government's actions included demonstrations, a number of ACLU actions, and the formation of the Electronic Music Defense and Education Fund, whose Web site (http://www.emdef.org) provides a timeline of legal developments and responses.

Similar governmental responses to rave in England began in the late 1980s, culminating with the passage of the Criminal Justice and Public Order Act of 1994, which defined a rave as a gathering of one hundred or more people playing amplified music "characterized by the emission of a succession of repetitive beats." See Reynolds 1999 and Thornton 1994 for further discussion. All world-wide-web pages cited 11 June 2004.

32. Concern with musical organization *is* evident in earlier ethnomusicological writing (for some examples from research on African music, see Locke 1982, Nketia 1974, and Koetting 1970); however, since the "paradigm shift" of the 1970s there has been a turn away from such approaches in favor of anthropologically based models emphasizing music in and as culture.

the conclusion. This design manifests itself in the grouping of chapters into three larger sections. Part I, entitled "Getting into the Groove" (introduction, ch. 1, and ch. 2), lays the foundation for the project as a whole. Chapter 1 considers the characteristics and practices through which electronic dance music is defined, as well as when, where, and how these practices arose. What musical and social circumstances informed the development of this style? Furthermore, what kinds of activities and technologies have been involved in its creation?

Chapter 2 focuses more specifically on conceptual frameworks involving rhythm and meter. What kinds of rhythms comprise the fabric of electronic dance music, and how do they relate to each other? How is meter realized in EDM, and how do these metrical behaviors shape the character of the music? How might existing ideas about rhythm and meter, both music-theoretical and fan-based, contribute to an understanding of EDM's temporal dimensions? Conversely, in what ways might EDM suggest alterations or revisions of these ideas?

Chapters 3 and 4 constitute part II, in which I explore two avenues of interpretive multiplicity, ambiguity and metrical dissonance. Both chapters center around detailed analyses of illustrative passages. In chapter 3, I describe ways in which the ambiguous structuring of rhythm patterns facilitates multiple metrical interpretations. Then, in chapter 4, I explore ways in which metrically "dissonant" layers may sound apart in relation to each other. In so doing, I draw on current theories of this phenomenon while also uncovering types of metrical dissonance distinctive to EDM. I conclude by suggesting several ways in which these musical practices resonate with broader meanings within EDM culture.

Large-scale features are the focus of chapters 5 and 6, which form part III, "Electronic Dance Music and the Epic." Chapter 5 considers how measures are organized into larger groupings and the various ways in which those groupings can be conveyed to listeners, as well as how and to what extent notions of hypermeter and phrase structure might shed light on the nature of these patterns as they are realized in EDM. I also comment on the role of multimeasure patterning in the art of DJing and the interaction of this aspect of design with metrical dissonance.

Chapter 6 completes the book's cyclical return, expanding the time-scale to consider the broad proportions of the record and the set. In this chapter I explain how the flexible approaches to musical structure characteristic of small-scale organization in EDM extend to its most expansive formal procedures and patterns. After addressing some of the methodological and conceptual implications of studying form in this repertory, I discuss how producers structure complete tracks and some of the recurring formal shapes that result. I then use participants' remarks about form as the basis for an exploration of the ways in which DJs organize and shape complete sets.

In addition to the explanations of methodology in appendices A and B and the nine transcriptions of complete tracks provided in appendix C, the end of the book contains a glossary of frequently used terms. For those outside of the field of music theory, I have provided definitions of music-theoretical concepts that play an important role in this work, while for those unfamiliar with electronic dance music, I have defined terms such as "producer," "sampler," and so on.

While the overall design of the book proceeds cyclically (from the broad to the specific and back again), its treatment of musical entities also unfolds in a linear fashion. I begin with the basic building blocks of rhythm and meter, individual rhythm patterns, addressing their characteristics and classification in isolation. I then turn to the question of how these patterns are combined to create meter as well as metrical conflict. From there I proceed to a consideration of multimeasure groups, then to form within complete tracks, and finally to the development and organization of entire DJ sets. Like a well-ordered DJ set, therefore, this discourse develops across time, while also being unified by recurring strands within the texture: pervasive principles of design that shape EDM at multiple structural levels, which I highlight as I proceed.

Before I conclude, I would like to offer a few notes of guidance for the reader. Because I am concerned with musical sound, listening to the recordings that accompany the majority of examples is essential. The contents of the compact disc are included as a separate list, and the track numbers for recordings of notated examples also are indicated in brackets in the caption of each example. In order to form an independent impression, I suggest listening to each recording prior to examining the transcription or reading my analysis, though the example should also be heard in conjunction with my discussion. Whenever possible, I have provided a recording of the entire track in addition to the short excerpts; I encourage the reader to listen to both, as my analytical claims about specific passages have certainly been shaped by the experience of hearing them in the context of the complete track. The full-track recordings also are important to the discussions of multimeasure patterning and form in chapters 5–6. See the discography for further information on all the recordings discussed in the book.

The History and Creation of Electronic Dance Music

Techno is a music based in experimentation;
It is sacred to no one race; it has no definitive sound.
It is music for the future of the human race.
Without this music there will be no peace, no love, no vision.
By simply communicating through sound,
Techno has brought people of all different nationalities
Together under one roof to enjoy themselves.
Isn't it obvious that music and dance
Are the keys to the universe?
So called primitive animals and tribal humans
Have known this for thousands of years!
We urge all brothers and sisters of the underground
To create and transmit their tones and frequencies
No matter how so called primitive their equipment may be
Transmit these tones and wreak havoc on the programmers!
—*Underground Resistance, excerpt from "Creed"*[1]

Electronic Dance Music and Its Histories

The term "electronic dance music" encompasses a broad range of music produced during the last two decades, including genres such as techno, house, drum 'n' bass, and trance. Although fans are very much aware of the differences between these types of music, they still view them as belonging to the same overall category, defined by particular practices of production and consumption and by

1. http://www.undergroundresistance.com, cited 21 June 2004.

certain shared musical characteristics.[2] After outlining these practices and characteristics, the first section of this chapter traces their emergence in the years
preceding EDM's rise and in the first decade of its development. I then turn
toward an exploration of the diverse creative roles and technologies involved in
realizing EDM as music, with particular attention to the activities of the DJ, the
producer, and the dancer.

One of the most distinctive characteristics of electronic dance music is the
way in which it is produced—namely, through the use of electronic technologies
such as synthesizers, drum machines, sequencers, and samplers. Although increasingly common in popular music in general in recent years, these technologies
have always formed the backbone of musical creation in EDM, in which a traditional instrument or a live vocal is the exception rather than the rule.

In other ways, however, live performance is essential to EDM, although as
with studio production it is always technologically mediated. The most pervasive
technologies in performance contexts are turntables, headphones, twelve-inch
vinyl records, and a mixing board, and the most familiar live performer is the DJ
(disc jockey). The tradition of DJing practiced in EDM involves more than simply
playing other people's records; rather, the DJ selects, combines, and manipulates
different parts of records into new compositions that differ substantially from
their source materials. In general, the exact course of a DJ's performance is not
predetermined, instead developing according to the demands of a specific situation, through interaction with a dancing audience. Although the DJ has always
been the most important figure in bringing music to fans throughout the history
of this music, within the last decade it has become increasingly common for
producers to perform as well, especially in events called "live PAs," in which
they manipulate studio technology in real time to (re)create their own music.[3]

Electronic dance music originated in the United States and first became

2. As a label for this category, "electronic dance music" (as well as the abbreviation "EDM")
has become increasingly common among fans In recent years. Durlng the 1980s, the most common
catchall term for EDM was "house music," while "techno" became more prevalent during the first
half of the 1990s. As EDM has become more and more diverse, however, these terms have come to
refer to specific genres. Another word, "electronica," has been widely used in mainstream journalism
since 1997, but most fans view this term with suspicion as a marketing label devised by the music
industry.

3. "PA" is almost always used in its abbreviated form. Some sources suggest that "PA" stands
for "public appearance" (Rietveld 1998: 89 n. 259) or "personal appearance" (Thornton 1996: 31),
while others (e.g., internet sites devoted to EDM) claim that the term stands for "performance artist."
As Thornton notes (1996: 31), the use of the adjective "live" to distinguish this type of performance
from DJing shows a curious persistence of the dichotomy between "live" and recorded music within
a tradition that challenges this distinction in a multitude of ways.

widely popular in the United Kingdom. Today, however, it is appreciated throughout the industrialized world—not only in Germany and Japan, but also in locales as diverse as Argentina, Australia, India, Israel, South Africa, and Thailand. Although the styles created and enjoyed can vary considerably from one place to another, certain musical characteristics are shared among almost all EDM. In general, it has a steady, relatively fast tempo—mostly in the range of 120–150 beats per minute (BPM), although certain genres regularly reach speeds of 180 BPM.[4] Except in certain ambient genres, a repeating bass drum pattern is almost always present. And finally, the majority of contemporary electronic dance music is instrumental.[5] Any vocal sounds that do occur are usually very brief samples (ranging in length from a very short part of a word, such as a single vowel or other vocal sound, to a single phrase) and are often subject to considerable timbral manipulation.[6] This instrumental focus—one source of the apparent abstraction I describe in the introduction (p. 11)—distinguishes EDM from almost all other commercial popular music produced in America and Europe since the birth of rock 'n' roll.

Although purely instrumental music has often been portrayed as "absolute," as refusing to articulate any meaning beyond its own patterning, listeners deal with the apparent abstraction of EDM by grounding it in the physical motions of dance.[7] This relationship to interpretive movement is one of its key defining features. Producers create music with the expectation that it will be played on the floor, where the crowd's response will determine its success or failure. DJs plan and shape their performances around this response, a major portion of which is dance (other ways of showing appreciation to the DJ include yelling, screaming, raising one's hands in the air, clapping, and whistling). And audiences associate this music with movement. While the extent to which listeners regularly experience EDM in a live dance context varies, with home listeners at one end and

4. The style of hardcore known as "gabba" or "gabber," popular during the early 1990s, was exceptionally fast, sometimes exceeding 200 BPM (Reynolds 1999: 283–85). During the 1980s, tempi in the range of 110–20 BPM also occurred in house and garage (Fikentscher 2000: 83 and 91).

5. Therefore, as mentioned in the introduction, I use the word "track" rather than "song" to refer to a single EDM composition. Both fans and journalists commonly use "track" in this sense as well. One potential area of confusion is the fact that the individual sounds *within* a composition are sometimes also called "tracks." (Krims 2000 uses this sense of "track" to discuss the texture of rap; this is also the type of track referenced by the term "multitrack recording.") In general, however, this usage is more specific to producers; I will describe individual sounds as "textural layers" instead.

6. Some exceptions to this general trend occur in drum 'n' bass/jungle, which sometimes includes rappers (MCs) who "hype" the crowd; certain styles of house music; and some of the most commercially successful EDM artists (such as Moby and Fatboy Slim), whose work often moves toward pop.

7. See Butler 2000 for further discussion of dance as a response to EDM's abstract qualities.

fans who *only* hear the music in clubs and raves at the other, most fans pursue these experiences on a fairly regular basis.[8] Furthermore, the experience of dancing creates a lexicon of physical memories that carry over into nondance contexts. Even when genres depart from direct connections to dance, they do so in ways that demonstrate their relatedness to dance-floor traditions: some music draws on the conventions of EDM, but manipulates them so much that the results are no longer suitable for the dance floor,[9] while other genres are written expressly for *not* dancing.[10]

Although humans have undoubtedly been using their bodies to interpret sound since the first music was made, electronic dance music is built around the uniquely modern practice of dancing to *recorded* music. The technologies that made this activity possible began to develop during the late nineteenth century, when Thomas Edison invented the phonograph (1877). Ten years later, Emil Berliner created the gramophone, which used flat discs instead of Edison's cylinders (Brewster and Broughton 2000: 20). By the turn of the century, these devices were affordable enough to be widely accessible (Chanan 1995: 27–28), but dancing was still very much linked with live music. This association started to break down during the 1920s and '30s, when the jukebox became prevalent across America (Brewster and Broughton 2000: 47–48). After World War II, however, the trend of dancing to recorded music picked up steam, becoming a "live" event in its own right due to the humanizing influence of the DJ.[11] According to Brewster and Broughton, the first documented occurrence of a DJ playing in public took place in 1943 in Otley, West Yorkshire, in the United Kingdom. The

8. These are informal comments based on my own experience. I have met fans (some of whom are very active as clubbers and ravers) who make statements such as "I only listen to dance music at parties," as well as those who have stopped going clubbing but continue to follow the music through personal listening.

9. This type of music might have a steady beat, but with an affect that is too low-key for the typical dance-floor audience, or it might take beat patterns characteristic of EDM and manipulate them until they are highly irregular.

10. Cf. McLeod 2001: 65. These genres have been described with a number of different names, including ambient, beatless, downtempo, and experimental. At times the term "electronica" has also been used to denote music that is more for listening than dancing, although more commonly it is used as a general term for any type of predominantly electronic popular music. These genres often omit the bass drum (hence the name "beatless") and also differ from other forms of EDM in terms of affect and tempo. Although often portrayed as home-listening music, much of this music first developed in association with dancing, either as music to be played in a venue's "chill room" (a place where dancers can take a break, offering comfortable furniture, softer music, and sometimes a cooler temperature) or as music to listen to *after* going dancing. See, for example, Reynolds 1999: 195–96.

11. Fikentscher portrays the liveness of technologically mediated dance music events in terms of "musical immediacy" (Fikentscher 2000: 15), a term that captures an essential quality of the events without relying on divisions between "live" and "recorded" music.

jockey involved, Jimmy Savile, later became the first DJ on the show *Top of the Pops*. The first live DJ events in the United States occurred during the 1950s, when radio DJs began to hold events called "platter parties" or "sock hops" as a way of promoting their shows (Brewster and Broughton 2000: 44–46 and 49).

Around the same time in France, bars called "discothèques" (which had first appeared during the war) became quite popular. In the 1960s, discothèques spread to London and America and began to develop some of the characteristics associated with modern nightclubs. No longer just a place where one heard recorded music, the discothèque became a special environment, distinguished by lights and a powerful sound system, which one attended for the expressed purpose of dancing. The DJ was now a central figure within the disco experience, the person who made recorded music immediate.[12]

Styles of dance also changed in significant ways during the 1960s. Dancing had previously been an activity for couples,[13] involving specific steps. With the advent of the Twist (1960) and the series of dance crazes that followed, movement became an individual phenomenon, requiring no training or choreography. Significantly, this allowed women to dance independently; at the same time, because dancers were no longer focused solely on their partners, it shifted attention onto the communal experience of the dance floor as a whole (Brewster and Broughton 2000: 54–55). Within the context of disco, this experience would become essential to gay liberation during the 1970s; it also was central to the social upheaval of the acid house movement in the United Kingdom during the late 1980s.

Although the term "discothèque" became widespread in the 1960s, it was not until the '70s that a style of music called disco developed. In the early years of this decade, DJs played a mixture of funk and soul at New York clubs such as the Sanctuary, the Loft, the Haven, and the Gallery, where the majority of the dancers were African American and gay. For several years the scene was a largely underground phenomenon, but between 1973 and 1976 it began to pick up steam, resulting in some 150–200 clubs in New York by the mid-1970s (Brewster and Broughton 2000: 155). At this point, narratives of disco's development begin to paint a picture of authenticity corrupted: as disco increased in popularity, it came to the attention of record company executives who seized upon it as a way of compensating for declining rock sales, and between 1976 and 1979 the record-buying public was bombarded with a deluge of disco releases. Long-

12. Brewster and Broughton 2000: 50 and 58. Fikentscher (2000: 22 and 35) refers to the confluence of these characteristics as "the disco concept."

13. More specifically, it was an activity for opposite-sex couples, an expectation that was often enforced legally.

forgotten stars released disco remakes of their hits and radio stations switched formats. Discos opened all over the country, and the scene was mythologized (and heterosexualized) in *Saturday Night Fever* (1977). The market became over-saturated, and crashed with a violence that still haunts the image of disco (and of dance music in general) even today. The event that seems to epitomize the antidisco backlash most effectively (it is mentioned in almost every account of disco's demise) occurred in Chicago on July 12, 1979. Radio DJ Steve Dahl, who had described disco as a "disease," held a promotional event called a "disco demolition" rally at a doubleheader between the Chicago White Sox and the Detroit Tigers.[14] Fans received reduced admission by giving up a disco record as they entered the park. The 10,000+ records that were collected were blown up on the field between games, an event that aroused the fervor of the crowd so much that a riot ensued and the second game had to be called off (Brewster and Broughton 2000: 268–69). As quickly as it had entered the mainstream, disco had become *déclassé*, and dance music returned to the underground.[15]

The disco era is significant for today's electronic dance music in several ways. First, it was during this era that the idea of spending an evening dancing in a club was first popularized across the world. Furthermore, most of the practices of musical creation associated with today's electronic dance music came into being during this time. It became commonplace for DJs to mix and overlap records to produce a continuous flow of sound, rather than allowing a record to die down before moving on to the next one.[16] They also would switch back and forth between two copies of the same record in order to extend it, as most records issued during the first part of the decade were very short, having been released according to pop-song standards. Other important DJ techniques developed during this time, which I will explain in detail later in this chapter, included beat matching (synchronizing the beats of two records), and the slip-cue (Brewster and Broughton 2000: 136–37).

Like almost every style of dance music to come after it, disco first developed on the dance floor, with studio production following after. In the early years, the records DJs played were mostly funk and soul; specifically "disco" records did not exist. However, because disco DJs favored certain styles of records over

14. Ironically, Chicago and Detroit soon became the leading centers of two new styles of dance music (house and techno, respectively) that have come to form the foundation of today's EDM.

15. This account of disco's history is largely based on that found in chapters 6 and 7 (pp. 124–202) of Brewster and Broughton 2000, an exceptionally detailed and comprehensive account. The same basic narrative appears in many other sources as well, however.

16. According to Brewster and Broughton (2000: 62), the first DJ to mix records was Terry Noel, who spun at the New York discothèque Arthur during the 1960s.

others, and because they combined records in unique ways, they created a distinctive "sound," which was eventually imitated in the studio. Studios also created song and record formats aimed specifically at the dance floor: namely, remixes and twelve-inch singles. The two phenomena arose around the same time and in conjunction with each other. The first person to remix disco singles was Tom Moulton, who would take tapes of songs, cut them up, and rearrange them so that the most danceable parts were extended.[17] At the time, singles were still released on seven-inch records, which were meant to be played at 45 RPM. Because this format could only hold a limited amount of material, it was not suitable for the remix, which often increased the length of a song quite substantially. Furthermore, because the seven-inch format forced the grooves closer together, the volume it could achieve was lower and the overall sound quality poorer than that of twelve-inch 33s. Producers discovered that the larger format allowed them to fit an entire remix or extended dance version of a song onto one side of a record and to achieve a richer, more resonant sound (especially in the bass, the register that affects dancers most physically), and record companies eventually began to utilize the format. The first commercially successful twelve-inch release was DJ Walter Gibbon's remix of Double Exposure's "Ten Percent," released on the Salsoul label in June 1976 (Brewster and Broughton 2000: 178–79). Nearly thirty years later, remixes are still widespread in dance music, and twelve-inch vinyl is still the format of choice.

Nevertheless, disco differed in many ways from the electronic dance music of the '80s and '90s. First of all, though it has often been characterized as "artificial," its production was not, by and large, electronic. Most disco records were made in record company studios with session musicians; even the most commercially successful releases list an array of performers on instruments such as drums, bass, lead guitar, rhythm guitar, grand piano, and miscellaneous percussion.[18]

17. Brewster and Broughton 2000: 175–76. The authors point out that, strictly speaking, this approach should be called "re-editing." Since it works with a single recording of an entire song, it differs from the remixing associated with EDM, in which the original multitrack recording is the object of manipulation. Brewster and Broughton do not explain when the latter technique became more common, but they do make it clear that remixes of some form were common from the mid-1970s on.

In Jamaica, reggae producers were creating remixes, which they called "versions" and "dubs," as early as 1971–72. Although no chain of influence between reggae and early disco remixes is apparent, reggae aesthetics did play a role in the genesis of hip-hop music (Brewster and Broughton 2000: 119–21), and all three styles emphasize the creative recombination of pre-existing materials through practices such as remixing and DJing.

18. This particular list is taken from the Village People EP *Go West,* which contains the hit title track as well as "In the Navy." The use of live drums made beat matching considerably challenging for 1970s DJs, since they had to take expressive timing variations into account. The drum machines used in most EDM since the 1980s simplify matters somewhat by making rhythm patterns quantitatively precise.

Synthesizers were used as well,[19] but they were not the predominant form of instrumentation.[20] Furthermore, disco was a resolutely vocal style; most disco releases were easily identifiable as "songs" rather than "tracks." And finally, as will be discussed further shortly, disco DJs worked with much more limited equipment than their '80s counterparts.

In the years following disco's decline in popularity, dance music seem to disappear from public view. Nevertheless, disco did not "die," for it was preserved and developed further within the communities with which it was originally associated. In clubs such as the Paradise Garage in New York City and the Warehouse in Chicago, DJs blended disco with other styles to create new variations on its sound. They also made use of new technologies to create dance music that was truly "electronic."

The Paradise Garage opened in 1977, when disco was still at its peak.[21] Like the early disco clubs, its clientele was largely African American and gay (Fikentscher 2000: 70). The force behind its musical menu was Larry Levan, a legendary DJ who played at the club until it closed in 1987. The style of music that he favored has since come to be called "garage," after the name of the club itself. Although Levan's selections were by all accounts eclectic, "garage" generally connotes a style that is a fairly direct continuation of disco, featuring vocals in a gospel or R&B style and the relatively "natural" feel of live instrumentals.[22] At the same time, garage did make use of the new technologies available during the early 1980s. For instance, the New York City Peech Boys' "Don't Make Me

19. The Village People recording just described, for instance, also lists performers on "electric keyboards" and "synthesizers." Synthesizers were also becoming increasingly common in rock and jazz during the 1970s; they were used by German bands such as Neu! and Kraftwerk and by jazz fusionists such as Herbie Hancock and Sun Ra, among others. See Simon Reynold's essay on "Krautrock" and Peter Shapiro's essay on "Jazz-Funk" in Shapiro 2000: 24–34 and 52–53.

20. One exception is the work of producers such as Giorgio Moroder and Patrick Cowley, whose work formed the basis of "hi-NRG," a genre popular in gay clubs throughout much of the 1980s. Like disco, hi-NRG relied on ecstatic vocals—a classic Moroder-produced track was Donna Summer's "I Feel Love," while Cowley produced Sylvester's "(You Make Me Feel) Mighty Real"—but its instrumentation was based almost exclusively on synthesizers and drum machines. See Shapiro 2000: 41–42. Like many authors making connections between disco and today's EDM, Shapiro seems to overemphasize the synthetic component of disco; although an increasingly prominent and persistent beat was an important part of disco, the "relentless four-to-the-floor machine beat" that he describes (p. 40) did not become commonplace until the 1980s.

21. This date comes from Brewster and Broughton 2000: 271. Fikentscher gives 1976 as the opening year (2000: 70).

22. Brewster and Broughton 2000: 82–83; Shapiro 2000: 219. One potential source of confusion is the fact that a style developing within the United Kingdom since the late 1990s has also come to be called "garage" (pronounced "gār-ridge"). It is sometimes differentiated with a geographical adjective ("U.K. garage") or alternately referred to as "two-step" (although some would argue that "two-step" is actually a subcategory of "U.K. garage").

Wait" (1982), often cited as an emblematic example of garage, includes live vocals, guitar, and piano but also features a variety of studio effects and a Linn drum machine in place of a live drummer (Fikentscher 2000: 90).

At the Warehouse in Chicago, another DJ-driven scene made even greater use of technology, while still preserving certain elements of disco. When the Warehouse opened in 1977, DJ Frankie Knuckles, a friend of Larry Levan, moved to the city specifically for the job. During the early years of the club, Knuckles played a mixture of classic disco and garage, as well as a largely electronic form of disco coming mainly from Italy.[23] As disco ceased to be commercially viable, he found himself short on releases, and so he began remixing tracks at home. He would work the results into his DJ performances with a reel-to-reel tape player. Eventually, he began to add elements to his mixes such as newly composed bass lines and drum tracks. As his style became more distinctive, it acquired a name: house music. As with garage, the term comes from the place where the music developed.

Although electronic music technology began to be popularized in the 1970s, it was still relatively expensive, cumbersome, and difficult to use during that time. During the formative years of house music, however, this situation began to change. A series of inexpensive machines from Japan's Roland corporation—in particular, the TB-303 bass line generator and the TR-808 and TR-909 drum machines—made production significantly more affordable and accessible. Musicians no longer needed to gain access to recording studios; instead, they could purchase their own equipment and create music at home. DJs such as Frankie Knuckles and Jesse Saunders also employed drum machines in their live performances, using the 808's resonant bass drum sound to intensify the beat of the record being played and to create transitions between records (Brewster and Broughton 2000: 307; Shapiro 2000: 75). The first vinyl releases in the house style began to appear in 1983 (Jesse Saunders's "On and On")[24] and 1984 (Jamie Principle's "Your Love"); by 1985, the trickle had become a flood.

House reveals its disco roots in the gospel style of its vocals and the funk of its bass lines. At the same time, its creators clearly found something attractive in the "unnatural" aesthetic of drum machines and synthesizers. Hence it is possible to speak of two streams of house—two related styles that coexist and commingle, and yet are identifiably distinct. On the one hand, there is "vocal" house, a style that—like garage—wears its disco ancestry on its sleeve. Vocal

23. This style is sometimes called "Italo-disco"; see, for example, Sicko 1999: 45–48.
24. Brewster and Broughton give 1984 as the date of this release (2000: 306), but Shapiro 2000 (p. 75) and Rietveld 1998 (p. 255) date it as 1983.

house productions can easily be described as songs. Although their instrumentation (unlike that of disco) is still largely electronic, they use features such as swing-quantized rhythms to create a more "natural" feel.[25] On the other hand, another style of house music, predominantly instrumental, utilizes the mechanistic capabilities of drum machines to their full advantage. These compositions are usually stark and minimal, eschewing not only sung melodies but also instrumental ones. Because drum-machine rhythms form their primary component, they are often called "drum tracks" or "rhythm tracks," or "tracks" for short; along these lines, works having these qualities are sometimes described as "tracky." Although this distinction between "songs" and "tracks" dates back to the mid-1980s, house musicians and fans still use these categories today.[26]

Around the same time that house was first created in Chicago, a somewhat different style of music, which eventually came to be called "techno," was developing in Detroit. The social circumstances in which the two genres emerged are similar in several ways; for instance, both types of music developed within large industrial cities in the American Midwest, and both were created by African Americans. At the same time, the formation of Detroit techno has been associated more with individual musicians than with particular clubs, and the milieu in which it arose was not a predominantly homosexual one. In spite of these differences, the musicians of the two cities have interacted with each other from the very beginning and continue to do so.

Techno developed within a scene that involved a great deal of musical cross-fertilization. During the late 1970s and early '80s, high school kids in northwestern Detroit—lacking clubs to attend—began organizing their own dance parties (Sicko 1999: 32–33). Attendance was usually at least several hundred people, and sometimes reached as high as 1200 (Sicko 1999: 37). These were DJed events where a wide range of music was played. Favorite styles included an assortment of electronic music, such as the highly synthesized disco still coming from Europe at the time, New Wave bands such as the Human League and Yellow Magic Orchestra, and technopop groups such as ABC (Sicko 1999: 44–51). Radio also played an important role in techno's development. Especially significant during the early years was the "Midnight Funk Association," a show hosted by Charles Johnson, whose on-air name was "the Electrifying Mojo." Johnson, whose show was on the air from 1977 to 1985, played a mixture of

25. If a rhythm is "quantized," it is quantitatively precise. Drum-machine rhythms almost always have this quality, since they are usually programmed rather than performed; however, some electronic technology features algorithms that introduce small variations in beat positions, mimicking the human effect of "swing."

26. See Shapiro 2000: 77–78 for a clear discussion of this distinction.

New Wave and futuristic funk;[27] significantly, he also gave heavy rotation to the German band Kraftwerk, who have often been cited as important precursors to techno.[28]

Listening to this radio show, and attending these parties, were three young men in the western suburb of Belleville named Juan Atkins, Derrick May, and Kevin Saunderson. Atkins, May, and Saunderson—now nicknamed the "Belleville Three"—formed their own DJ collective, which they called "Deep Space" (Sicko 1999: 56–58). Gradually, they also began to make electronic music of their own, eventually becoming the first producers to release techno records.[29] Although the three recorded independently, they were friends, having met in high school. Atkins was the first to release records, although his initial forays occurred within a rock context. In 1981, he formed a band called Cybotron with guitarist Richard ("Rik") Davis. Their initial release, "Alleys of Your Mind," was an early example of what might be called "proto-techno."[30] Both Atkins and Davis were very interested in questions of technology and the future, and they spent significant amounts of time discussing these matters from a philosophical perspective and reading works such as Alvin Toffler's 1980 book *The Third Wave* (Sicko 1999: 70). These themes are reflected in their song titles ("Cosmic Cars," "Industrial Lies"), in the name Cybotron (a merger of "cyborg" and "cyclotron" [Sicko 1999: 70]), in their lyrics, and the technological focus of their instrumentation. In 1983, they released an album, *Enter* (reissued under the title *Clear* in 1990), but they broke up shortly thereafter because Davis wanted to pursue a more rock-based approach.

In 1985, Atkins decided to skirt the music industry altogether and produce

27. A characteristic example of "futuristic funk" would be Parliament's "Flashlight," which was the first song to feature a synthesized bass line (Shapiro 2000: 231). The work of George Clinton and Parliament was also explicitly futuristic in its lyrical content.

28. Kraftwerk, whose seminal releases include *Autobahn* (1974), *Trans-Europe Express* (1977), and *Computer World* (1981), were one of the first groups to use exclusively synthesized instrumentation; as Simon Reynolds writes in his essay in *Modulations,* "they staked everything on the idea that the synthesizer was the future and won" (Shapiro 2000: 33). As mentioned in the introduction (p. 7 n. 4), one of techno's first producers, Derrick May, is often quoted as saying, "The music is just like Detroit—a complete mistake. It's like George Clinton and Kraftwerk stuck in an elevator" (Cosgrove 1988: 86). May has subsequently claimed that he was unaware of Kraftwerk's music when he first began to experiment with synthesizers (Sicko 1999: 70–71).

29. A fourth member of the collective from Belleville, Eddie "Flashin' " Fowlkes, also played a significant role in early techno production. He has not been emphasized as an originator of the music to the same extent, however, perhaps because he released fewer records than the "Belleville Three" (Barr 2000: 126).

30. The first proto-techno record, released just before "Alleys of Your Mind," was "Sharevari" by A Number of Names (Sicko 1999: 71). Although largely electronic in instrumentation, "Sharevari" is still a pop song in format, with a clear verse/chorus structure.

records on his own, an approach that has been characteristic of techno ever since. He began recording tracks independently and formed his own label (Metroplex) to release them. His first single, released under the name Model 500, was entitled "No UFOs"; it is frequently described as the first techno record. Unlike "Alleys of Your Mind" and "Sharevari," it shows no obvious relationship to rock or pop. Its instrumentation is entirely electronic, with stark drum-machine rhythms standing out as its most prominent feature. In fact, with the exception of the bass line, it contains little in the way of melody or pitch at all. There are no traces of verse/chorus structure, and the only words in the track, which do not appear for nearly two minutes, are rhythmically chanted rather than sung (and often heavily manipulated). In a reversal of conventional associations, Atkins presents UFOs as a symbol of hope:

> They say, "There is no hope"
> They say, "No UFOs"
> Why is no head held high?
> Maybe you'll see them fly[31]

Not long after the release of "No UFOs," Kevin Saunderson formed his own record label, KMS records. In the coming years, he would issue releases under names as diverse as Reese, Reese and Santonio, Reese Project, Keynotes, Tronik House, Inner City, Inter City, and E Dancer.[32] In 1986, Eddie Fowlkes released "Goodbye Kiss," the second Metroplex release. In the same year, Derrick May also formed a label, Transmat, on which he recorded now-classic singles such as "Nude Photo" and "Strings of Life" (1987). Both were released under the name Rythim is Rythim.[33]

During these early years, the scenes in Detroit and Chicago were relatively isolated phenomena—confined to their respective cities, and largely underground in character. It was in the United Kingdom that the music of these cities first became widely popular. In 1985 and 1986, DJs in England found house singles

31. Atkins has commented on the song's meaning as follows: "The government always tries to cover up the fact that there could be other life in the galaxy. To me, the system is bent on keeping people in despair, hopeless, not wanting to achieve anything, so if you keep your head up high maybe you'll start realizing things that you never thought possible, and seeing a UFO is probably the ultimate impossibility" (quoted in Shapiro 2000: 116).

32. Shapiro 2000: 116. "KMS" stands for Kevin Maurice Saunderson, and "Reese" is a nickname for "Maurice" (Sicko 1999: 82). Saunderson has said that he used as many names as possible in order to make the Detroit scene appear bigger than it was (Shapiro 2000: 116). However, his approach also fits in with an aesthetic of anonymity that has dominated techno production since its earliest days. Even today, producers frequently use multiple aliases for their various projects.

33. This name is sometimes spelled "Rhythim is Rhythim"; for instance, see Sicko 1999. I have used the spelling given on the 1997 release *Innovator.*

in import record stores and began to play them in the clubs where they worked (Rietveld 1998: 40–45). The music increased in popularity during 1987, while around the same time certain DJs and promoters began to foster a new approach to clubbing. Figures such as Paul Oakenfold and Danny Rampling had been transformed by their experiences in clubs on the resort island of Ibiza, where they had danced until dawn and experimented with the drug Ecstasy. Oakenfold, Rampling, and others began to recreate these events at clubs in London (Reynolds 1999: 58–61). Their endeavors were limited, however, by the fact that English clubs were required to close at 2 A.M. (hence, after-hours events were unlicensed); furthermore, the events were becoming so popular that clubs began to seem too small (Rietveld 1998: 54). All-night events, which came to be called "raves," began to spring up in illegal locations such as warehouses and fields. In 1988, the combination of house music and raving exploded in popularity, culminating in a time that has been dubbed the "second summer of love." By 1989, raving had become a mass-cultural phenomenon among British youth.

In the early 1990s, U.S. promoters who had heard about English raves starting holding similar events in cities such as New York, Los Angeles, and San Francisco.[34] The phenomenon spread quickly, and rave-like events now occur across the country—not only in major metropolitan areas, but also in the Arizona desert, in small Midwestern towns, and in a range of other locations. Although the term "rave" is difficult to define (and most dance-music fans in America no longer use the term, instead describing events as "parties"), it generally refers to a one-time, one-location, all-night dance party. In contrast to news portrayals, contemporary raves are defined neither by illegality nor by drug use. As a phenomenon, the "rave" is just one part of the history of electronic dance music, and one of many environments in which EDM now occurs in America and the rest of the world.[35] Although media accounts have tended to collapse all of these contexts into this most controversial one (thus the frequent use of nonsensical terms such as "rave club"), EDM is part of a wide variety of "scenes," all of

34. Raves began to appear in other locations as early as 1992; for instance, it was during that year that they first occurred in North Carolina, where I was living at the time.

35. I have already mentioned clubs, which are distinguished from raves as geographically stable locations that (usually) close earlier, as well as music festivals and bars. Also relevant is the "club night," a recurring (usually weekly) event on a particular night, often featuring a specific genre of EDM, which takes place either in the same club every week or in a venue that changes with the date. Another type of event, the "circuit party," is similar to a rave in that it lasts all night and occurs independently of clubs. However, the audience at a circuit party consists largely of gay men in their twenties, thirties, and forties, whereas raves involve a mix of sexualities and genders and a younger crowd (typically ranging in age from about sixteen to twenty-four).

which feature different crowds, different practices and behaviors, different values, and different musical styles.

The first genre of American dance music to become popular in the United Kingdom was Chicago house. Although music from Detroit was soon imported as well, it was often treated as subcategory of house, and for many years the most common English term for electronic dance music in general was "house" or "acid house."[36] Despite the social and musical differences of the two cities— which are less than three hundred miles apart—it was clear that the two styles were related. During the formative years of techno and house, the musicians involved interacted in various ways. The Belleville Three often visited Chicago to sell their music, and Derrick May lived there for nearly a year around 1984 (Brewster and Broughton 2000: 320, 329).[37] In fact, he even sold Frankie Knuckles a TR-909 drum machine at one point (Shapiro 2000: 116).

As English journalists and record companies became more aware of the distinction between the two cities' musical styles, they began to emphasize the Detroit style as a separate genre. Part of this process was the newfound use of "techno" as a term. This development seems to have been driven in part by marketing forces. In 1988, Neil Rushton issued a compilation of Detroit material, originally entitled *The House Sound of Detroit*. Wishing to emphasize his product as distinct from that of other labels featuring Chicago producers, he changed the name to *Techno! The New Dance Sound of Detroit*. The musicians played an important part in this process as well, though: they had already been using "techno" as an adjective, and Atkins recorded a track called "Techno Music" for the compilation (Brewster and Broughton 2000: 331–32).[38]

Related tensions between diverse local forces, and between local and global

36. Acid house was a track-oriented style of Chicago house in which distorted bass-line sounds from the Roland TB-303 played a prominent role. It was so popular in the U.K. that "acid house" often functioned as a catchall term for house music as a whole. I comment further on the origins of the term on p. 69. Sicko points out that some producers from Chicago and Detroit (he cites Derrick May and Marshall Jefferson as examples) objected strongly to the association of their music with drug-taking; he describes the Detroit techno scene in the 1980s as almost entirely drug-free and attributes this condition in part to the scourge of the contemporaneous crack epidemic (Sicko 1999: 116–17).

37. It is less clear whether Chicago musicians visited Detroit; no such visits are described in current literature on the history of house and techno.

38. Cybotron had also recorded a track called "Techno City" in 1984 (Brewster and Broughton 2000: 332). Ironically, however, it was guitar-driven; in fact, Davis's choice of this track as the band's next single was one of the reasons Atkins chose to leave the project (Shapiro 2000: 116). In addition, Alvin Toffler uses the epithet "The Techno-Rebels" in *The Third Wave* to characterize individuals who re-envision traditional modes of interacting with technology (Toffler 1980: 149–54).

forces, are also evident in historical accounts of EDM's development. In Rietveld's book, for example, "house music" is sometimes used to refer quite specifically to Chicago house and its offshoots and at other times as a catch-all term for electronic dance music in general (resulting in the coinage of curious terms such as "gabber house" [p. 4] and "techno house" [p. 84] to refer to specific sub-genres). Dan Sicko generally uses "techno" as a term for a particular Detroit-based genre, but a broader sense of the term comes into play when he applies it to artists such as the Chemical Brothers and Björk. Fikentscher, in turn, claims that "UDM is essentially a post-1970s, post-disco phenomenon, based in New York" (2000: 6). And many scholarly sources coming from the United Kingdom (e.g., Pini 2001) tend to speak quite broadly about "rave."

More broadly, these tensions call into question the unity that characterizes most historical narratives of EDM. As the account I have provided reflects the information provided in currently available sources, it is also characterized by this unity. Nor do I have sufficient space in which to offer an alternative account, having chosen to focus primarily on music rather than history. However, I would like to suggest that future works that do focus on the historical dimensions of EDM might concentrate more on the dynamic forces that have shaped its development and less on individual figures.

This comment also raises questions about how gender might have shaped narratives of EDM's development. Existing accounts tend to emphasize the creativity of a few individuals, and they often include elements of heroic struggle as well: obstacles to be overcome, and technology to be conquered. These emphases are evident not only in the actual accounts, but also in the titles that frame them (e.g., *Techno Rebels: The Renegades of Electronic Funk* [Sicko 1999]). It is not just that the heroes of these stories (the specific individuals involved) are male, but that the stories themselves are masculine kinds of stories. Although this gendered mode of discourse is particularly noticeable in writing on Detroit techno, and less so in the more scene-based accounts of the origins of disco, garage, and house within gay subcultures, we might consider what other types of stories might be possible as we move toward increasingly precise histories of EDM.

The account I have provided focuses on the first genres of electronic dance music to develop: garage, house, and techno, which are still considered foundational genres today. In the interest of space, I will not trace their histories beyond the 1980s, though I will remark briefly upon the considerable diversification that occurred within EDM during the 1990s. One of the most significant developments of the decade was jungle/drum 'n' bass, a genre that combines accelerated drum patterns ("breakbeats") sampled from the percussion-only sections ("breaks") of old funk records with half-tempo bass lines influenced by reggae.[39] More generally, electronic dance music since the 1990s has been characterized by a dramatic increase in the number of genres under its fold and the terms used to describe them.[40] By the turn of the century, genre labels in use included trance, progressive house, nu-NRG, deep house, tech-house, minimal techno, glitch-hop, IDM, two-step, happy hardcore, big beat, funky breaks, electro, and breakbeat—to name just a few. To describe the complex interaction of musical and social processes that led to the development of each of these genres would take us far afield, though I will offer a broad system for characterizing genres in rhythmic and metrical terms in the following chapter. In the next section of this chapter, I turn to a consideration of the activities and technologies involved in creating electronic dance music.

The Creation of Electronic Dance Music

MODES OF CREATIVE INTERACTION

The many styles of electronic dance music, while sonically quite diverse, share a common set of approaches to musical creation. In the following section, I explain these approaches from a functional perspective, emphasizing three key modes of interaction with EDM: that of the recording artist, that of the performing artist, and that of the performing audience. Most commonly, the recording artist is the producer, although remixers can serve in this capacity as well. The prototypical performing artist is the DJ; less commonly, producers also perform live. And finally, EDM audiences also perform musically through dance. I begin my discussion of these functions with a brief overview of the roles of producer and DJ, and then turn to a more in-depth treatment of all the roles I have mentioned. I

39. I present the terms "jungle" and "drum 'n' bass" together because both are used as catch-all terms for the genre. "Jungle" was the first term used, but some claimed that it was racist, hence, "drum 'n' bass" arose as a more neutral alternative. McLeod (2001: 71–72) claims that this move was part of a strategy of cultural appropriation of jungle by whites; as a term, "drum 'n' bass" was less "identity-specific" and more "universal." While this seems possible in theory, McLeod does not cite specific instances to support this assertion. In any event, "jungle" is still widely used. Some fans and musicians treat the two terms as synonyms, while others claim that they refer to different styles of music. In interviews I found that members of the latter group varied considerably in terms of the characteristics they ascribed to each style.

40. This development might be situated within a broader trend that scholars of popular music have described; Bradby, for instance, speaks of "the collapse of rock music's metaproject of youth and rebellion and subsequent dispersion into a proliferation of genres and styles" (Bradby 1993: 162).

explain the principal musical activities involved as well as the technologies through which they are mediated. In this way the reader can begin the detailed musical discussion of the following chapters with a clear sense of how this music comes about.

In any given performance situation, the functions of recording artist, performing artist, and audience are distinct. Each record that the DJ plays was made by a particular person or group of persons (the producer or producers), and the DJ is never a part of the dance floor while performing. Within the broader social contexts of EDM, however, it is common for individuals to occupy multiple roles. Many DJs also do production work (especially remixing), for instance, and many producers perform as DJs. The dynamics of the electronic dance music industry encourage this interaction: producers who perform as DJs gain opportunities to appear in public, while DJs who experiment with production have a ready-made laboratory in which to test their results (hence it is common for DJs to play their own recordings). The skills required for the two crafts are interdependent as well: producers must make records that work on the dance floor, and DJs must have a thorough understanding of how such records are made.[41]

Furthermore, a considerable percentage of the audience at a given EDM event will have some experience with DJing or production. Some may be "bedroom DJs," who never play in public, or producers who create music solely for their own enjoyment. Others may be amateur performers who play for free (or for very little) at local and regional events. Semiprofessional or aspiring professional DJs or producers may be in attendance; these artists have begun to establish a reputation outside of their immediate environment and to make money from their EDM activities, although they usually maintain some other job to make ends meet. Such a high degree of participation in music-making is possible for a variety of reasons. First, one can be a producer or a DJ on one's own; there is no need to form a band, organize rehearsals, or gain access to music-industry recording studios. Second, the technology required is relatively inexpensive; although professionals might have more pieces of equipment, some of which would be costly enough to be beyond the reach of amateurs, cheap forms of studio and DJ technology are widely available. Third, as with classical music, the abstraction of EDM may make DJing and production particularly appealing as hands-on ways of getting to know the music better; working with an instrument (whether acoustic or electronic) in performance or composition is one way of grounding music

41. That is, they must understand how individual records (and records in general) are put together structurally; they do not need to understand specific production methods.

in the body. However, these observations stem from my field research in Indiana; in locations with larger clubbing crowds, it may be less common for audiences to contain large numbers of DJs and producers.

Of the roles I have outlined, the one that conforms most closely to conventional notions of a musical creator is that of the producer. The meaning of this term in electronic dance music differs somewhat from its connotations in the majority of contemporary popular music, where it generally refers to someone who oversees the process of recording in a studio. Whereas this type of producer can have a significant impact on the sound of a recording, s/he is not generally thought of as a songwriter. In most EDM, however, technology is integrated directly into the act of composition, and the person who creates music usually records it as well. Hence, although I have chosen the term "recording artist" as the clearest expression of what the producer does, the distinctions between producer, songwriter, and recording artist begin to break down in this tradition; the EDM producer embodies all of these roles.[42] The producer also might be described as a composer, for much of what s/he does is compositional in a quite traditional sense, but I prefer the term used within the culture for at least two reasons: first, the figure of "composer" leaves out the element of recording, essential to modern popular-music production; and second, the act of DJing is also compositional, as I will now explain.

The DJ plays an exceptionally significant part in controlling the sound of electronic dance music. Much more than a person who simply plays records, the EDM DJ functions as an intermediary between the producer and the audience, the person who makes technologically mediated music immediate. DJs listen to the records producers have made, choose certain ones of them, and arrange them in a particular order to create a single continuous performance (a "set") of an hour or more in length. A set is a unity: not only do DJs create an unbroken flow of sound, they also minimize the distinctions between individual tracks, so that the emphasis is on the larger whole rather than its components. Furthermore, the DJ's arrangements within the set are intentionally novel; one of the primary goals of DJing is to create something new from diverse sources. To this end, DJs combine tracks in unexpected ways; they layer *parts* of tracks on top of parts of other tracks (for instance, the bass line of one record with a single measure of another record's vocal line); and they create collage-like pastiches by cutting back and forth between records. They also alter individual tracks, often considerably.

42. As a result, the person creating electronic dance music has much more direct control over the technology involved in its production than a typical pop star. Although EDM seems to involve greater technological mediation, its use of technology is very "hands-on."

Hence, DJing is a compositional act—both in the literal sense of the Latin root *componere* ("to put together") and in a broader, more modern sense—even though DJs do not create music "from scratch."[43]

Lest I overemphasize this compositional side, I hasten to point out that programming, or track selection, is also an important part of DJing. This involves playing the right music at the right time (for the right audience), as well as choosing tracks that work well together. Although the latter aspect of this process is still compositional in focus, the former emphasizes the DJ's role as a sort of *über*-connoisseur—a person who chooses just the right entrée from the musical menu. In this capacity, the DJ might, for example, play a favorite track—one that much of the audience would recognize—by a well-known artist at a climactic point in the evening. In general, accounts of earlier types of (electronic) dance music emphasize programming over composition. Writers attempting to capture the ecstasy of the disco dance floor (e.g., Holleran 1978) during the 1970s often describe the joy of hearing a particular track at a particular moment; programming was clearly a major emphasis in New York gay clubs in the 1980s as well, as Fikentscher's (2000) account reveals. Since the 1990s, the compositional side of DJing has become more prominent, and it has become much less common to hear identifiable, discrete tracks within a DJ's set. However, programming is still emphasized to a considerable degree within certain genres.

Before I turn to a more detailed discussion of the musical figures I have presented, some words about the people who embody these roles are in order. As in many other music-cultures, those with primary control over the creation of electronic dance music (including both DJs and producers) are predominantly male. This fact raises a number of questions for authors writing about EDM. One practical concern involves the manner in which the DJ is referenced. Several studies (e.g., Brewster and Broughton 2000, Fikentscher 2000), after noting that most DJs are male, explain that they will always use male pronouns to refer to "him." I find this approach problematic for several reasons. First, the number of female DJs and producers has increased significantly since the 1990s, although women are still the minority in both professions. It is no longer true, as Brewster and Broughton baldly assert (2000: x), that "98 percent of DJs have a penis."[44]

---

43. However, as is well known, DJs do create music from scrat*ching* records, producing carefully controlled variations in pitch. Scratching is pervasive in many turntable-based styles, but not especially common in most EDM cultures.

44. For further discussion of the position of female DJs in recent years, see Rietveld (1998: 111 n. 326) and Brewster and Broughton (2000: 376–78). In their most recent book (2003), in a chapter entitled "How to Be a Girl" (every chapter title begins with the phrase "How to . . ."), Brewster and Broughton offer some decidedly problematic advice to aspiring female DJs.

Second, the voices of women form an important part of this study; three of the twelve original interviews were with women DJs (DJ Shiva, Mystik, and Vixen Swift), all of whom are quoted herein. Third, I will often be speaking of DJs in a general manner, and I wish to avoid using the defining power of language to suggest that "the DJ" in an abstract sense is male. Hence I will avoid using gendered pronouns to refer to the DJ; when pronouns are necessary, I will use "s/he" (to be read "she or he") or "his and her."

A significant number of works do address issues of gender and sexuality in EDM culture in depth; indeed, this area is probably the most thoroughly explored within EDM research. Nevertheless, the focus of these works has tended to revolve around a fairly constrained set of questions. In particular, scholars have considered whether EDM cultures might be empowering and liberating or whether they perpetuate sexist power structures, as well as how and why they might be liberating for particular groups of people (women and sexual minorities). As I mentioned earlier in this chapter, however, we might also consider the roles played by gender in accounts of EDM's creation and development, as well as a host of other questions: How are constructions of gender different or similar among the various EDM subcultures? How are genres gendered, both individually and in relation to each other? How do the discursive practices through which genres are defined reflect beliefs about gender and gendered constructions of power? How does gender inform practices related to technology, as well as interactions between DJs and audiences? And finally, how does gender relate to rhythm and other musical qualities of EDM?[45] Although space does not allow me to do more than raise these questions, I wish to bring them up not only as potential avenues for future research, but also to indicate that more is at stake than simply the biological status of EDM musicians.

THE DJ

DJs make music with an array of technology. Although the exact features and brands of their equipment may vary, certain components are common to almost all DJ setups—namely, a pair of headphones, two turntables, and a mixing board (or "mixer"). The mixing board, a simplified version of the equipment used in

45. Scholarly descriptions of popular music often depict its "beat" as masculine (it is persistent and penetrative); in the realm of popular discourse, the All Music Guide notes that "what tied [all the genres of dance music] together was their emphasis on rhythm—in each dance subgenre, from Disco to House to Rave, the beat is *king*" (http://www.allmusic.com/cg/amg.dll; cited 17 June 2004; emphasis mine). One might ask how these characterizations could be reconciled with EDM's emphasis on tone color (considered a "secondary" parameter in most theoretical accounts) and the way in which it envelopes audiences in ambient sound. More obviously, dance has a long history as a gendered activity that is certainly relevant to such debates.

Example 1.1. Technics SL-1200 MK2 turntable.
Courtesy of Technics USA.

recording studios, is usually placed between the turntables.[46] This equipment is plugged into the venue's sound system, so that the music the DJ plays is amplified through loudspeakers. Example 1.1 shows a Technics SL-1200 series turntable (the most commonly used turntable in electronic dance music), and example 1.2 presents a high-end mixing board, the Pioneer DJM-600.[47]

The DJ uses this equipment to create a continuous flow of music. There is never any silence between records; instead, records are overlaid, or "mixed," in a variety of ways. The development of this continuity completes a merger of music and environment that has become essential to the modern-day club. It also helps position the DJ as a creator rather than a mere presenter, since it leads to the set being perceived as a whole shaped by the DJ rather than as a

46. Although two is the standard number of turntables, it has become increasingly common in recent years for virtuoso DJs to use three or even four.

47. For additional information about the Technics SL-1200, the following sites are helpful: http://www.panasonic.com/consumer_electronics/technics_dj/default.asp; http://www.1200s.com; and http://www.backspin.org/home.html. For additional information about the DJM-600, visit http://www.pioneerprodj.com. All pages cited 16 June 2004.

series of songs recorded by other artists. Mixing in its most basic form is sequential: the end of one record overlaps with the beginning of the next.[48] The amount of time involved in the mix can vary considerably, however: the DJ might mix the second half of record A with the first half of record B, or play the two records together in their entirety. Alternately, the DJ might jump back and forth rapidly *between* records rather than overlapping them.[49]

The mixing board facilitates this process in a variety of ways. First, each turntable is connected to a separate channel on the mixing board, thereby allowing the DJ to control the volume of each record independently with a slider that moves up and down (often called a "vertical fader"). These sliders—one for each of the four channels, which are labeled at the top of the mixer—appear in the bottom half of example 1.2.[50] In addition to the vertical faders, DJ mixing boards always contain another slider called a cross fader, which moves horizontally (see the bottom of ex. 1.2). The cross fader controls the balance between two channels: the further it is to one side, the more the audience will hear of one channel and the less of the other; if it is in the middle, the two channels will be balanced equally.[51] On some mixers the DJ can adjust the "curve" or sharpness of the fader (see the three shapes pictured just above the cross fader on the DJM-600). It is up to the DJ to determine whether to employ the vertical faders, the cross fader, or both in combination; in general, the vertical faders allow greater flexibility, but the cross fader is easier to use.

Besides controlling the volume of each record in the mix, the DJ is also able to manipulate the texture of individual records with the knobs found above the vertical faders. DJs call these controls "EQs" (short for "equalizers"), a term that I will use as well. Each EQ knob controls a different range of the frequency spectrum, most commonly divided into high, middle, and low.[52] DJs use the EQs for both textural and timbral purposes. Timbral manipulation can serve a variety of functions: it can be a way of adjusting the sound of a record to the acoustics of a particular room and sound system; it can help two records blend more

48. I will hereafter distinguish the order of records presented in a mix with letters: "record A," "record B," and so on.
49. This style of mixing, most commonly called "cutting" or "cutting back and forth," is more characteristic of hip hop; in EDM DJing it is used mainly as a temporary variation from the more common practice of presenting records in vertical combination.
50. The rightmost slider controls the master volume.
51. DJ mixing boards usually have two to four channels, as well as separate inputs for a microphone (rarely used in most EDM genres) and headphones. On mixers with more than two channels, the DJ must choose which two channels are assigned to the cross fader.
52. The uppermost knob on most mixing boards—called "gain" or "trim"—adjusts the overall strength of the signal coming into each channel.

Example 1.2. Pioneer DJM-600 mixing board.
Courtesy of Pioneer Electronics (USA), Inc.

effectively; it can call attention to an interesting part of a record; and it can gradually intensify (and possibly distort) a sound through a process called "tweaking" (to be discussed further in chapter 6). Textural manipulation occurs when the DJ uses the EQs to remove a certain part of the record. Usually this is the bass drum, though the DJ might remove other parts to make a mix work more effectively. For instance, if two synthesizer lines create too much pitch dissonance, one of them could be excised from the mix.

The aesthetic of continuity that dominates EDM mixing requires not only that records be played continuously with no intervening silence, but also that the same tempo be maintained from one record to the next. This is possible because of certain conventions of EDM DJing and composition—DJs usually focus on a particular genre in their sets, and most records within a genre will fall within a relatively narrow tempo range—and because of technological innovations in turntable design. Unlike turntables intended for home listening, which play records at speeds of either 33 or 45 rotations per minute, the turntables used in EDM DJing allow continuous tempo adjustment. This is done with a slider (usually vertical), which can be seen on the bottom right side of the turntable shown in example 1.1.[53] The tempo variation allowed usually ranges from +8 to −8 percent, although some DJs take their turntables apart and modify them to obtain a wider range of variation.

DJs maintain a constant tempo through a process called "beat matching" (or, less commonly, "beat mixing"). Fundamental to EDM mixing, like learning to play one's violin in tune, beat matching is a core skill that must be mastered before more advanced techniques can be attempted. The "beat" referred to is usually a literal force within the music—the steady quarter notes of the bass drum—although in more syncopated genres (e.g., jungle/drum 'n' bass) its presence may have to be inferred. To match the beats of record B with those of record A, the DJ listens to record B (or to the combination of A and B) through headphones, while keeping the mixing board on a setting that allows the audience to hear record A only. The slider is then used to adjust the tempo of record B so that the two records are moving at exactly the same speed. In addition, the beats must be synchronized, which is accomplished by pushing the record very slightly forward or backward.[54]

Another component of mixing, rarely mentioned in written descriptions of the process, but equally important, is the alignment of larger periodicities: measures, hypermeasures, and formal sections.[55] To accomplish this alignment, a technique known as "slip-cueing" becomes crucial. Once the DJ has "cued up" record B through beat matching, s/he holds it in place with a finger. A "slipmat" made of nonabrasive material such as felt allows the cued record to remain stationary while the turntable spins underneath it. The DJ then lets it go when record A reaches the desired point of synchronization. Some DJs also rock the

53. As adjusting the tempo also affects the pitch of the record, this device is also frequently referred to as the "pitch control." Because most DJs use this slider primarily to adjust tempo, however, I will describe it as the "tempo control" or the "tempo adjustment."

54. This is usually done with a finger applied to the outer rim of the record, although for certain purposes some DJs prefer to turn the spindle of the turntable instead.

55. I discuss the roles of hypermeter and form in DJing in detail in chapters 5 and 6.

record back and forth in time with the first record's beat while holding it in this manner.

The process of beat matching requires great precision. Beats that might seem to be synchronized will gradually go out of phase if they are not aligned *exactly.* In a repertoire characterized by perpetual machine-generated rhythms, unmatched beats stand out like a sore thumb; one DJ described their sound to me as "like shoes in a dryer." EDM audiences are also quite sensitive to the importance of beat matching; a "train wreck," a term dancers use for an obviously unsuccessful mix, can clear the floor instantly.

The virtuosity and precision associated with contemporary DJing have been facilitated by improvements in the construction and design of the turntable. After the first major innovation, continuous tempo adjustment, another important development was the direct-drive motor. Turntables used for home listening are belt-driven: the motor controls a belt, which causes the "deck" (the turntable surface) to turn. Because this method of control is indirect, it affords less power and accuracy: when a belt-driven turntable is switched on, it takes a considerable amount of time to reach full speed; in addition, belt-driven decks tend to fluctuate slightly in tempo as a record plays—a behavior that might not be noticeable when listening to a single record, but that becomes a serious liability when trying to coordinate two records precisely. Stopping a belt-driven turntable for a slip-cue also strains the belt. With a "direct-drive" turntable, the motor is connected directly to the deck. As a result, the record never varies in speed, and the DJ is able to stop and start a record instantaneously, at whatever speed is desired, thereby allowing much more fast-paced and flexible mixing.

Features such as continuous tempo adjustment and the direct-drive turntable began to appear during the 1970s. They first became widespread, however, in 1979, when the Technics SL-1200 series turntable appeared on the market. In addition to continuous tempo adjustment and a direct-drive motor, the Technics SL-1200 is designed so that the loud, resonant bass sounds characteristic of EDM will not cause it to skip. It quickly became the industry standard, to the extent that turntable technology has hardly changed since its introduction.[56]

In addition to the standard turntables, headphones, and mixing board, DJs may utilize a variety of supplementary equipment. Perhaps the most common supplementary device is the effects processor, which allows the DJ to manipulate records with effects such as delay, reverb, echo, pan, and flange. In written

56. Fikentscher 2000: 36. The turntable depicted in example 1.1 is the SL-1200MK2, the most commonly used model in the United States. The "international version," the SL-1210MK2, is virtually identical except that it features different voltage switches and is black.

discourse, these effects are often referred to collectively as "EFX." An effects unit may be a separate device plugged into the mixing board or built into the board itself. Free-standing devices can be controlled in a variety of ways; in addition to the standard knobs and sliders, there are units featuring touch-pads, track balls, and even an infra-red laser beam that allows three-dimensional manipulation along x, y, and z axes.[57] The DJM-600, for instance, contains an on-board effects processor, which is manipulated through a set of controls running along the right side of the machine (see ex. 1.2). These controls also include a sampler, another device that may be on-board or free-standing. The sampler allows the DJ to extract a short excerpt from a record (or, for that matter, from any sound source connected to the sampler) and introduce it into the mix; if an effects unit is also present, the sound can be manipulated as well. Less commonly, some DJs employ drum machines and other instruments in their sets, in the manner of the early Chicago house DJs. An example of a recent recording incorporating a number of these elements is Richie Hawtin's DJ mix entitled *Decks, EFX & 909* (NovaMute 3055–2, 1999). On this recording Hawtin utilizes three turntables, an effects processor, and Roland TR-909 drum machine, playing portions of thirty-eight records in approximately one hour.

As previously described, twelve-inch vinyl is the standard format for electronic dance music. In order to achieve maximum power and resonance by spreading out the grooves of the record, most twelve-inch dance singles are considerably shorter than a rock album; they typically contain between two and five tracks, distributed between the record's two sides. Tracks range from four to ten minutes in length, with lengths of about six minutes being particularly common. The number of unique tracks (i.e., those that have a distinct title) varies: usually there are one or two originally titled tracks plus various alternate mixes or remixes, but in some cases all the tracks are unique.

During the 1970s, when the twelve-inch format developed, vinyl was still the standard medium for singles throughout the popular music industry; dance music differed only in the size of its releases (twelve versus seven inch singles). In the 1980s, however, a new medium, the compact disc, soon surpassed other formats in popularity. Yet vinyl continued to be the material of choice within EDM. Though dual CD players with variable speed control have been available for some time, these devices do not allow the tactile control essential to modern DJing. As the techniques I have described illustrate, DJs find the beat and cue

57. An example of this laser-based technology is the Alesis AirFx (http://www.djgear.com/alesisairfx.html; cited 17 June 2004). At the 2002 Detroit Electronic Music Festival, I saw The Advent use this type of processor (I cannot confirm the specific brand) within a live DJ set. It is controlled in a manner similar to that of the theremin, except that only one hand is used.

records by touching them directly *with their hands,* and advanced techniques such as scratching are even more dependent on manual interaction. Within the last few years, however, new CD players aimed at the DJ market have been released. A picture of one such "digital turntable," the Pioneer CDJ-1000, is shown in example 1.3. Though the CD enters via a slot in the front, the top of the device features a round interface that can be controlled like a turntable; significantly, it also looks very much like a turntable (though smaller), and can be plugged into a mixing board in place of or in addition to vinyl turntables. These features make its use in DJ sets much more viable, and there are increasing signs of its popularity among DJs.

Another recent technology (released July 2002) is Final Scratch, a device created by Stanton (a turntable manufacturing company) that allows DJs to mix with digital files in formats such as .mp3 and .wav. Final Scratch involves software installed on a computer, which the DJ plugs into the mixing board, and specially adapted records (still made of vinyl), which the DJ uses to manipulate the files. Example 1.4 shows a potential Final Scratch setup. The turntables and mixing board are standard; it is the software and records that allow the files to be manipulated.

Example 1.3. Pioneer CDJ-1000.
Courtesy of Pioneer Electronics (USA), Inc.

Example 1.4. Final Scratch setup on two turntables and a mixing board.
Courtesy of Stanton Magnetics.

Although these new devices may one day render the twelve-inch record obsolete, at the time of writing vinyl and the analog turntable remain the technologies of choice for electronic dance music. In combination with a mixing board and other devices, they allow the DJ great flexibility and have fostered considerable compositional creativity.

THE PRODUCER

Although the music the DJ plays begins its life in the recording studio, the DJ is a much more visible figure than the producer. Because an EDM recording artist appearing in public is still the exception rather than the rule, the DJ's performance is much easier to identify with a specific person than the producer's recording. The producer is also imbricated in a dynamic that favors relatively generic music: knowing that DJs will minimize the distinctions between tracks in their sets, producers make tracks that work well in this context. In a typical DJ set, the audience will be able to identify only a few tracks by name; producers aim for name recognition with DJs more than with the general public. They also obscure their identities by recording under multiple names.[58] As I noted in the introduction, one result of the producer's anonymity is a substantial failure on the part of contemporary writing (both scholarly and journalistic) to address EDM production in any detail. In the following paragraphs I begin to address this gap by explaining some of the technical components involved, while in chapter 6 I will explore how this equipment is used in relation to aspects of rhythm, meter, and form.

The materials used to make electronic dance music are diverse, varying considerably from producer to producer and constantly developing as technology improves. Four main functions—synthesis, processing, sampling, and sequencing—are essential to production. Each function occurs in both hardware and software manifestations: on the one hand, there are machines called synthesizers, effects processors, samplers, and sequencers; on the other, there are computer programs that fulfill the same functions. Only rarely are these categories strictly maintained: most technology fulfills several functions (even if one is primary), and most pieces of equipment contain software as well.[59] It will be most productive, therefore, to begin exploring this topic from a function-based perspective. I will then consider how the various functions are manifested in specific machines.

The first two functions I will discuss are synthesis and processing. Synthesis is the electronic generation of sound, while processing refers to its modification. These two capacities were embodied in the earliest synthesizers, which consisted of signal sources—oscillators and noise generators—that were in turn modified by signal processors such as amplifiers, gates, and filters. Sound processing today still makes use of these basic techniques,[60] although it has diversified considerably to include a set of standard "effects" such as delay, reverb, and flange, as well as any other technique a producer can imagine and implement.

Synthesis can be either analog or digital. Sampling, however, is largely a digital phenomenon, involving the conversion of an analog sound to digital information through periodic "snapshots" of its electrical signal (and the reversal of this process when sound is generated). In the context of electronic dance

58. An extreme example of this phenomenon is the Detroit techno and electro group Drexciya, who released records for years without ever appearing publicly, allowing themselves to be photographed, or identifying their names.

59. By "pieces of equipment," I mean music-making equipment other than a personal computer, whose function is usually thought of in more general terms. Computers always involve hardware too, of course. The difference is one of emphasis: a computer contains a great deal of software, while its hardware is mostly hidden, whereas a drum machine is manipulated primarily through its hardware interface, and any software it uses is relatively minimal.

60. For instance, Adam Jay, a producer whom I interviewed, showed me how he uses separate hardware filters in home recording.

music, a "sample" is a recording of any sound captured through this technique, and "sampling" refers more generally to the process of obtaining sounds in this manner.

Samples become a part of EDM in several different ways. First of all, many of the sounds stored in electronic keyboards and drum machines are not synthesized at all; rather, they are samples of acoustic instruments loaded into the instruments by their manufacturers.[61] EDM producers also use externally derived samples as electronic instruments. For instance, jungle/drum 'n' bass producers often construct intricate drum patterns from multiple sound sources; every drum hit that appears in a particular measure might come from a different source. Although these sources are often percussion-based (a typical example would be a drum solo from a 1970s funk recording), this is certainly not a requirement; any sound imaginable can be chosen and recontextualized as a percussion instrument. And, finally, EDM tracks sometimes contain samples of discrete "sound bytes": for instance, excerpts from speeches (such as the "I Have a Dream" speech by Dr. Martin Luther King Jr.), lines from movies, and snippets of musical popular culture (such as the theme from *Dr. Who*). Extensive use of this type of sampling peaked during the late '80s and early '90s, when sampling was such an important part of track construction that the aesthetic of the period has been described as "sampladelic" (Reynolds 1999: 41–43). During this time, large portions of other works (entire bass lines, choruses) were borrowed freely, and some tracks were formed largely from collages of samples. Since then, sampling has become more discreet (in part in response to lawsuits that made it clear that obvious samples would require payment of copyright fees), although it is still an important part of EDM production.

The fourth function essential to EDM production is sequencing. A sequencer is a hardware or software device that controls the instruments and events that occur in a track. It records and carries out a series of directions (a "sequence") programmed by the producer. The sequence tells each instrument when to play and how,[62] and it also determines formal features. For instance, it might direct a particular group of instruments to play for sixteen bars, and then indicate that a new group should enter and play for eight bars. Eventually, an entire track is

---

61. The similarity of the samples to their real-world counterparts depends on a variety of factors, including the way in which the sample is created and the degree to which it is manipulated (either by the makers of the equipment or by the producer). In general, EDM producers favor "synthetic" sounds, and they select and modify samples accordingly.

62. An "instrument" in this context can refer to a discrete piece of hardware (e.g., a synthesizer), but it usually refers to an individual instrumental sound. On any given piece of hardware, such as a synthesizer or a drum machine, there may be a large number of "instruments" in play at one time.

put together through series of directions of this type. Sequencers are strongly associated with MIDI (Musical Instrument Digital Interface), a standard set of equipment specifications that allows electronic instruments of diverse types and brands to communicate with each other. In this context, a sequencer records MIDI data—messages such as note-on, note-off, pitch bend, and key velocity— which it then deploys to create music with the instruments under its control. However, sequencers did exist prior to MIDI, as did several other instruments (such as the Roland TR-808 drum machine) that are still widely used in EDM. Producers wishing to incorporate these instruments into MIDI setups can retrofit them with adapters, or they can avoid MIDI altogether by using vintage instruments exclusively.[63]

The various functions associated with EDM production appear in a broad cross-section of musical instruments. A few instruments bear some resemblance to traditional acoustic instruments (namely, the piano), but most do not. Instruments develop as rapidly as technology itself, though EDM producers do not hesitate to make use of equipment from the 1970s and '80s as well. Because so many different products exist, categorizing instruments can be difficult, but certain types do occur more often than others. In the following paragraphs I discuss four common instrumental types: the keyboard, the drum machine, the sampler-sequencer, and the computer.

The term "synthesizer" usually connotes some sort of keyboard instrument, and the earliest synthesizers were indeed keyboard-operated. Today, however, sound synthesis (both analog and digital) occurs on a variety of equipment, while keyboards in turn may incorporate many other functions. In the context of EDM production, then, a keyboard is simply a particular type of interface. Its performance capacity is exploited only to a limited extent; instead, it is used primarily as a tool for building and deploying sounds.

Most keyboards come with banks of preprogrammed sounds or "patches"; these may be created strictly through synthesis, through short samples of acoustic instruments, or through a combination of the two. Users may add patches derived from other sources (huge numbers of them are available online), and they can program their own sounds. They can also modify the patches in a variety of ways: they might choose a different waveform, change the shape of an envelope, or apply a signal processor such as a filter. These activities are essential to production, as using unmodified presets is frowned upon.

63. Vince Clarke, an electronic musician who has played a pivotal role in Depeche Mode, Yaz, and Erasure, describes using a setup of the latter type in Rule 1999: 171.

Although sequencing is not their primary function, keyboards generally contain some sort of sequencer, whose capacities will vary from the severely limited to the relatively advanced. In addition, many keyboard instruments also allow users to load in and manipulate their own samples. In fact, the earliest instruments capable of sampling external sound sources had keyboard interfaces,[64] and since then certain keyboard instruments have emphasized sampling as much as or more than the other functions traditionally associated with synthesizers.

The advantages of the keyboard as an interface are several. For some producers, it offers a more intuitive way of inputting music than pressing buttons, turning knobs, and operating a mouse. Sounds can be recorded in real time, thereby incorporating expressive variations in timing, and then edited.[65] Most keyboards today are sensitive to "velocity" (the speed or force with which a key is pressed) and "aftertouch" (additional pressure on a key that has already been depressed). Although pianists might imagine these features affecting dynamics (which they certainly can), they are equally capable of controlling any other parameter on the keyboard; for instance, a certain amount of aftertouch might be used to trigger a filter. Contemporary keyboards are usually "polyphonic" as well, meaning that more than one key can be depressed simultaneously. In addition, multiple instruments can be mapped to different parts of the keyboard: for instance, one octave might contain the bass line sound, another the instrument used for the main melodic riff, and a third a synthesized string sound.

Another musical instrument used extensively in electronic dance music is the drum machine. In essence, the drum machine is a synthesizer devoted exclusively to percussion sounds, although it does not use a keyboard interface. Although its sounds may come from analog or digital synthesis or from samples of acoustic instruments, it usually contains an array of preset sounds modeled on (and named after) acoustic percussion instruments such as the bass drum, open and closed hi-hat cymbals, snare drums, tom-toms, and claves. On the machines favored by EDM producers, however, the resemblance of these sounds to "real-world" instruments is often largely nominal.

64. An example is the Fairlight CMI (Computer Music Instrument), the first commercially available digital sampler (released 1979). The Fairlight was adopted by some artists, but it was prohibitively expensive; digital sampling did not become viable for most producers until the introduction of much cheaper technology in the mid- to late 1980s.
65. If expressive timing variations are not desired, the producer can instruct the keyboard to quantize the rhythms as they are recorded.

Example 1.5. Roland TR-808 drum machine.
Courtesy of Roland Corporation U.S.

Certain drum machines released during the early 1980s have had a particularly significant influence on electronic dance music. The two most important of these, both of which were made by the Roland corporation, are the TR-808 and the TR-909.[66] Approximately 12,000 TR-808 machines were produced from 1980–83, and just 10,000 TR-909s were manufactured between 1983 and '84 (Rule 1999: 81 and 95). In spite of their age and their small, short-lived production runs, these machines are still widely used today; they are constantly sold and resold on the secondhand market.

The 808 and the 909 are very similar in design; I will use the somewhat simpler 808 as an example (see ex. 1.5). To create a rhythm pattern using this machine, the producer first chooses a percussion sound from one of the twelve categories provided. These instruments are labeled individually across the top half of the machine, where there are knobs for adjusting their levels as well as additional features such as decay, tuning, and timbre. The rhythm can then be

66. "TR" stands for "transistor rhythm." The Vintage Synth Explorer, www.vintagesynth.org, provides photographs and information about these and many other influential drum machines and synths (cited 26 September 2004).

input either by tapping it in or through a process called step entry.[67] The sixteen buttons running along the bottom of the instrument control "steps" in a sequential pattern. By default, they represent sixteenth notes in a 4/4 measure (see the row of numbers above the buttons), though other smallest values (e.g., eighth-note triplets) can be mapped to them, and the length of the measure can be adjusted by defining any step as the last. The producer creates a rhythm by pressing the button that corresponds to each attack's position in the measure; when depressed, the button lights up and the machine plays the sound that has been selected. For instance, to program a four-quarter pattern in 4/4 time, one would press buttons 1, 5, 9, and 13. This pattern will then repeat infinitely until "stop" is pressed. To create patterns beyond a single measure, the producer specifies the number of each measure involved and then programs them individually.

The design of the 808 clearly offers a number of advantages to the dance music producer. First, its programming interface is simple and hands-on, yet flexible enough to allow considerable variety. Second, it automatically produces perfectly quantized rhythms, which are an asset in music that is to be beat-matched. Third, it can generate rhythms endlessly. In addition to saving drummers from dying of exhaustion (as they might if they had to play all the drum parts heard in a typical evening at a club), this last capacity has had certain far-reaching aesthetic consequences, which I will explore further in subsequent chapters.

The sampler-sequencer (or sequencer-sampler) is a machine used primarily for creating and organizing entire tracks. This instrumental category is much more loosely defined than "keyboard" or "drum machine"; depending on whom one asks, the same type of machine might also be called simply a "sampler" or a "sequencer." Typically, however, these machines have powerful sampling *and* sequencing capabilities. An example is the Akai MPC-2000, pictured in example 1.6.

The MPC-2000 is one of the devices used by Indianapolis producer Adam Jay, whom I interviewed as part of the field research for this project. At the time of our interview (spring 2002), it was the centerpiece of his recording studio. It has all the functions of a keyboard and a drum machine along with powerful

67. Other names for step entry include "step writing" and "step sequencing." On some later drum machines, the button(s) used for tapping in patterns respond to variations in velocity and expressive timing. On the 808 and 909, however, tapping simply enters the pattern, which is always strictly quantized. (The 909 does allow shuffle, which will add varying degrees of "swing"; however, these timing variations are also determined electronically rather than through performance.) In general, drum machines are not performance instruments; they are usually programmed rather than played.

Example 1.6. Akai MPC-2000 sampler-sequencer.
Courtesy of Akai Professional America.

sequencing and sampling capabilities. It contains various tools for sample editing (including a waveform display), as well as sufficient memory for storing the types of samples used in contemporary EDM. It is also capable of recording sequences of up to 300,000 notes. Notes can be entered through step entry, through linear recording, or through loop recording.[68] The interface of the MPC-2000 is not as intuitive as a keyboard for functions such as note entry,[69] but it is more intuitive than certain other types of technology commonly used in EDM production. This is largely because of its sixteen "pads," the large buttons found in the bottom right corner of the machine. The pads serve multiple functions, but one of their most important is to facilitate real-time performance of patterns during recording.

68. In loop (or looped) recording, the producer specifies a certain duration to be repeated infinitely during recording. With each pass through the loop, new elements are added. This is an especially common technique for building up drum parts (Pellman 1994: 160).

69. One interesting characteristic possibly related to the way machines such as the MPC-2000 de-emphasize pitch entry is that those using them may begin to treat pitch as a timbral function. Adam Jay, for example, spoke several times of "pitching sounds up and down" in the context of a discussion of effects.

Different instrumental sounds can be assigned to each pad, which (unlike the buttons on a TR-909 or 808), respond to varying degrees of velocity. As a result, producers can enter patterns by playing them rather than programming them. Hence this type of hardware sampler-sequencer is much more "hands-on" than the computerized versions that are its main competition.[70]

A fourth type of machine involved in EDM production is the personal computer. As computers have become more powerful and less expensive throughout the past decade, their use has become increasingly commonplace. Software is also more available than ever; some commonly used programs at the time of writing include Pro Tools, Acid Pro, and Sound Forge.[71] Any of the primary functions of EDM production can be accomplished through software; in addition, there are "virtual" versions of commonly used equipment such as drum machines and keyboards.[72] One advantage of computers is the ease of cut-and-paste editing, as well as the huge amounts of memory available. The extent to which EDM producers utilize computers varies considerably, however. Some, such as Adam Jay (at the time of our interview), do not use them at all; others use them exclusively; and many others use them in combination with hardware such as drum machines and keyboards.

TO WHAT END TECHNOLOGY? RE-ENVISIONING "TECHNO" THROUGH MUSIC-MAKING PRACTICES

In the popular press, electronic dance music is often portrayed as "high-tech" music made with the latest technology. As this discussion illustrates, however, this characterization is overly simplistic. On the one hand, it is true that technological innovations such as the variable speed turntable and the digital sampler have had major impacts on EDM's development,[73] and that many EDM musicians

70. The MPC-2000, released in 1997, is not a vintage instrument, although it was recently replaced by an updated model, the MPC-2000XL. The English producers known as the Chemical Brothers (Tom Rowlands and Ed Simons) have also described using the MPC-3000 (a related product with additional features) in their studio work and "jamming" on it in live performance (Rule 1999: 13).

71. For additional information about Pro Tools, visit http://www.digidesign.com; for further information on Acid Pro and Sound Forge, visit http://mediasoftware.sonypictures.com. Both pages cited 17 June 2004.

72. Some of these virtual versions are based on specific instruments, and may even include a graphic interface that looks like the instrument. Even when this is not the case, many programs include samples or imitations of sounds from vintage instruments such as the 808 and the 909.

73. One might also argue that these technologies were welcomed because they reflected musical practices already in place. DJs were already mixing records continuously prior to the introduction of the variable speed turntable, and they were creating sound collages through turntable wizardry and tape editing long before the invention of the digital sampler. See Brewster and Broughton 2000 for further discussion of sampling with respect to turntable virtuosity and tape editing.

have welcomed new inventions (e.g., Final Scratch) with open arms. On the other hand, analog synthesizers, pre-MIDI drum machines, and vinyl records are also essential to music-making in EDM. Clearly, obsolete technology is just as much a part of EDM's fetishization of the machine as is the latest gizmo, and the simple tool can be just as important as the most complex of devices.[74]

The very notion of technology itself is premised on the idea that humans create tools to fulfill some necessary function or to enable some useful task. In their interactions with technology, however, EDM musicians have often explored the gaps between this ideal and its realization. Not only have they relished machines that appear to have outlived their usefulness, they also have made a widespread practice of what might be termed the "creative perversion" of technology.[75] In this capacity, they have frequently used machines in ways their makers never intended, and they have used them "incorrectly" in order to achieve surprising new results. The most commonly cited example of this phenomenon is their use of the Roland TB-303 bass line generator (called the "TB-303 Bass Line" by its manufacturer, with "TB" standing for "transistor bass"), pictured in example 1.7.

The TB-303 is an extremely basic analog synthesizer, designed specifically for the production of bass lines. It was meant to function as a sort of portable accompanist, which guitarists could use in place of a live bassist when practicing or playing solo gigs (Shapiro 2000: 193). Produced in 1982, it was promoted along with the TR-606, a similarly simplistic drum machine. This equipment was intended to be cheap and functional. The sound of a TB-303, however, does not resemble any bass guitar, either real or imaginary, and its interface is unreliable and difficult to use.[76] The machine was never successful in a rock context, and it was soon discontinued.

Electronic dance musicians, however, were not concerned with reproducing the sound of "real" instruments. Entranced by the otherworldliness of its timbres, Chicago house musicians such as DJ Pierre used the 303's signal processing controls (the knobs running across the top of the machine) to modify parameters such as resonance and decay. The results, which sounded even *less* like a bass

74. Technologies such as the TR-909 drum machine and the TB-303 bass line generator (to be discussed further shortly) are not obsolete simply because they were made during the 1980s. The TR-909 was also obsolete within the larger music industry soon after its production due to the rise of all-digital machines (Shapiro 2000: 192), and the TB-303 was hardly ever used *except* in electronic dance music.

75. I derive this term from Brewster and Broughton 2000: 315.

76. The 303's "keyboard" cannot be played; its "keys" are actually buttons set on top of a keyboard-shaped interface, and they are quite small (the entire instrument is approximately one foot in width). Rather, the device must be programmed, with pitches and rhythms entered separately.

Example 1.7. Roland TB-303 Bass Line.
Courtesy of Roland Corporation U.S.

guitar, have been described with a variety of adjectives, some of the most common being "buzzy" and "squelchy."[77] In more technical terms, its sound is very resonant, emphasizing a rich palette of overtones (the sawtooth is one of its waveforms), and its envelope is constantly in flux (because producers use the knobs to quickly diminish and replenish the range of partials). Records that employed this sound came to be called "acid tracks," and the overall style came to be known as "acid house."[78] Acid house became hugely popular in England, and the sounds of the 303 continue to pervade electronic dance music today.

Electronic instruments such as synthesizers and drum machines are often

77. Both terms are used in Shapiro 2000: 193. For instances of "squelch," see Sicko 1999: 104, Reynolds 1999: 32, and Brewster and Broughton 2000: 315.

78. The origins of the adjective "acid" are unclear. Some sources claim that when dancers first heard the music, they found it so bizarre that they thought the club's punch had been spiked with LSD (Shapiro 2000: 76). Reynolds (1999: 32) also describes the punch-spiking as a "rumor," while Brewster and Broughton (2000: 316) assert it as fact. Although there does not seem to be any conclusive evidence linking the music's reception or creation to LSD use (and in England it was much more strongly associated with Ecstasy use), the sound of the music is clearly psychedelic in character.

portrayed as substitutes for "real" instruments and human performers. With the 303, this tendency is evident in the manufacturer's own characterization of the product. However, technology is rarely used in this manner in EDM. Producers steer clear of sounds that approximate acoustic instruments, preferring to use electronic machines for their own special sonic attributes. In a 1997 interview (reprinted in Rule 1999: 8), the Chemical Brothers express this attitude very clearly:

> This idea of having to replicate the sound of, I don't know, a great piano or whatever. I mean, if you want that, get the real thing. For us, synthesizers are for making sounds that no other machines can make—not for copying other sounds. It's all about making sounds that no one has ever heard before.

HYBRID ROLES

Some of the musically creative activities that occur in electronic dance music blur the boundaries between the normally clearly defined roles of recording artist and performing artist. Two of the most common of these hybrid roles, which I will explore briefly in the following section, are those of remixer and live PA.

Technically, remixing is a type of production work. In practice, however, it changes music in much the same way as DJing, and it is generally done by people who are DJs. In fact, many DJs who do not produce "original" work still create remixes. Remixes may be "authorized" or "bootlegged," depending upon whether they are sanctioned by the producer of the remixed track. Today, the vast majority of them are authorized; in fact, they are usually solicited by the producer. To start, the producer gives the remixer a master recording of the track, which will contain a separate recording of each instrumental or vocal line. The remixer uses these as raw material, while also adding his or her own material. The extent to which the remix departs from the original recording can vary considerably. Some remixes keep the structure of the original track largely intact and simply add a few new elements (e.g., new percussion parts, or a different synth line). This approach is especially common when DJs are asked to remix Top 40 pop songs. However, it is much more common for the remixer to radically reconstruct the track. Elements from the master recording will be chopped up, processed, and reordered, and sometimes so many new elements will be added that it will be difficult to detect any features of the original track at all.

My description of remixing preserves a clear distinction between the original recording and its remixes. In practice, however, this boundary is often quite blurry. In many cases, no time interval separates the primary recording and its remixes; when a track is first released, its twelve-inch commonly contains the "original" version of a track *as well as* several remixes by different artists. To complicate the picture further, some twelve-inches contain multiple versions of a track by its original producer, thereby undermining any effort to identify a single recording as authoritative. In any event, distinctions between all these types of mixes are of little or no concern to DJs, who simply choose the mix that they and their audiences like best. A remix of a track may be a much bigger hit than its "original," which may receive little or no club play at all.[79]

In between the DJ's performance and the producer's recording is the "live PA," a term used to describe live performances by producers. The term does not refer to performances by producers *as DJs* but, rather, to the real-time use of studio technology during a live event. Live PAs may occur at music festivals, at rave-like events, and at "concerts" given by the most commercially successful EDM performers;[80] they do not usually occur as part of a regular evening at a club. Just as the equipment producers use in the studio varies, so, too, does the technology employed in these performances. Some producers actually "play" synthesizers and other equipment: for instance, at a performance by Timeline Live (a group of musicians from the Underground Resistance label) that I attended in Detroit on May 31, 2004, one musician ("Mad" Mike Banks) played keyboards and another drummed with his hands on an electronic drum pad. A third musician mixed additional sounds using CD turntables, and projections of visual images were also closely coordinated (both rhythmically and thematically) with the music. In other live PAs, the musicians sit in front of a laptop computer while the music blasts out of huge speaker stacks surrounding them; I observed one such performance in this style by Nobukaza Takemura at the 2001 Detroit Electronic Music Festival.[81] The extent to which the live PA is improvised also varies considerably. Many producers recreate their own tracks in more or less complete form when performing live. In this type of performance, tracks are usually played continuously in the manner of a DJ set, though they are created with sequencers and other technology rather than played from recordings; two producers whom I interviewed, Stanley and Neal Blue, perform live PAs of this type.[82] Others may

79. An example of this phenomenon is Timo Maas's remix of "Dooms Night" by Azzido Da Bass, which I will analyze in subsequent chapters. For further discussion of remixing, see Fikentscher 2000: 48–54.

80. These performers include figures such as Moby, Chemical Brothers, and The Prodigy. As part of their championing by the larger music industry, these acts have been expected to conform, at least to a certain extent, to rock conventions; hence they appear in public, go "on tour," have live shows similar in some respects to rock concerts, and often contain more than one member (thus mimicking a "band" in some respects).

81. Takemura is one of a number of Japanese EDM artists described in Loubet 2000.

82. Adam Jay also performs both DJ sets and live PAs, although our interview focused largely on his studio work.

simply improvise with loops (short repeating patterns) stored in their computer or sequencer.[83]

THE DANCER

Dancers, whom I have described as the "performing audience" (p. 47), form a third side of the triangle of creative activity in electronic dance music. Constructing this network in three parts is unusual; most scholarship has portrayed the world of music in binary terms, maintaining a conceptual separation between music's creator and its audience. The division between creation and reception is fundamental to musicology, for instance, and a similar dichotomy between production and consumption has long been a part of popular music studies. However, there are several reasons why dance, as practiced within EDM, should be viewed as a creative musical performance. First, in contrast to many other dance-based traditions (e.g., ballet), EDM dancers at a live event can have a significant impact upon the sounds that unfold. Successful DJs are highly attuned to the crowd's behavior: most do not play prearranged sets, instead preferring to shape their performance as the evening unfolds in order to get a maximal response from the people on the floor. As a result, the audience's actions—whether or not they dance, the intensity with which they dance, and the other physical and verbal cues that they give to the DJ—can affect what music will be played, when it will be played, and how it will be played.

Furthermore, communication flows in both linear and lateral directions: that is, not only between audience and DJ, but also within the audience itself. Individual dancers collaborate with the DJ and with each other to create a sense of "vibe"—a powerful affective quality associated with the experience of going dancing—among those present. Although the type of vibe sought out may vary depending on the style of music played, the people in attendance, and the type of event, this sense of communal energy is an essential part of an effective event. Most dance music fans will still appreciate a performance that is musically interesting and technically solid, but they will feel something lacking if the audience does not cooperate in generating a vibe to surround it.[84]

At the same time, the audience does not have direct control over the music that is played. They cannot select the music; they can only respond to what the DJ offers them. Nevertheless, their participation remains both creative and mu-

83. The recently released product Live 4 from Ableton, an audio sequencing program that can be played in real time, encourages live improvisation with a computer; see www.ableton.com for more information (cited 17 June 2004).

84. Fikentscher references the concept of vibe, which he defines as a "collective energy," quite frequently; see especially pp. 80–82 (Fikentscher 2000).

sical. In a quite specific sense, the dancer's motions are rhythmic; they add a counterpoint to the sounding patterns of the music. Moreover, to dance to this music is to interpret it. On the dance floor, motion is largely an individually determined phenomenon. There are no predetermined steps or choreography; instead, each dancer must shape his or her response to the music as it unfolds. Hence Fikentscher's description of EDM dance as "musicking in movement" seems particularly appropriate. As he notes, "musicking in sound and musicking in movement happen simultaneously and in relation to each other" (2000: 58).[85]

The focus of this activity is interpretive movement rather than physical display. EDM dance is not a spectator sport; in fact, standing around watching is generally discouraged.[86] Some people dance in small groups or pairs, though the extent of interaction involved can vary considerably. "Dancing together" might mean simply dancing near each other, responding to each other's motions without actually touching, or physically interacting through dance. Even when dancers do interact, however, the primary focal points of EDM dancing are physical and musical expression rather than "ritualized courtship" (Fikentscher 2000: 66). The majority of dancers on the floor will be on their own, even though friends may be nearby. Some dancers also use accessories, such as light "toys" that blink, flash, or glow; in this way, dance can acquire another dimension of technological mediation.

The individualistic nature of EDM dancing should not be overemphasized, however. Being one among a crowd of dancers is clearly a communal experience, one that can bring on powerful emotions.[87] Furthermore, there are common patterns of motion in EDM,[88] and many dancers are influenced by the ways in which others around them move. These themes—individualism in the midst of a communal context—come to the fore in the following excerpt from an interview with

85. Fikentscher derives the concept of "musicking" from Small 1987, who posits the term as a way of conceptualizing music as an *activity*.

86. See also Malbon 1999. Also relevant, however, are Pini's references to "to-be-looked-at-ness," a term she uses to refer to women's cultivation of a sense of visual spectacle for themselves within EDM environments—although her interest is in this phenomenon as a particular expression of femininity rather than a practice related specifically to dance (Pini 2001: 121–25).

87. For further discussion of the communal aspects of EDM dancing, see Fikentscher 2000 (esp. ch. 4) and Malbon 1999 (esp. 70–133).

88. Aside from many unnamed ways of moving, there are also certain styles of dance known by descriptive names (e.g., "liquid"). Break dancing, a virtuosic style that arose as a part of hip hop during the 1970s, is still popular among some EDM fans, although it occurs only sporadically in most EDM environments. There are also ways of moving associated with particular genres; in particular, ravers often describe a unique style of dancing associated with drum 'n' bass. Although all of these dance styles may involve certain repertoires of moves, the way in which they are combined into a dance is still individually determined. See Buckland 2002 for some interesting descriptions of dancers' movements.

DJ Impact (who, as a part-time teacher of Latin dance as well as a clubber, was able to offer particularly clear descriptions of his experiences):

> Mark Butler: You say you have "moves." Did you think about how you're going to move ahead of time, before you heard the music, or is it something you came up with then, or ...?
>
> DJ Impact: Normally what happens is, it depends on the audience or the place I'm dancing. I adjust to the people I'm around. If they're doing a certain dance style—like, you go to a rave and people are pulling out glow sticks and doing funky things with their hands or whatever ... if that's where it's happening, then I normally incorporate that and try to do something similar. Most of my dance teaching, just like anything, I learn from watching others. I come up with moves on my own every once in a while, but the majority of my moves that I have are I guess stolen—if you want to say that (but I don't necessarily consider my dancing "stolen" from other people)—but the small phrases that I do are stolen. And that's how I learn. I learn through observation.
>
> Mark Butler: So you feel like you sort of have a repertoire of ways of moving?
>
> DJ Impact: Yeah, there's definitely ... I can see myself doing, repeatedly, certain patterns. And when I notice myself doing that I try to stop and do something different, because obviously if I'm noticing then probably someone else is thinking "Well, he does the same stuff over and over again." If they're paying attention, which most of the time people aren't. They're too engrossed in their own dancing.

In his comments, DJ Impact describes a number of negotiations between individual and communal aspects of dancing. On the one hand, he wants his dancing to blend in with that of the crowd as a whole, and he learns from the ways others move. On the other hand, he is concerned that his dancing should appear sufficiently distinctive, while also believing that most of those around him are primarily focused on their own experiences.

In commenting on the role of dance within EDM, I have emphasized elements that I believe to be essential to an understanding of the musical phenomena that I will describe: in particular, the creative and musical capacities in which dancers are involved, as well as the balance between and among individual and communal forces within live musical events. Many more questions might be pursued at length: for instance, how and to what extent might particular ways of moving correlate to particular musical phenomena, and how might these physical behaviors be understood as rhythmic or otherwise musical phenomena in their own right? These are immensely complicated questions that no current study of EDM has addressed in any depth, although several recent studies have made important contributions toward our understanding of the aesthetic and cultural criteria that shape dance as a general practice. In the spirit of the comments offered in the introduction, it would be desirable to see scholars account not only for specific musical practices but also for specific ways of moving in relation to those practices. It is toward the first of these goals that I will now direct my attention.

Conceptualizing Rhythm and Meter in Electronic Dance Music

a couple of people on this list tend to say that "oh, I don't like the 4/4 beat ..." when talking about their preference to breaks and/or jungle over house and techno.

a little lesson for you guys:

4/4 is a time signature that ALL dance music uses ... the ONLY exception may be towards IDM producers ...

no one in dance uses 3/4
no one in dance uses 6/8

even the recent rash of sounds that SOUND like 3/4 or 6/8 are using 4/4 time signatures with a TRIPLET note value causing a swingy feel reminiscent of that one 80s song Dr. Who....

so, please, stop saying breaks and jungle don't use 4/4 ... they do ... if it's standard contemporary music, 90% of the time it's using a 4/4 time signature.

Grunge was quick to utilize 5/4 and 7/4 ... Tori Amos constantly uses alternate time sigs ... and I'm sure countless other non-pop-oriented artists use it...

but no one in standard dance music does...

(by the way, there's nothing especially wondrous or difficult in doing alt time sigs...)

—"That Reminds Me ... (A Small Lesson in Music Theory),"
posting by "Chocolate" to IU-Ravers electronic mailing list, 5 August 2003

In this self-described "lesson in music theory," Chocolate, an Indianapolis house DJ, references and responds to a larger discourse about meter in electronic dance music. Noting a distinction that many fans make between breaks and jungle, on the one hand, and house and techno, on the other—a distinction based on the perceived metrical characteristics of these genres—he offers a corrective: in actuality, *all* dance music uses 4/4.

In so doing, Chocolate evokes a central paradox of discourse on electronic dance music. Not only do fans and musicians reference the temporal qualities of EDM with great frequency; they also use these qualities to justify basic personal reactions to the music, reactions involving fundamental distinctions between genres they like and identify with and those they disdain. In making these judgments, they discriminate between the metrical characteristics of various styles. At the same time, they sometimes describe the music in ways that flatten out the differences between these styles. Chocolate is not alone in claiming 4/4 as *the* meter of electronic dance music; many of the people whom I interviewed also made statements to the effect of "all dance music is in 4/4 time." In this chapter I wish to respond to these remarks, initiating a broader discussion that will reverberate through the rest of this text. I will be concerned with rhythm and meter in a broad sense: with the ways that those who listen to the music have described and categorized its rhythmic and metrical attributes, and with music-theoretical concepts that can clarify these phenomena as they occur in this repertory. Without suggesting that claims of "4/4 time" are factually incorrect, I will propose a re-evaluation of this category, one that portrays meter as multivalent rather than monolithic. In short, the meter of electronic dance music cannot be understood as any one thing but, rather, as a network of possibilities enabling the diverse experiences of time that clearly matter so much to those who love this music.

Taxonomies of Rhythm

In stores that sell electronic dance music, records are divided according to genre, with separate bins for techno, house, trance, and so on. Genre classifications are made on the basis of musical traits, as well as on the reputations of record label and producer. Drawing on ideas and terminology from both music theorists and EDM fans, the following section will suggest some classification systems specific to the rhythmic characteristics of electronic dance music. My purpose is not to place beats into boxes but, rather, to explore some conceptual schemata that can be used to frame and enrich actual musical experiences. I will be speaking mostly of "rhythm," which I use broadly to refer to any phenomena involving musically organized time; however, my discussion will also make reference to "meter." Although I will refine and clarify my conception of meter throughout this chapter, for now it will suffice to say that I regard it as a specific subcategory of rhythm having to do with the measurement of time.

BREAKBEATS VERSUS FOUR-ON-THE-FLOOR

Fans and musicians often divide electronic dance music into two broad categories on the basis of its metrical characteristics. This division is clearly evident in the quotation that introduced this chapter, where genres are divided into "breaks and/or jungle" versus "house and techno." Drawing on two of the most commonly used terms employed in this discourse, I will describe these categories as "breakbeat-driven" and "four-on-the-floor." The latter term comes from rock, in which a performer playing a drum set would need to depress the foot pedal on the bass drum (the "kick" drum) four times per measure in order to play a four-quarter-note pattern. The constant stream of steady bass-drum quarter notes that results is the distinguishing feature of four-on-the-floor genres, and the term continues to be used within EDM even though the only feet hitting the floor are those of the dancers. The primary genres within this category are techno, house, and trance.

Breakbeat-driven genres of electronic dance music include hardcore, jungle/drum 'n' bass, and big beat, as well as a category known simply as "breakbeat" or "breaks." Breakbeats are drum patterns sampled from the percussion-only sections, or "breaks," of old funk records. As in hip-hop music, where the practice of sampling breakbeats began, some of the most widely used breaks in EDM come from James Brown tracks, especially "Funky Drummer" (1970), "Give It Up or Turn It a Loose" (1969), and "Think (About It)" by Lyn Collins (produced by Brown in 1972). Even more common, especially in jungle/drum 'n' bass, is a break from a 1969 recording of the familiar gospel song "Amen Brother" by The Winstons (Shapiro 2000: 153), which fans and musicians commonly refer to as the " 'Amen' break." When used in EDM, breakbeats are sped up, often considerably. The amount of acceleration depends on the genre: the breakbeats heard in jungle/drum 'n' bass are *much* faster than the original (for instance, they might be accelerated from 92 BPM to 160), whereas in slower genres such as big beat and breakbeat the tempo change is more moderate (e.g., an increase of 20–30 BPM).

Breakbeat-driven tracks depart from four-on-the-floor styles in several ways. First, they include entire drum-set patterns rather than just one instrument. Second, because they originate within live percussion, their rhythms may include expressive timing variations, which do not occur in programmed drum-machine rhythms. Third, breakbeat rhythms tend to de-emphasize strong beats, instead placing considerable stress on metrically weak locations. In example 2.1, a transcription of the "Amen" break, the only instrument with an even rhythm is the hi-hat, which sounds out steady eighths. It is much less prominent than the other two instruments, however. The most apparent syncopation occurs in the snare drum, which presents strong dynamic accents on beats 2 and 4 (the "backbeats") during the first two and one-half measures. In between these backbeat hits, it lands on weak sixteenth-note beats. Except for the hi-hat eighths, the only strong beat receiving an articulation is beat one, played by the bass drum during the first three measures.

Another characteristic of breakbeats seen in example 2.1 is irregularity. The beginning of this break sets up a clear accentual pattern, followed through the first two and one-half measures (see the bass-plus-snare composite rhythm transcribed on the lowest staff). During the second part of the break, however, the drummer severely disrupts the regularity of this patterning. Beginning in the second half of measure 3, several factors conspire to create a moment of initiation that competes with the previously established downbeat. Specifically, the bass-drum arrives on the "and" of beat 3, the backbeat snare hit shifts to the "and" of beat 4, and the downbeat that should occur at the start of measure 4 is not articulated by either of the two main percussion instruments. As the analysis of rhythm patterns in relation to instrumentation shows, a motive previously found on beats 1–2 (motive *a*, where dots indicate sixteenth-note subdivisions of the beat) now seems to begin on the "and" of 3. Although the backbeat pattern described as motive *b* remains constant through this disruption (presenting an unusual scenario in which an accented offbeat seems to *confirm* a particular

Example 2.1. The Winstons, "Amen Brother," drum break (1.24–1.33).

metrical organization), the conflict created by the shifted *a* reappears at the end of measure 4.

The rhythmic characteristics I have described also appear in electronic dance music based on sampled breakbeats. However, whereas the breaks in funk form just a small portion of a track (such as four or eight measures), breakbeats permeate the fabric of genres such as jungle/drum 'n' bass. Producers sample short excerpts from a break (two measures is a typical length) and set them to repeat continuously. Because a single breakbeat is already a multipart pattern, it usually appears individually; producers do not layer breakbeats on top of each other. They preserve a sense of irregularity, however, by suddenly changing the pattern at various points during the track. The new breakbeat usually presents a quite different accentual scheme, thereby preventing the listener from getting overly comfortable with a particular pattern.[1]

Although most styles of electronic dance music can be classified as either four-on-the-floor or breakbeat-based, some genres blend the two approaches. "Happy hardcore," for instance, layers very fast breakbeats over a pounding bass drum, while "speed garage" combines elements of house and jungle.[2] Other styles elude this taxonomy altogether. Ambient, or "downtempo," is slow and often beatless, whereas the label "IDM" (for avant-garde "intelligent dance music") seems to be based more on an association with individualistic experimentation than on a particular set of musical characteristics.

PURE AND MIXED SPANS

In distinguishing between four-on-the-floor and breakbeat-driven styles, fans divide genres on the basis of the rhythmic characteristics of prominent instrumental patterns. Regardless of their differences, however, these rhythms share certain aspects of design. First, as is the case with almost all instrumental patterns in EDM, they are presented as cycles. In describing them as such, I mean to highlight the periodic repetition of an ordered sequence of events, as evoked in the following definition of "cycle" from the *Oxford English Dictionary:* "a period in which a certain round of events or phenomena is completed, recurring in the same order in succeeding periods of the same length." Second, the duration of

1. In genres such as jungle/drum 'n' bass, the rhythmic characteristics of breakbeats have been preserved even as producers have begun to turn away from sampling complete multipart patterns in favor of constructing their own patterns. In this newer approach, often referred to as "breakbeat science," producers use many very short samples—for example, a single snare drum hit instead of an entire drum-set pattern—which they usually alter in the studio (for example, snare hits are often reversed). In this way, complex breakbeat-like patterns are cobbled together from an array of diverse sources. See Shapiro 2000: 139–47 for further discussion.

2. See Reynolds 1999: 378–80, for further discussion.

a cycle, expressed in terms of a common denominator underlying its rhythms, is almost always duple. Rhythms occur in groups of two, four, eight, sixteen, thirty-two, and sixty-four from the smallest level (usually the sixteenth note) to the largest (including hypermeasures as long as sixteen bars).

Other authors have occasionally commented on this fact; for instance, Fikentscher observes that the "tempo" of underground dance music "is in almost all cases structured in 4/4 meter, as well as larger musical phrases which are simple divisions or, more often, multiples of four measures: 2, 4, 8, 16, 24, 32 etc." (Fikentscher 2000: 83). To note that these durations are multiples of two or four, however, does not fully describe their distinctive qualities; in most cases, they also share a property that Richard Cohn has described as "pure" (Cohn 1992a and 1992b). According to Cohn, pure spans—which include values such as 2, 4, 8, 16, and 32 (but not 24)—are based on a power of a single prime integer. Depending on whether the integer involved is two or three, spans can be further classified as either "pure duple" or "pure triple" (Cohn 1992a: 194). A measure of 4/4 meter, for instance, constitutes a pure-duple span, whereas 9/8 affords an example of pure triple.

Although pure-duple values are common in EDM and other types of popular music, music theorists have tended to downplay their interpretive possibilities in favor of what Cohn calls "mixed" spans—that is, durations based on two or more different primes. Scholars have frequently suggested that the ability to be divided by both two and three makes durations such as six and twelve inherently more capable of supporting complex rhythmic and metrical phenomena. Cohn, for instance, describes pure spans as "safe, stable, and hermetic," whereas mixed spans "invite conflict, instability, confusion" (Cohn 1992a: 195). In a second article, he reiterates this contrast, noting that "the potential metric interpretations for a span of mixed length are plural. Consequently, mixed meters have a potential for instability that is denied to pure meters, which admit but a single metric interpretation" (Cohn 1992b: 11). In light of these claims, a key question raised at the beginning of this work, and reiterated at the outset of this chapter, takes on a more specific cast. The question becomes not simply "how does electronic dance music create diverse experiences of time?," but more specifically, how does it create rich temporal experiences within *pure-duple contexts*? I will begin to answer this question in the following section.

EVEN, DIATONIC, AND SYNCOPATED RHYTHMS

When the pure spans of electronic dance music are divided into actual rhythm patterns, at least three distinct approaches, which I will term "even," "diatonic," and "syncopated," become evident. Rhythms in the first of these categories tend to reinforce the pure-duple quality of EDM spans by dividing them equally. Table 2.1 shows some of the most common even rhythms, along with the instruments with which they are most commonly associated. In addition to presenting the rhythms in musical notation, I show the positions of each rhythmic attack based on a sixteenth-note common pulse. The latter technique allows the rhythms to be considered apart from notational implications of active silence (rests), particular beat divisions (ties and beaming), and sustained durations.

In four-on-the-floor genres, the bass drum pattern 1/5/9/13 is almost universal. The 5/13 backbeat, pervasive in rock, is somewhat less common in EDM; when it does occur, it usually adopts the characteristic rock instrument, the snare drum. In disco, this backbeat pattern is often articulated by handclaps instead. EDM genres with roots in disco (house, garage) frequently preserve this instrumentation, though with drum-machine "handclaps"; "harder" styles such as techno tend to avoid this disco reference. More common than the 5/13 pattern is 3/7/11/15, usually played by a hi-hat cymbal but occasionally with snares. In trance, this rhythm is commonly articulated by synth "stabs" (short, percussive attacks).

These prototypes can be transformed in several ways, thus broadening the rhythmic palette without altering the patterns so much as to change them into another category (diatonic or syncopated). Rests may be substituted for attacks (or vice versa), or the even distribution of two equal durations may be shifted so that one is longer than the other (e.g., a two-eighths pattern can become dotted-eighth/sixteenth). But the most common transformation that preserves this category is to further subdivide even rhythms evenly.

Music based exclusively on even rhythms would clearly be quite limited. One important way in which electronic dance musicians have introduced variety, therefore, is by dividing spans asymmetrically. Table 2.2 shows the most common asymmetrical divisions of a whole-note span, the usual length of a measure in EDM; numerical values are given in most-reduced form. All of the asymmetrical

Table 2.1. Common even rhythms in electronic dance music.

Rhythm in Musical Notation	Attack Positions of Rhythm	Most Common Instrumental Associations
♩ ♩ ♩ ♩	1/5/9/13	Bass drum
𝄽 ♩ 𝄽 ♩	5/13	Snare drum; handclaps
𝄾 ♪ 𝄾 ♪ 𝄾 ♪ 𝄾 ♪	3/7/11/15	Hi-hat (open or closed); also snare drum or synth "stabs"
♬♬ ♬♬ ♬♬ ♬♬	All	Hi-hat (closed)

Table 2.2. Common asymmetrical rhythms.

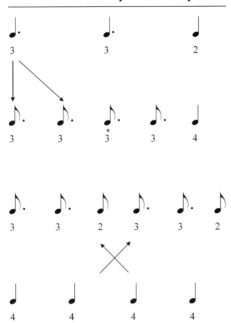

rhythms in the table can be derived from the first 3+3+2 (♪=1) through processes of diminution. In the pattern 3+3+3+3+4 (♪=1), the dotted-quarter spans of the original pattern are divided in half, as suggested by the arrows pointing downward. The 3+3+2 rhythms of the third row, meanwhile, are exact diminutions of the complete first pattern.

Two additional means of varying the patterns are shown as well. First, 3+3+3+3+4 may be shifted so that the downbeat coincides with the third dotted-eighth (see asterisk); in this case, the first two dotted-eighths usually function as an anacrusis. In spite of the clear downbeat, the pattern still seems to begin with the first "3"; in effect, the pattern-beginning and the measure-beginning do not coincide. Second, as the 3+3+2 patterns of the third row (♪=1) divide half-note spans, they can function as rhythmic cells within a larger whole-note span. As suggested by the arrows pointing upward from the fourth row, either cell can be replaced by a variant, such as the even rhythm 4+4.

Many other asymmetrical divisions of pure spans are possible, of course. The sixteen-pulse cycles found in electronic dance music, for example, might be divided into 3+2+4+3+4 or 5+4+4+3. These rhythms, however, differ in several important ways from patterns such as 3+3+2 and 3+3+3+3+4. The latter patterns have a property that music theorists, following mathematicians, have described as "maximal evenness" (see especially Clough and Douthett 1991). In simple terms, this means that their attacks are distributed as evenly as possible throughout the measure. Hence, 3+3+3+3+4 is a maximally even distribution of five attacks among sixteen pulses, whereas 3+2+4+3+4 is not. Likewise, 3+3+2 is a maximally even distribution of three attacks among eight pulses, whereas the rhythm 2+4+2 (♩ ♩ ♩) is not. Of course, many of the "even" rhythms I describe above, such as the four-on-the-floor pattern, are also maximally even; what is significant about asymmetrical patterns is that they are maximally even without being *absolutely* even. In musical terms, this means that they can create interest by dividing the measure irregularly, and yet they are still *almost* as regular as metrical patterns.

Patterns such as 3+3+2 have at least two other distinctive properties in addition to maximal evenness. First, they are also maximally *individuated*. This means that any given note forms a unique network of relationships with the other notes in the pattern. For example, in the pattern 2+1+2+1+2, a maximally even variant of 3+3+2, the fourth note begins exactly five pulses after the first, three pulses after the second, two pulses after the third, and one pulse before the last note. No other note within the pattern has the same set of relations to its surrounding notes. Of course, other patterns that are not maximally even can also be individuated in this way: for instance, the even rhythm ♩♪♪♩ is not maximally even, but it is maximally individuated. In this pattern, however, it is easy to rank the notes hierarchically in terms of metrical strength: assuming a musical context in which a quarter-note pulse is referential, the first note falls on the strongest beat, the fourth note on the second strongest, the second note on a weak beat, and the third on a weaker beat. In contrast, it is much more difficult to order the notes in the 2+1+2+1+2 pattern (♩♪♩♪♩) in this way. The first note ("the one") and the last stand out as more important than the others, but hierarchy is less apparent within the pattern.[3]

These rhythms occur in other repertories as well: for instance, the drum ensemble music of sub-Saharan Africa, Cuban *son,* and certain strains of rock music. Much of the research on their properties has centered on West African music, which forms a common point of heritage among these styles. In the most frequently discussed African styles, asymmetrical patterns tend to present an odd number of attacks within an even number of pulses: for instance, five or seven attacks within twelve pulses, three or five attacks within eight pulses, and seven

3. My discussion of maximal evenness and individuation is based primarily on Rahn 1996: 77–80. See also Butler 2001: paragraphs 30–31.

or nine attacks within sixteen pulses (see Rahn 1996: 78). The same tendency occurs in the pure-duple spans of electronic dance music; for instance, 3+3+2 presents three attacks within an eight-pulse span, while 3+3+3+3+4 presents five attacks within a sixteen-pulse span. Moreover, the presence of these rhythms cannot be traced directly to the spans in which they occur: in contrast to five- or seven-pulse spans (associated with repertories such as Eastern European folk music), which *must* be divided asymmetrically, eight-, twelve-, and sixteen-pulse spans can be divided with absolute evenness; indeed, in the duple meters of common-practice Western music, even divisions prevail, and the asymmetrical rhythms I have described are extremely rare. Hence, dividing even-pulsed spans asymmetrically seems to suggest a particular strategy for creating rhythmic interest. The asymmetrical patterns that occur in EDM are distinctive as a result of their special properties, yet they are also perfectly compatible with even rhythms (Rahn 1996: 77).

As a descriptor for rhythms such as 3+3+2, the term "asymmetrical" is problematic in various ways. First, I am using this term to refer to a special *subclass* of asymmetrical patterns rather than to all of them. Second, some of the patterns I have discussed are not, strictly speaking, asymmetrical. The patterns 3+3+4+3+3 and 2+1+2+1+2, for example, present durations that form a palindrome (Butler 2001: n. 39). Hence I prefer the term "diatonic rhythms," first presented by Rahn in his 1996 article "Turning the Analysis Around: Africa-Derived Rhythms and Europe-Derived Music Theory."[4] The adjective "diatonic" is appropriate because, as Rahn and others have pointed out, these rhythms share properties such as maximal evenness and individuation with the diatonic scale.[5]

I will describe a third class of rhythms in electronic dance music as "syncopated." In its most general sense, "syncopation" typically refers to phenomenal accentuation in metrically weak locations.[6] When I speak of "syncopated rhythms" as a class, however, I invoke a more specific sense of the term, as I explain in the following paragraphs.

4. In an earlier article (1987), Rahn uses the adjective "asymmetrical" instead.
5. The diatonic scale is a maximally even distribution of seven notes among twelve pitch classes, and the seven possible arrangements of this distribution correspond to the seven modes. Within the diatonic scale, each pitch has a unique intervallic relationship to every other pitch. See especially Pressing 1983, which focuses specifically on pitch-rhythm analogies, and Clough and Douthett 1991, which explores the property of maximal evenness within diatonic sets in general.
6. Following Lerdahl and Jackendoff, I use the term "phenomenal accent" to refer to "any event at the musical surface that gives emphasis or stress to a moment in the musical flow" (Lerdahl and Jackendoff 1983: 17). Lester (1986) has specified various categories of phenomenal accent, such as dynamic, durational, density, registral, ornamental, new-event, and harmonic accents.

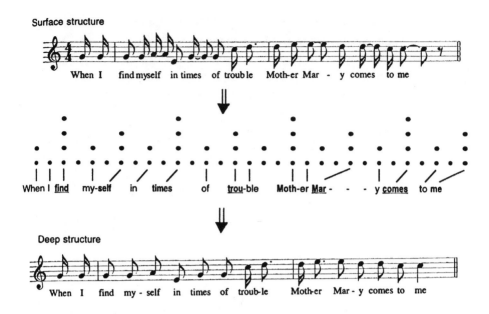

Example 2.2. Temperley's analysis of the deep and surface rhythmic structure of "Let It Be," opening phrase (Temperley 1999: 29).

In spite of the emergence of broad theories of metrical conflict (e.g., Krebs 1999), music-theoretical research on rhythm and meter has done little to address syncopation as a particular phenomenon. Although the term has been defined clearly enough as some sort of deviation from a metrical background, the ways in which a syncopated rhythm might *relate to* such a background remain understudied. In an effort to address this issue, David Temperley (1999) argues that the syncopations that occur in rock can be best understood as displacements from specific metrical beats.[7] For instance, in his analysis of the opening melody of the Beatles' "Let It Be" (reproduced in ex. 2.2), he argues that the syncopations found on almost half of the syllables in this phrase are actually perceived as backward displacements (indicated by diagonal slashes), which we normalize as we infer the melody's underlying rhythmic structure.

7. Temperley is not alone in emphasizing displacement in relation to syncopation; the theoretical roots of this association date back at least as far as the fourth species of Fux's *Gradus ad Parnassum* (1725). However, Temperley makes it clear (1999: 20) that he wishes to argue for a mechanics of displacement that is particular to rock. This research is also presented in chapter 9 of Temperley 2001.

Example 2.3. James Brown, "Funky Drummer," patterns used during drum break (5.34–5.55).

Temperley argues that syncopations of this sort actually *reinforce* the meter rather than disrupting it (1999: 26). In this view, syncopations are, at a fundamental level, embellishments of the metrical structure. Drawing on this general view, I would like to claim that certain types of rhythms are defined by a dynamic tension between our perception of a note's position and our sense of where it *should* be. This interplay creates a kind of gravitational pull toward the beat, a sort of negative emphasis on the position from which the note is displaced.

In EDM, syncopated rhythms occur most often in breakbeats. Consider, for instance, example 2.3, a transcription of the patterns used during the drum break in James Brown's "Funky Drummer."[8] The break is eight measures long; pattern a is used in measures 1, 2, 3, and 6, while the slightly varied a' (identical except for an additional attack by the bass drum) occurs in measures 4–5 and 7–8. The resulting sequence is a a a a' a' a a' a'.

Syncopation in a general sense (accentuation on a weak beat) occurs in this break in the snare drum, which creates dynamic and durational accents on beats 2 and 4. In rock, funk, and other traditions with roots in African-American musical practice, strong phenomenal accents on the second and fourth beats of the measure are so pervasive that this trait can be regarded as normative—hence, audiences within these traditions tend to clap on these beats rather than on 1 and 3—and there is little reason to regard the attacks on beats 2 and 4 as belonging elsewhere.[9]

The snare-drum part in this break also provides examples of "syncopated"

8. The break has a total length of eight measures, but EDM producers have often used shorter segments when sampling it.
9. Temperley's silence regarding this widespread pattern represents a significant lacuna in his article (if indeed it is intended as a general model of syncopation in rock).

rhythms in the narrower sense. As the break unfolds, the marked timbral differences between the three drum sounds make it easy for the listener to "tune in" closely to particular strands within the texture, while the interlocking rhythmic attacks enable an alternate focus on the composite rhythm. Regarding these as equally viable modes of attending, I will address some possible outcomes of each perspective in turn. Concentrating first on the snare drum as an individual pattern, I notice the way in which its second and third hits seem to dance about beat 3 without actually landing on it. The second hit seems early, while the third seems late. Through these behaviors, however, both attacks call attention to where they should be, in so doing invoking the presence of the unarticulated beat.[10] Focusing on the overall composite rhythm, it becomes somewhat more difficult to hear the third attack as coming after beat 3; rather, this and the following snare hit become part of a three-note anacrustic gesture leading into beat 4 (see the combined snare and bass drum rhythms on the bottom line). The second attack's pull toward beat 3 remains quite palpable, however.

Many of the same characteristics, including the circling about beat 3 and the anacrusis leading into beat 4, are evident in the first part of the "Amen" break (ex. 2.1). In both patterns, the snare and bass drums create irregular, shifting patterns of accentuation within the measure. These rhythms are not diatonic, however.[11] Instead, the syncopations that result are best understood as phenomenal accents occurring on weak beats, and in many cases as decorations of stronger beats. These syncopations ultimately reinforce our sense of the meter by pushing and pulling against it.

In positing certain rhythms as "syncopated" and others as "diatonic," I have implicitly suggested that diatonic rhythms are not syncopated in the same way that breakbeat patterns are. This distinction deserves further examination, as most music-theoretical approaches to rhythm and meter would explain patterns such as $3+3+2$ as syncopations against an evenly spaced metrical background.

10. I prefer temporal terms such as "early" and "late" to the spatial emphasis of "displacement." Moreover, events may only be displaced backward in Temperley's model, a condition that derives from his focus on vocal melodies (if displacements were allowed in both directions, two syllables might fall on the same beat in the deep structure). This vocal focus is rarely pertinent to EDM contexts, however. In the case of the third snare hit of the "Funky Drummer" break, a forward shift would read this attack as embellishing the "and" of beat 3 on a deep level; it seems much more plausible that we would experience it as gravitating toward a stronger beat.

11. In both breaks, none of the patterns played by the snare drum and the bass drum are maximally even or individuated, either individually or in combination. It is possible to find a $3+2+3$ division ($\flat$ =1) of the half-note span between beats 2 and 4 in both breaks, but it is difficult to *hear* the pattern in this way: the three sixteenths formed by the composite rhythm seem to lead into beat 4 rather than functioning as the start of a new group.

I do not deny that the irregularity of diatonic rhythms can become apparent when they are juxtaposed with the even rhythms generally associated with meter; in my view, however, diatonic rhythms are not heard as *subordinate* to an underlying metrical structure. Rather than being measured against an absolutely even, strictly regular norm, they create their own kind of evenness through their distinctive structural properties. This unique type of evenness will be evident in subsequent analytical examples: we will see that 3+3+2 can retain a quality of "almost triple" even when combined with pure-duple rhythms, and that in certain situations it may even be perceptually indistinguishable from pure-triple rhythms such as 3+3+3.[12] Interestingly, similar referential qualities have been ascribed to the diatonic rhythms that occur in African music.[13] For instance, Jay Rahn writes:

> [Asymmetrical] ostinatos . . . are not mere outgrowths of the referential meters of the pieces in which they occur. In each case, they represent persistent deviations from the divisive patterns that accompany them. . . . Ethnomusicologists have observed that African musicians say these sorts of asymmetrical time lines represent an audible point of reference for the ensemble as a whole. That is, in some instances, African performers apparently find their point of rhythmic orientation within a dense texture not with respect to a pulsating pattern or a divisive, unsyncopated pattern, but rather in relation to a seemingly syncopated pattern that appears to deviate constantly from the meter of the piece. (Rahn 1996: 25)

The musical contexts in which diatonic and syncopated rhythms appear also highlight their perceptual differences. As previously noted, syncopated rhythms occur most often in breakbeats, where they are part of a network of interrelated patterns. Though individual rhythms within the network tend to be highly syncopated, the overall composite rhythm usually expresses the meter clearly. In addition, breakbeats are often irregular in presentation: either they change from measure to measure, or the producer shifts to a new pattern at various points within a track. In contrast, diatonic rhythms—like the timelines of African music—tend to appear in individual instrumental lines and are usually repeated over and over without variation.

---

12. See especially the discussion of example 3.6 on p. 132 (which relates back to example 3.1, pp. 124–25).

13. In African music, diatonic rhythms often function as the "timeline," a repeating pattern (usually played on a bell or similar instrument) that serves as the rhythmic foundation of a piece of music. In this context, therefore, a seemingly irregular, asymmetrical pattern functions as the timekeeper rather than an even, pure-duple drum beat.

"Beats Were Meant to Be Felt and Not Heard": Meter in Relation to Texture and Instrumentation

The rhythmic and metrical characteristics of electronic dance music are closely connected to the instrumental sounds through which they are realized and the overall texture in which they are imbricated. In fact, the fundamental unit of musical structure in EDM is a repeating pattern associated with a particular instrument, which fans and musicians describe as a "loop." Most tracks are composed primarily (if not entirely) of loops, and any of the three basic rhythmic types (even, diatonic, or syncopated) may be used within a loop. The primary indicator of loop-based structure is cyclical repetition: if the rhythm of a certain part of the texture varies freely, with no discernible pattern of repetition, it is probably not a loop.[14] Nonlooping patterns do occur in EDM, particularly in tracks incorporating live vocals, but loop-based structure is much more common.

Although many popular-music styles with roots in African-American music make use of cyclical repetition, the pervasiveness of loop-based structure in EDM sets it apart. As Temperley illustrates, vocal melodies in rock create rhythm patterns that vary freely. In funk, a style that has served as the basis for many of the breakbeats used in EDM, drum patterns still reflect the idiosyncrasies of a live performer. In EDM, however, the vast majority of rhythms unfold as constantly repeating patterns. As a fundamental structural idea, this cyclical repetition manifests itself on multiple levels: not only in loops, but also in sequences, and ultimately within the structure of a complete track, as embodied in the form of a continuously revolving record.

Loops vary in length: they can be as short as a single sixteenth note, or as long as sixteen bars. For instance, in example 4.7 (ch. 4, p. 143) the hi-hat repeats after a single quarter note, while the drum and synth 1 patterns each last for a whole note. Synth 2, due to a variation in the sixth measure, repeats every eight bars. Generally, the term "loop" refers to a single instrumental pattern (or to a single repeating sample, as with looped breakbeats), though multiple loops can be combined into repeating sequences. For the sake of consistency, I always analyze the length of a loop based on the shortest possible unit of repetition. In some cases, the producer may actually be using longer units of repetition; for instance, the drum pattern in example 4.7 could be based on a four-measure loop, even though the listener only hears one measure being repeated. I will consider the ramifications of producer-based repetition in detail in chapter

14. The locked groove, described in the introduction, is the ultimate realization of the principle of looping—a manifestation of EDM's essential structural unit in both physical and musical terms.

6; for the time being, it is sufficient to note that EDM producers regularly create textures based on a variety of cyclical durations.

As table 2.1 illustrated, the characteristic rhythm patterns of EDM often appear in conjunction with particular instruments. Some of these instruments play especially important roles in shaping the rhythmic and metrical profile of a track. This is especially true of the bass drum, the loudest and most resonant sound within the texture; in fact, it is often the bass drum pattern that fans refer to when they describe "the beat" in electronic dance music. Music theorists studying rhythm and meter, in contrast, have tended to view beats much more abstractly. Most influential in this regard has been Lerdahl and Jackendoff's *A Generative Theory of Tonal Music* (1983). In this work, the authors characterize beats as durationless time points, claiming that they form the basis of meter by providing a background grid against which the rhythms of a piece are measured. "Beats are idealizations, utilized by the performer and inferred by the listener from the musical signal," they write (Lerdahl and Jackendoff 1983: 18). In other words, beats are cognitive entities; they should be felt and not heard.

In electronic dance music, however—and especially within four-on-the-floor genres—beats are richly present within the music. The beat is not only heard, but also physically felt, as well as enacted through bodily motion. Moreover, playing with the beat is essential to the metrical, textural, and formal processes that occur in EDM. This play occurs within a variety of musical contexts, including individual tracks as well as complete DJ sets, and it can be created by the producer or by the disc jockey. The most common phenomenon involving the beat is the removal of the bass drum—followed, of course, by its eventual return. This dynamic of removal and return is pervasive within EDM, appearing at some point in nearly every track. I will use several different words to describe this procedure in all its varying dimensions. At a broad level, I will speak of bass drum "removals" or "cuts," general terms that refer to any way in which the bass drum might be taken out of a track. However, I also will make use of two more specific expressions: "breakdowns" and "withholding the beat." "Break-down" is a term that fans and musicians use to describe sections of a track in which the bass drum is absent.[15] Although bass drum removals can be quite short

15. They also frequently describe such sections using the shortened term "break." I have already used "break" in my discussion of breakbeats, however. In that context it referred to the percussion-only section of a song (and did not imply the absence of the bass drum in any way); it was also used as a synonym for "breakbeat." (In addition, "breaks" can be used to denote certain genres that rely on breakbeats, such as "funky breaks.") To avoid confusion, I will use "break" only in its breakbeat-related senses (e.g., as a term for the percussion-only section of a track), while "breakdown" will always refer to sections in which the bass drum is absent. However, the reader should realize that dance music fans regularly use "break" in all of these ways; in fact, examples of

(e.g., one measure, or even a single beat), a breakdown is usually somewhat longer, typically lasting for at least four measures, and sometimes going on for a minute or longer. In addition to the removal of the bass drum, breakdowns may be associated with a host of other features, some of which are genre-specific. Trance breakdowns, for example, are often quite long, and tend to introduce an "ambient" feel through the use of sustained synth lines or strings without accompanying drumbeats. Another characteristic of breakdowns common to many genres is timbral manipulation; for instance, the producer might gradually turn up the delay as the breakdown unfolds. In sum, the term implies a particular kind of formal section as well as the removal of the bass drum.

"Withholding the beat" is a new expression, which I use to refer to a particular DJ-specific phenomenon. Withholding the beat occurs when the DJ removes the bass drum during a live performance.[16] Audience interplay is an essential part of this phenomenon. The crowd seems to actively anticipate the return of the beat: during its absence, they look toward the DJ as if to see what will happen next, and their dancing becomes tentative or breaks off. When the bass drum comes back, however, they dance with greater energy than in any other portion of the track, while enthusiastically expressing their appreciation to the DJ. Furthermore, as the term suggests, withholding can involve an element of teasing between DJ and audience. The DJ heightens the audience's desire for the beat, which represents the music in its most essential form, by taking it away and giving it back at carefully controlled intervals.

As a phenomenon, withholding the beat is both textural and metrical. Removing the bass drum takes away the loudest and most resonant element of the texture, and it can also call the metrical organization of a passage into question, as subsequent analyses will reveal. Moreover, withholdings most commonly occur at the end of a metrical unit: in the last beat of a measure, in the last measure of a four-bar group, or in the last four measures of a sixteen-bar group.[17] In fact, this anacrustic orientation is broadly characteristic of electronic dance music in

---

"breaks" as a term for the removal of the bass drum will appear in several interview excerpts in later chapters.

16. Technically, a withholding is also a kind of breakdown. However, the former term connotes a specific *action* (cutting the bass drum out within a live performance) rather than a type of section. In addition, "breakdown" generally suggests something created by the producer (and thus inherent in the record's structure), although in theory it could also be used to describe a beatless section created by a DJ (and in practice it can be difficult to tell the difference between DJ- and producer-based breakdowns while listening to a live performance).

17. Throughout the text, I use "bar" adjectivally as it appears in this sentence and within the term "bar line," reserving "measure" for all other uses. These choices are stylistic; I do not intend any semantic distinction between "bars" and "measures."

general. Emulating the kinetic emphases of Berry (1985) and Hasty (1997), I use "anacrusis" and its adjectival derivative to refer not simply to the upbeat as the final position in a measure, but more specifically to a part of the measure that has an energetic quality of leading *to* the downbeat. A similar quality inheres in EDM's most common diatonic rhythms: when 3+3+2 and 3+3+3+3+4 divide a whole-note span, they will only align with quarter-note beats in two places—the upbeat and the downbeat. This feature distinguishes these diatonic rhythms from less common variants such as 3+2+3. Moreover, this particular dynamic of returning to an orienting beat after an interval of rhythmic contrast is also typical of certain styles that have influenced EDM's development, especially funk;[18] George Clinton and other funk musicians have referred to the phenomenon in spiritually elevated terms as "the One" (Stewart 2000: 311). In this regard, the cyclical quality of rhythm patterns in EDM should be understood not so much in terms of a strict analogy to the circle (as a geometric design that has no distinct beginning or end), but rather in the broader sense suggested by the *OED* definition of a cycle as "a round or series which returns upon itself."

In order to address relationships between rhythm, meter, and texture more fully, it will be useful first to consider the texture of electronic dance music on its own. The vast majority of contemporary popular music features solo singers with a backing band, resulting in a predominance of melody-and-accompaniment textures. Such arrangements are extremely common in classical music, too, although in the latter repertory literal voices are often replaced by instrumental ones. The percussion-based textures of EDM, however, are not dominated by any single "voice"; instead, they are heterogeneous, with all the parts being more or less equal. In most rock and pop, drums remain in the background, where their function is to provide a steady beat and establish the meter; the singer (and, in passages such as guitar solos, the singer's instrumental surrogates) is the real focus of attention. But in electronic dance music (and especially in techno), drums *are* the music, to the extent that the few melodic elements that are present (e.g., the riffs) frequently assume a percussive role as well.

Texture also stands out as a primary compositional parameter in EDM because of its clarity. Instrumental sounds typically have distinctive timbres and registers, so that they are heard as individual layers rather than combining into groups.[19] Rhythm highlights this tendency further, as the pattern played by each

18. See example 2.3, where on-beat bass-drum attacks occur *only* on the downbeat; example 2.1 is similar, but with an additional emphasis on the four-*bar* level due to the syncopation that occurs in the last measure.
19. Because of this individuality, a "textural layer" in the context of electronic dance music usually consists of a single electronic instrument such as a hi-hat or a bass drum. (According to

layer is almost always unique. The occurrence of rhythms in repeating cycles, meanwhile, makes the individuality of each pattern more directly perceptible.

To a certain extent, one might trace this textural individuality back to the recording process, which involves multichannel environments that allow many different textural layers to be controlled independently. However, the widespread use of similar technology in other genres with markedly different results suggests that a distinct aesthetic is at work in EDM. Whereas other popular musicians have used technologies such as MIDI to synchronize parts and to combine instruments into groups, EDM producers seem to cherish the ability of these tools to make layers distinct.

The manipulation of textural layers is a central component of the art of DJing as well. The most obvious manifestation of this phenomenon is the practice of mixing two or more records together. To be a successful DJ, one must be able not only to match beats, but also to choose records that will work well when played simultaneously. The portions of a DJ set in which two different records overlap is called "the mix," and good DJs are said to be capable of "riding" the mix for long periods of time. If the records are mixed well, the audience will not be able to tell that the sounds are coming from different sources. Instead of hearing two different records, they will hear an integrated combination of sounds—a hybrid that is often called "the third record."

In general, then, although it is possible to view each record in the mix as a distinct textural "layer," the goal of mixing is not to highlight the two records as distinct entities but, rather, to blend them as smoothly as possible. At the level of the individual record, however, manipulation of textural layers is both explicit and frequent. Because the controls on the mixing board ("EQs") allow the DJ to adjust the high, middle, and low range of each record separately, the DJ can manipulate layers *within* individual records as well as between discrete tracks. Although the most common type of textural manipulation involving the EQs is withholding the beat, other parts of the texture may be removed as well (or, alternately, augmented in volume).

In sum, texture in EDM consists of a number of quite distinct layers, relatively equal in prominence, that are constantly in flux. These textural characteristics do not exist in isolation, but rather are intimately intertwined with rhythmic and metrical processes. In fact, this close relationship is also evident in individual tracks at a fundamental structural level *prior* to their manipulation by a DJ.

Maury Yeston, timbre is "the criterion by which rhythmic sub-patterns may be differentiated most easily" [1976: 41].) Exceptional cases in which a layer consists of more than one sound will be noted as they appear.

Example 2.4, which consists of excerpts from the beginning of the track "Jerical" by Jeff Mills, will illustrate the interaction of texture with rhythm and meter in a complete musical passage.

"Jerical" opens with two textural layers: a steady stream of quarter notes in the bass drum, and a sixteenth/eighth-note pattern played by a hi-hat cymbal (ex. 2.4a). The bass-drum pattern establishes the tactus at a tempo of approximately ♩=135,[20] while the combination of bass drum and hi-hat creates a sense of eighth-note motion. In this way, the beginning of the song sets up the beat and tells us that its division is simple rather than compound, but does not provide any information about how these beats should be grouped into measures.[21] The entrance of the next textural layer, another hi-hat pattern, does not clarify matters either. In fact, its added emphasis on the eighth-note offbeats may even raise doubts about the primacy of the bass drum as tactus (ex. 2.4b).[22] The fourth layer to enter, a snare drum, further subdivides the beat into sixteenth notes (ex. 2.4c), while the fifth—handclaps—provides the first definitive articulation of a periodicity above that of the quarter note (the half note; see ex. 2.4d). As the sixteenth iteration of the handclap pattern begins, all parts are abruptly cut off. The return of all layers two beats later marks the first major formal articulation of the work.

The next two patterns to enter, Riffs 1a and 1b,[23] are not only the first sounds with definite pitch in the track but also the first to articulate whole-note durations (ex. 2.4e). With their entrance, the texture of the work is complete. Listeners familiar with the style of techno will realize that the number of parts present is typical of a work at its fullest. In fact, only one other layer—a bass line—appears in the track, and not until more than a minute later.

The opening of "Jerical" reveals several ways in which techno's distinctive approach to textural layering is connected to its rhythmic and metrical attributes.

20. Here I use the term "tactus" in the sense of basic pulse, following the definition given by Lerdahl and Jackendoff: "[The tactus] is the level of beats that is conducted and with which one most naturally coordinates foot-tapping and dance steps. . . . The tactus is invariably between about 40 and 160 beats per minute" (1983: 71, 73).

21. It is for this reason that the duration of the example is indicated only in terms of the total number of quarter notes.

22. Nevertheless, the entrance of the new pattern after thirty-two quarter notes—a pure-duple value—does at least suggest that a duple hearing is more likely here. Example 2.4b uses dotted bar lines to indicate this possibility. In this and similar examples, a number (in this case, 7) used in combination with the measure repeat sign indicates the repetition of a pattern for a given number of times after its initial statement.

23. Because the two patterns, which are very similar in timbre, are always presented in combination, they are labeled 1a and 1b rather than 1 and 2. As such, they can be considered a single composite layer in the texture rather than two distinct layers.

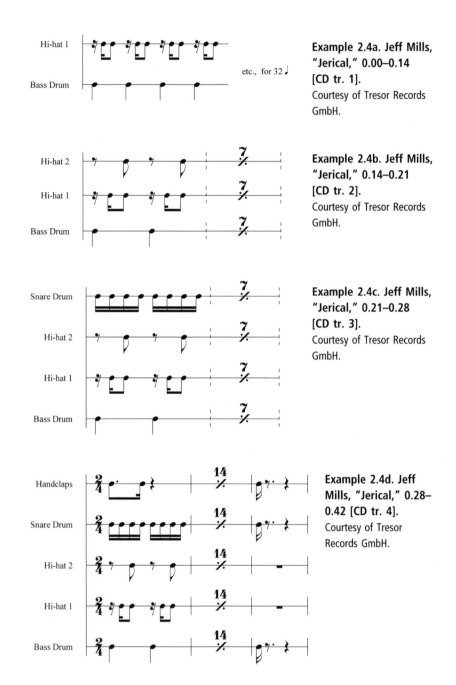

Example 2.4a. Jeff Mills, "Jerical," 0.00–0.14 [CD tr. 1]. Courtesy of Tresor Records GmbH.

Example 2.4b. Jeff Mills, "Jerical," 0.14–0.21 [CD tr. 2]. Courtesy of Tresor Records GmbH.

Example 2.4c. Jeff Mills, "Jerical," 0.21–0.28 [CD tr. 3]. Courtesy of Tresor Records GmbH.

Example 2.4d. Jeff Mills, "Jerical," 0.28–0.42 [CD tr. 4]. Courtesy of Tresor Records GmbH.

Riff 1a

Riff 1b

Handclaps

Snare Drum

Hi-hat 2

Hi-hat 1

Bass Drum

Example 2.4e. Jeff Mills, "Jerical," 0.42–1.06 [CD tr. 5]. Courtesy of Tresor Records GmbH.

etc.

First, each layer of the texture presents not only a distinctive rhythmic pattern but also a unique rhythmic *value.* The bass drum, for example, articulates quarter notes (and *only* quarter notes), while the hi-hats fill in eighth-note attacks on the offbeats. The snare drum articulates sixteenth notes, the handclaps half notes, and the composite riff whole notes. In every case except the hi-hats, which work in combination with the bass drum, the distinctive value articulated stems from the unit of repetition—that is, the duration of the loop.

This example also illustrates the existence of parallels between textural and metrical *processes* in electronic dance music. As described in the preceding paragraphs, the opening of "Jerical" leads us through a course of textural completion, beginning with two sparse percussion patterns and concluding with a rich, multilayered texture typical of the style. Significantly, this textural completion is accompanied by a metrical completion: it is only with the arrival of riffs 1a and b that the music begins to unambiguously express 4/4, the normative meter for the style.

Theoretical Points of Departure

Thus far I have emphasized the special qualities of EDM's rhythm patterns as well as their behavior both individually and in combination with each other (that is, in conjunction with texture). Although I have already been exploring music-theoretical concepts, as expressed in discourse about EDM and in published research, I would now like to focus in greater detail on three key theoretical issues: the relationship between rhythm and meter, conceptualizing meter in terms of "layers of motion," and the musical processes involved in establishing a sense of meter. Drawing more heavily than I have thus far on the work of particular theorists, I will explore each of these concerns in turn, thus laying the groundwork for the return of these issues in subsequent chapters.

RHYTHM AND METER: SHALL THE TWAIN NEVER MEET?

In the heading to the previous section ("Beats Were Meant to Be Felt and Not Heard"), I referenced Lerdahl and Jackendoff's notion of meter as grid. In portraying meter as a background hierarchy of equidistant, durationless beats that persists without variation throughout a work, Lerdahl and Jackendoff set up an opposition between metrical structure and another mode of musical organization that they describe as "grouping structure." Their formulation of this separation in *A Generative Theory of Tonal Music* (or *GTTM*, 1983) has been highly influential, having come to assume an almost axiomatic status in music-theoretical research on rhythm and meter through the past two decades.[24]

Not surprisingly, this dichotomy also plays a role in recent popular-music research, where it has often been mapped onto textural divisions between melody and accompaniment. Several music theorists have emphasized the timekeeping role of drums in rock. John Covach, for instance, writes that "rock listeners tend to take their tempo and metric bearings from the drums and bass" (Covach 1997a: 11), and David Temperley claims that "in rock, the accompanying instruments usually establish the metre of a song quite clearly" (Temperley 1999: 26). In fact, in Temperley's model, which is closely based on the *GTTM* approach, the tension between the accompanying instruments and the soloist is essential. He treats the drums and other accompanying instruments as "meter"—fixed, predictable, and therefore inherently uninteresting (he never even transcribes them)—and the solo melody as "rhythm"—syncopated, and changing from measure to measure (although ultimately reducible to the same "deep structure" as the meter).[25]

A wide variety of music-theoretical sources—*GTTM* foremost among them—

---

24. While Lerdahl and Jackendoff speak of a separation between meter and grouping, the distinction is more frequently expressed in general terms as a division between meter and *rhythm*. Hence when I speak of a separation between "rhythm and meter" or vice versa, I mean to include Lerdahl and Jackendoff's approach.
25. See esp. pp. 25–30.

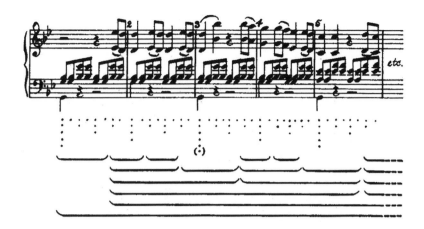

Example 2.5. Lerdahl and Jackendoff 1983, example 2.14a.

ascribe these same qualities to rhythm and meter in classical music. Rhythm is treated as a fluctuating foreground phenomenon heard against an unchanging metrical background. Although most scholars of classical music—unlike Temperley—do not explicitly associate the rhythm/meter distinction with texture, this distinction is strikingly apparent in the melody-and-accompaniment textures of the works that they select as paradigmatic. For instance, consider example 2.5, an excerpt from Lerdahl and Jackendoff's oft-cited analysis of the first movement of Mozart's Symphony in G Minor K. 550. Although the metrical structure, indicated by the dots, can be inferred from the melody alone, it corresponds directly to the patterns seen in the accompaniment. Only the hypothetical sixth level actually requires the melody's input. Meanwhile, the grouping structure, indicated by the slurs beneath the example, is derived almost entirely from the melody.

In contrast, electronic dance music—and especially techno—is difficult to divide into rhythm and meter along textural lines, as it is comprised almost entirely of percussive elements. In this way, it poses an interesting challenge to the aforementioned dichotomies. As long as our tendency to hear drums as timekeepers remains active, we will hear a number of different times being kept at once, rather than a variety of patterns measured against a singular dominant time. In an earlier work, I described this quality as follows:

> Although almost all EDM can be transcribed in 4/4 (or, less commonly, 2/4), the ways in which the music is layered, in combination with its persistent repetition of rhythmic patterns over long spans of time, encourage the listener to attend to the periodicities of individual layers rather than focusing on how those layers deviate from a single underlying structure.

These observations suggest a shift in emphasis, a change in the way rhythm is viewed with respect to meter in electronic dance music. Rhythm begins to seem not so much like a foreground phenomenon embellishing some deep background structure, but rather as a structurally significant element in its own right. (Butler 2001: paragraphs 27–28)

As I have already suggested without explicitly invoking the rhythm/meter distinction (pp. 88–89), this structural independence is particularly evident in diatonic rhythms. Patterns such as $3+3+3+3+4$ and $3+3+2$ stand out from the even patterns generally associated with meter due to their irregular division of the measure, yet they are similar to even, "metrical" patterns in certain ways. Because their attacks are spaced as evenly as possible throughout the measure, they are *almost* as regular as metrical beats. In addition, they repeat as regularly and persistently as the other patterns within the texture, a feature that distinguishes them from the constantly changing rhythms that Temperley and other authors contrast with "metrical" drumbeats.

Theories based on a rhythm-meter distinction have generally shown little interest in dealing with these sorts of patterns, often simply noting the presence of rhythms that dissonate with the meter without attempting to theorize their relationship to the metrical "framework." Lerdahl and Jackendoff, for instance, remark only that "the listener's cognitive task is to match the given pattern of phenomenal accentuation as closely as possible to a permissible pattern of metrical accentuation; where the two patterns diverge, the result is syncopation, ambiguity, or some other kind of rhythmic complexity" (1983: 18). The work that focuses on metrical "dissonances" more extensively than any other, Krebs's *Fantasy Pieces* (1999), only addresses layers comprised of a single duration; asymmetrical patterns such as $3+3+3+3+4$ and $3+3+2$ are not considered.[26]

In the past few years in music theory, a critical re-evaluation of the separation of rhythm and meter has begun to emerge, suggesting new ways of conceptualizing the relationships between irregularity and regularity, "surface" and "background" that rhythm/meter divisions purport to address. This trend has been generated largely by the publication of Christopher Hasty's *Meter as Rhythm* (1997), which aims to dissolve these divisions through the introduction of a new metrical concept, "projection." In the context of electronic dance music, Hasty's approach is valuable not only for the broad perspectives it offers on metrical experience, but also for its ability to address effectively the hybrid qualities of

26. In a review of Krebs's book, Frank Samarotto notes that "Krebs's layers are in principle regular, but perhaps it could be useful to define some layers as irregular, in the manner of additive rhythms" (Samarotto 2000: paragraph 4.3).

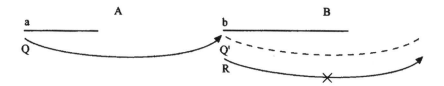

Example 2.6. Projection.

diatonic rhythms.[27] In the following paragraphs, I will outline the key tenets of Hasty's theory and then apply them to illustrate how a projective approach can comment on the irregularity of diatonic patterns (a characteristic that other theories would classify as rhythmic in nature) without ignoring their metrical aspects.

Hasty claims that meter occurs when listeners replicate the duration of an event through a process of "projection." See example 2.6, a reproduction of his example 7.2 (Hasty 1997: 85). In this diagram, capital letters A and B represent two events. At first, the listener does not know how long A will last. When B begins, however, the duration of A becomes definite; it now has the potential to be replicated by B. The solid arrow Q shows this projective potential; the projec*ted* duration is shown by the dotted line Q' (Hasty 1997: 84–86).

Hasty conceptualizes meter not as a series of timepoints but in terms of events, which he classifies as beginnings, continuations, or anacruses (symbolized respectively as |, \, and /). He also discusses a special subclass of continuation, deferral, which occurs in triple meter (ex. 2.7). In Hasty's view, triple meter (or "unequal measure") is articulated through two special processes: (1) the denial

a. Denial of potential half-note duration   b. Deferral

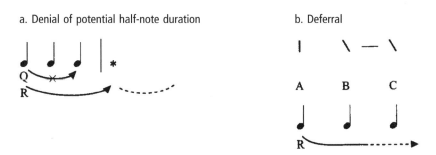

Example 2.7. Processes involved in unequal measure.

27. Asymmetrical patterns are not a particular point of focus within Hasty's book, although he does analyze various five-pulse patterns (1997: 140–47) as well as numerous complex twentieth-century examples.

of a potential half-note projection (Q in ex. 2.7a), and (2) the extension of the continuation begun with the second quarter-note duration (indicated by the symbol \—\ in ex. 2.7b). In this way, the completion of the projection set up by the first two quarter notes is *deferred* through the measure.

Whereas other methods tend to describe regular, even patterns as "meter" and irregular patterns as "rhythm" or "grouping," a projective approach enables the explanation of both phenomena using the same concept. This capability becomes especially helpful when analyzing diatonic rhythms, as example 2.8 illustrates.[28]

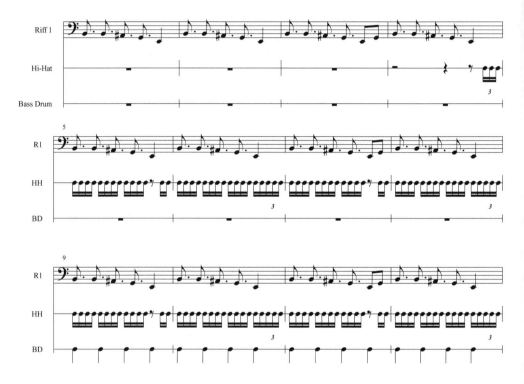

Example 2.8. 808 State, "Cubik (Kings County Perspective)," mm. 1–12 (0.01–0.24) [CD tr. 6].
Courtesy of ZTT Music.

This transcription shows a 3+3+3+3+4 rhythm as it appears in the context of an electronic dance music track, the classic "Cubik" by 808 State. The pattern,

28. All transcriptions of "Cubik are based on the "Kings County Perspective" mix, which includes additional production by Frankie Bones and Tommy Musto.

the track's signature riff, is heard first alone and then in combination with hi-hat sixteenth notes and quarter-note drumbeats. Example 2.9 reveals several ways in which Hasty's approach highlights interesting attributes of the pattern. In part *a,* a recomposition, the duration of the final quarter note is extended by two sixteenths, which significantly reduces the motive's rhythmic asymmetry (in fact, it could be made completely symmetrical if this note were simply replaced with two more dotted eighths) and produces triple meter with its characteristic deferral.[29] Why does such a minor change produce such striking results? Because this hearing is already latent within the pattern as it actually sounds.

The pattern begins with a series of evenly spaced articulations that set up and then realize a number of projections of equal duration; see Q–Q', R–R', and S–S' in example 2.9b. As these projections unfold, there is nothing to suggest that they are *not* metrical (and, in Hastian terms, they are). The motive also projects and then realizes a larger dotted-quarter note projection (Q–Q' in ex. 2.9a); this behavior implies the continuation R–R'—which, if realized, would form triple meter as shown in example 2.9a.

What makes this pattern interesting, however, is that it does *not* realize this triple-meter implication. The promise of the projected duration R' is never fulfilled; instead, the motive begins again before the duration of R' is completed. In this sense, R' is interrupted, as shown by the vertical line cutting it off in example 2.9c, and the second measure of the pattern seems to arrive too soon. Accordingly, the deferral associated with triple meter is also denied, as indicated by the *x* through the deferral sign (cf. Hasty 1997: 143–44). On a lower level, however, the quarter-note duration that ends the measure is too *long* in comparison to the preceding dotted eighths, resulting in a projection that is incomplete without being actively denied (see T–T' in ex. 2.9b). Were this overly long duration "fixed," the result would be quintuple meter, as shown by the recomposition in example 2.9d.

Similar phenomena occur with another common asymmetrical pattern, 3+3+2. This rhythm also suggests the possibility of triple meter (ex. 2.10a), but then presents an interruption instead (ex. 2.10b). Unlike the more complex 3+3+3+3+4, however, 3+3+2 does not create projections that are denied by an overly *lengthy* duration. For this reason, the simpler pattern only suggests one alternate interpretation rather than two.

Analyzing diatonic rhythms in this manner provides a detailed account of each pattern's distinctive projective profile as well as of the cognitive processes that may be involved in its perception. Furthermore, this approach explains each

29. In example 2.9a, dotted note values are used for easier comparison with examples 2.9b and 2.9c; considered in isolation, the pattern would be more effectively rendered in 3/4.

a. Triple-meter recomposition

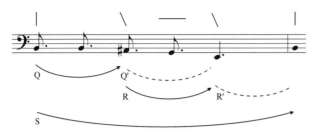

b. Lower-level projections

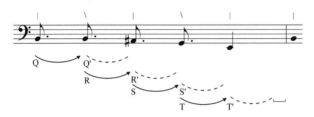

c. Higher-level projections

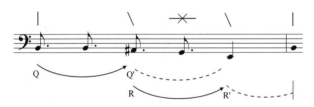

d. Quintuple-meter recomposition

Example 2.9. Synth motive from "Cubik" with projective analyses.
Courtesy of ZTT Music.

a. Triple-meter recomposition

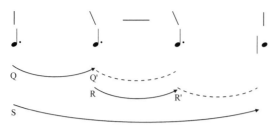

b. Original pattern

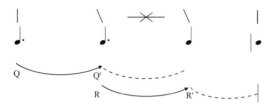

Example 2.10. Interpretations of 3+3+2.

rhythm's *positive* attributes rather than simply noting departures from a regular framework. In this regard, I should note that in problematizing certain aspects of the rhythm/meter separation I do not intend to suggest that listeners never use a regular "background" to measure and evaluate a less regular "surface." Indeed, I have suggested that a strategy very much like this comes into play when listeners experience breakbeats and similar rhythms as "syncopated." However, I have tried to frame this strategy as just one possible window into what might be called "metering"; I have positioned it as a particular orientation involving "hearing against" rather than as the sole arbiter of rhythmic experience.

In one sense, Hasty's theory might seem to be an odd choice for the analysis of electronic dance music. If the repertoire to which he has devoted the most attention is any indicator, it seems that his theory was first developed as a way of analyzing highly irregular twentieth-century compositions, whereas EDM is often extremely regular—at times, almost like a musical realization of Lerdahl and Jackendoff's grid.[30] If the works Hasty analyzes call for meter as rhythm, electronic dance music seems to suggest rhythm as meter. At the same time, a projective approach might also provide a way of coming full circle: meter as rhythm as meter (and so on). Hence we might say that Hasty's theory is useful

30. This is especially true of its four-on-the-floor genres, and less applicable to breakbeat-derived styles.

in this instance *because of* EDM's closeness to the grid. A projective account of meter can show how—in spite of its regularity—EDM is *not* the grid, and can suggest some of the reasons why listeners find this very regular music interesting.

LAYERING TEXTURE, LAYERING TIME

Hasty, like Rahn, devotes considerable attention to the characteristics of individual rhythms. However, the textural dynamism of EDM hinges in large part upon play and interaction *amongst* patterns. In theorizing this "layering," I draw in particular upon the work of Harald Krebs (1987, 1997, 1999), who—building on ideas first articulated by Maury Yeston (1976)—has developed a model in which meter is conceived of as the union of several different layers of motion.[31] According to Krebs (1999: 22), usually at least three metrical layers are present: the pulse layer (the fastest regular layer of motion) and two or more slower-moving interpretive layers (which group the pulse layer into larger units). In 3/4 meter, for instance, there is a pulse layer consisting of eighth-note motion, an interpretive layer of quarter-note motion, and a slower interpretive layer of dotted-half-note motion (ex. 2.11). Any sort of phenomenal accent can articulate these layers. Krebs measures interpretive layers in terms of the number of pulse-layer attacks they contain, describing the resulting number as the "cardinality" of the layer (Krebs 1999: 23). He then uses the abbreviation "*n*-layer" to refer to this cardinality; according to this system, example 2.11 would be said to contain a 2-layer and a 6-layer.

In this example, all layers of motion are neatly aligned. However, Krebs's primary focus is on layers that do *not* align, which fall under the rubric of "metrical dissonance" in his theory.[32] Krebs first describes the possibility of metrical dissonance as follows:

> A set of layers aligns when each pulse of each interpretive layer coincides with a pulse of every faster-moving layer. This state of alignment always exists when only one interpretive layer is imposed on a pulse layer. Two or more interpretive layers, however, may or may not align with each other. (Krebs 1999: 29)

If interpretive layers are aligned, they are metrically "consonant," but if not, the result is metrical dissonance. Those layers that form the meter of a work—its

---

31. Krebs defines a layer of motion as a "series of regularly recurring pulses" (1999: 23). I employ this understanding of the term throughout. Note, however, that the term "pulse layer" has a special meaning in Krebs's approach, as defined in the following sentence in the main text.

32. I will briefly explain Krebs's approach to this topic in the following paragraphs, and then return to treat it exhaustively in chapter 4.

Pulse Layer

Interpretive Layer 1

Interpretive Layer 2

etc.

Example 2.11. 3/4 meter in Krebs's model.

"normative metrical consonance" (1999: 30)—are "metrical layers," whereas dissonant layers are "antimetrical."

Krebs defines two categories of metrical dissonance: displacement dissonance and grouping dissonance.[33] Displacement dissonance occurs when two layers of the same cardinality are not aligned; according to Krebs, the metrical layer usually functions as a reference point from which the antimetrical layer appears to be displaced (1999: 34). He presents the following passage (ex. 2.12) as an initial example of the phenomenon:

Example 2.12. Schumann, *Papillons,* op. 2 no. 10, mm. 24–28 (Krebs ex. 2.8).

Krebs's analytical markings indicate the presence of two different 3-layers (where $\downarrow$ =1): a metrical 3-layer coinciding with the downbeat, and an antimetrical 3-layer beginning with the last quarter note in each measure.[34] He describes this particular dissonance as D3+2, where "D" stands for displacement dissonance,

33. As Krebs points out, these terms were first proposed by Peter Kaminsky (1989); in an earlier article entitled "Some Extensions of the Concepts of Metrical Consonance and Dissonance" (1987), Krebs describes them as type B and type A dissonances, respectively.

34. Krebs always bases the numerical values used in his analyses on multiples of a durational unit common to all of the layers discussed. As in this example, this unit does not always correspond to the actual pulse layer.

"3" for the cardinality of the layers, and "2" for the amount of displacement (the "displacement index"). Arguing that most displacements are heard in a forward direction (following the direction of musical flow), he indicates the displacement in positive terms, though he does acknowledge that contextual factors may occasionally lead to a "backward" displacement (i.e., a situation in which the antimetrical layer is heard to initiate *before* the metrical layer). This is indicated with a minus sign: e.g., D3–1 (1999: 35–36).[35]

Grouping dissonance arises when two layers of *different* cardinalities are combined. For instance, in example 2.13, the accompaniment articulates a 2-layer while the right-hand pattern creates a 3-layer.[36]

Example 2.13. Schumann, "Préambule" from *Carnaval,* mm. 28–32 (Krebs ex. 2.7).

Krebs describes grouping dissonances in terms of the ratio formed by the competing layers; the dissonance in example 2.13, for instance, would be described as G3/2. All grouping dissonances will eventually align—and they almost always do, although it is theoretically possible that a piece of music could contain a dissonance that would fail to reach a point of alignment before the end of the work. Following Horlacher (1992: 174) and Yeston (1976: 140), Krebs describes the span from one point of alignment to another as the "cycle" (1999: 32).

In electronic dance music, layers of motion often correspond directly or almost directly to textural layers. In "Jerical" (ex. 2.4a–e), for instance, the combination of bass drum and hi-hats articulates the eighth-note pulse layer, while the bass drum by itself expresses the first interpretive layer (quarter notes). The

35. Krebs's position is exactly the opposite of that taken by Temperley, who always analyzes syncopations as backward displacements (recall ex. 2.2, p. 86, and n. 10, p. 88).
36. As indicated by the 3-layer between the staves, a D3+1 displacement dissonance is also suggested. The parentheses around the first three numbers indicate that these pulses are weakly articulated.

Example 2.14. Schumann, String Quartet op. 41 no. 3, II, mm. 193–96 (Krebs ex. 2.2).

handclaps articulate a second interpretive layer (half notes), and riffs 1a and b sound out a third layer (the whole note, corresponding to the level of the measure).[37] Layers of motion also frequently associate with distinct textural layers in the music that Krebs analyzes. In example 2.14, for instance, the inner voices are the main force articulating the eighth-note layer, while the first violin melody sounds out the quarter-note layer and the low cello notes express the dotted half note. As in "Jerical," each layer of motion is associated with a particular instrument or instrumental group as well as a characteristic register.

In the string quartet, however, textural layers sometimes articulate more than one metrical layer. Registral accents in the inner voices, for example, create quarter-note emphases, and melodic new-event accents reinforce the dotted-half-note layer in the first violin. Moreover, Krebs's analysis also indicates an anti-metrical dotted-half-note layer starting on beat two of the first violin part. One might question whether the dynamic accent on beat two really creates a separate "layer." The term implies a certain constancy, the continuing presence of a distinct musical entity, whereas this phenomenal accent on a weak beat can be integrated into the prevailing meter quite easily.[38]

In contrast, the association between metrical and textural layers is excep-

37. The sixteenth notes played by the snare drum form another metrical layer, which—because it is faster than the pulse layer—Krebs would describe as a "micropulse" layer (1999: 23).

38. The looseness of this approach, whereby any perturbation is said to form a metrically dissonant "layer," is one of the main points of critique voiced by Robert Hatten in a recent review of *Fantasy Pieces* (Hatten 2002: see esp. 276–78). Hatten's commentary focuses on examples such as this one, in which relatively non-disruptive syncopations are analyzed as displacement dissonances. (He does not take issue with Krebs's analyses of grouping dissonances.) He argues for a clear distinction between syncopation and displacement dissonance, writing that "actual metrical displacement reorients one layer's perceived downbeat, creating a sense of displacement between contradictory metrical fields, fields that set up distinct hierarchies of metrical accent; syncopation achieves its dislocating effect by means of various phenomenal accents that work against, but do not contradict,

OHIO UNIVERSITY
MUSIC/DANCE LIBRARY

tionally strong in EDM. In "Jerical," for instance, the bass drum expresses the quarter-note layer *only,* and for the first forty-two seconds it is also *the only part* that articulates this particular layer.[39] Likewise, the snares articulate sixteenths only, and in the passage represented in example 2.4c they are the only part to do so. This trend continues throughout the texture, with each instrument articulating one distinct layer of the meter. Although the degree to which this phenomenon is manifested in this track might be somewhat unusual, it is nonetheless indicative of a tendency that is quite common in EDM, especially in techno. Hence, although it is easy to find examples in which a recurring syncopation might be analyzed as a separate layer of motion,[40] I reserve the term "layer" for instances that are more or less concrete—that is, for cases in which metrical layers are strongly associated with textural layers.

Questions of concreteness versus abstractness also arise when considering possible similarities between Krebs's layered conception of meter and Lerdahl and Jackendoff's grid-based view. Although the Yeston/Krebs approach is not identical to that of *GTTM,* it is related, in that one way of producing a grid is through the combination of several different layers of motion.[41] In fact, Hasty presents just this sort of grid as the first example of his book (ex. 1.1a, p. 14), in which he contrasts a set of metrical levels in 3/4 meter—quite similar to my example 2.11—to a rhythm pattern involving a variety of durations. In his discussion of the example, entitled "meter as a system of coordinated periodicities versus rhythm as variegated pattern," he emphasizes the abstract regularity of meter in such models: "We might imagine that several pulse 'levels' or 'strata' shown in the example . . . provide a set of coordinated periodicities that can be sampled by the actual rhythm. . . . It would appear that none of the metrical levels shown beneath the rhythm in example 1.1a is to be understood as a succession of actual sounding durations" (Hasty 1997: 14).

Krebs does take pains to distance himself from the notion of meter as an inexpressive grid, however:

> We frequently refer to the most pervasive metrical consonance of a work as "the meter." The meter in a broader sense, however, includes not only that

---

the downbeat (or more generally, the hierarchy of metrical accents) of the primary metrical field" (Hatten 2002: 277).

39. The hi-hats may also be said to articulate another quarter-note layer that is not aligned with the bass drum pattern.

40. In example 2.4e, for instance, the high *E*s in riff 1b could be said to form an antimetrical half-note layer.

41. Krebs does explicitly relate his own approach to that of Lerdahl and Jackendoff by characterizing their model as a layered one (Krebs 1999: 22).

consonance but also the various conflicts against it, and processes such as those that I have described—in fact, the entire metrical progression of the work. Meter in this sense is not a monolithic, inflexible grid, but is as organic and expressive as any other component of music. (Krebs 1999: 112, 114; cf. 23)

Finding this inclusive view of meter valuable, I consistently aim to treat layers of motion as real musical phenomena rather than abstract components of a given metrical framework. In electronic dance music, moreover, these layers reveal themselves as evolving elements that are constantly in flux, as the following section will reveal.

METRICAL PROCESSES

Works from the common-practice period typically establish meter almost immediately at their outset; to borrow a term from cognitive psychology, "entrainment" occurs quickly and efficiently. Consequently, theorists studying this repertoire have devoted little attention to metrical layers, instead preferring (as Krebs does) to focus on the antimetrical, "dissonant" layers that appear against them. Electronic dance music, however, features a great deal of play with the metrical layers themselves. The construction of meter is foregrounded as a *process.* Often just one or two layers are present, especially at the beginning of tracks. The track "Panikattack" by Plastikman (Richie Hawtin), for instance, begins as follows (ex. 2.15):

Example 2.15. Plastikman, "Panikattack," 0.00–0.16 [CD tr. 7].
Courtesy of Plus 8 Records, Ltd.

The pattern does not give the listener any clues about the grouping of the quarter notes; one could choose to count in a number of different meters. Nor does it imply any particular beat division; in fact, notating the passage in quarter notes is to a certain extent arbitrary, as the articulations could just as easily be dotted-quarters or eighths. In this sense, the meter is *underdetermined:* there is not enough information to make a decision about beat division or metrical type.

This example, which fans classify as "minimal techno," clearly adopts an aesthetic of radical simplicity. Nevertheless, metrical underdetermination is common in electronic dance music, especially in techno. Although most tracks begin with at least two instrumental patterns rather than a single pattern as seen in the "Plastikman" example, these two patterns are usually sufficient to establish only two metrical layers—the first interpretive layer and the pulse layer (i.e., the tactus and its beat division). This procedure can be seen in the opening of Dave Angel's "Bounce Back" (ex. 2.16), in which the bass drum establishes a quarter-note pulse and the hi-hat establishes an eighth-note subdivision. This sort of beginning tells us that the beat division is duple, but it does not provide any information about metrical type.

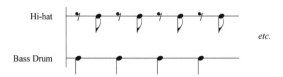

Example 2.16. Dave Angel, "Bounce Back," opening.

From this sort of passage EDM compositions often move on to a stage in which a larger grouping is suggested. Often the duration of this grouping is the half note rather than the whole note. See example 2.17, which represents the second phase of Plastikman's "Panikattack."[42]

Example 2.17. Plastikman, "Panikattack," 0.16–1.54 [CD tr. 8].
Courtesy of Plus 8 Records, Ltd.

This phenomenon also occurs in example 2.4d. Because most EDM tracks eventually end up in 4/4 rather than 2/4, such passages will most likely still be heard as underdetermined; those familiar with the style will expect a whole-note layer to arrive at some point. In "Jerical," whose process of metrical and textural

---

42. Within the highly repetitive and sparse texture that characterizes this passage, musical interest is created through a gradual dynamic and timbral change in the drum sound. Note also how the drum establishes the eighth-note beat division at the same time as the half-note layer.

completion I have already described, the whole-note layer does eventually appear, although it never occurs in the minimal "Panikattack." This emphasis on constructive processes is an important way in which electronic dance music draws the listener in and sustains interest within a minimal, repetitive context.

Conclusion: Re-evaluating "4/4"

As I conclude, I would like to return to the quotation with which I opened this chapter, and specifically to Chocolate's assertion that "4/4 is a time signature that all dance music uses." I want to focus on the category of "4/4," the purported representative of "the meter" of electronic dance music. Although such ascriptions might initially seem transparent, closer examination suggests at least four possible meanings associated with these kinds of statements about meter in EDM:

1. When EDM is created, the producer sets the time signature on the equipment to 4/4.
2. During listening, EDM can be counted in 4/4 most easily.
3. Patterns in EDM occur in fours (at a variety of levels).
4. Techno and other four-on-the-floor genres have a pure-duple quality, in contrast to syncopated, breakbeat-driven genres such as jungle/drum 'n' bass.

In terms of production, it is true that most sequencing programs (as well as other software/hardware used to make EDM) require a time signature to be chosen, and the patterning that occurs in EDM suggests that 4/4 is the most commonly chosen signature. This choice, however, is comparable to a classical composer's decision to write a particular time signature at the beginning of a score: while notational conventions may require such a choice, the mere act of inscription does not necessitate *perception* of the indicated meter.[43] Music theorists often speak of a discrepancy between "perceived" and "notated" meter; in EDM, this distinction might be reformulated in terms of perceived versus *programmed* meter.

In fact, producers can create a sense of other meters even in cases where

---

43. Most interviewees referred to "time signatures" rather than "meter." In an EDM context, where notation is rarely associated with musical performance or appreciation, the use of notational terminology to describe an aspect of musical experience is striking. While undoubtedly a matter of which music-theoretical terminology is most familiar to non-theorists, the tendency also reveals the continuing strength of the association between music theory and notation.

the equipment itself seems to physically restrict the available choices. For instance, classic drum machines such as the Roland TR-808 and 909, with their sixteen-button interfaces, seem to favor pure-duple metrical constructions. Other meters are possible, however; in fact, the creators of these machines inscribed this possibility directly onto the face of the equipment. On the TR-808, for instance (ex. 1.5, p. 64), four rows of rhythmic groupings appear above the sixteen buttons. The bottom two rows express pure-duple divisions of quarter notes, but the third and fourth express triple values based on groups of three eighth notes (at two different levels). In addition, a row of numbers beneath the buttons suggests the possibility of a twelve-pulse cycle. These groupings could be realized in several different ways. In a context in which each button corresponds to an eighth-note value, for instance, "mixed-span" meters such as 12/8, 6/8, or 3/4 could be created by setting the twelfth step as the last. Alternately, triple groupings (e.g., dotted quarter notes) could be used within a sixteen-step cycle, resulting in patterns that will only align with a 4/4 meter in increments of three: every three quarter-note beats, every three measures, and so on.[44] With additional instruments, potential configurations multiply; Graham Massey of 808 State told me about using a drum machine in "stop-nine time" (i.e., a nine-step pattern) in combination with a sequencer running in sixteen-bar cycles, as well as the use of 6/8 in combination with 4/4 in the track "Cobra Bora."[45]

With regard to claims about patterning and counting in EDM, one could argue that the predominance of 4/4 meter in the texturally complete sections of tracks might lead listeners to count in 4/4 even when certain cues are absent. This is certainly a possibility; because loops tend to occur in multiples of four, listeners who count in duple will eventually be rewarded, even in the absence of whole-note groupings. Recall examples 2.4b and 2.4c, where I used dotted bar lines to suggest that the sixteen-quarter duration of each textural configuration could encourage a duple hearing. In both cases, however, neither passage suggests anything more than this general category of "duple"; if such a meter is experienced, it is unclear whether 4/4 or 2/4 would be more likely. Moreover, markedly underdetermined beginnings such as the one that occurs in example 2.4a do not provide *any* cues beyond the quarter-note level.

Undoubtedly some listeners will still choose to count such passages in 4/4 and to feel the particular qualities associated with this meter even when they

44. I discuss this possibility further in chapter 4.
45. Massey has frequently commented on the use of unusual meters in 808 State's music; for instance, in a posting to the 808 State online discussion board on June 18, 2004, he remarks, "I always thought 'Cobra Bora' could have stood a chance. It was sometimes played at Hot Night at the Hacienda despite its funny time signature."

are not literally present in the music. Yet there is evidence to suggest that others cherish the stark neutrality of ungrouped beats. DJ Shiva, for instance, consistently referred to durations in terms of beats, even when the numbers involved were large; she would speak of sixty-four beats instead of sixteen measures, or of 128 beats instead of thirty-two measures. She also indicated that she prefers to count in terms of beats rather than measures. When I asked Graham Massey about the length of the sequences used in a particular track, he replied that they were "thirty-two beats" (rather than eight bars). Fans of electronic dance music, meanwhile, commonly refer to the music simply as "beats." In one sense, these usages reflect the fact that EDM is percussion music, a repertoire in which rhythm and beats are strongly emphasized. In a broader sense, however, they also reflect the music's tendency to foreground beats in themselves apart from any larger metrical context.

In combination with the examples I have presented, these statements suggest that an ongoing dialectic between fully formed "meter" and pure, unadorned "beats" is a pervasive characteristic of electronic dance music in general and of techno in particular. Although tracks often begin with underdetermined passages, it is true that the majority of EDM tracks eventually come to articulate some full-fledged version of 4/4 meter. However, the likely eventuality of 4/4 does not mean that it should be treated as a given, for to do so would be to ignore the processes of gradual metrical construction that are so essential to the music.

Nor does it mean that all 4/4 meters are the same. Within the broad category delimited by the referent "4/4," meter can be realized in a variety of ways. I follow Hasty in treating these differences of articulation as metrical in nature, rather than cordoning them off into a separate category of "rhythm." These two possible approaches also play a role in fans' discourse about meter and genre in EDM: although Chocolate is clearly in favor of a singular category of 4/4 for all dance music, he also references the way in which other fans use "4/4" much more freely to contrast four-on-the-floor styles such as techno and house with the syncopated rhythms of jungle/drum 'n' bass. In a posting to the same mailing list from February 2002, "ian7408" makes just this sort of comparison:

> Yes, there are a lot of junglists down in Bton . . . but I've been to a few house parties in the last few months that have had 4/4 music out the ass. Actually I only really remember one jungle DJ spinnin' . . . but other than that, it's almost all been 4/4 music. I've heard lots of house and hard trance. . . .[46]

46. "jungle in bton. . . . ," posting by ian7408 to IU-Ravers electronic mailing list, 11 February 2002. "Bton" refers to Bloomington, Indiana, and the expression "house party" to a party in a house (no particular connection to house music is implied).

In a technical sense, Chocolate's critique of such statements is correct: jungle, which is created with the same technology as techno, is also produced with a 4/4 time signature, and the length of its measures can be expressed in terms of pure-duple multiples of quarter notes, eighth notes, and sixteenth notes. However, the listeners who make these comparisons are also responding to perceived musical differences in a sensitive way; their references to 4/4 meter seem to describe a particular metrical *quality* rather than a metrical type. Phrases such as "4/4 music" contrast the metrical characteristics of four-on-the-floor genres with those based on breakbeats. In techno and other types of "4/4 music," even rhythms predominate, so that 4/4 meter and its subdivisions are much more apparent on the musical surface. Quasi-regular diatonic rhythms are also common. Jungle and drum 'n' bass, by contrast, are dominated by irregular, syncopated breakbeats; as a result, although they can still be understood in a 4/4 context, the pure-duple quality ascribed to techno is much less noticeable in these styles.

The category of "4/4," therefore, clearly references multiple qualities and experiences of meter. Although most EDM can be transcribed in measures of pure-duple duration, and often with a 4/4 time signature,[47] it cannot be reduced to a singular metrical type. The various kinds of rhythms that form its beats offer different windows into temporal experience, as listeners' categorizations of rhythmic and metrical qualities illustrate. Nor does 4/4 have universal governance within individual EDM tracks; the ways in which DJs and producers construct and deconstruct meter and texture reveal sensitivity to the components that constitute these musical dimensions as well as an interest in shaping time through gradually unfolding processes. Moreover, rhythm and meter in EDM intersect in interesting ways with existing theoretical views of these phenomena, providing a challenge to their traditional separation while also demonstrating allegiances with other layered styles. On the whole, electronic dance music suggests a turn away from the search for complex (metrical) structures that has occupied so much of music theorists' attention in favor of a reorientation toward the possibilities afforded by metrical experience. As a structure, meter in EDM appears unproblematic; as a phenomenon, it is rich.

47. I say "often" because there are cases in which a notation that indicates four regularly recurring quarter-note beats might constitute a misrepresentation; for instance, in situations where diatonic rhythms dominate, signatures such as 3+3+2/8 might be more accurate.

Electronic Dance Music
and
Interpretive Multiplicity

In the first part of this book, I outlined the intellectual history of research on electronic dance music, making a case for studying it *as music;* traced its historical emergence along with the musical and technological practices involved in its creation; and explored its fundamental rhythmic and metrical characteristics from a theoretical perspective. At the conclusion of the previous chapter, I emphasized the diverse experiential possibilities afforded by meter in EDM. I will continue to develop this theme in part II, focusing on the particular ways in which EDM enables multiple musical interpretations through ambiguity and metrical dissonance. I would like to begin this exploration with a musical illustration of these two dimensions.

In this passage shown in example II.1, an excerpt from the Chemical Brothers' track "Piku,"[1] the textural layering characteristic of so much electronic dance music is immediately apparent. The two components of the texture, the synthesizer and the snare drum, are distinguished by timbre and by rhythm, as well as by the presence of definite pitch in the synth part only.

The metrical attributes of this passage, however, are considerably more com-

1. For more extended discussion of this track, see Butler 2001: paragraphs 4–9.

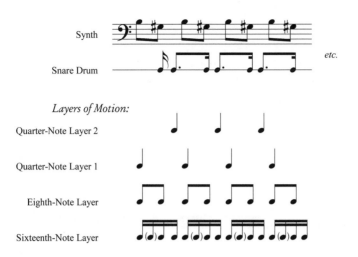

Example II.1. The Chemical Brothers, "Piku," opening (0.05–0.31).

plicated. As the analysis beneath the transcription indicates, several different metrical layers are present: a sixteenth-note layer suggested by the composite rhythm, an eighth-note layer corresponding directly to the synth part, and two different quarter-note layers (one suggested by durational accents in the snare drum, and the other by melodic high points in the synth part). These last two layers, however, are not aligned. Furthermore, the passage demonstrates at least two different kinds of ambiguity. First, because of the absence of layers moving at a rate slower than the quarter note, the metrical organization of the excerpt is underdetermined. Although the sixteenth-note and eighth-note layers tell us that the beat division is duple, the passage does not provide any information about metrical type; each quarter-note layer may be grouped in a variety of ways. Second, because the excerpt occurs before the meter has been clearly established, it is unclear which of the two quarter-note layers is referential. Rather than superimposing a "dissonant" layer on top of a previously established set of "consonant" metrical layers, the creators of the music present two relatively equal layers at once. As a result, listeners are free to choose either layer as regulative, and to change their minds as the passage unfolds.

The most noticeable aspects of this excerpt—ambiguity and metrical dissonance—are widespread within electronic dance music as a whole. In the next two chapters I will discuss these attributes further, focusing on ambiguity in chapter 3 and on various types of metrical dissonance in chapter 4. As subsequent discussion will reveal, I do not regard these phenomena as mutually exclusive;

rather, I treat them separately for the sake of organizational clarity. At the close of chapter 4, I will bring these themes together, focusing on the distinctive ways in which ambiguity and metrical dissonance are manifested in electronic dance music as well as their broader implications for our understanding of rhythm and meter in general.

Ambiguity

Ambiguity and Musical Analysis

Many different types of human creative output have been described as "ambiguous," and music is certainly no exception. The second edition of the *Oxford English Dictionary* gives the following "objective" senses of the word:

1. Doubtful, questionable; indistinct, obscure, not clearly defined.
2. Of words or other significant indications: Admitting more than one interpretation, or explanation; of double meaning, or of several possible meanings; equivocal. (The commonest use.)
3. Of doubtful position or classification, as partaking of two characters or being on the boundary line between.

As the following discussion will show, each of these three meanings is relevant in various ways to experiences of rhythm and meter in electronic dance music. Furthermore, all three senses have appeared in music-theoretical writing on ambiguity. Music theorists often disagree on the precise qualities that constitute ambiguity, however. Before embarking on an analytical exploration of specific instances of ambiguity, I wish to briefly consider some of these sites of disagreement. The *OED* definition will serve as a guide for my discussion, a point of departure to which I will return throughout the chapter.

As the *OED* suggests, ambiguity is most commonly defined as a state in which two or more meanings or interpretations are possible. Music theorists writing on ambiguity have also tended to favor this sense of the word, often to the exclusion of other meanings. Both Agawu (1994) and Levy (1995), for instance, take pains to distinguish ambiguity from "vagueness," a notion that corresponds most closely to the first of the above senses. Agawu writes that "although they are liable to be confused in ordinary discourse, ambiguity and vagueness do not mean the same thing" (Agawu 1994: 90), and Levy describes ambiguity as "diametrically opposed to vagueness" (Levy 1995: 151–52). Levy makes a further distinction between ambiguity and uncertainty: ambiguity is not synonymous with uncertainty but, rather, is a quite specific subclass of it. Curiously, however, neither author gives a reason for excluding vagueness from definitions of ambiguity; they seem to feel that simply distinguishing between these two causes of uncertainty is reason enough.

On a broader level, scholars also have raised questions about ambiguity in relation to the purposes of music theory. Agawu, for instance, maintains that the function of music theory (and of analysis based in theory) is to *dis*ambiguate; "theory-based analysis," he writes, "necessarily includes a mechanism for resolving ambiguities at all levels of structure" (Agawu 1994: 107). Taking this argument to its logical extreme, he denies the existence of any sort of ambiguity in music, on the grounds that musical factors always favor one interpretation over another. He concludes that "an analysis that terminates in undecidability represents a conscious or subconscious retreat from theory" and that "while ambiguity may exist as an abstract phenomenon, it does not exist in concrete musical situations" (Agawu 1994: 107).

Agawu bases these claims on two rather severe limitations to the notion of ambiguity. First, he requires the competing meanings involved in an ambiguous state to be *absolutely* equivocal; if there is any factor that might tip the scale in one direction, then the situation is not truly ambiguous. "A musical situation," he writes, "is ambiguous if and only if its two (or more) meanings are comparably or equally plausible" (Agawu 1994: 89). Second, he seems to believe that a truly ambiguous piece of music must leave the listener (and the analyst) undecided even *after* the piece has ended. He claims, for instance, that "to interpret a musical event as ambiguous does not mean that I do not know its meaning, or that there are innumerable possibilities for its meaning; the claim is rather that the event remains ambiguous *after* a reflective analytical exercise" (Agawu 1994: 93; original italics); he describes this condition as a "final-state awareness of ambiguity" (104).

Agawu's emphasis on the hierarchical resolution of ambiguous situations at all levels resonates strongly with a Schenkerian view of tonal structure, in which all of the events within a piece of music must ultimately be explained in relation to a single tonic triad. After all, the central activity of Schenkerian analysis—the "reflective analytical exercise" of making a graph—involves continually making precise decisions as to the weight of particular musical events in relation to other events at multiple structural levels. Situated thus within the intellectual traditions of music theory, Agawu's perspective on ambiguity, and especially his insistence on some sort of unified final state, appears unrelentingly structuralist, in the sense described by Lydia Goehr (1992), who speaks of a view of musical construction based on the "plastic arts." This approach treats a piece of music as a single, permanent object, comparable to a sculpture, rather than as an experience unfolding in time.[1]

Theorists also have questioned the relationship of ambiguity to a work's aesthetics. In one sense, a claim of ambiguity might be taken as a sign of artistic inadequacy, as evidence of a failure to communicate clearly. Levy, however, argues that ambiguity is central to the aesthetic experience of certain works. Focusing on situations in which musical events seem to signify both beginnings and endings, she writes that "it is likely that part of the affective experience for an engaged listener resides in the attempt cognitively to separate out the overlapped meanings or functions" (Levy 1995: 167). Furthermore, in contrast to Agawu, she claims that such ambiguities should not be resolved;[2] rather, it is the duty of the performer to "let them live": "If a listener is to be enabled to experience the pleasurable tensions of such ambiguities, the performer must convey both functions as fully as possible" (Levy 1995: 167).

The view of ambiguity I wish to develop is both broadly based and positive. I include all three types of ambiguity mentioned in the *OED* definition (and illustrate each of these with examples from EDM compositions), allowing for situations in which two or more meanings are more or less comparable in plausibility without requiring an exact balance between them. Nor do I regard ambiguity as an artistic deficiency; in fact, one goal of my discussion is to reveal ways in which ambiguous passages can bring nuance to electronic dance music. Furthermore, the view of ambiguity that underlies this study is processive: I do not require a "final-state" awareness of ambiguity, but rather hold that ambiguity is perceived within a particular moment or time span in a musical process. In this approach— which centers on a musical experience rather than an object—the experience of ambiguity is not negated by subsequent events such as eventual "resolution."[3]

I classify the phenomena discussed in this chapter into two broad categories: ambiguity of beginning, and ambiguity of metrical type. Ambiguity of metrical type may be the result of underdetermination, of competing metrical divisions (e.g., diatonic vs. even), and of simultaneously stated metrical types of relatively equal strength. Ambiguity of beginning, which I will discuss first, may involve meter (primarily in the form of ambiguity regarding downbeat location) as well as a type of organization that theorists have often described as "grouping."

1. For a view of ambiguity informed by cognitive and computer science (and admitting the possibility of both synchronic and diachronic ambiguity), see Temperley 2001.

2. This contrast is not exact, since Agawu focuses on the role of the analyst, whereas Levy discusses the performer. However, one could easily argue that the conscientious performer Levy has in mind is, in effect, a performer-analyst. Furthermore, Agawu expresses direct opposition to Levy's viewpoint (without making specific reference to her work) on pp. 98–99; see especially n. 17.

3. As further discussion will reveal, however, many ambiguous passages in EDM do not resolve.

Ambiguity of Beginning

One of the most common types of ambiguity in electronic dance music involves situations in which the metrical type of a pattern is clear but the location of its beginning point is not. In this respect, ambiguity of beginning might be considered a type of "functional" (Thomson 1983; Levy 1995) or "syntactic" ambiguity (Levy 1995), because the rhythmic and metrical function of the elements within a musical excerpt is, for various reasons, unclear. The passage transcribed below, from the track "Televised Green Smoke" by Detroit techno DJ and producer Carl Craig, provides a simple example of ambiguity of beginning. Although example 3.1a shows the measure beginning with the first eighth note in drum 1, the downbeat can just as easily be heard on the second eighth, as shown in example 3.1b.[4]

a. Downbeat beginning on the first eighth note in drum 1

b. Downbeat beginning with the combination of drums 1 and 2

Example 3.1. Carl Craig, "Televised Green Smoke," mm. 1–15 (0.00–0.15), two possible downbeat locations. [CD tr. 9].
Courtesy of Planet E Communications, Inc.

4. This track contains two drum sounds that are pitched much more definitely than is usually the case; in my transcriptions, I have represented their pitches as accurately as possible, although what is shown should still be regarded as an approximation. Panning is also very evident in the first three instrumental parts; the labels "center," "right," and "left" in transcriptions of this track indicate the respective positions of these sounds in the stereo field. Because of these stereophonic aspects, readers having difficulty hearing drum 2 in the audio example are advised to situate themselves closer to the left speaker; this will isolate drum 2 from drum 1, which is heard only through the right speaker.

Placement on the second eighth is supported by the density accents that occur when the two parts sound together, as well as by the general tendency of short-long patterns to function anacrustically in triple-meter contexts. At the same time, the larger context of the piece supports placement on the first eighth, since the downbeat location remains in this position when the next textural layer (not shown) is added. As this information is not available to the listener while the opening passage unfolds, however, the second interpretation remains equally viable.

The opening of "Televised Green Smoke" also illustrates one way in which extreme simplicity can foster ambiguity. In this case, the ambiguity of downbeat location provides a minimal example of either/or ambiguity, which would fall within the rubric of the second OED sense (two competing interpretations). There are just two attacks, and one or the other must be chosen as the downbeat. Nevertheless, the simplicity of the example does not diminish the effect of this ambiguity; in fact, it seems to make it starker. Because the pattern has few rhythmic components, its downbeat orientation determines much of its overall affect.

Although this simple type of ambiguity occurs frequently in electronic dance music, and especially in techno, more involved examples are also common. The opening loops of James Ruskin's "Connected" provide an interesting illustration.[5] Example 3.2 shows three different interpretations of the pattern's downbeat location. All three interpretations are plausible: interpretation a coincides with the beginning of the track; interpretation b is supported by melodic high-point accents (the first F# is a downbeat); and interpretation c has the advantage of grouping identical pitches together. Although there are also factors that work against particular interpretations—interpretation b places the snare drum on sixteenth-note offbeats, and interpretation c requires the first four notes of the track to be heard as upbeats—none of these details are sufficient to override the positive evidence. Hence, individual listeners may tend toward different interpretations, choosing among these hearings depending on their inclinations.

Throughout this book I point out numerous examples that, like this one, can be experienced in more than one way. In this respect I diverge from more traditional music-theoretical approaches—which, as Agawu's article illustrates, have tended to prefer singular interpretations. In many cases, rather than iden-

5. This track also contains a hi-hat playing steady eighths in alignment with the snare. I have not transcribed this part, however, because I do not find it to be perceptually salient. The hi-hat is so low in the mix that it is difficult to discern unless one listens very closely through headphones; most listeners will hear two instruments as shown above, with the hi-hat sounding like a reverberation in the snare drum part.

a. Interpretation a

b. Interpretation b

c. Interpretation c

Example 3.2. James Ruskin, "Connected," three interpretations of opening loops (0.00–0.15). [CD tr. 10].
Courtesy of Tresor Records GmbH.

tifying one interpretation as "correct," I prefer to claim that listeners will hear differently depending on their own inclinations and that multiple hearings are viable. (Note that I do not claim that *all* hearings are equally viable.) Rather than evasion or indecision, this choice stems from a deep conviction rooted in experiences of listening to electronic dance music; in fact, in presenting the examples discussed in this text to other listeners, I have often been surprised at the variety of responses I have received.[6] Invoking a distinction first suggested by Andrew Imbrie (1973), I view some of these listeners as "conservative" and others as "radical"; when presented with conflicting cues, conservative listeners tend to hold onto previously established metrical interpretations for as long as pos-

6. Example 3.2c, for instance, arose from discussion with another music theorist (a skilled listener with perfect pitch who had spent many years studying rhythm and meter); expecting listeners to insist on one of two possible interpretations (exx. 3.2a and 3.2b), I was surprised to find that some gravitated toward a *third* interpretation!

sible, whereas radicals move on to new interpretations more readily. Moreover, individual listeners may also interpret the same musical configuration in multiple ways as its cycles unfold; the repetitiveness of electronic dance music gives listeners plenty of time to experiment with different ways of hearing.[7]

In music-theoretical discussions, ambiguity is frequently discovered at "deep" levels, where it tends to serve as a stand-in for complexity. Much of the significance of ambiguous structuring in electronic dance music, however, lies in its potential for drawing the listener in. Rather than demanding a particular way of hearing from the listener, passages such as the one heard in example 3.2 encourage each of us to seek out our own preferred interpretation—to actively participate in the construal of our musical experience. In highlighting these qualities, and in choosing not to endorse a singular interpretation in situations in which multiple hearings are possible, I am not retreating from the practice of theory, as suggested by Agawu (1994: 99), but rather seeking to highlight a characteristic that is central to the aesthetics of electronic dance music—namely, its structural and interpretive openness.

The multiplicity of the opening passage of "Connected" is further verified by the next musical event. As it turns out, none of the competing interpretations shown in example 3.2 are favored within the context of the complete piece, for the entrance of a new textural layer (the bass drum) results in a new hearing (ex. 3.3).

Example 3.3. James Ruskin, "Connected," second textural combination (0.15–0.58). [CD tr. 11].
Courtesy of Tresor Records GmbH.

This turn of events is interesting in at least two different ways. First, as I will discuss further in the following chapter, the entrance of the bass drum in an

7. Horlacher (2004) observes a similar emphasis in the music of Steve Reich.

EDM track often results in a decisive metrical interpretation. In this case, the entrance of the bass drum also places the snares in positions 3/7/9/13, more typical for the style than the various possibilities shown in example 3.2.[8] Second, this clarification of the metrical organization occurs without resolving the ambiguities experienced during the opening of the track. Instead of reinforcing one of the previously suggested possibilities, the bass drum presents yet another way of hearing the passage. The initial ambiguity is never resolved with a "final-state" awareness of a "correct" interpretation.

At the same time, none of the patterns heard in example 3.3 are particularly downbeat-oriented. For this reason, one can just as easily hear them organized as follows (ex. 3.4).[9]

Example 3.4. James Ruskin, "Connected," alternate interpretation of second textural combination (0.15–0.58).
Courtesy of Tresor Records GmbH.

Given the factors cited in support of example 3.3, one might reasonably question the validity of this interpretation. However, its aural veracity can easily be tested by "dropping the needle" at a random point between 0.15 and 0.58. One can

8. In addition, the rest of the song's loops begin in sync (or almost in sync) with the downbeat as shown in example 3.3. This does not necessarily mean that the subsequent loops *articulate* this downbeat, however, but simply that their entrances into the texture coincide with it. While this observation suggests that the producer treated this point as the beginning of the measure when programming the track, it does not mean that he intended for it to be audible as such (or that it will stand out as the downbeat to listeners).

9. A third possibility, corresponding to a displacement of example 3.2c, would be to hear the downbeat falling on what appears to be the fourth beat of example 3.4. This hearing is not viable, however, because it works against the pure-duple tendencies of techno. Listeners familiar with the stylistic conventions of this music will most likely hear the downbeat falling either *with* the entrance of the bass drum (as in ex. 3.3) or two beats after it (as in ex. 3.4).

easily hear either metrical organization depending on where the recording begins.[10]

An adherent of Lerdahl and Jackendoff's approach might claim that the ambiguity encountered in this example is not strictly metrical, but rather a question of *grouping* in relation to meter. If we compare the two transcriptions visually, the meter does not seem to change, and the percussion parts would presumably sound the same regardless of where they begin with respect to the bass line. According to this line of thought, what is at issue is whether or not the bass line's pattern is synchronized with the meter; grouping and meter are considerably more out of sync in the first interpretation, in which the bass line begins on an upbeat.

Alternately, we can avoid the grouping/meter separation and regard all the differences between the two hearings as metrical in nature. If we follow this path, the anacrustic orientation of example 3.3 will seem just as metrical a characteristic as the location of the downbeat. The absence of a score also makes the meter/grouping distinction harder to maintain in passages such as this one. If we had a textual artifact to tell us that "the meter" is that shown in example 3.3, then it might be easier to view the grouping of the bass line as out of sync with this meter. In the absence of such an object, however, distinctions between questions of beginning-point location (where does the bass line begin with respect to the meter?) and questions of metrical accent (where does the downbeat fall?) begin to seem less relevant.[11]

Ambiguity of Metrical Type

In the next type of ambiguity I will discuss—ambiguity of metrical type—it is not the beginning points of patterns or the location of beginning points in relation to some other pattern that is in question but, rather, the larger context in which the patterns are to be interpreted. I already introduced one of the most common sources of this type of ambiguity, underdetermination, in the previous chapter. Underdetermination usually occurs when one or more layers of motion needed

10. One might imagine testing a similar ambiguity in a classical work by asking the performers to begin in the middle of the score. This would be incorrect within the traditions of classical performance practice, however, whereas DJs are free to begin a record wherever they want.

11. My comments here are not meant to suggest that the score validates the distinction. After all, Hasty's challenge focuses on Western art music, a tradition in which the use of scores is pervasive. Rather, I wish to note that this distinction is even *harder* to maintain when the score is absent.

to make a decisive metrical interpretation are absent; in such a case, the meter is "not clearly defined" as in the first sense of ambiguity described by the *OED*.[12] Underdetermination may involve a total lack of information regarding metrical type: for instance, in the beginning of "Panikattack" (ex. 2.15), only one metrical layer is present, leaving the grouping of that layer entirely to the imagination of the listener. If two layers of motion are present, the passage may establish a clear beat division without specifying a measure-level grouping of the beats (as in the beginning of "Bounce Back," ex. 2.16). Less commonly, a passage may suggest "duple" or "triple" without indicating whether the beat division is simple or compound. This type of underdetermination occurs in example 3.1. Although I have notated this passage in 3/8, the meter could just as easily be some other triple meter, such as 3/4 or 9/8.

Underdetermined passages often occur at the beginning or end of a track, where they enable smoother transitions between records. Stripping records down to their beats alone makes it much easier to match beats, and having a relatively small number of textural elements decreases the likelihood of a clash created by conflicting rhythm or pitch patterns. However, they can also occur within tracks, and underdetermination is particularly evident within certain genres, such as minimal techno.

I have also discussed the intermingling of even "4/4 rhythms" with diatonic rhythms such as $3+3+3+3+4$. With reference to the *OED* definition, this situation can be understood as an example of the third sense of ambiguity, described as "of doubtful position or classification, as partaking of two characters or being on the boundary line." In such cases, the music partakes of more than one projective profile, and it is not always clear which is referential. I presented one example of this phenomenon in the previous chapter ("Cubik," ex. 2.9), but numerous others may be found. Throughout the track "Reborn" by Walt J, for instance, $3+3+2$ patterns and duple rhythms mix together freely at the half-note level, occurring both in vertical combination (ex. 3.5a) and horizontal juxtaposition (ex. 3.5b; ex. 3.5a, snare drum).

While ambiguity of metrical type can arise through underdetermination or through ambiguity of metrical division (diatonic vs. even), another, more complex situation involves the *reinterpretation* of metrical type. Reinterpretations occur when the entrance of a new textural layer calls a prior metrical interpretation

---

12. As such, underdetermination is a clear example of musical vagueness (pun intended). While Agawu (1994: 90) doubts that examples of musical vagueness exist, the passages about to be discussed clearly illustrate the phenomenon.

a. 1.33–1.47

b. 2.23–2.37

Example 3.5. Walt J, "Reborn."

into question. While the actual process of reinterpretation is not, strictly speaking, an example of ambiguity, reinterpretation is often made possible through the ambiguity of a particular pattern within the texture. A particularly beautiful example of this phenomenon occurs in Carl Craig's "Televised Green Smoke." As previously described, this track begins with two drum sounds that clearly suggest some sort of triple meter. The beat division of the pulses is uncertain, however, as is the beginning point of the pattern (ex. 3.1). When a third drum sound enters in measure 16, however, a quite different interpretation is suggested, as shown below (see ex. 3.6; compare with ex. 3.1a).

Example 3.6. Carl Craig, "Televised Green Smoke," mm. 16–31 (0.15–0.31). [CD tr. 12].
Courtesy of Planet E Communications, Inc.

Although drums 1 and 2 appear to differ from their counterparts in the first transcription, they do not actually change. What changes is the metrical context in which they are interpreted. After the entrance of drum 3, it becomes apparent that drums 1 and 2 do *not* divide the measures of example 3.1 into three equal parts; in fact, a more quantitatively accurate transcription would depict them as the first two articulations of a 3+3+2 pattern. When heard in isolation, however, they evoke triple meter. My transcriptions reflect this difference, aiming to show the most likely perception of the two passages rather than a purely descriptive representation of "what happens."[13]

The tendency to hear triple meter in the opening measures of "Televised Green Smoke" supports my earlier contention (ch. 2, p. 89) that 3+3+2 may sometimes be perceptually indistinguishable from pure-triple rhythms such as

13. In the case of the opening passage, the ostensibly objective nature of a descriptive transcription would be misleading, since it is highly unlikely that a 3+3+2 organization would be perceived in the drum 1 and 2 parts when they are first presented.

Example 3.7. 3+3+(2) written in 3/8 meter.

3+3+3. Whereas the realization of this implication is usually denied by an interruption, as shown in the projective analysis of example 2.10, in certain situations listeners may be more attuned to a sense of "threeness" and less concerned with precise comparison of durational quantities. In fact, the triple-meter implications of the 3+3+2 pattern are so strong in this example that conservative listeners may continue to feel triple even after the entrance of drum 3.[14] In this way, differences between listener reactions highlight the perceptual implications of this diatonic rhythm.

Another factor enabling the perception of 3+3+2 as triple is the very small durational difference between this rhythm and a pure-triple pattern like the one shown in example 3.1a. Example 3.7 shows how a 3+3+(2) pattern like that of example 3.6 (drum 1) would appear if written in 3/8. In comparison, each of the first two articulations in example 3.1a is just one sixty-fourth note shorter in duration.

The ambiguity involved in example 3.6 comes about through a capacity for dual meaning inherent within the 3+3+2 pattern. This capacity facilitates the dramatic reinterpretation experienced by radical listeners as well as the triple versus diatonic ambiguity that creeps into conservative hearings. The 3+3+2 pattern is enabled for ambiguity in both structural and perceptual ways; in other words, it is *structured* so that we can *hear* it in a variety of ways depending on the context. This fact is not significant in itself, since many rhythm patterns can be interpreted differently depending on the context in which they are presented. Its usage in this passage *is* noteworthy, however, because it illustrates one way in which electronic dance musicians explicitly foreground the ambiguity of these patterns in their compositions.

"Televised Green Smoke" presents two different metrical types in succession. In other cases, conflicting metrical types may occur simultaneously. An interesting example occurs in Kenny Larkin's generically titled composition "Track." As my interpretation of the polymetrical passage in "Track" can best be understood within the larger context that surrounds it, I will begin with an exploration of

14. Those not yet convinced by example 3.6 should listen to the rest of the track, in which the 3+3+2 organization becomes increasingly clear.

the music that precedes this passage. Analyzing "Track" in this way also enables the chapter to conclude with an analysis of an extended musical passage.

The first sound with a definite beat articulation in "Track" is a low synth sound (ex. 3.8). A slight accent on the first E♭ suggests triple meter. Although the beat division is not specified, I have notated the example in 9/8 for the sake of consistency with subsequent transcriptions.[15]

Example 3.8. Kenny Larkin, "Track," Synth 1 part. [CD tr. 13].
Courtesy of Kenny Larkin.

After about twenty seconds, another sound begins to fade in. Example 3.9 shows how this new sound (synth 2) relates to the initial E♭s.

Example 3.9. Kenny Larkin, "Track," 0.20ff. [CD tr. 14].
Courtesy of Kenny Larkin.

Synth 2's pattern reinforces both of the layers suggested by synth 1: that formed by the recurring E♭s, and the interpretive layer that groups these notes into threes. It also suggests an eighth-note pulse layer, thereby moving toward Krebs's three-layer model of meter. However, both patterns are still relatively underdetermined, in that the only factor defining the bar line is a weak dynamic accent. Without this accent, any other note within the patterns could function as a beginning.

15. Transcriptions of this track have been simplified considerably for the sake of clarity. The beginning of the track, for instance, also contains a steady sound that rotates continuously through the stereo field (a sort of *Ur*-loop) as well as various other intermittent sounds. In addition, all of the passages shown in examples 3.8–12 contain minor variations in dynamics and timbre that are too irregular to be notated.

The next section plays on the accentual ambiguity of synth 2's pattern, as a third pattern aligns with the first two as shown in example 3.10.

Example 3.10. Kenny Larkin, "Track," 0.32ff. [CD tr. 15].
Courtesy of Kenny Larkin.

The use of grace notes may create some minor uncertainty about the location of beginning points in synth 3's pattern (hence recalling the ambiguity of beginning referenced earlier), especially given that the number of grace notes often varies in an irregular manner.[16] At the same time, the introduction and pitch resolution of the dissonant D♭s creates directed motion toward E♭. As synth 3 increases in volume, therefore, it gradually becomes easier to hear it as the downbeat-forming loop rather than synth 2.[17] This new interpretation is shown in example 3.11.

Example 3.11. Kenny Larkin, "Track," 1.00ff. (previous pattern with shifted downbeat). [CD tr. 16].
Courtesy of Kenny Larkin.

16. At times, E♭ is also included as a grace note, creating a neighbor-note figure E♭-D♭-E♭.
17. I begin to experience this change around 1:00, although other listeners may hear it sooner or later.

In the fourth section of "Track," which begins around 1:46, a new synthesizer pattern immediately comes across as duple, thereby creating a sense of uncertainty as to the metrical type of the passage (ex. 3.12).[18]

Example 3.12. Kenny Larkin, "Track," 1.46ff. [CD tr. 17].
Courtesy of Kenny Larkin.

If we were to apply Krebs's approach to this passage, we would interpret synth 4's pattern as a dissonant "antimetrical" layer that is heard against the 9/8 "metrical" layer. However, although the fact that 9/8 has been the primary meter of the piece for nearly two minutes does support such an argument, this interpretation fails to capture an essential quality of this passage and others like it in electronic dance music. Rather than hearing a dissonant layer in conflict with a dominant one, we are more likely to hear two clearly incommensurate layers of relatively equal importance; instead of immediately favoring one of the layers as dominant, we suspend judgment for a while, waiting to see which one will emerge as regulative. The passage therefore presents an example of the type of ambiguity in which two or more interpretations are equally possible. And process plays a crucial role in shaping these expectations of meter: the behavior of the piece thus far, as well as general stylistic familiarity with EDM, encourages us to defer judgment. We have already heard three different textural combinations, each of which was followed by the entrance of a new pattern that either clarified or contradicted the previous accentual organization (which was often tenuous to

18. In addition to the 4/4 vs. 9/8 ambiguity, synth 4's part is also underdetermined. When considered in isolation, it could just as easily be 2/4; the only reason to prefer 4/4 is that the four-quarter level aligns with the beginning of the most prominent 9/8 pattern.

begin with). These tendencies suggest not only that synth 3, in spite of its seniority in the time-world of the piece, holds little promise as a dominant pattern—but also that if we keep waiting, a clarification will eventually arrive.

The repetitive nature of electronic dance music, in combination with the almost constant presence of a loud, insistent bass drum within its texture, may lead to perceptions of its use of rhythm as homogeneous and simplistic. In pointing out these instances of ambiguity, I wish to counteract this tendency by highlighting important arenas of rhythmic and metrical subtlety. I contend that many of the nuances of EDM rely on ambiguous structuring to achieve their effects. The consequences of ambiguity in this music, therefore, are both formal and aesthetic. Moreover, they hail the listener in a way that is also social: metrically ambiguous sections encourage the listener to *construe the meter actively* rather than absorb metrical information passively. On the dance floor, this construction occurs in and between bodies as well as in minds. In so doing, dancers and listeners challenge the oft-expressed contention that rhythm in dance music (in general, not just in EDM) must be simple and obvious—a view that hinges upon a conception of the dancers as passive recipients of the rhythms they are given. Rather, EDM is consistently written in a way that promotes active participation in the construction of musical experience, generating interpretations that are both individual and multiple. This emphasis on the nexus between musical design and musical participation will resurface frequently through our exploration of ways in which grooves can be unlocked.

Metrical Dissonance

Adam Jay: In beats, my single bars usually have two to four beats.
Mark Butler: OK. So you do sometimes think of them as two beats?
Adam Jay: Yeah. [*counting*] 1–2–1–2—tech-house uses that a lot.
Mark Butler: Oh really?
Adam Jay: Yeah. And, my friend [name deleted] writes techno tracks in 3/4....
Mark Butler: Really? OK—I want to hear about this!
Adam Jay: [*laughs*] A lot of people don't buy his records. But he's a compositional genius. If I'm mixing his records, and I start his 3/4 record at a certain time, a really long way away ... it'll line up! [*laughs*] And between then, it'll just sound weird. And it's amazing.

—*Interview, 22 March 2002*

Viewed individually, each layer of motion within an EDM track shapes time in a particular way. Viewed collectively, layers work together to construct meter. Yet as Adam Jay notes, the mechanisms within this clockwork do not always tell the same time. Some cogs, of different sizes, move apart and then back together at regular intervals. Other gears, although identical in size, articulate displaced cycles that never align. For the listener, these elements offer divergent paths through the pure-duple landscape. I explore these avenues of interpretive multiplicity in this chapter, framing them as instances of metrical dissonance. Categories based on displacement and grouping serve as starting points for broader discussions of nonalignment as a general phenomenon. Some might argue that the harmonically based metaphor of "dissonance" is inappropriate for this rhythmically oriented music, an objection that I will address in further detail later in the chapter. In the sense of the Latin root *dis-sonans,* however, the notion of "sounding apart" is not only literally applicable to certain interactions between layers in EDM; it also resonates with the cultural and musical practices through which this music is created and appreciated in numerous ways.

Displacement Phenomena

In EDM, layers of motion often begin at different moments. If these layers are identical in duration (Krebs's "cardinality"), they will never align, resulting in persistent displacement. As a broad category, phenomena involving displacement in EDM include simple displacement dissonance, processes resulting in metrical displacement, and particular DJ techniques. I will begin with the most straight-forward examples, which involve percussion patterns that are displaced with respect to each other. In James Ruskin's "Connected," for instance (ex. 4.1), the snare drum creates a D2+1 dissonance ($\flat$=1) with the bass drum.[1]

Example 4.1. James Ruskin, "Connected," 0.15–0.58, displacement dissonance.
[CD tr. 11].
Courtesy of Tresor Records GmbH.

Likewise, the common pattern of snare drum hits on beats 2 and 4 of a 4/4 measure might be understood as creating a D2+1 dissonance ($\downarrow$=1) in relation to bass-drum attacks on 1 and 3. In each case, timbral and registral differences sharpen the contrast between the layers.

---

1. Examples 4.1–4.3 correspond to examples 3.3–3.5, with analytical marks added to highlight the presence of metrical dissonance.

Less binary examples of displacement dissonance occur in Kenny Larkin's "Track." Example 4.2 shows how the entrance of synth 3 results in a D3+2 displacement dissonance ($\flat$=1).

Example 4.2. Kenny Larkin, "Track," 0.32ff., displacement dissonance. [CD tr. 15].
Courtesy of Kenny Larkin.

Except for its limited pitch material, this excerpt is similar to many common-practice examples. As Krebs's analyses illustrate, however, layers of motion tend to retain their function as "metrical" or "antimetrical" throughout the individual works of that era. In contrast, layers in electronic dance music often change identity as new interpretive contexts emerge. In "Track," for instance, synth 3—which was initially antimetrical (ex. 4.2)—gradually increases in volume until *it* begins to function as the metrical layer. In this hearing, synth 2 and synth 1—the former metrical layers—now create a D3+1 dissonance with the synth 3 part (ex. 4.3).

Example 4.3. Kenny Larkin, "Track," 1.00ff., displacement dissonance. [CD tr. 16].
Courtesy of Kenny Larkin.

As with previous examples involving the gradual construction of meter, a key stylistic feature of these metrically dissonant passages is a heightened emphasis on *process.* In fact, one of EDM's most distinctive phenomena involving displacement is a process that I call "turning the beat around" (or "TBA").[2] This procedure can best be illustrated through musical examples. I will begin with an excerpt from Underworld's "Cups." The passage shown below begins about forty-four seconds into the track. As meter is ambiguous at the beginning of the track because of long sustained notes and a rubato tempo, example 4.4 represents the first passage in which beat articulations are definite.[3]

Example 4.4. Underworld, "Cups," 0.44–0.59. [CD tr. 18].
Words and Music by Karl Hyde, Richard Smith and Darren Emerson. Copyright © 1999 Smith Hyde Productions and Sherlock Holmes Music Ltd. This arrangement Copyright © 2004 Smith Hyde Productions and Sherlock Holmes Music Ltd. All Rights for Smith Hyde Productions in the United States and Canada Administered by Chrysalis Songs. All Rights for Sherlock Holmes Music Ltd. Administered by Sony/ATV Music Publishing, 8 Music Square West, Nashville, TN 37203. International Copyright Secured. All Rights Reserved.

In this excerpt, the combination of synth and hi-hat unambiguously asserts 4/4 meter. Pattern repetition in the synth articulates the level of the measure, while the hi-hat marks the quarter-note beats.

At the end of the passage shown above a new textural layer, a drum, enters.

2. In an earlier work (Butler 2001), I use "metrical reinterpretation" as a technical term for this phenomenon, while "turning the beat around" functions as a poetic description of its quality. The latter term also references dance music's roots in disco through allusion to Vicki Sue Robinson's 1977 classic "Turn the Beat Around" (RCA PD-11029). In the present work I use "turning the beat around" in a sense that is both poetic and technical, while discarding "metrical reinterpretation." The latter term is insufficiently distinguished from the "reinterpretation of metrical type" discussed in chapter 3, and it has already been used in a different sense by Rothstein (1989) to describe a hypermetrical phenomenon in which the last bar of one hypermeasure simultaneously functions as the first bar of the next hypermeasure.

3. The synthesized strings heard during the opening of this track are still sustaining their last note as the synth and hi-hat enter; however, they have faded out by 0.58.

The drum is not synchronized with the synth and hi-hat patterns, however; instead, it begins one eighth note earlier, as shown in example 4.5.

Example 4.5. Underworld, "Cups," entrance of drumbeat (0.55–1.00). [CD tr. 19].
Words and Music by Karl Hyde, Richard Smith and Darren Emerson. Copyright © 1999 Smith Hyde Productions and Sherlock Holmes Music Ltd. This arrangement Copyright © 2004 Smith Hyde Productions and Sherlock Holmes Music Ltd. All Rights for Smith Hyde Productions in the United States and Canada Administered by Chrysalis Songs. All Rights for Sherlock Holmes Music Ltd. Administered by Sony/ATV Music Publishing, 8 Music Square West, Nashville, TN 37203. International Copyright Secured. All Rights Reserved.

Because the drum is noticeably louder and more resonant than the other two parts, it can more easily function as referential. As a result, the downbeat seems to shift, resulting in the interpretation shown in example 4.6.

Example 4.6. Underworld, "Cups," 0.59–1.13. [CD tr. 20].
Words and Music by Karl Hyde, Richard Smith and Darren Emerson. Copyright © 1999 Smith Hyde Productions and Sherlock Holmes Music Ltd. This arrangement Copyright © 2004 Smith Hyde Productions and Sherlock Holmes Music Ltd. All Rights for Smith Hyde Productions in the United States and Canada Administered by Chrysalis Songs. All Rights for Sherlock Holmes Music Ltd. Administered by Sony/ATV Music Publishing, 8 Music Square West, Nashville, TN 37203. International Copyright Secured. All Rights Reserved.

The evidence for this hearing is not yet conclusive; conservative listeners may be unwilling to give up on the previously established downbeat location just yet.[4] After eight bars of the drumbeat, however, the new interpretation becomes definitive, as a second synthesizer pattern begins to reinforce the downbeat of the drum pattern (ex. 4.7).

Example 4.7. Underworld, "Cups," 1.13–1.28. [CD tr. 21].

Words and Music by Karl Hyde, Richard Smith and Darren Emerson. Copyright © 1999 Smith Hyde Productions and Sherlock Holmes Music Ltd. This arrangement Copyright © 2004 Smith Hyde Productions and Sherlock Holmes Music Ltd. All Rights for Smith Hyde Productions in the United States and Canada Administered by Chrysalis Songs. All Rights for Sherlock Holmes Music Ltd. Administered by Sony/ATV Music Publishing, 8 Music Square West, Nashville, TN 37203. International Copyright Secured. All Rights Reserved.

4. In example 4.6, the lack of a strong downbeat orientation in the drum pattern and the fact that the articulations of this pattern occur on weak beats of the previously established meter support a conservative hearing. At the same time, the tendency of low drumbeats to occur on the beats in EDM (and of hi-hats to occur on the offbeats) supports a radical hearing, as does the fact that the drum pattern begins one eighth note *before* the synth and hi-hat patterns (if it were an eighth-note backbeat, it would more logically begin on the "and" of beat one).

The conflicting interpretations created by the new textural layers in examples 4.6 and 4.7 result in D8+1 displacement dissonance; the 8s found in the examples indicate the boundaries of the various 8-layers. As the foregoing discussion reveals, however, turning the beat around involves much more than just a state of displacement dissonance. First, it is part of a process—a process that is both textural and metrical. Two different phases are involved: (a) the presentation of a particular textural layer or combination of layers, and (b) the entrance of an additional textural layer that results in a new metrical interpretation. Second, though the listener may not arrive at a new interpretation immediately, the entrance of the reinterpreting layer is abrupt. It does not fade in gradually, for our sense of the beat turning around relies on a sudden challenge to what we previously assumed to be stable.[5] (This claim implies that conservative listeners will also feel something amiss while listening to example 4.6, even if they do not relinquish the downbeat just yet.) Finally, a third specific dimension of turning the beat around is the transformation of a seemingly clear downbeat into an offbeat and vice versa.

The type of turning the beat around seen in "Cups" is also bilaterally symmetrical. In other words, the bass drum pattern is based on a completely symmetrical division of a 4/4 measure (if the anacrustic sixteenth note is treated as an embellishment); the hi-hat contains the same pattern spaced evenly between the quarter-note attacks; and when the beat turns around, offbeats map onto beats and beats onto offbeats. This is the most common type of TBA. Also typical is the placement of the passage near the beginning of a track, in association with a gradual buildup of the texture. However, the phenomenon can also be precipitated by the entrance of the bass drum after a texturally sparse passage within a track, as occurs in Mario Più's "Communication." Examples 4.8–9 show how this transformation arises.

Measures 81–96 consist of four statements of a four-bar snare drum loop (SD2) in combination with riff 1—a single repeating synth attack that begins on the pitch A but is subsequently distorted through timbral manipulation. See example 4.8, which begins with the last of these four statements. An additional snare (SD3) enters in measure 97. The durations of this sound keep dividing in half: it begins with steady eighth-note attacks, which subsequently turn into

---

5. According to this reasoning, the downbeat relocation represented in example 4.3 is not, properly speaking, an instance of turning the beat around. That change might be better described as "downbeat drift": the reinterpreting part (synth 3) fades in so gradually that a precise moment of transformation does not stand out; instead, one slowly becomes aware of counting with the new pattern. A similar gradual transformation occurs in the Aril Brikha track "Read Only Memory" (from *Deeparture in Time*, 1999).

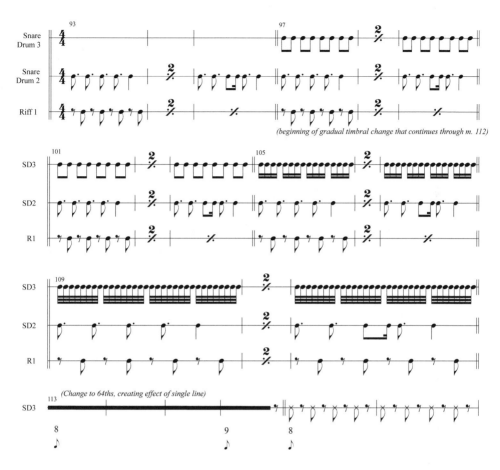

Example 4.8. Mario Più, "Communication," mm. 93–118 (2.43–3.30). [CD tr. 22].
Courtesy of Warner-Chappell Music.

sixteenths, then thirty-seconds, and finally sixty-fourths. By measure 113, the articulations of individual notes in this pattern are no longer perceptible; instead, we hear a single sustained sound (though the rapid sixty-fourth notes that comprise it create a reticulated effect). At the same time, the riff and snare drum 2 drop out.

The transformation of snare drum 3 and the removal of the other layers significantly undermine the metrical determinacy of measures 113–16. The patterns that permeated the preceding measures expressed eighth-note, quarter-note, whole-note, and four-bar layers of motion quite clearly. The disappearance of these patterns leaves us with a single sound that is continuous, lengthy, and undivided. It is theoretically possible, of course, that some listeners will continue to count quarter notes and whole notes (beats and measures) as it unfolds, but it will certainly be difficult for them to perpetuate these projections with any precision when the music does nothing to articulate them.

Near the end of the passage shown in example 4.8, a portion of the distorted snare drum 3 sound is extracted and used as a beat (mm. 117–18). After the indeterminacy of the preceding measures, the reconfigured snare drum 3 functions effectively as a new beginning. For this reason, I have placed it at the start of a measure, even though a quantitatively precise transcription (one that preserves measures of eight eighth notes irregardless of perception) would put the first eighth-note attack on the "and" of beat 1.

The projective dynamics of the passage leading up to this moment also influence its metrical qualities. As the twenty-bar span of measures 81–112 unfolds, the snare drum 2 loop consistently projects a four-bar duration (indicated by double bar lines in the example). The entrance of snare drum 3 in measure 97 and the sudden changes associated with its rhythmic accelerations in measures 105 and 109 enhance the determinacy of this duration, although the continual presence of riff 1 on the offbeats (and the absence of an orienting bass-drum tactus) provides a metrically disruptive undercurrent. When the riff evaporates in measure 113, therefore, the textural foregrounding of snare drum 3 allows us to focus without interference on the four-bar duration that we have been projecting. Although the continuous, undivided quality of this sound works against the perception of beats and measures, projections of the larger duration can easily continue. In fact, although the passage shown in measures 113–16 is actually one eighth note longer than the other four-bar spans in the transcription, I would argue that all of these four-bar durations are experienced as equal.[6] According to this interpretation, when snare drum 3 reenters with an explicit pulse in measure 117, it will not seem "early," nor will measure 116 sound "too long."[7] Unless the listener decides to hold on doggedly to a quarter-note pulse, s/he will instead be focused on a series of beginnings that arrive without any disruption whatsoever.

Within the space of two measures, however, there *is* a strong disruption, when

6. In this regard I follow Hasty, who argues that "more or less equal durations" may be perceived as equivalent in certain situations (1997: 86 and 94). The ability of the ear to forgive minor durational differences as it searches for metrical consistency is applicable to examples 3.1 and 3.6 as well.

7. More obviously, I also do not mean to suggest that measure 116 is in compound triple meter (9/8), but rather that its literal duration is equivalent to nine of the eighth notes established in the preceding measures.

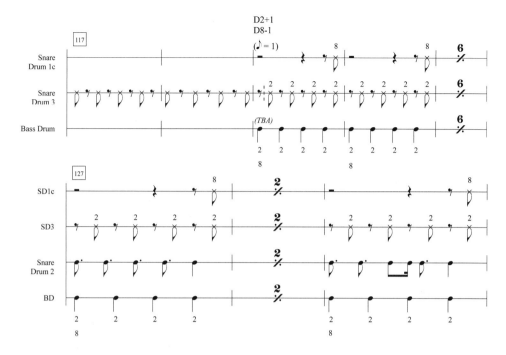

Example 4.9. Mario Più, "Communication," mm. 117–30 (3.26–3.50). [CD tr. 23].

Courtesy of Warner-Chappell Music.

the newly established beat is turned around (ex. 4.9). As in "Cups," a drumbeat seems to enter an eighth note too soon, causing beat and backbeat to reverse their accentual roles. As a result, two related displacement dissonances occur: D8–1 between the bass drum and snare drum 1c, and D2+1 between the bass drum and snare drum 3. The transcription now shows measure 118 as consisting of seven eighth notes, thereby compensating for the extra eighth in measure 116.

Not all examples of turning the beat around in electronic dance music are as symmetrical as those seen in "Cups" and "Communication." For instance, in Carl Craig's "Televised Green Smoke," just after the passage shown in example 3.6, the bass drum enters and turns the beat around. Example 4.10a, which corresponds to the audio excerpt, shows how the bass drum enters after sixteen measures of drums 1–3; example 4.10b shows the end of the passage reinterpreted.[8]

8. When the bass drum enters this passage, it is accompanied by a hi-hat, which I have chosen to omit in the interest of clarity. Within the track as a whole, the hi-hat does not play a particularly significant role in shaping meter, as it consists mostly of continuous streams of eighth-note or quarter-note motion.

a. Entrance of bass drum with respect to previous patterns (0:15–0:32)

b. The end of example 4.10a reinterpreted

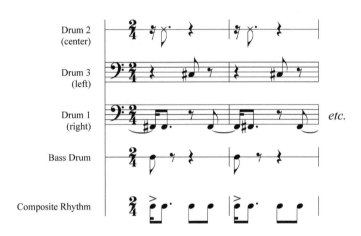

Example 4.10. Carl Craig, "Televised Green Smoke," turning the beat around. [CD tr. 24].
Courtesy of Planet E Communications, Inc.

In this example, the beat still shifts by an eighth note (although the bass drum now enters an eighth note too *late* rather than too early). Because the parts do not interweave in the same way, however, the effect is not one of binary reversal. One reason for this difference is the prevalence of asymmetrical rhythms in the passage leading up to the TBA; another is the less frequent iteration of the bass drum (it recurs at the half note level only). The reinterpretation that occurs at this moment also brings an end to the asymmetrical measure divisions; hence, the meter is shown as 2/4 beginning in example 4.10b.

This TBA is similar to the one in "Cups," however, in that it is initially ambiguous. Some listeners may not hear the beat turn around when the bass drum first enters; it is possible for a conservative listener to hold on to the previous metrical interpretation. Nevertheless, just as in "Cups," the reinterpreted hearing does eventually become definitive, and once again it is a multimeasure synth pattern (beginning around 1:19) that clarifies matters.

There is another dimension to the ambiguity of the Craig example, a curious situation for which there is no apparent analogue in the classical repertoire. One's interpretation of the passage may change significantly depending on the stereo equipment with which it is played. Listening to example 4.10 through the speakers on my home stereo or computer, I find the first interpretation much more convincing; I do not hear the beat turn around until synth 2 enters at 1:19. If I listen through headphones, however, the beat turns around as soon as the bass drum enters. This seems to indicate that the power of the bass drum to turn the beat around is closely related to its resonance, which is much more noticeable when the sound source is close to one's ears. One might also expect the beat to turn around more quickly if the example were played on a dance club's stereo system. This sort of situational variability is not unique to this example: aspects of EDM compositions often vary according to the materials used to realize them, in some cases generating significant interpretive differences. Hence, although electronic sound production is often described in terms of the control it affords the composer (through the elimination of performance variation), for the listener it can lead to experiences that are *less* rather than more determinate. The absence of a score further heightens this flexibility. In contrast to the theoretical tendency to portray particular musical interpretations as singular, permanent structures (e.g., "the voice-leading structure," "the metrical structure"), this variability points directly toward the role of the listener in construing the music.

When the beat turns around in Kenny Larkin's "Track," bilateral symmetry is absent altogether. Instead, the bass drum is displaced by a sixteenth note,[9] as shown in example 4.11.

9. Krebs suggests that one factor affecting the intensity of a displacement dissonance is its proximity to a state of alignment (Krebs 1999: 57). According to this criterion, the sixteenth-note displacement effected in "Track" should be more intense than the eighth-note displacements seen in previous examples.

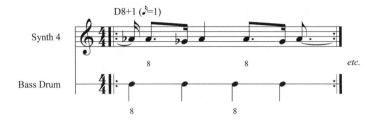

Example 4.11. Kenny Larkin, "Track," 2.18ff. [CD tr. 25].
Courtesy of Kenny Larkin.

This particular TBA has an unusually complex relationship to its surrounding material. Typically, turning the beat around creates surprise by introducing an unexpected change in a seemingly straightforward passage. The passage preceding example 4.11, however, is anything but straightforward, suggesting the possibility of two different meters at the same time without putting forth one or the other as dominant (recall ex. 3.12). We might expect the bass drum to resolve this ambiguity, given that it so often provides a decisive metrical interpretation. Nevertheless, the bass drum's reply to the question posed by synth 4—which pattern is dominant?—is a firm "none of the above." It refuses to align itself with either pattern, instead creating a downbeat in an entirely new location. Like James Ruskin's "Connected" (ex. 3.2), its ambiguity is never resolved directly, leaving us without a "final-state" resolution.

At the same time, the entrance of the bass drum and its attendant reinterpretation are much clearer than those of the prior patterns in this passage. Because the bass drum is the first pattern that does not fade in gradually, it has a definite beginning, and it also plays a more significant role in determining accentuation as the lowest and most resonant instrument.[10] After its entrance, the meter is relatively clear for most of the rest of the track, although the projective profiles of the 9/8 patterns continue to be heard in combination with 4/4.

Although downbeat relocation is the most palpable element of turning the beat around, the phenomenon involves more than that, as certain counterexamples reveal. When playing Walt J's "Reborn" (ex. 3.5) as the eighth track in a DJ mix, for instance, Juan Atkins creates a downbeat two beats earlier than expected by eliminating half a measure. Call-and-response alternation between the bass line/hi-hat/bass drum and the snare drum firmly establishes a whole-

10. A similar kind of transformation occurs in "Televised Green Smoke." The triple/3+3+2 ambiguity discussed with respect to example 3.6 is not resolved directly, but there is a move toward greater clarity in example 4.10.

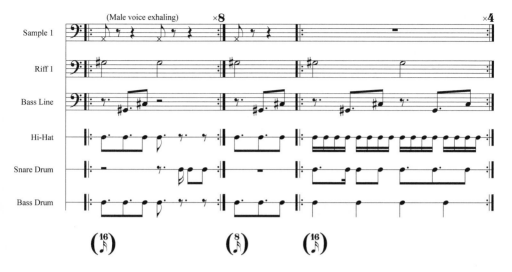

Example 4.12. Walt J, "Reborn" (as mixed by Juan Atkins on *WaxTrax! Mastermix Vol. 1*), 1.30–1.53.

note layer of motion prior to this change (see the first one-bar configuration in ex. 4.12). The opening pattern, however, is subsequently truncated, leading to a relocation of the downbeat.[11] After this change, the snare drum reestablishes a sense of whole-note motion through a 3+3+2 variation (♪=1) in the second half of its pattern. Although the downbeat's shift is certainly striking, at least two of the aspects associated with TBA are lacking. First, there are no new textural layers; instead, previously stated layers simply enter two beats early. Second, there is no beat/offbeat reversal; the beat simply moves to another pulse (the second strongest) within the tactus. Because of these factors (and because the whole-note layer was never articulated very strongly), the effect of this change is much less striking; although the downbeat of the last textural configuration does seem to arrive too soon, it does not turn the beat around.

Although turning the beat around is usually associated with the addition of textural layers, its effects can be reversed through their removal as well. For example, at the end of "Track" (not shown; 6:25), Larkin removes the bass drum, thereby allowing the synth lines to determine the meter once more. The result is a hearing like that of example 3.11 (with occasional allusions to ex. 3.12 as synth 4 fades in and out of the texture). This phenomenon, which might be

11. The change described here is specific to this studio-produced DJ mix; it does not occur in the unmixed track.

termed a "reverse TBA," is less dramatic than turning the beat around, which involves the explicit contradiction of a previously established pulse. A similar turn of events arises in measures 175–76 of "Communication" (not shown; 5:09–12), which are comparable to measures 117–18 of example 4.9. Here the extraction of the bass drum from the texture returns snare drum 3 to the fore; if one is willing to adopt a completely radical approach and hear the snare as referential, then the beat will turn around when the bass drum reappears in measure 177. It is much more difficult to place our trust in the snare this time around, however, for our perception of the passage will be shaded by our memory of what happened the last time the snare seemed to promise a beat. It is also significant that the use of snare drum 3 as a beat in measure 117 is new, whereas in measure 175 we have already heard forty-eight measures (mm. 119–66) in which it functioned as a backbeat. Thus, although TBA can be associated with textural decrescendos, it is more strongly associated with the *addition* of textural layers.

In addition to the displacement of musical patterns that occurs with turning the beat around, certain DJ techniques involve the *physical* displacement of records. In the most widespread of these practices, which I will describe as the "double-copy effect" (dance music fans and DJs generally describe it simply as "double copies"), the DJ plays two copies of the same record at once, with each record beginning at a different point. In the following passage (from a joint interview with the ethnomusicologist Cornelia Fales), DJ Shiva describes how this technique might come about:

> *Cornelia Fales:* And what are you doing at a climax then?
> *DJ Shiva:* Just find the most absolutely floor-wrecking track I can find and just ... Sometimes maybe even find that track and then do double copies. Start chopping between records.
> *Cornelia Fales:* "Double copies" is when you have the same thing on both turntables?
> *DJ Shiva:* [Agrees] ... What you can do—this is the most simple way to do it—is ... you can set it—I don't know how to describe it—on the half beat. So you've got this one going [taps] *tap tap tap tap* [now "brings in" second record, doubling the speed of the tapping and using two hands] *tap **tap** tap **tap** tap **tap** tap*. And what's happening is, you're not hearing that the whole time; you can cut. So you can make it go *"boom* boom *boom* boom *boom* boom *boom* boom" [making the pitch of every other "boom" slightly higher]; you can do weird effects; you can do little off-shuffle beats.

Although certainly less common than turning the beat around, I have heard the double-copy effect put into practice in live performances (such as Dave Clarke's set at the 2002 Detroit Electronic Music Festival) and recordings of live sets (such as DJ T-1000's 1998 mix entitled *Live Sabotage: Live in Belgium*). Its sound is also mimicked in certain studio-produced records, as the journalist Dan Sicko notes in his description of "Sharevari" (1981), a seminal track by A Number of Names that is often considered to be one of the first Detroit techno records.[12]

> As for the musical inspiration behind "Sharevari," one doesn't have to look any further than one of the staples of the high school scene: Detroit DJs would work two copies of Kano's "Holly Dolly," repeating the spare intro over and over again[13] and doubling up on the chorus of "Holly . . . Dolly." What A Number of Names did was to mimic this interpretation of the Italo-disco classic, building on the raw rhythm track (mostly a pronounced hand clap) and the female vocal as it would sound coming from two alternating copies of the same record: "Chari Chari . . . Vari Vari." (1999: 52–53)

Example 4.13 illustrates this effect in musical notation. Here a female voice (panned right) represents the first record, while an echo of this voice (panned left) suggests the presence of a second record.[14]

Although the double-copy effect clearly results from a process of displacement, it is not, properly speaking, a type of metrical dissonance. While the second record's pattern does seem to offer a set of alternate beginning points, it is difficult to hear it as a separate layer. In other examples of displacement dissonance involving identical nonaligned patterns, the layers are at least differentiated by timbre. In "Sharevari," however, both timbre and rhythmic pattern are identical. Furthermore, the metrical layers of the song are well established before the effect begins. Rather than two distinct layers in a dissonant relationship, this procedure evokes an echo or a pattern dividing in half (diminution). Like displacement dissonance, however, the double-copy effect does function as a source of musical intensification (as DJ Shiva's comments make apparent). Furthermore, it also involves bilateral symmetry: the desired placement of the second record is usually in the middle of a rhythmic cycle; in "Sharevari," for instance, the

12. In references to this track, I use the spelling given by Sicko; the 2001 re-release of the original (with new remixes) cited in my discography uses the title "Shari Vari." According to Sicko (1999: 35, 51–52), the name, originally spelled "Charivari," referred to a Detroit social club and to a New York clothing-store chain (rather than to the medieval mock-serenade) and was changed to avoid conflicts with these parties.

13. As this comment indicates, DJs might also play two copies of the same record in order to extend the length of a favorite track. In this procedure they alternate between two records; for example, they might play the intro first on one record and then on another, thus making it last twice as long. This strategy, which has become less necessary since the advent of extended dance mixes, differs from the double-copy effect, which does not make the track longer because the second record comes in on the first record's weak beats.

14. In Juan Atkins's rendition of this track in his DJ set entitled *WaxTrax! Mastermix Vol. 1*, he appears to compound the effect by playing double copies of "Sharevari" itself; echoes not found in the original mix occur in the second chorus, resulting in the doubling of the male voice as well.

Example 4.13. A Number of Names, "Sharevari," first chorus (0.32–0.47).

displacement occurs exactly in the middle of the metrical half-note layer. In tracks with a strong quarter-note layer, the DJ often brings in the second record on the eighth-note backbeats.

For some readers, this discussion may evoke certain techniques used in the music of the minimalist composer Steve Reich. This comparison is not an idle one, for EDM musicians and art-music composers (including Reich) have collaborated several times in recent years.[15] In terms of musical procedures, both the "phasing" of minimalism and the "double copies" of electronic dance music use multiple sound sources to simultaneously present repeating rhythm patterns, thereby allowing the patterns to go out of alignment with each other. And the doubling of rhythmic values that occurs in "Sharevari" recalls the diminution that takes place at the midpoint of Reich's phases (at the moment, for example, where the combination of the two parts in *Piano Phase* results in steady thirty-second notes).[16] However, significant differences surround the ways in which these techniques are presented. In general, Reich places much more emphasis on an audible process of going out of phase. Repeating patterns in his works tend to start in alignment and then go out of phase very slowly, lingering in the in-between condition before returning to a state of rhythmic alignment.[17] In EDM, however, the goal of using double copies is to hit a particular point of displacement and keep the music there for a while as the audience savors the distinctive effect. Gradual changes in alignment are avoided: these suggest a failure to beat-match, and they make the music difficult to dance to. Instead, the DJ cues up the displaced record at the desired point and *then* brings it into the mix. When "phasing" occurs in EDM (see n. 16), the tempo alteration is kept to a minimum, so that the audience only hears a delay between the records rather than a separation, and the effect is applied for a relatively short amount of time.

Grouping Dissonance

When layers of motion differ in cardinality, they have the potential to create grouping dissonances of varying complexity. In electronic dance music, the simplest examples of grouping dissonance usually involve eighth-note or quarter-note triplets within a 4/4 context. Both types occur in Sensorama's "Harz," along with an interesting twist: the quarter-note triplet is subsequently altered to a

15. The CD *Reich Remixed* (Arthrob/Nonesuch 79552–2), containing remixes of Reich's work by eight EDM DJs and producers, was released in 1999. Another minimalist composer involved in this trend is Philip Glass, who orchestrated the track "Icct Hedral" by Aphex Twin. Recordings of the music of Pierre Henry and Iannis Xenakis featuring EDM remixes alongside original versions of the composers' works have also been released in recent years.

16. EDM DJs actually use the term "phasing" to describe *another* practice involving multiple copies of records, in which they begin the two records in unison and then gradually speed one record up until it is very slightly out of phase, thus creating the effect of a delay.

17. In *Piano Phase,* for instance, Reich directly encourages the performers to remain in the out-of-phase state for as long as possible.

3+3+2 pattern (compare the bass lines of ex. 4.14a and b), thus opening a new window onto the close relationship between 3+3+2 and triple rhythms. The presence of these divergent rhythm patterns helps imbue the track with a sense of metrical diversity.

Nevertheless, the sense of conflict created by such dissonances remains relatively minor. Their cycles—the time spans bounded by their points of alignment—are short in duration: quarter-note triplets align with the quarter-note tactus after

a. 0.34–0.41

b. 2.49–3.03

Example 4.14. Sensorama, "Harz" (as mixed by Stacey Pullen on *DJ Kicks*).

a half note, and eighth-note triplets match up with the eighth-note pulse layer after only a quarter note. More significantly, these cyclical durations both correspond to and align with the principal metrical layers in clear and consistent ways. Such behavior is also typical of common-practice literature. In almost every example of grouping dissonance presented in Krebs's *Fantasy Pieces,* for instance, the cycle aligns with a metrical layer—either the pulse layer, the tactus, the half-measure (in the case of quadruple meter), or the bar line—or with the first hypermetrical layer (i.e., the two-bar level). In fact, this tendency appears to be so widespread that Krebs does not find it necessary to remark on it.

In the repertoire that music theorists have studied the most, therefore, the periodic alignment of grouping dissonance actually tends to *reinforce* important metrical junctures. And whereas this reinforcement also can occur in EDM, as example 4.14 illustrates, other dissonances work against the meter in ways that scholarship has not yet addressed. In example 4.15, for instance, a constant series of attacks in the synthesizer groups eighth notes into threes against the clear

Example 4.15. Azzido Da Bass, "Dooms Night (Timo Maas Mix)," embedded grouping dissonance.

4/4 meter of the other instruments. The result is a G3/2 dissonance with a cycle of three quarter-note beats, a duration that would be extremely unusual in a common-practice work in 4/4. Because this duration is incommensurate with the meter, it generates a larger dissonance with a three-*measure* cycle. I have labeled this dissonance G4/3, with the quarter note equal to one; as indicated by the larger numerals running along the outer tiers of the staff system, the alignment points of the initial dissonance form the 3-layer of this larger dissonance, whereas the downbeats of each measure form its 4-layer.[18]

I describe this configuration, in which one grouping dissonance is nested within another whose common durational unit is larger, as an *embedded* grouping dissonance (EGD). At least three distinct dimensions are involved in embedded grouping dissonance: first, the presentation of more than one grouping dissonance at the same time; second, the presentation of grouping dissonance on more than one metrical level; and third, a causal relationship in which the noncongruence of the lower-level dissonance's cycle *generates* the larger dissonance.

Although electronic dance musicians may realize these conditions in a variety of ways, the embedded grouping dissonances found in this repertory consistently involve a fundamental conflict between the pure-duple values of 4/4 meter and a pure-triple dissonance. The pure-triple layer often consists of dotted quarter notes, as in example 4.15, but other rhythmic values may occur. Throughout most of the Detroit-techno track shown in example 4.16a, for instance, the voice moves in steady dotted eighths, creating a 3-layer that combines with the drumbeat's 4-layer to produce a G4/3 grouping dissonance. This dissonance moves through two complete cycles, shown by brackets and dotted lines at the points where the layers converge. A third cycle is left unfinished when the dotted-eighth-note motion breaks off in the second measure.

As in the previous example, the lower-level cycle in this excerpt lasts for three beats, thereby creating a larger G4/3 dissonance in which the quarter note equals "one." If the slower moving layers of this dissonance, indicated by larger numerals in the outer tiers, were allowed to continue, they would return to a point of alignment every three measures. Instead, however, the cessation of the

18. In order to present the dissonance as clearly as possible, example 4.15 places the first attack of the synthesizer on the downbeat. In the recorded track, the synth actually enters on the "and" of beat 1, at a point comparable to the fifth measure of the example, and then continues to cycle through the dissonance in the order shown. A further complicating factor is the two-bar length of the bass line, which only aligns with the three-bar cycle of the larger dissonance after six measures (hence the length of the example). I discuss the use of metrical dissonance in relation to multimeasure patterning in "Dooms Night" in detail in chapters 5 and 6.

a. The dissonance as realized

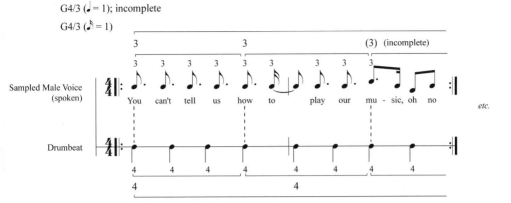

b. Asymmetrical divisions of the two-bar span

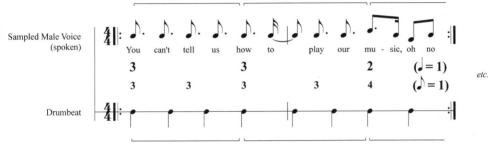

Example 4.16. Reese and Santonio, "How to Play Our Music," embedded grouping dissonance.

dotted-eighth-note motion leads to a "resolution" of the dissonance in the *second* measure of the pattern, thereby reinforcing rather than subverting the two-bar hypermeter. Although this behavior might recall dissonance treatment in common-practice music, the two-bar patterning of this passage is still realized in a way that is especially characteristic of EDM. As shown in example 4.16b, the beginning point of each lower-level cycle divides the two-bar span asymmetrically into durations of 3, 3, and 2 quarter notes—or, if the eighth note is taken as the common durational unit, into the pattern 3+3+3+3+4. These rhythms are augmentations of the asymmetrical patterns shown in table 2.2.

Moreover, the 3+3+2 and 3+3+3+3+4 divisions also correspond to the accentual pattern of the lyrics; in response to the meter, they seem to reinforce the defiant message conveyed by the text.

In examples 4.15 and 16, the dissonant layer is generated through the repetition of a single duration. In other cases, distinctive patterning highlights the pure-triple quality of the dissonance. In example 4.17a, an excerpt from "Connected" by James Ruskin, a dotted-quarter duration like that found in example 4.15 is divided into a quarter-eighth rhythm, thus making the triple subdivision of the 3/2 dissonance explicit.

Riff 2 is not the only layer creating metrical dissonance in this track, however. Example 4.17b, a more detailed transcription of the same passage, shows how an additional riff presents *another* EGD. This dissonance, a double G4/3 in which the sixteenth note is the common durational unit of the smaller dissonance, is like that seen in example 4.16 except that both of its cycles reach completion.[19]

Though the two riffs are dissonant with each other, they interlock in an interesting manner: the E in riff 3 always falls exactly between the F♯ and the A in riff 2. Because riff 3 is much softer dynamically, and because its F♯ occurs almost simultaneously with the F♯ in riff 2, it does not stand out clearly as a separate pattern. Instead, the combination of the two patterns suggests the resultant line A–F♯–E, indicated by the lines connecting riffs 2 and 3.

In describing the relationships between the hi-hat and the two riffs in this track, I have analyzed the hi-hat as a 4-layer in example 4.17b and as a 2-layer in example 4.17a, a difference that results from my preference for describing dissonances in the most reduced form possible. This strategy highlights the presence of differently sized manifestations of the same dissonance. The dissonance G4/3, for instance, occurs three times in this passage: once between riff 2 and the hi-hat (♩=1) and twice between riff 3 and the hi-hat (♪=1 and ♩=1). Keeping the dissonances reduced also clarifies embedded relationships—e.g., the way in which one G4/3 generates another (ex. 4.17b), or the way in which the 3-layer in a G3/2 dissonance can generate a larger-level G4/3 (ex. 4.17a).

At the same time, describing all the dissonances in a given work in terms of a single common durational unit can simplify discussion of complex textures. In this passage, for instance, preserving the sixteenth note as a common value reveals the array of dissonances shown in example 4.17c, which can be summarized as follows:

19. The snare drum and bass drum shown in example 3.3 are absent in this passage. As a result, the bass line assumes a different metrical position (comparable to ex. 3.2b), and the hi-hat becomes more audible.

a. Riff 2 as dissonant layer

b. Riff 3 as additional dissonant layer

c. All metrical dissonances interpreted in terms of a common durational unit

**Example 4.17. James Ruskin, "Connected," embedded grouping dissonance.
[CD tr. 26].**
Courtesy of Tresor Records GmbH.

1. G4/3 (riff 3 + hi-hat)
2. G6/4 (riff 2 + hi-hat)
3. G16/12 (riff 2 + hi-hat; riff 3 + hi-hat)
4. D12+8 or D12−4 (riff 2 + riff 3)

In addition, the common-unit approach can clarify certain relationships between dissonant layers. In the case of this track, it shows that the two G16/12 dissonances are augmentations (by four) of G4/3, while also bringing out the higher-level displacement between riffs 2 and 3.[20] Hence, although the "most-reduced" approach is generally the simplest and most effective way to highlight the embedded quality of these dissonances, preserving a single common durational unit can also be useful in certain circumstances.

I previously described three key features of embedded grouping dissonance: (1) the simultaneous presentation of multiple grouping dissonances, (2) the presentation of grouping dissonance at multiple metrical levels, and (3) a causal relationship in which the cyclical noncongruence of the lower-level dissonance generates the larger dissonance. These distinctive qualities come to the fore when EGD is considered in light of previous music-theoretical discussions, which describe *similar* occurrences without addressing this specific phenomenon. Krebs, for instance, has used the term "compound dissonance" to describe passages that contain more than two conflicting layers of motion (Krebs 1999: 59), as in example 4.18a, in which nonaligned 3-layers combine with a 2-layer to form G3/2 and D3+2 dissonances. Like an embedded grouping dissonance, this passage presents multiple metrical dissonances at the same time; however, it is not based solely on grouping dissonance. In fact, almost all of the examples of compound dissonance in *Fantasy Pieces* involve combinations of grouping and displacement dissonance or multiple displacement dissonances rather than grouping dissonances *only*.[21] Hence, although EGDs certainly qualify as a type of "compound" dissonance, this category does not sufficiently account for their specific attributes.

Another concept, Richard Cohn's "double hemiola," appears to be more closely related; in fact, Cohn describes the double hemiola as "embed[ding] a 2:3 relation at two levels simultaneously" (Cohn 1992b: 13). In a recent article he defines this concept more formally as "the relationship between symmetrical divisions of a time-span that simultaneously bear 3:2 conflicts at two adjacent

---

20. For another instance of quadruple augmentation, see example 4.16a.
21. "Connected" also contains both grouping and displacement dissonance, as discussed with respect to example 4.17c. In this passage, however, displacement dissonance is a secondary phenomenon generated through the simultaneous presentation of multiple embedded grouping dissonances. Each embedded dissonance is, in itself, generated solely through grouping.

a. Krebs's compound dissonance (Schumann, Piano Sonata op. 11, III, mm. 51–56; see Krebs 1999: 96)

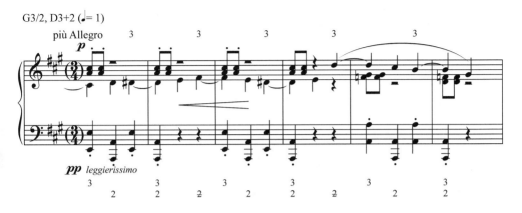

b. Cohn's double hemiola (Brahms, Violin Sonata op. 78, I, m. 235; see Cohn 2001: 304)

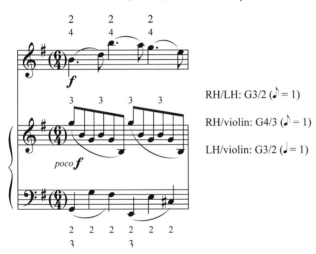

RH/LH: G3/2 ($\flat$ = 1)

RH/violin: G4/3 ($\flat$ = 1)

LH/violin: G3/2 ($\bullet$ = 1)

Example 4.18. Related phenomena in current music-theoretical literature.

levels of the metric hierarchy" (Cohn 2001: 295). Example 4.18b presents an example from that article; for the sake of consistency, I have analyzed it using Krebs's methodology, adding dissonance labels throughout the passage. According to this analysis, the right hand of the piano forms a G3/2 dissonance with the left hand; the left hand forms a larger G3/2 dissonance with the violin; and the right hand forms G4/3 with the violin. Unlike example 4.18a, therefore, this excerpt satisfies the first two conditions associated with embedded grouping dissonance: it presents more than one grouping dissonance at the same time, and the dissonances occur at multiple metrical levels. It does not, however, meet the third condition, for there are no generative relationships between the dissonances. The cycle of the smaller G3/2 dissonance, for instance, has no special relationship to the larger G3/2; although the dotted-half-note duration defined by the cycle of the former does correspond to the 3-layer of the latter, the 2-layer of the larger G3/2 is articulated through independent contextual means. Furthermore, all of the dissonances respect the boundary of the bar line. The key factor, it seems, is the relationship between the meter and the dissonance. If the meter, like the 6/4 that underlies this example, is built to allow multiple groupings, dissonances can occur without disrupting it excessively. If the meter is not designed in this manner, a tiny disagreement can have far-reaching consequences, the fundamental incommensurability of pure duple and pure triple extending outward to progressively larger levels.[22]

Although I have defined EGD specifically as a type of grouping dissonance, other types of embedded dissonance are possible, of course. For instance, if every other 8-layer in example 4.7 were doubled by a 16-layer, an embedded displacement dissonance would occur. Another possibility, which might be termed "mixed

22. For instance, while discussion of embedded dissonances has thus far been limited to two levels (which, in all of the examples considered, led to a higher-level mixed span consisting of twelve quarter-note beats), the combination of pure-triple dissonance with an insistently pure-duple meter will continue to produce conflict at subsequent levels. The aforementioned twelve-quarter span, for example, will create a larger conflict between its three-measure duration and a four-bar hypermeter. This dissonance, in turn, will only align after every twelve measures, thus generating a conflict between twelve- and sixteen-bar hypermeasures. (The length of the cycle of such a dissonance, 192 measures, corresponds approximately to the duration of an average EDM track.) The mixed spans involved in these dissonances are therefore inherently different from those found in common-practice music, since they can never be reconciled with the meter.

A further (although less significant) point is that the values involved in an embedded grouping dissonance need not be exclusively hemiolic. In theory, conflicts such as 7/4 or 11/3 could also generate dissonances of this type. These dissonances would quickly produce cycles of extreme length, however, thereby stretching the limits of perceptibility. For instance, in the case of a recurring 7-layer within 4/4 meter, where $\quarternote = 1$, the first embedded cycle would take twenty-eight bars to reach a point of alignment. These hypotheticals aside, all of the embedded grouping dissonances I have observed in electronic dance music involve conflicts between duple and triple values.

embedded dissonance," involves displaced grouping dissonances in which the duration of the cycle *is* a factor of the number of pulses in the measure; for an example, see Krebs's example 8.14c, a passage in 3/4 meter in which the dotted-quarter cycle of a G4/3 dissonance ($\eighth=1$) begins on beat *two,* creating D3+1 at the quarter-note level.[23] In general, however, embedded dissonances involving displacement are much more dependent on contextual factors for their articulation, whereas embedded grouping dissonances consistently involve a generative relationship in which the duration of the measure is noncongruent with the length of a grouping dissonance's cycle.

Another intriguing feature of the embedded grouping dissonances that occur in EDM is the way in which they create complex arrays of dissonance with a very limited number of rhythmic values. In fact, when all the layers involved in dissonances in examples 4.15–18 are considered as a group, the only surface-level durations to be found are eighths, dotted eighths, quarters, and dotted quarters.[24] In classical music, grouping dissonances in common time generally involve tuplets; in fact, it is actually *impossible* to create a grouping dissonance whose cycles align with pure-duple meter without employing tuplets. In contrast, the embedded grouping dissonances found in EDM always use durations common to 4/4 meter, and all of the attacks articulating these dissonances coincide with metrical "beats" in the classic *GTTM* sense.

One possible explanation for this situation lies in technology: the most commonly used durations are those that can be entered with the sixteen buttons of a drum machine. As previously described (ch. 1, pp. 63–65, ch. 2, pp. 113–14), the drum machines most popular with EDM producers have featured hands-on interfaces oriented toward 4/4 meter. Yet tracks such as "Connected" complicate the assumption, often implicit in beliefs about the relationship between technology and authenticity, that simply designed machines lead to simplistic music. By re-envisioning the meaning of the pure-triple groupings etched onto the surfaces of the 808 and the 909—which are explained prosaically in their manuals as

23. Krebs does not describe this or any of the examples in his book as embedded; as previously noted, almost all of his examples of grouping dissonance involve a cycle that both corresponds to and aligns with a metrical layer or the first hypermetrical layer. To verify this observation, I examined every grouping dissonance he presents, finding just eight possible exceptions. Of these, three are drawn from the work of Charles Ives (exx. 8.37 and 8.38a–b), while the rest are atypical of the common practice in various ways. Two are "mixed" embedded dissonances (exx. 8.14c and 8.33); three are drawn from etudes (exx. 2.20, 3.11, and 8.14c), the repetitive nature of which often encourages groupings of figuration into unusual values such as five; and two involve "subliminal" dissonance in which the notated meter is not articulated at all (exx. 2.20–21).

24. When each example is considered individually, the range of durations is even smaller. Example 4.16, for instance, begins with just two note values (the quarter and the dotted-eighth).

rubrics for meters such as 6/8 and 12/8—producers have been able to utilize a few basic units to generate complex dissonances within the seemingly restrictive context of pure-duple meter. In so doing, they have continued a tradition of creatively misappropriating technology that dates back at least as far as the 303's first overdriven squelch. Paradoxically, however, their actions also simultaneously realize the fundamental premise of the drum machine, for it is the manufacturing of endlessly repeating rhythms that enables these complex dissonances. Seeing beyond the manufacturer's unimaginative marketing of machines such as the 909 as simple substitutes for human drummers, producers have unveiled this technology's potential for generating endlessly repeating patterns *of different sizes,* beginning in different places, creating a constantly shifting kaleidoscope of texture and accentuation.

Conclusion: Interpretive Multiplicity and Musical Style; or, The Emancipation of Metrical Dissonance

Electronic dance music invites listeners to chart their way through an interpretively open soundscape in which ambiguous structuring and divergent metrical paths enable diverse experiences of time. And although ambiguity and metrical dissonance occur in many repertories, EDM realizes them in particular ways, in association with a broader constellation of distinctive musical behaviors. More than simple examples of displacement and grouping dissonance, phenomena such as turning the beat around and embedded grouping dissonance suggest extensions and expansions of current metrical dissonance theory. As I conclude part II, I would like to consider how the realization of ambiguity and metrical dissonance in EDM exemplifies the characteristic features of the style as a whole, how these phenomena open windows onto conceptualizations of rhythm and meter in general, and how these aspects of musical patterning both inform and respond to certain practices and meanings within EDM cultures.

Both turning the beat around and embedded grouping dissonance are inextricably intertwined with EDM's cyclical, loop-based structure. The essence of this structure is *modular:* musical entities are selected from a moderate number of elements, relatively simple and functional in design, that can be combined and juxtaposed in many different ways. Recall, for instance, how the simplest examples of turning the beat around involved two identical or nearly identical rhythm patterns. The generic nature of such loops allows them to be combined with other textural elements with flexibility and ease, to easily assume different metrical functions, and to form either side of the binary reversal seen in so many examples of TBA. Moreover, by constructing a pattern from as few as two different durations, producers can create intense metrical dissonance. The simplicity of these rhythmic building blocks—rather than indicating a lack of skill or knowledge on the part of the producer—serves a larger design principle. The operation of divergent loops in embedded grouping dissonances also reveals the degree to which cyclical structure is intertwined with repetition: the lower-level dissonance must be repeated several times before the larger dissonance will complete its cycle, while further repetition gives the listener more time to process the two dissonances and their relationship to the meter.

Current analytical approaches to common-practice music portray metrical dissonances as a combination of metrical and antimetrical layers, with a clear distinction maintained between the two. EDM subverts this hierarchy in favor of interpretive multiplicity by presenting layers that sound apart without clearly specifying one or the other as dominant. This ambiguity often arises from underdetermination. For instance, when a displaced combination of bass drum and hi-hat in Dave Angel's "Bounce Back" (ex. 2.16) creates a D2+1 conflict ($\flat$=1), the lack of an articulation at the whole-note level allows the "dissonant" hi-hat pattern to compete much more strongly with the metrical bass-drum layer; if we focus on the hi-hat, we may hear it as the beat. Although most listeners will probably gravitate toward the bass drum at some point, since it usually articulates the tactus in four-on-the-floor genres, the fact that the two competing patterns are rhythmically identical makes it easier to follow the hi-hat down an alternate path. In examples such as "Piku" (ex. II.1), meanwhile, the metrical/antimetrical distinction is truly undecidable: here the combination of two patterns makes the pulse layer clear; the individual patterns express unique quarter-note groupings; and neither instrument articulates durations beyond that of the quarter.[25]

Even in a situation in which all the layers necessary for meter are present, ambiguity between metrical and antimetrical layers may result from the way in which layers unfold across time. In "Track," for instance, a single layer (synth 3) participates in three different metrical dissonances—first as an antimetrical layer (ex. 3.10), then as a metrical one (ex. 3.11), and finally in a situation in which such distinctions are not especially relevant (ex. 3.12). In contrast, antimetrical and metrical layers almost always *retain* their respective functions in the works

25. Given the absence of a decisive metrical interpretation, we might follow Krebs's dictum that "where there is no metrical framework, the layer initiated earlier usually functions as the referential layer" (261, n. 20). This seems like a reasonable principle, but it is difficult to apply in this case given that both layers begin almost simultaneously and at a low volume. It is also worth noting that the principle remains untested within the context of Krebs's book, as none of his examples fall into this category.

addressed by current metrical dissonance theory. Krebs's examples illustrate this tendency quite clearly: he returns to particular works frequently throughout the course of his book, yet the identity of each metrical dissonance remains constant throughout its various appearances. Although he does discuss process in *Fantasy Pieces* as well—in fact, "metrical progressions and processes" are the subject of an entire chapter—his emphases are rather different. He divides processes involving metrical dissonance into three categories, organized around an axis of consonance and dissonance: "consonance-to-dissonance" processes, processes within a dissonant state, and "dissonance-to-consonance" processes. In spite of the prominence given to process as a concept, many of the procedures he discusses seem relatively static; they are described as changes from one metrical "state" to another, and some of these states are not contiguous.[26]

In addition, in the repertory that Krebs considers, metrical layers are usually associated with a single time signature throughout a work. Krebs assumes that the meter indicated by this signature remains in effect even in passages where it is not expressed on the musical surface.[27] This premise—which suggests a sort of "monometricality" analogous to the oft-discussed notion of monotonality—is most evident in his discussion of "subliminal dissonance,"[28] a phenomenon that occurs when the music does not express the notated meter at all. Krebs believes that this meter—the "primary metrical consonance" (1999: 30) of the work— can still be felt within such passages, and that the performer should emphasize it in subtle ways. Electronic dance music eschews this monometricality as a norm in at least two significant ways: first, through the simultaneous or successive suggestion of two different meters (as heard in "Track"), and second, through turning the beat around. Although TBA does not create two different meters, it does transform metrical layers into antimetrical ones, thereby challenging the tendency to hear a single metrical consonance as "primary" throughout an entire work.

Such transformations also subvert easy mappings of the adjectives "conso-

26. Processes involving a single dissonance, such as intensification and "preparation," are more frequently continuous, however.

27. While it is not unheard of for changes in meter to occur in common-practice works, such changes are usually presented as variants of the primary meter—in which case it is often only the beat division that changes (imagine a set of variations in 2/4 in which one variation changes to 6/8)—or they occur after the principal formal closure of the piece (for instance, when a work in duple meter changes to triple during the coda).

28. See esp. Krebs 1999: 46–52. Krebs does note that some of Schumann's works create the effect of "a disjointed dialogue between different meters, rather than one of a unifying, consistently present metrical layer" (1999: 98). However, as revealed by the discussion that follows this statement, he still assumes that such works contain subliminal dissonance resulting from the tension between the notated meter and the expressed meter, and that the notated meter is ultimately primary.

nant/dissonant" onto the binary "metrical/antimetrical." Turning the beat around, for example, clearly begins in a state of consonance. When the reinterpreting layer enters, displacement dissonance results, yet it is the relocation of the downbeat—rather than the displacement that follows this relocation—that is the most significant feature of the process. Furthermore, when a displaced layer repeats throughout a track, the strength of its dissonance may slowly dissipate as the track unfolds.[29] It may also be obscured by the entrance of additional textural layers—as occurs in "Cups"—although the displaced layer usually remains subtly present and may be exposed when the obscuring layers are removed. This gradual dissipation of dissonance (the mirror image of the fade-ins heard in "Track") contrasts significantly with the changes in consonance and dissonance heard in classical works, where there is usually a distinct moment when the metrical state changes. In addition, although many of the ambiguous states that I have described are not dissonant, it does not seem entirely appropriate to describe them as consonant either, for the latter term implies a sense of stability that is often lacking. The opening of "Connected" (ex. 3.2), for instance, does not contain grouping or displacement dissonance, yet all of the potential metrical interpretations seem so tenuous that they hardly deserve the appellation "consonant."

Current theories based on analogies between pitch and metrical dissonances tend to invoke not only the character but also the behavior and function of those dissonances. Put more specifically, metrical dissonances, like pitch dissonances, (a) must resolve and (b) are embellishing in function. Krebs writes that "the term 'metrical dissonance' suggests that, by analogy with pitch theory, dissonance is ornamental and could be subjected to a reductive process to expose underlying consonances."[30] Although his analogy loosens somewhat with respect to resolution—specific dissonances do not require specific resolutions, and many metrical dissonances "resolve" simply through the removal of the dissonant layer—it is clearly characteristic for the pieces he discusses to end in a state of metrical consonance (see Krebs 1999: 108ff. for further discussion). And if metrical dis-

29. The rate at which this process occurs depends upon the degree to which the displaced layer's pattern "meshes" with the new metrical context. For instance, the snare drum heard on the offbeats after the TBA in "Communication" (ex. 4.9) will be integrated into the new metrical context rather quickly: since its pattern is the same as that of the bass drum, it can be heard not only as a displaced quarter-note layer but also as a completion of the metrical eighth-note layer. Given the prominence of the bass drum, it seems misleading to claim that the snare drum is still dissonant in measure 158, when the snare-plus-bass combination has been repeated for forty measures. As the displaced layers discussed in the other examples of TBA are more distinctive, however, they tend to maintain their independent status for longer.

30. Krebs 1999: 83. This view also resonates strongly with the approach to syncopation expressed in Temperley 1999.

sonance is embellishing, then its existence will usually be temporary as well. In contrast, dissonant layers in electronic dance music usually become a permanent part of the piece. A mixture of "metrical" and dissonant layers is normative, and works often end by highlighting the dissonant states with which they began. In short, dissonant layers behave much like metrical layers, and thus may be considered structural.[31] Metrical dissonance is "emancipated" from its need to resolve.

If metrical dissonances do not behave like pitch dissonances, perhaps the term "dissonance" should be discarded altogether. This is the route suggested by Robert Walser, who—in a critique of the way in which "musicologists and music theorists tend to discuss rhythm"—writes that:

> Not only is [rhythm] customarily assumed to be cognitive and disembodied, but Western music theory's traditional emphasis on harmony has led many music theorists to conceive of rhythm through harmonic metaphors. Terms like "metric dissonance" and "dissonant strata" suggest that rhythmic conflicts must always be resolved, whether in performance or analysis. There seems to be no place for tensions that remain unresolved, differences that can coexist. (Walser 1995: 214 n. 20)

I would argue, however, that "dissonance" remains useful as a way of describing the sounds I have discussed. When two layers do not align, their relationship will always be "dissonant" even if they cannot be categorized as "structural" versus "embellishing." Moreover, this dissonance, this "sounding apart," is in a certain sense *more* applicable to metrical phenomena than to pitch. Dissonant layers of motion do quite literally *sound apart,* whereas intervals and harmonies, when so described, are being portrayed in qualitative, evocative terms (although the naturalization of "dissonance" as a music-theoretical concept tends to veil this poetic strategy). By reevaluating metrical "dissonance" through considering it in a new light,[32] we can arrive at a place where metrical dissonances can "remain unresolved," and different—even conflicting—layers can "coexist."

In EDM, metrical dissonance can call particular attention to the independent quality of textural and metrical layers. In many cases, dissonant layers seem to float relatively freely rather than being bound by a strict hierarchy. Although this effect of independence can occur with any type of metrical dissonance, it is particularly noticeable with embedded grouping dissonance. Dance music pro-

---

31. This claim also relates to my discussion of diatonic rhythms in chapter 2.
32. In fact, Walser—presumably inspired by Attali—effects a similar maneuver with "noise" in his own essay, subverting its position as a descriptor of things-that-are-not (music) by delineating its positive attributes.

ducers often find interesting ways to explore the tension between the common rhythmic values found in these dissonances and the pure-triple groupings they create. For instance, they might foreground the complete regularity of the dissonant layer through lengthy breakdowns in which all or most of the other parts are removed. In Timo Maas's remix of "Dooms Night," for example, the dissonant synth line first enters the track during a forty-three-second breakdown (0.43–1.26) in which it is the *only* layer present. Because it has not been heard before, it seems completely consonant and regular; one has no idea that it will subsequently form the basis of 3/2 and 4/3 grouping dissonances. At the end of the breakdown, however, the percussion patterns (along with the bass line) suddenly return, placing the synth line in a highly dissonant context, as shown in example 4.15. This play between the exposed solo synth and its superposition against a percussive backdrop continues throughout the rest of the track, in which breakdowns continue to alternate with full-texture sections.

In James Ruskin's "Connected," the dissonance created by riff 2 stands out even more sharply from the metrical layers, as the quarter-eighth pattern creates an especially strong triple-meter effect. The presence of definite pitch also draws attention to the dissonant layer. Moreover, because the meter itself is not articulated as strongly in this track as it is in "Dooms Night," it is easier to hear this layer apart from the metrical context; throughout much of the track, it seems to hover independently above the rest of the music. A further contributing factor, the relationship between the dissonant layers and the track's primary drumbeat, plays an even more significant role. In previous discussion of the embedded grouping dissonance in this track, I analyzed a passage in which the bass drum was absent (ex. 4.17), thereby enabling this complex EGD to be heard and discussed with greater clarity. When the bass and snare drums reenter the texture after this breakdown, they place riffs 2 and 3 in an even *more* dissonant relationship to the meter, for the grouping dissonances they create are now *displaced* as well (see ex. 4.19; compare to ex. 4.17). This additional relationship intensifies the independence of the dissonant layers: as a result of the displacement, riff 2 never shares an attack with the bass drum or snare drum; it skips across the surface of the music without once alighting upon the beat or its eighth-note subdivisions.[33]

33. Although the entry of the snare drum obscures the presence of the hi-hat considerably, it is still audible upon close listening. I thank student Bryson Kern, a jazz percussionist, for calling attention to the displaced quality of this EGD. As comparison of examples 3.3, 4.17, and 4.19 will reveal, the downbeat shifts during and after the breakdown, effecting a reverse-TBA followed by a TBA. As in the Maas, the breakdown seems to call attention to the presence of 4/4 rhythmic values in the dissonant layers. When Ruskin removes the bass drum, the remaining layers seem more

Example 4.19. Displaced embedded grouping dissonance in James Ruskin, "Connected." [CD tr. 27].
Courtesy of Tresor Records GmbH.

When a dissonant layer seems to function independently from the metrical context, I describe the resulting effect as "dissociation." Dissociation is not involuntary; the degree to which a dissonant layer separates will depend on how closely the listener focuses on it, as well as on its relationship to the meter and the strength with which the metrical context is asserted. Nevertheless, the music does *invite* dissociation; its combination of highly distinct patterns repeating noncongruent durations over long spans of time encourages the listener to explore the different projective worlds that are available. If we always choose to hear a particular textural combination in the same way, we will probably become bored; however, if we choose to focus first on this pattern, then on that one, and finally on the combination between the two, we can find more than enough richness to keep our attention engaged.[34]

Although dissociation is most noticeable in grouping dissonance, it also can take place with displacement dissonances. In fact, a particular dissociative effect

---

precisely aligned than before, creating a sort of hocket effect in which a highly active composite rhythm is articulated by constantly shifting arrays of textural combinations.

34. Lynne Rogers (1989, 1992, 1995) has also written about "dissociation" in the music of Stravinsky. While we each use the term to describe passages involving nonaligned strata, she emphasizes dissociation as a structural technique involving pitch, which she defines as "the superimposition of distinctive, harmonically independent layers of musical material" (1995, 477; cf. 1992, 202). In contrast, I employ the term to characterize a perceptual and aesthetic effect, focusing on listeners' experiences of dissonant layers.

is noticeable with turning the beat around. Although the original patterns will be heard as displaced after the downbeat shifts, they still retain their previous projective profiles; we can still hear them as *beginning* a particular duration. This effect is noticeable in both "Cups" (exx. 4.6–7) and "Track" (exx. 4.2–3 and 4.11). In each case, although it is clear that the downbeat shifts, it takes us a while to integrate the old patterns into the new metrical context, and we can still enter the pre-TBA world of the shifted patterns through selective attention.

The experiential qualities of dissociation as a metrical process also suggest broader roles for the phenomenon within electronic dance music culture. First, dissociation can imbue the music with a psychedelic aesthetic, regardless of how listeners choose to experience it. Don Dresser, a dance music fan whom I interviewed, told me that "there's some emphasis in the culture on just having a psychedelic atmosphere . . . , using that to take you into a similar place without the chemicals." In this context, the effect of certain layers being outside the meter mirrors one's sense of being outside of reality. This also relates to the "virtual reality" of a dance club—the way the environment is artificially constructed. In a typical club, the outside world is completely shut out. Conventional indicators of the passage of time, such as clocks, are avoided. Windows are covered; the walls are painted black; and entrances and exits are isolated from the actual club environment as much as possible. As in the movie theater (another darkened setting), the goal is to create the effect of another world.

Furthermore, the dissociative effects of metrical dissonance operate within a larger environment which serves to dis*orient* the clubber in many ways. Clubbing is not like watching a film or reading a book, where one's attention is (at least ostensibly) directed toward a single object or experience. Rather, there is total sensory overload. The music is extremely loud, to the point of being physically overwhelming. Lights are flashing. Smoke is released onto the dance floor, contributing to a collapse between the club's "effects" and the actual "reality" of the environment. The experience is decentralized as well. One can come and go as one chooses, participate in whatever activities one chooses, attend to the music or not, and attend to whichever part of the music one finds most interesting. In the following passage, Buckland captures many of these qualities in a description of a particular clubbing experience:

> There was no architectural, scopophilic, sexual, or aural center to the club. . . .
> I found it difficult to get a sense of the mass of movement from the outside,
> because on the outer margins of the area, dancers were more diffuse in critical
> mass, density, and energy. . . . I wandered deeper onto the floor in search of
> dance. With few markers to orient my position, the club neutralized typical

reference points. As a result of the initial deliberate disorientation effect produced by darkness, flashing lights, and pounding music, the circulation of bodies in the space became a prominent marker and shaper of not only orientation, but of the nature and energy of the populated club. (Buckland 2002: 57–58)

In the realm of rhythm and meter, ambiguity resonates with notions of decentralization, and metrical dissonance with effects of disorientation. For the listener/clubber, the value of these disorienting, decentralized effects lies in their ability to encourage—perhaps even to *necessitate*—the active determination of one's own (musical) experience. Buckland captures this dynamic in cultural terms through the notion of *world-making:* "After entering a club, I found that many were disorienting spaces within which participants had to orient themselves in order to recognize and make a lifeworld" (2002: 56). "The lifeworld produced by movement was not fixed, but fluidly determined by the moving participant. The participant actively created the club and the experience, rather than being its passive consumer" (2002: 61).

In electronic dance music, this active determination plays out in at least one more realm of significance, and one in which passivity might be most expected: namely, technology. The dissociative effect of metrically dissonant layers highlights the presence of technology in this repertory, for part of the layers' perceived independence may stem from their performance by machines. In styles featuring traditional performance techniques, metrical dissonances must be executed by a single performer or ensemble, requiring a cognitive and performative integration that surely affects the way in which the dissonance is played in certain subtle but perceptible ways. In electronic dance music, however, dissonant layers can unfold independently with absolute precision, thereby exposing a gap between the mechanistic aesthetic of the music and the ways in which humans interact with it. This dialectic can be understood as part of a broader critique; although EDM musicians have clearly embraced technology in many ways, their optimism regarding its promise is often tempered with a note of wariness. Detroit-techno pioneer Juan Atkins, for instance, points out that "with technology, there's a lot of good things, but by the same token, it enables the powers that be to have more control" (Reynolds 1999: 19), and key Atkins influence Alvin Toffler, re-envisioning the model of human-technological interaction set in place by the Industrial Revolution, speaks of a group of "techno-rebels" who argue that "either we control technology or it controls us" (Toffler 1980: 152). Through their constant exploration of the tension between these two possibilities, EDM musicians and audiences reveal a genre defined not so much by the machines with which is made as by an ongoing commentary on the interaction of humans *with* these machines. As part of this trend, ambiguity and metrical dissonance represent not only particular ways of solving a musical problem (the need for variety within pure-duple contexts) but also a culturally specific strategy for creating meaning through musical sound.

Electronic
Dance Music
and the Epic

Contemporary pop music is, to a large extent, the domain of the miniature. Most of the songs that one hears on American commercial radio, for instance, are closely constrained in length, rarely lasting more than four minutes. Within this narrow time span, the songwriter must capture the listener's attention with a distinctive hook or groove. Each single is constructed efficiently from a small amount of musical material, and, as an emblem of a particular artist or band, is more or less self-contained. As one moves away from the mainstream, one begins to find exceptions to these characteristics: "jam bands" such as Phish often feature much longer songs, and many indie- and prog-rock groups have tended toward lengthier forms as well. For the most part, however, relatively short, self-contained songs are widespread outside of the top forty as well as within it.

The prevalence of these conditions makes their almost complete absence in electronic dance music all the more striking. A performance of electronic dance music does not present "songs" per se, but rather a collection of relatively generic "tracks." An average audience member would be able to describe the style of the music being played in considerable detail but would not typically be able to identify either the producer or the track name of more than a few records (unless s/he is a DJ who performs in that style). Furthermore, it is often difficult to tell where one record ends and another begins, as one of the main goals of DJing is to make the distinctions between tracks imperceptible.[1] In these ways, EDM eschews both the name recognition and the song-oriented format of many other popular genres in favor of an open, continuous structure. Even more striking, however, are the epic dimensions of this music. DJ sets almost always last for at least one hour; however, sets ranging from two to six hours are not uncommon, and even longer performances are possible. Danny Tenaglia, for instance, is known for his twelve-hour sets.[2] Although individual tracks are much shorter—typically around five to seven minutes in length—they are only the starting point for a musical experience that is often Wagnerian in scope. In part III, I will address the ways in which these large-scale dimensions are manifested in electronic dance music. Beginning with multimeasure patterning in chapter 5 and then moving outward in chapter 6 to consider the form of entire tracks and complete DJ sets, I will show how particular approaches to these musical dimensions can play important roles in distinguishing the styles of particular artists and genres and how their structured organization enables the shaping of time on an expanded scale.

1. As previously noted (ch. 1, p. 50), this does not mean that track *selection* (which tracks are played) is unimportant, but simply that most contemporary DJs focus more on choosing records that have the right sound and mood for a particular moment than on playing tracks that are recognizable to the audience.

2. For a description of one such marathon performance, see Mike Gwertzman, review of Carl Cox and Danny Tenaglia, Twilo, New York City, *Urb: Future Music Culture,* May 2001, 44. The shorter one-hour set is more common at raves and similar events, which typically feature a large number of performers (presumably in order to attract as many people as possible by covering a broad spectrum of genres). Longer sets are more typical of clubs, where the DJ is usually either a regular employee or a star brought in for a period of "residency." Raves introduce the epic in their own way, however: in spite of the shorter sets, the events themselves are quite long; 10 P.M. to 6 A.M. is a typical time frame, but twelve-hour events are not uncommon. Although one would hear many different performances on such an occasion, they would be part of a single uninterrupted musical experience; sets are usually performed continuously, with no intervening silence.

5 Multimeasure Patterning

In electronic dance music, the patterning of small groups of measures serves as a bridge between the local territory of the measure and the large-scale proportions of complete tracks and DJ sets. The ways in which multimeasure groupings unfold reveal distinctive characteristics of this repertory as well as commonalities with other styles. In this chapter I will consider particular techniques involved in the creation of these groupings along with various ways in which they are made manifest to the listener. I will begin with an explanation of notational techniques I have developed to represent these patterns, followed by an overview of two exemplary tracks. I will then theorize multimeasure patterning in relation to existing music-theoretical concepts of "hypermeter" and "phrasing." Along the way, I touch upon relationships between this patterning, DJ practice, and the "pure-duple" tendencies of temporal organization in EDM, and I conclude by exploring interactions between multimeasure patterning and the effects of metrical dissonance.

Notational Techniques

Appendix C includes visual representations of each track discussed in part III. Unlike the shorter examples interspersed throughout the book, these transcriptions aim to be exhaustive, representing every sound that occurs in the course of a track. The tracks are arranged in alphabetical order based on the first word of the producer's name. I present information in two formats, the "sound palette" and the "textural graph." In the following paragraphs, I will explain these formats using transcriptions of Dave Angel's "Sighting" (pp. 280–86) as examples.

A *sound palette* is a key that presents a notated version of the sounds heard in a track (see pp. 280–81). Within the sound palette (and within the transcriptions more generally), I categorize sounds as "rhythmic," "articulative," or "atmospheric." "Rhythmic" sounds are loops, which are repetitive and (in techno at least) generally short; their function is more rhythmic than melodic.[1] "Articulative" sounds are brief and intermittent; they usually appear at or near structural boundaries, such as the beginning of a measure or multimeasure group. The most common type of articulative sound is the "sound-byte" type of sample (cf. ch. 1, p. 61). "Atmospheric" sounds are hazy and dynamically soft and generally lack clear rhythmic articulations. Their function is to fill in the texture and contribute to the mood. Although they sometimes appear at regular intervals, in most cases no pattern of repetition is discernible. Within each of these categories, I present sounds in the order in which they appear. After presenting all the sounds, I list the track's loops in order from shortest to longest.

The material presented within each pair of repeat signs represents a loop, not a measure. The content of each loop is based on the shortest repeating pattern within a particular instrumental sound. The duration involved in each repetition is shown in the column entitled "loop length." As explained in chapter 2 (p. 90), the loops used by the producer may or may not coincide with the shortest possible unit of repetition; I do not make any claims about whether the loops that appear in the sound palettes match those used by the producers.

Some loops seem to be variants of other patterns with the same instrumental sound; in such cases I label the different versions with lowercase letters (see Bass Drum 1a, 1b, and 1c in "Sighting"). In addition, certain other loops involve two patterns of the same timbre that always occur simultaneously. In most cases of this phenomenon, I label the two patterns *a* and *b* (see Riff 2a and b); if the two sounds present very distinct lines, I use the numbers *1* and *2* instead (see Tom-Tom 1 and 2). Information presented in the "Other Comments" column addresses timbre and other distinctive characteristics that are not easily expressed in notation.

The next format shown in conjunction with "Sighting," the *textural graph* (pp. 282–86), shows how the textural configuration changes from measure to measure. I use a different kind of patterning for each element of the texture, naming sounds with the abbreviations given in table A.1 of appendix A.[2] In addition, boxes around patterns show repetition at the level of the measure or

---

1. For some genres, the term "melodic" might be employed as an additional category. However, since most of the pitched elements in techno function in rhythmic ways, this classification is not useful for the examples I discuss.
2. I use the abbreviation "EFX" (for "effects") whenever the timbre of a sound is modified in a way that seems rhythmically significant. In "Sighting," for example, the sudden addition of reverb in measure 65 creates a timbral and textural change that marks the beginning of a multimeasure group.

larger. I do not show shorter patterns of repetition, which would encumber the graph with excessive detail, but I do indicate the length of each pattern's loop at the right side of every row. The measure numbers used are always based on 4/4 meter, and the page is arranged in a way that emphasizes pure-duple organization (there are sixteen measures per line). In addition, the timing of the recording (based on the compact disc player's display) appears beneath every fourth bar. These units of measurements serve only as reference points, however. Although—as should be clear from the recurring emphases of my discussion—I do *not* view 4/4 meter as a given, discussion of multimeasure patterning and form within complete tracks cannot proceed without agreement upon some common point of reference. In cases where articulations of the 4/4 bar line are entirely absent, I show the projected meter above the 4/4 "ruler"; examples occur in "Dooms Night" (pp. 268 and 271) and "Televised Green Smoke" (p. 276).

I use bar-graph style notation only for looping patterns. I show intermittent articulative and atmospheric sounds by printing the name of the instrument in the measure in which it appears. These sounds often occur either just before or just after the beginning of a measure, in which case a short arrow points forward or backward to the relevant downbeat.

Two Exemplary Tracks

How do electronic dance musicians organize measures into larger groupings, and how (and to what extent) do they convey those groupings to listeners? I will begin to answer these questions through the examples provided by two tracks, Reese and Santonio's "How to Play Our Music," and Jeff Mills's "Jerical." In "How to Play Our Music" (pp. 318–23), multimeasure patterning is extremely regular. The clarity with which the measure is articulated aids the listener in tracking this patterning. As shown in the sound palette, only two of the track's loops are shorter than a measure. Three loops last exactly one measure, and most of the longer loops also articulate the whole-note layer quite clearly. The two-bar and eight-bar layers are not difficult to follow either: every other eight-bar passage contains four iterations of a distinctive two-bar sample, the track's only vocal element (see textural graph). Although two- and four-bar patterns are not always explicitly articulated (mm. 1–8, mm. 17–24), they divide the eight-bar span evenly when they do occur (mm. 121–92).

"Jerical" (pp. 299–303) also uses pure-duple multimeasure groups almost exclusively. However, four-, eight-, and sixteen-bar groups are mixed together much more freely, so that pure-duple nesting is not consistent across the track. The first sixty-four measures, for instance, are grouped (in order) into 8, 4, 4, 8, 16, 16, 4, and 4 measures; notice how the sixteen-measure groups cut across the rows of the textural graph rather than aligning as they do in the Reese and Santonio track. In addition, none of the track's nine loops articulate durations longer than the measure, and six of the nine patterns repeat at periodicities shorter than the measure. As a result, multimeasure patterning is relatively underdetermined.

These examples reveal several different ways in which electronic dance musicians create multimeasure patterning. The most direct method involves the use of loops that last for more than one measure, such as the two-measure sample 1 and the four-measure sample 2 from "How to Play Our Music." In EDM genres other than techno—especially trance—patterns lasting as long as sixteen and even thirty-two measures are not uncommon; for instance, a trance track might have a sixteen-measure bass line in which each four-bar subdivision implies a single harmony. Patterns of this length are less common in techno—perhaps because the music favors rhythm over pitch, and lengthy patterns are less memorable without a pitch component. Using short, simple patterns also contributes to the music's stark effect. Indeed, many of the multimeasure loops used in techno and other types of EDM are essentially one-measure loops in which a larger grouping is produced through an occasional variation (almost always during the fourth measure); for instance, see the sample 2 pattern in "How to Play Our Music."

Producers and DJs also generate multimeasure patterning through the addition and removal of textural elements. Although less direct than the use of patterning within textural elements, the timing of these textural changes is the most common means through which multimeasure groups are formed in techno. In "Jerical," for instance, this is the *only* method used, since none of the loops are longer than a measure.

Clearly, some textural changes have more pronounced effects than others. In particular, the most dramatic changes in a track tend to stem from the removal or addition of the bass line or the bass drum. The activity of the bass drum also can have significant formal implications, as I will explain further in chapter 6. In general, however, the heterogeneous texture of EDM makes it difficult to rank elements strictly in order of importance. The prominence of any given instrument within the mix depends on a variety of factors, including volume, timbre, and the extent to which definite pitch is used, as well as on the number and prominence of other textural elements.

A further way in which multimeasure patterns may be demarcated is through the use of articulative sounds. As described earlier, these sounds do not occur as continuous entities, but instead appear intermittently, usually at the boundaries of multimeasure groups. "Jerical" and "How to Play Our Music" do not contain any articulative sounds; for an example, observe the behavior of the synth 1 part in James Ruskin's "Connected" (see textural graph, pp. 295–98).

An Ontology of Multimeasure Patterns: Hypermeter, Phrasing, and Other Ways of Thinking "in Four"

Thus far, I have referred to the multimeasure units that occur in electronic dance music in general terms, describing them simply as "patterns" or "groups." I adopted this strategy because I wanted the initial characterization of their behavior to be independent from the particular musical implications of existing theoretical taxonomies. I would now like to address the nature of these entities in more detail, focusing on the intersections between music-theoretical categories, the insights afforded by analysis, and musicians' remarks about musical structures and practices.

Music theorists have traditionally classified multimeasure patterns either as hypermeasures or phrases, a division that reflects the more fundamental distinction between meter and rhythm (or meter and grouping) found in so many approaches. To what degree might multimeasure patterns in EDM be considered hypermetrical or phrase-like? I will begin with the latter category, the *phrase*. Although phrases are rhythmic events, in that they unfold in time and shape it in a particular way, most music theorists define the phrase primarily in harmonic and tonal terms. A phrase projects tonal motion: it progresses from one harmony to another, either ending on a different harmony or returning to the one with which it began. Furthermore, a phrase closes with a cadence, which carries varying degrees of finality according to its harmonic progression and the scale-degree motion of its uppermost voice.

Electronic dance music, however, is not harmonically driven. This is particularly true of techno: some tracks do not contain any sounds with definite pitch, and most contain only a small number of pitched sounds, each of which is limited to a few repeating notes. In general, pitch patterns tend to be more riff-like than melodic. As a result, pitches in the bass line may seem to belong to one chord rather than several; if they do imply more than one harmony, the resulting progression may or may not be a conventional tonal one. Additional synth lines are generally consonant with the implied harmonies, although they sometimes seem quite independent and dissonant. In general, the characteristics of techno's melodic patterns suggest that producers conceive of each line independently. When they put the lines together, they tend to choose combinations that are relatively consonant, but they do not seem to be especially concerned with establishing a sense of harmonic progression or tonal motion.[3] Repetition also plays a role here: any tonal motion expressed by the bass line will be established quickly and then repeated throughout much of the rest of the track; tonality is not structured hierarchically within the record as a whole.

A striking corollary of techno's rejection of harmonic patterning is its almost total lack of cadences. Although tracks do contain passages that allow for the release of energy, the music flows continuously, never stopping for a moment of rest. The reasons for this relentlessness are both aesthetic and technological. In most musical styles, phrase structure has vocal origins; a phrase is often defined intuitively as the amount of music that can be (or should be) sung in one breath, and the cadence as a point at which one pauses to breathe. The mechanistic ethos that pervades techno and other EDM genres, however, favors the removal of this human element. Its creators have fully exploited the capacity of machines to generate music endlessly without ever needing to breathe or rest.

It is clear, then, that techno does not exhibit phrase structure in the conventional music-theoretical sense. Nevertheless, its perpetual motion is not without internal divisions that tend to parse the music into phrase-like lengths. Not surprisingly, practicing musicians sometimes describe these units as "phrases" and their shaping and delineation as "phrasing." In my discussions with DJs and producers, I learned that musicians are very much aware of multimeasure patterning in EDM, and furthermore, that they regard this patterning as a important structural feature of the music, one that is essential to its production and performance. DJ Shiva, for instance, referenced phrasing several times during our interview, first describing the practice during a discussion of what makes a DJ good:

> *Mark Butler:* What do you think makes a DJ good?
> *DJ Shiva:* Oh wow. … A lot of shit. I think it helps when DJs have some basic knowledge of music. Anybody can string records together and learn to beat-match, but . . . insofar as composition, a lot of people don't pay attention to composition, like how you phrase things, how you emphasize certain sounds and certain bits and how you not only program the music itself but, it's like you have to do that *and* pay attention to what the crowd is responding to.

---

3. I speak primarily of "techno" rather than "EDM" in this and the following paragraphs because certain genres (especially trance), while still emphasizing rhythm, involve pitch to a greater degree. There are exceptions to the tendencies I describe in techno as well; in particular, distinct melody lines and harmonic progressions play a more important role in certain strands of Detroit techno. Aztec Mystic's 1999 track "Knights of the Jaguar," for instance, is based on the repeating progression i iv i⁶ V. The progression occupies sixteen 2/4 bars (or possibly eight 4/4 bars), with changes occurring every four bars. Above the bass line, synthesizers present short riffs and extended string lines that strongly recall the sound of early Detroit techno tracks such as Derrick May's "Strings of Life."

Later in the interview, she elaborates further on the concept of phrasing, suggesting that it involves aligning the larger formal divisions of each record in the mix:

> *DJ Shiva:* But when you're layering two records over each other, you layer the outro beats and the intro beats of the next song, and then the breaks all fall in the same spots. So it locks. As opposed to people who just throw on a record, and things are just happening willy-nilly all over the place, which sounds sloppy. And a lot of people still do that. A lot of big-name DJs do that. I *hate* it. They're all like, "It's experimental." No it's not; it's just phrased badly.

Shortly after this statement, I ask a follow-up question:

> *Mark Butler:* So when you are talking about phrasing, is that the sort of thing you mean: the larger groupings in the music?
> *DJ Shiva:* Uh-huh. Just having them all lock in together, and mesh, instead of being all over the place. I hate it when people drop the 1 beat of the next record on the 15 over here. It's just like everything sounds off. It's like this [*hand gesture indicating nonalignment*]—they all sort of just drift instead of being locked on, basically.

In *Phrase Rhythm in Tonal Music,* William Rothstein notes that musicians often use the term "phrasing" to describe "the delineation and internal shaping of *phrases* . . . by a musical performer," including "both the joining of notes into phrases and the separation of these phrases from each other" (Rothstein 1989: 11; original emphasis). "Phrasing" can also refer to the technical aspects of articulation, such as staccato, legato, and tonguing. Rothstein eventually excludes the term "phrasing" from his book, wishing to make a clear distinction between the actual structural units (phrases, which are a primary focus of his study) and the ways in which they are brought out. This division makes sense within the interpretive tradition of classical music, in which it is assumed that compositions have a certain phrase structure written into them, which performers are responsible for discovering and articulating. In electronic dance music, however, performers do not simply bring out multimeasure patterns; they also play an active role in *creating* them. This aspect is clearly evident in DJ Shiva's discussion of phrasing; significantly, she always uses a verb or a noun derived from a verb to describe the concept. The DJ does not just articulate "the phrasing"; s/he also "phrases" the music itself. Therefore, without describing EDM's multimeasure patterns as "phrases," I will use the term "phrasing" to refer to the active shaping and creation of multimeasure patterns.

Music theorists often describe multimeasure patterns that are not strictly phrase-like as "hypermeasures." This term was first used by Edward Cone in his 1968 book *Musical Form and Musical Performance.* Characteristically, Cone does not present an isolated definition of the term for analytical contemplation, but rather weaves elegant delineations of the concept throughout two different essays. His most succinct summation of hypermeter appears in the following passage:

> In Romantic music, on the other hand, one can find long stretches in which the measures combine into phrases that are themselves metrically conceived—into what I call hypermeasures. This is especially likely to occur whenever several measures in succession exhibit similarity of motivic, harmonic, and rhythmic construction. These almost demand to be counted as units. The desire of the measure to behave as a single beat, already noticeable in very fast Beethoven scherzos, is here intensified—and not only in very fast tempos. (Cone 1968: 79)

This description associates a number of distinctive characteristics with hypermeasures. In particular, measures are "counted as units," behaving "as a single beat," thereby forming larger groupings that are metrical in their design. In retrospect, Cone's observations appear prescient, for the concept of the hypermeasure as a measure writ large has become a crucial issue in modern accounts of multimeasure patterning. The strictness of this model varies considerably: some theorists use the term "hypermeasure" quite loosely to refer to any sort of large-scale pattern other than a phrase, whereas others require the hypermeasure to possess all the qualities associated with meter. Within the latter group, there is additional diversity resulting from varying accounts of the measure's behavior.

In *A Generative Theory of Tonal Music,* Lerdahl and Jackendoff present a relatively neutral conception of hypermeter, defining it simply as "a level larger than the notated measure" (Lerdahl and Jackendoff 1983: 20). Although this implies that their strict definition of meter as the regular alternation of strong and weak beats should carry over to these larger levels, their grid-based approach results in less emphasis on qualitative aspects such as strong/weak distinctions and more on meter as pattern replication. As a result, their discussion of hypermeter is largely focused on explaining hypermetrical irregularities.

The influence of Lerdahl and Jackendoff's separation between grouping and meter looms large (both literally and figuratively) in William Rothstein's treatment of hypermeter. After establishing this distinction at the outset of *Phrase Rhythm in Tonal Music,* Rothstein applies it to the next level up by formulating a strict division between phrases and hypermeasures.[4] Hypermeasures are "by definition predictable and regular," whereas phrases are "living, breathing things [that]

---

4. Significantly, this separation is not a part of Cone's original formulation of hypermeter; as seen in the previous quotation from *Musical Form and Musical Performance,* Cone describe hypermeasures as "phrases that are themselves metrically conceived." At the same time, Rothstein unites the notions of phrase structure and hypermeter in the broadest concept informing his book, that of *phrase rhythm.*

resist simple arithmetical interpretation" (Rothstein 1989: 22). In other words, measures are to hypermeasures as grouping (or rhythm) is to phrases. Rothstein's conception of hypermeter is based on a rather literal application of this analogy; he defines hypermeasures as "suprameasure units that are perceived *as if* they were measures, because they exhibit a regular alternation of strong and weak 'beats' analogous to that of single (in this case 4/4) measures" (Rothstein 1989: 8; original emphasis). At the same time, his exploration of this analogy is exceptionally detailed, resulting in a much more thorough account of the qualitative aspects of hypermeter than those found in works such as *GTTM.*

Christopher Hasty advocates a balanced view of the relationship between measures and hypermeasures (Hasty 1997: 174–97). On the one hand, he points out that the measure/hypermeasure analogy cannot always be maintained with the utmost strictness: at times, we may perceive multimeasure patterns without experiencing every quality associated with meter at the level of the bar.[5] For Hasty, these qualities encompass concepts such as beginning, continuation, anacrusis, deferral, and (most important) projection. Thus we might be aware of a three-bar hypermeasure without experiencing a strong sense of deferral in the third bar, or we might know that two eight-bar durations are "the same" without actually forming accurate eight-bar projections. On the other hand, Hasty insists that these concepts *are* relevant in many cases. He emphasizes this relevance by eliminating the terminological distinction between "measures" and "hypermeasures" when discussing metrical formations of various sizes (Hasty 1997: 183), instead using the term "bar measures" to refer to measures in the conventional sense and descriptors such as "two-bar measure," "four-bar measure," and so on to denote lengthier metrical patterns.

Music theorists, therefore, vary considerably in their conceptions of hypermeter. Some require the hypermeasure to behave exactly like the measure, whereas others acknowledge more general characteristics such as the perception of lengthy multimeasure patterns as the same or the tendency to count measures as if they were beats. Rather than a detriment, this theoretical diversity proves useful for EDM, which reveals a range of approaches to hypermetrical construction. At times, the music exhibits characteristics that correspond to even the strictest definition of hypermeter. Throughout the passage shown in example 5.1, two- and eight-bar hypermeasures can be heard with ease. The loops of the bass line, snare drum 1a and b, and sample 1 all articulate the two-bar level, while

5. He also provides an enlightening discussion of some ways in which this analogy is loosened in Rothstein's work; see esp. 179–81.

textural changes delineate the eight-bar level.[6] Within each eight-bar hypermeasure, metrical qualities associated with 4/4 meter begin to emerge: the second and fourth two-bar units can be heard as weak continuations of the beginnings initiated by the first and third units, and on a larger level, the third unit can be understood as weaker than the first.

On the other hand, multimeasure patterning may be barely perceptible in EDM, even when it clearly plays a role in the music's construction. For instance, the textural graph of "Jerical" (pp. 300–303) shows that textural changes always occur after a multiple of four measures; as a result, it is possible to count in four-bar hypermeasures if one so chooses. Mills's stark compositional approach certainly does nothing to encourage the *perception* of these hypermeasures, however. For the most part, the track consists of undivided eight- and sixteen-bar spans; only occasionally (mm. 13, 17, 61, 65, 133, and 137) do changes occur at the four-bar level.

Example 5.1. Reese and Santonio, "How to Play Our Music," mm. 33–56 (1.01–1.48).

6. The missing four-bar level is also completed through textural changes that begin in measure 57 (see textural graph, p. 320).

And the textural changes that demarcate longer spans are sometimes weak as well; for example, the only factor differentiating the two halves of the thirty-two-bar span in measures 25–56 is the removal of the handclap—a change that is hardly striking.[7] The listener who wishes to hear measures combining into larger patterns (and qualitative distinctions within these patterns) is further obstructed by the brevity of the track's loops, which never last for more than a measure (and for the most part are much shorter). It seems, therefore, that the "hardness" of this track stems not only from its timbre and speed ($\quarternote = 139$), but also from an insistent, almost single-minded focus on the relentless *beat* (the quarter note) and its immediately adjacent metrical neighbors.[8]

As these examples illustrate, the factors that give rise to multimeasure patterning in EDM vary in strength and in the extent to which they evoke specifically metrical qualities. The weakest means of articulating a multimeasure unit is through the addition or removal of a textural element; within this category, the former technique is much stronger than the latter. For the most part, the instrumentation of the element in question is not important, unless the bass line or the bass drum is involved. Of these two sounds, the bass drum plays a particularly important role in the metrical interpretation of a track; either adding or subtracting it can strongly mark a moment for significance.

Most of the textural changes that occur in EDM involve an element either entering or leaving the mix for a reasonably extended period of time—at a minimum, four measures. Some changes are more short-lived, however. This type of alteration usually reflects EDM's tendency toward anacrustic orientation: variations almost always occur just before a metrical or hypermetrical downbeat, and they tend to articulate hypermeter and formal divisions much more effectively than gradual changes in instrumentation. Typically involving the removal of the bass drum (although other elements may participate as well), they last for 1–2 beats or 1–2 measures. (As noted in ch. 2, pp. 91–92, longer bass-drum removals that suggest a distinct formal section will be described as "breakdowns.") Two characteristic examples occur in "Jerical." First, Mills cuts all parts for two beats just before measure 25 (see textural graph, pp. 300–303); he then applies the same procedure to a single beat as he approaches measure 101.[9] In the first

---

7. Measures 81–96 offer a similar division of a sixteen-bar group.

8. Fans often describe Jeff Mills's style of music as "hard techno" (although "hardness" as an aesthetic quality is frequently associated with techno in general as well).

9. The two examples differ slightly in that the first removal begins just after a beat has been reached, whereas the second excises a beat in its entirety. Nevertheless, it still seems reasonable to describe the first removal as lasting two beats, since the change involved creates a silence spanning two beats (from beat 3 to the next downbeat).

Example 5.2. 808 State, "Cubik (Kings County Perspective)," mm. 131–38 (4.14–4.30). [CD tr. 28].
Courtesy of ZTT Music.

case, the anacrusis comes at the end of a relatively clear eight-bar hypermeasure and initiates a sixteen-measure group in which texture reaches a peak of density. In the second case, the removal divides an otherwise undifferentiated eight-bar span in half.

Both two-beat and four-beat (one-measure) cuts occur frequently in "Cubik." In addition to emphasizing a hypermetrical downbeat, the cuts that occur in example 5.2 foreground a single element in the texture—usually a sound that has just entered the mix—by preserving it while all the other parts drop out. The particular elements cast into relief here are synth 2' (m. 134) and riff 4 (m. 138).

Stronger than the effects of most textural changes, however, are the hypermetrical articulations that come about through pattern repetition. By using loops that recur across multimeasure spans, producers can express large-scale patterning directly. Loop lengths also may work *in combination* with textural change to effect a sense of hypermeter. In the following passage from "Cubik," for instance, the use of one-measure loops in combination with regular textural changes at

Example 5.3. 808 State, "Cubik (Kings County Perspective)," mm. 17–24 (0.32–0.47). [CD tr. 29].
Courtesy of ZTT Music.

the four-bar level is enough to enable the perception of four-bar hypermeasures even though none of the loops last longer than a measure (ex. 5.3).[10]

The strength of hypermetrical articulations also depends upon the time spans involved and the extent to which definite pitch is used. When multimeasure patterning is created by pitch, longer loops seem to result in a stronger sense of hypermeter, but when this patterning is expressed only through textural change, the perceptibility of hypermetrical units diminishes as the amount of time between changes increases. In fact, the use of pitched loops generally makes hy-

10. This description of loop lengths is not absolutely precise: one pattern (hi-hat 1) does last for two measures. However, this loop consists primarily of a repeating sixteenth note, with occasional variations suggesting larger (one- and two-measure) periodicities. It is also rather low in the mix at this point.

permeter much clearer, especially when the loops have a well-defined melodic profile (in contrast to shorter and more percussive "riffs").

Of the various sorts of pitched loops that occur in electronic dance music, the type that has the greatest potential for delineating hypermeter is the bass line. Melodic bass lines—especially those that suggest a distinct harmonic progression—can carry the listener across longer time spans, making the projection of eight- and sixteen-bar durations easier. The rarity of extended harmonic progressions in techno, however, differentiates it significantly from the repertoire on which most music theorists have focused. In classical music of the common-practice period, hypermeter occurs in conjunction with phrases and periods; these entities, which provide a continuous thread through the hypermeasure, are demarcated to a large extent by harmony. In this context, tonal motion marks the hypermeasure as well as the phrase, projecting a clearly defined relationship between the (hyper)meter and the harmonic changes. In techno, however, hypermeasures are often harmonically static, generally limiting any tonal motion to one or two measures in length. The bass line of "How to Play Our Music" (ex. 5.1) illustrates these tendencies quite well: though technically two measures long because of small rhythmic and melodic variations, it confines its tonal motion to a single measure.[11] Because of this tonal stasis, techno relies more on other kinds of pattern repetition to create a sense of hypermeter, and the units within a hypermeasure are often quite similar to each other (if not identical).[12] Although the metrical position might still be very clear at any given moment (for example, one can immediately sense which "beat" of the hypermeasure is occurring), qualitative distinctions between measures tend to be somewhat attenuated.

Because of the extent to which realizations of "hypermeter" can vary in EDM, I will reserve this term and its cognates for structures that have at least a degree of measure-like quality. At a minimum, the metrical position should be clear to the listener even if the individual measures are too homogeneous to stand out as "upbeats," "afterbeats," and so on. Meanwhile, I will continue to use terms such as "multimeasure patterning" or "multimeasure grouping" to describe structures larger than the measure that do not meet these criteria. These include patterns created solely by textural changes or articulative sounds as well as other compositional designs that may not be immediately perceptible.

11. The implied progression might be analyzed as i iv i⁶ V i (understanding the E at the end of the first measure as a harmonically insignificant upbeat). On the other hand, one could also claim that the bass line is simply an arpeggiation of the tonic harmony (with E functioning as an incomplete neighbor), which would imply that it lacks tonal motion altogether.

12. Similar examples might be found in the music of twentieth-century composers, as well as in medieval music employing repeating cycles.

In fact, multimeasure patterns in EDM *do* reflect attributes of the measure in many ways, though these qualities usually relate more closely to the distinctive metrical characteristics of this repertory than to "meter" as defined by music theorists. Anacrustic orientation, for instance—as exemplified by bass-drum removals—can occur not only at the end of a measure but also at the close of a multimeasure group. Moreover, the tendency toward underdetermination seen locally in the measure is mirrored at the next level by the fact that large-scale patterning is often too general to be described as "hypermetrical."

Another correspondence involves the duple nature of meter in techno and other four-on-the-floor genres. It is clear that when fans describe techno as "4/4 music," they are not simply referring to the level of the measure. Because techno is based almost exclusively on pure-duple values, enabling it to be counted "in four" at a variety of levels, the distinction between "metrical" and "hypermetrical" often becomes irrelevant to listeners.[13] In their discussions of metrical structure in electronic dance music, interviewees tended to move freely from one level of meter to another (although follow-up questions revealed that they were clearly aware of the difference between the measure and other levels). In general, they noted that "techno has a four-count structure" or that "everything happens in four" without worrying about whether the "four" refers to the beat, the measure, or the hypermeasure. A good example of this free approach to "fourness" occurs in the following excerpt from an interview with Mystik and Jimmi Journey:

> *Mark Butler:* When you're taking the bass out, how do you decide how long to keep it out?
> *Mystik:* A lot of times it goes … It depends on the song. It goes of course in fours. Sometimes I'll drop it out at … Well, there's four sets of four, and at the end of the last four I'll drop it out maybe for four beats, and you bring it back in—and that's perfect timing. It's all a timing thing—you can't just drop it out any time you want and have it sound right. It's got to be on beat.

Mystik first refers generally to "four sets of four," without specifying whether beats, measures, or larger patterns are involved, but her subsequent mention of beats led me to believe that she was referring to four sets of four-beat measures. In fact, however, she meant four sets of *four-measure* groups, as she explained shortly thereafter:

> *Mark Butler:* How much do you all think about larger groups? Obviously it starts with beat matching, but that's [*counting as if with a typical bass-drum beat*]

13. This distinction is also weakened in the absence of notational support.

"1 2 3 4," whatever. ... And then you can start thinking about the groups of measures, and a lot of times there are four-measure groups, but do you think about as much as like sixteen-measure groups? . . .
Mystik: Yeah.
Mark Butler: Is that something you aim for ...
Mystik: Yeah—well, when I said ...
Mark Butler: or do you think more in terms of four-measure groups?
Mystik: Oh, no—what I meant when I said that, I meant, four ... I meant sixteen-measure groups.
Mark Butler: Four sets of four measures.
Mystik: Yeah, four sets of four-measure groups.

In addition to showing the importance of "fourness" at multiple levels of organization, Mystik's reference to "sets" of measures suggests that she is describing a hypermetrical phenomenon.

From a perceptual standpoint, this sense of "fourness" may be more salient than the level at which it appears. "Cubik," for instance, moves from four-bar hypermeasures in measures 1–32 to an eight-bar hypermeasure in measures 33–40 (see textural graph, pp. 290–93). Yet because this new hypermeasure is still "in four" (riff 2 provides a two-bar group by which to count), it does not seem strikingly different; there is a sort of equivalency between it and the previous four-bar hypermeasures. At the same time, when we move from a hypermeasure to a duration of the same length in which hypermeter is absent, the span without large-scale metrical organization will seem longer, even though the two durations are identical in terms of clock time. One can experience this phenomenon in measures 103–26 of "Cubik," in which the eight-bar hypermeasures of measures 103–18 give way to measures 119–26, which lack strong groupings beyond the level of the measure.

Interactions between Multimeasure Patterning and Metrical Dissonance

Hypermeter, like meter, is conceived of as fundamentally regular in most music-theoretical approaches. In the music that these theories address, hypermeter usually forms patterns based on pure-duple values, with lengths of two, four, and eight measures being most prevalent.[14] In the midst of this regularity, how-

14. Regular three-bar hypermeasures can also occur, although these are less common; for discussion of an example from the scherzo movement of Beethoven's ninth symphony, see Cohn 1992a. Rothstein (1989: 37–40) also provides a few examples of recurring five-bar hypermeter, which is quite rare.

ever, isolated hypermeasures consisting of three, five, or six measures do occasionally appear. The explanation of such irregularities has become a major focus of contemporary work on hypermeter. In electronic dance music, however, regularity and repetition extend to metrically dissonant patterns as well as consonant ones. In the following section, I will consider the hypermetrical dimensions of metrical dissonance in EDM both in relation to existing explanatory concepts and independently, eventually arguing that the ways in which hypermeter is or is not articulated can have significant effects on the character of particular dissonances.

Most commonly, music theorists have interpreted hypermetrical irregularities as transformations of regular background structures. Lerdahl and Jackendoff, for instance, claim that departures from a work's prevailing hypermeter usually occur through a process of "metrical deletion." Their concept of metrical deletion is in turn related to two grouping phenomena known as "overlap" and "elision" (Lerdahl and Jackendoff 1983: 99–104, 55–62). Overlap occurs when an event functions simultaneously as the end of one group and the beginning of another, as in the beginning of measures 3 and 5 in example 5.4, a reproduction of Lerdahl and Jackendoff's example 3.25 (1983: 56).

Example 5.4. Mozart, Piano Sonata in C major K. 279, I, mm. 1–5, overlap.

Elision is essentially the same as overlap, except that the balance between the two groups is asymmetrical: typically, the second group enters much more forcefully, so that the end of the first group seems to have been obscured.[15] The third

15. Rothstein, who also provides substantial discussion of these techniques (1989: 44–51), does not distinguish between overlap and elision, but instead uses the more general term "phrase overlap" (or "subphrase overlap") to refer to both phenomena.

and fourth measures of example 5.5 provide a characteristic illustration (Lerdahl and Jackendoff 1983: 100).

Example 5.5. Haydn, Symphony No. 104, I, mm. 13–19.

The metrical analysis shown beneath this example reveals the unusual feature of its treatment of hypermeter: in measures 15–16, two strong beats occur in succession at the two-bar level. Lerdahl and Jackendoff explain this discrepancy by claiming that a measure has been deleted from the underlying prototype; compared to measure 16, the missing measure would be weak, with an accentual pattern like that of measure 14. Rothstein, following Schenker's discussion of "reinterpretation" in *Der Freie Satz,* describes this transformation as "metrical reinterpretation," a phenomenon that occurs when "the last bar of one hypermeasure is treated simultaneously as the first bar of a new hypermeasure" (Rothstein 1989: 52). Although this definition emphasizes simultaneity, Rothstein's choice of terminology implies a processual component—that is, the measure in question is first experienced as weak, but then comes to function as strong as the listener becomes aware of the new metrical context.

There is an obvious correlation between the process of metrical deletion/reinterpretation and turning the beat around, as both phenomena involve the creation of a pattern of strong/weak accentuation and its subsequent reversal. In the examples discussed by Lerdahl, Jackendoff, and Rothstein, however, the transformation is confined solely to the domain of hypermeter, whereas in EDM, it is the *beat*—the tactus—that is reinterpreted.[16] This difference explains, in part, why the shift involved in turning the beat around is much more jarring and immediate than the hypermetrical reinterpretations seen in the classical repertory.

16. For examples of reinterpretations at lower metrical levels in Stravinsky's *Les Noces,* see Horlacher 1995.

At the same time, considering the hypermetrical dimensions of turning the beat around also sheds light on its distinctive effect. For instance, recall the passage leading up to the TBA in Underworld's "Cups" (ex. 5.6).

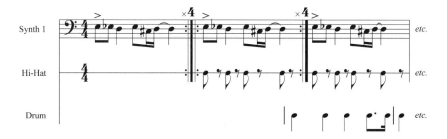

Example 5.6. Underworld, "Cups," 0.44–1.06. [CD tr. 30].
Words and Music by Karl Hyde, Richard Smith and Darren Emerson. Copyright © 1999 Smith Hyde Productions and Sherlock Holmes Music Ltd. This arrangement Copyright © 2004 Smith Hyde Productions and Sherlock Holmes Music Ltd. All Rights for Smith Hyde Productions in the United States and Canada Administered by Chrysalis Songs. All Rights for Sherlock Holmes Music Ltd. Administered by Sony/ATV Music Publishing, 8 Music Square West, Nashville, TN 37203. International Copyright Secured. All Rights Reserved.

In the beginning of this excerpt, textural changes create a very clear sense of four-bar patterning, which some listeners may experience as hypermeter. Furthermore, when the drumbeat enters, it appears near a hypermetrical juncture. Yet it shifts the pattern of accentuation not by a *measure,* but by a single eighth note. As a result, there is a wide discrepancy between the various metrical levels emphasized in the passage. In Krebsian terms, the largest level—the four-whole-note layer—is particularly prominent, but the shift is most noticeable at the smallest level—the eighth-note layer. It is also significant that the shift takes place *before* the downbeat:[17] according to Rothstein (1989: 48), "a phrase overlap is most likely to occur when the first of two phrases ends either at (or just after) a hypermetrical downbeat." When an overlap (and its resultant reinterpretation) occurs with or after such a downbeat, we still get to experience the downbeat we were expecting, though eventually we come to understand the new element as more strongly accented. When the beat is turned around before a downbeat,

17. With the exception of "Televised Green Smoke," all of the examples of TBA presented in chapter 4 involve an element entering *before* an expected accent.

however, the accent we were expecting is actively *denied,* resulting in a much more disruptive effect.

In turning the beat around, multimeasure patterning works in conjunction with a form of displacement dissonance. How does large-scale metrical structure interact with EDM's distinctive embedded grouping dissonances? One possibility was seen in "How to Play Our Music" (ex. 4.16), in which the EGD "resolved" every two measures, thus preserving (and bolstering) the work's two-bar hypermeter. Most EDM producers do not adopt this strategy, however, instead preferring to allow EGDs to spin out in an endless series of cycles that will never synchronize with pure-duple hypermeter. And within this general trend, considerable variety exists. In particular, the way in which the producer articulates patterns larger than the measure can have a significant effect on the character of the dissonance.

One reason why the dissonant layers that appear in James Ruskin's "Connected" (pp. 294–98) are able to function as independently as they do is the remarkable underdetermination of the track's 4/4 metrical context. This underdetermination affects the higher metrical levels as well; indeed, the first major obstacle to the perception of hypermeter in the track is the ambiguity of the whole-note layer. The work's multimeasure patterning is also obscured by the weakness of the factors articulating it. Because none of the loops in "Connected" last for more than a measure, longer durations are expressed *only* through textural changes. The strongest changes are the one-bar bass drum removals that lead to measures 113 and 161; aside from these cuts, the only forces delineating multimeasure patterning are occasional articulative sounds (synth 1, synth 3) and general changes in instrumentation (e.g., the entrance of the bass drum in m. 9), which Ruskin sometimes veils with gradual fade-ins (as with riffs 2 and 3). Furthermore, the changes that do occur are often spaced quite widely apart: only one appears after less than eight bars, and several arrive after sixteen bars or longer. Hence, an especially wide gap separates the local-level motion of the track's loops from its large-scale patterning. Ironically, the only loop that *can* be said to demarcate a multimeasure pattern is riff 2—the source of the embedded grouping dissonance—through its consistent alignment with every third downbeat.

In the Timo Maas mix of "Dooms Night" by Azzido Da Bass (pp. 266–72), however, both meter and hypermeter *are* very clear. All metrical layers from the eighth to the whole note are established almost immediately at the beginning of the track, and the sixteenth note is added just eight measures later when the ma-

18. One exception to this general state of consonance is synth 1. This pattern, which forms an embedded grouping dissonance in the same manner as synth 3 (both parts consist of repeating

racas enter.[18] When the dissonant layer (synth 3) first appears in conjunction with the percussion parts (m. 49), it is accompanied by a new consonant element, the bass line (refer also to ex. 4.15). The bass line expresses a clear two-bar hypermeter, and four-bar hypermeasures are quite perceptible throughout its iterations as well. In certain passages, articulative elements demarcate these larger units (synth 1 entrances, mm. 65–73 and 117–32), whereas in other cases the clarity of the double-whole-note layer seems to encourage the listener to hear the two-bar units in pairs (e.g., mm. 49–64, in which none of the loops actually repeat or change at four-bar intervals).

Because meter and hypermeter are articulated so strongly in "Dooms Night," the dissonant synth riff seems to stand in stark opposition to the other layers; its effect is truly "antimetrical." Furthermore, the clarity of hypermeter in particular foregrounds the incommensurability of the pure-triple dissonance with the pure-duple values found in the other parts. Although the dissonant layer will align with a metrical beat every three beats, and with a downbeat every three bars, it will only align with a four-bar hypermetrical downbeat every *twelve* bars.

By contrast, the layer that functions as a dissonance in measures 49–88 (synth 3) first appears during the breakdown of measures 25–48. Except for a few articulative and atmospheric sounds, it first emerges as a solo instrument, generating no dissonant effect at all.[19] In fact, the length of this passage suggests that the producers wanted the synth to seem as consonant as possible at first. Within the forty-three-second breakdown, synth 3 is heard a total of sixty-three times, and it is clear from the context that it would appear a sixty-fourth time were it not for the one-beat removal that precedes measure 49. Sixty-four, of course, is a pure-duple value; given the prevalence of such values in the first part of the track, as well as the clarity of 4/4 meter, it seems likely that listeners

---

dotted quarter notes), first appears in measure 17. The dissonance created by synth 1 is much less disruptive, however, since it is dynamically soft and always fades out after a few iterations. For this reason, it is classified as an atmospheric sound, whereas synth 3 is rhythmic. Interestingly, whenever synth 1 appears in conjunction with synth 3, the two patterns are not aligned.

19. Krebs would most likely claim that the change that begins in measure 25 would result in an indirect dissonance—a perceived conflict between the metrical structure of the preceding passage and the new interpretation with which it is juxtaposed—which would be perceptible through the first few measures of the breakdown. He also tends to analyze similar passages in the music of Schumann and others as subliminally dissonant. An indirect dissonance does indeed occur here, but a subliminal dissonance seems unlikely; the passage is so long that the opening meter will probably fade from most listeners' minds. Nevertheless, two factors that support a subliminal hearing are (1) the entrances of two atmospheric sounds near the downbeats of measures 33 and 41—these sounds divide the twenty-four-bar span roughly into three eight-bar units, although their prominence is minimal in comparison to that of synth 3—and (2) the fact that the passage preceding the breakdown is exactly twenty-four bars (also divided into eight-bar units).

would also apply a pure-duple hearing to this stream of attacks. This interpretation would result in sixteen 4/4 measures, although the measures would be longer (in clock time) than those heard in the first part of the track. In the textural graph, this alternate metrical structure is shown above measures 25–49, which are enclosed in parentheses to indicate that their status at this point is relatively hypothetical.

The ratio of the sixteen measures of synth 3 with the twenty-four measures implied by the primary metrical consonance is 2:3, a relationship that seems to have a special status as an organizing factor in the track. At the lowest level, 2:3 is the ratio between the quarter note and the dotted quarter note, the superposition that functions as the primary generator of metrical dissonance in the work. Because of the embedded nature of the dissonance, the ratio radiates outward, appearing again in the relationship between the two-bar hypermeter and the three-bar cycle formed by the larger dissonance, and finally in the 16:24 ratio just described.[20] The 16:24 relationship governs the third breakdown (mm. 157–80) as well.

One also can argue for another type of 2:3 ratio in the second breakdown (mm. 89–116), which is unusual in several respects. In terms of the 4/4 meter of the track as a whole, it lasts for twenty-eight bars, making it the only formal section in the track that does not last for a multiple of eight measures.[21] In addition, it contains a dramatic accelerando that crests in measure 112; measures 113–16 consist of a swirling mix of effects ("EFX") that lead to the return of the groove in measure 117. The accelerando makes it difficult to characterize the metrical behavior of synth 3 in the passage. In all, the synth attack is heard 116 times. Because it dissolves into continuous sound four measures before the end of the passage, however, it is possible to imagine that it actually continues to accelerate, eventually merging into a single unbroken tone. Hence, one might argue that the passage is actually *twice as long* as the other breakdowns—that is, thirty-two measures of synth 3 against forty-eight "regular" measures—with

20. Because the twelve-bar span has special significance as the smallest duration allowing alignment between the three-bar dissonant cycle and the four-bar hypermeter, one might also argue for an additional intermediate level formed by eight bars of synth 3 in relation to twelve bars of the primary metrical consonance.

21. In addition to the textural graph, refer to the form chart (p. 273), which consists of rows that should be read from left to right. The arrangement of blocks on the page highlights similarities between three types of formal sections: percussion-only sections ("grooves"), breakdowns in which synth 3 is heard as a solo instrument, and dissonant combinations of synth 3 and the groove. The duration of each section in measures is indicated by a number at the right of each box, while numbers beneath the box suggest probable internal divisions. Numbers above each box indicate the starting beat of each sequence (a feature that will be explained in the following chapter) and the number of iterations of synth 3 found within the section.

the acceleration causing the measures to take up less and less clock time. The sixteen missing articulations at the end of the synth 3 pattern (technically, it should sound 132 times rather than 116) can be understood to have taken place within measures 113–16.

In conclusion, it is clear that thinking hypermetrically can shed light not only on the nature of multimeasure patterning in EDM but also on some of the unique qualities of its metrical dissonances. The distinctive effects associated with these dissonances often depend to a large extent on the ways in which individual works articulate multimeasure patterning. More than simple examples of overlap or reinterpretation, phenomena such as turning the beat around and embedded grouping dissonance call attention to both small- and large-scale dimensions of musical time and the interactions between them. Aspects distinctive to the re-alization of measures in this repertory, such as underdetermination, anacrustic orientation, and heightened emphasis on process, also guide higher levels of temporal organization. I will continue to explore this expansion of the time-scale in the following chapter, showing how multimeasure patterns combine to form sequences, records, and sets.

Form from the
Record to the Set

"Form" in Theory and Practice

As our discussion of rhythm and meter moves toward increasingly lengthy spans of time, we begin to approach notions of what music theorists conventionally call "form." Although the concept of form properly includes every level of musical patterning, the majority of formal discussions concentrate on broader entities such as complete pieces of music or major sections within works. This is the sense in which I invoke the term here. While I will still focus upon rhythmic and metrical phenomena, I will now begin to address larger structures, with particular emphasis on complete tracks and their combination.

Form inheres within a number of different realms in electronic dance music. On one end of the spectrum, there is the form of a single track; on the other, that of the complete set. Considerable variety exists within each of these categories: tracks can be experienced in their original versions as well as transformed and combined with other records, and sets can arise in live performance contexts or in the studio. Each of these factors has significant formal implications and presents particular analytical challenges. This chapter attempts to negotiate this formal diversity by blending detailed analysis of individual, unmixed tracks with discussion of DJs' and producers' roles in creating and shaping form. Much of the latter material will be presented directly in the words of musicians who shared their insights with me.

The music-theoretical study of form has a long history. Although the term has accrued a great deal of semantic richness over the years, it remains general enough to be useful in a variety of contexts. Nevertheless, I would like to address some of its potential implications before applying it to a repertoire quite different from that usually addressed by theorists. The first of these implications concerns the role of tonality, which American music theorists, influenced by Schenkerian perspectives on musical structure, have tended to view as the driving force behind form. Because pitch material is not usually a significant organizing factor in EDM, its form tends to be determined more by patterns of rhythm, meter, and texture. Its characteristics also work against the usual separation between form as a rhythmic phenomenon and meter as pattern replication, because meter plays such a significant role in determining the form of the music at all levels. In addition, the absence of tonal implication makes it more difficult to interpret form teleologically. Although expectations—for example, the return of a hypermetrical downbeat—may be created and fulfilled, they do not usually govern entire works.

Second, the music-theoretical study of form has tended to revolve around certain formal "types": binary, ternary, rondo, and sonata-allegro form, to name just a few. The reader should not assume that my use of the word "form" implies the presence of any of these types within electronic dance music. Although I will reveal the presence of certain characteristic formal shapes within EDM tracks and sets and demonstrate that both producers and DJs are aware of these shapes and their roles in creating them, these formal patterns do not necessarily have specific names or any direct relationship to the formal types of classical music.

Conceptions of form in classical music tend to be premised on an object-like conception of the musical work. A piece of music is assumed to have a single fixed structure, with a clearly defined beginning and end that separate it from other musical works, and to be associated with a concrete physical object (the score).[1] In EDM, it is certainly possible to map these characteristics onto individual tracks in isolation; indeed, the physical representation of an EDM composition is in some senses more concrete than a classical score, since its acoustical information is etched directly into its grooves. DJ Shiva, in fact, told me that it is possible to "read" a track's form by looking at it: "The cool thing is . . . if you take a twelve-inch techno record and look at it, you can actually read the record according to the grooves. The grooves are wider cut when there's a beat going. When it breaks down—when there's no beat—they're thinner. You can actually read it." Nevertheless, It Is ultImately more productive and accurate to conceive of the structure of an EDM work as *open*. Within the (re)mix culture of EDM, works cannot be associated with a single definitive recording in the manner of songs in rock. Although participants clearly viewed individual tracks as exhibiting

1. The fact that music theorists often argue about the structure of a work highlights the importance of determining just what that structure is. Although there may be disagreements about the structure of a work and its interpretation, these do not prevent us from imagining it to have a stable identity. For further discussion of conceptions of the musical work in the classical tradition, see Goehr 1992. To the criteria that Goehr associates with the "work-concept," I would add the importance of definite boundaries.

particular formal behaviors, which DJs had to understand in order to create effective sets, this understanding was situated within consistent expectations regarding the larger context in which tracks would function. Participants frequently described records as "tools" to be employed in sets. For instance, the producer and live performer Stanley noted that techno in particular "is treated a lot more as a tool for the DJs," while DJ Shiva argued that DJing is not "just records strung end-to-end; it's not single records; you're taking basically a bunch of blunt little tools and making an entire piece out of it." Adam Jay, in turn, repeatedly spoke of ways in which his records were designed to work well within DJ sets. For these reasons, the tracks that I am analyzing should be understood as starting points for DJ sets. This does not mean that their form cannot or should not be analyzed. As subsequent comments will reveal, DJs regard understanding and attending to formal patterning as essential parts of their craft, and this craft starts with individual tracks as its core ingredients. Yet the tradition of organicism so important to classical works does not govern the creation and reception of EDM, even though one may find unity within a given track. Instead, records are designed in ways that allow them to be combined and juxtaposed with great flexibility.

In live performance, electronic dance music is most often improvised rather than planned out in advance. Improvisation also can play a role in production, as subsequent discussion will reveal. The analytical tradition of music theory, however, has developed in relation to composed works and generally involves close examination of musical scores. How might the differences between these two modes of musical creation—improvisation and composition—affect approaches to form in EDM?

Some scholars have suggested that improvisations are not really so different from compositions. The ethnomusicologist Bruno Nettl, for example, considers improvisation to be a rapidly executed form of composition. He asks: "Should we not then speak perhaps of rapid and slow composition rather than of composition juxtaposed to improvisation?" (Nettl 1974: 6). Other writers, such as the jazz scholar Frank Tirro, have taken this idea further, suggesting that transcriptions of improvisations can be studied as if they were musical scores. Tirro argues that certain types of improvisation are compositional because of the coherent, teleological nature of their organization. He writes that "there can be little doubt that these transcribed improvisations are indeed compositions, each following musical laws that govern the progress of the work" (Tirro 1974: 305).

By contrast, many authors have raised strong objections to such approaches, and to the structural analysis of improvised music in general. Setting up oppositions between "composed creative products"—a term that Sawyer (1996: 281) uses to refer to the scores of Western classical music—and the *processes* involved in live improvisation, they argue that traditional methods of music theory and musicology such as Schenkerian analysis are inappropriate for the analysis of improvised music because they are based on static scores rather than dynamic processes. John Brownell, for example, objects to compositionally based analyses on the grounds that "the object in the analysis of improvisation is itself a phantom, and rather than analysing [*sic*] music, what ends up being analyzed is the frozen *record* of a process" (Brownell 1994: 15). Keith Sawyer suggests that it is the score, which he calls a "text artifact" (1996: 271), rather than musical sound, that has generally been the object of structural analysis. Both authors feel that this type of analysis fails to capture the essential indeterminacy of an unfolding improvisation, a quality that Sawyer theorizes with the term "contingence." In other words, although it is possible to describe the structure of an improvisation after the fact, this structure is not predetermined but, rather, emerges during the performance and is subject to change at any moment.

Sawyer and Brownell are correct to point out that a transcription of an improvised performance is not the same as a musical score created by a composer, and that some analytical methods may favor certain aesthetic or musical qualities at the expense of others. Nevertheless, although the tendency of some authors to equate various types of improvisation with classical compositions is unfortunate, it is simplistic to assume that any analysis that considers musical structure and involves notation will automatically result in an inappropriate transfer of aesthetic values from the classical world. Sensitive analysts, aware of the ways in which musical traditions differ, can and should avoid such slippage.

The competing interests of this debate suggest two different yet complementary analytical orientations. One possibility is to study the decisions made during an improvisation, considering the process involved from the perspective of the performer-creator. This is the approach advocated by Sawyer and Brownell. Another possibility is to concentrate on the sounds created by the performer, considering the results of the improvisation from the perspective of the listener. The latter approach *can* be product-oriented—centered on a transcription of the improvisation—but it need not be exclusively so, for one can also consider the processes involved in listening to the work as it unfolds (and, more generally, of interacting with the DJ as an audience member). After all, from the listener's perspective, *all* music (including composed music) is a contingent phenomenon; as Christopher Hasty has written, "a piece of music, while it is going on, is incomplete and not fully determinate" (Hasty 1997: 3).

These approaches are equally valid, and they should not be regarded as mutually exclusive. Ideally, improvised genres should be studied from the perspectives of both the listener *and* the performer/creator, taking into account the decisions made by the DJ as well as the resulting patterns of sound. However, authors should not feel obliged to accomplish both tasks within the confines of a single study. Rather, such a broad-based understanding should be the *shared* goal of scholars studying improvised genres as they approach their subjects from multiple disciplinary perspectives.

The Organization of Complete Tracks

Having addressed some of the practical and philosophical concerns relevant to a study of "form" in EDM, I will now begin to consider the music's large-scale features in more detail. I will focus first on the ways in which individual tracks are structured, and then upon the combination of those tracks into complete sets.

THE ROLE OF THE SEQUENCE IN PRODUCTION

In highlighting the many different ways in which people may interact with electronic dance music, I have tried to emphasize the distinctive vantage points offered by each position. The perspectives associated with each possible role—whether one is dancing, listening at home, DJing, producing, or analyzing as a music theorist—overlap and intersect to varying degrees. For example, certain details of a track's construction will be immediately obvious to both listener and producer, while others—though still impacting the experience of everyone who hears the music—will be known only to the person who created it. One such feature that occurs in almost all electronic dance music is the *sequence.*

As described in chapter 1, a *sequencer* is a type of technology that directs the instruments within a track. In essence, it controls the form of a work; in the hands of the producer, it tells each instrument whether or not to play and when. A track composed in this manner will consist of a series of *sequences:* units in which a particular configuration of instruments is directed to play for a set amount of time, usually specified in measures.

In electronic dance music, sequences tend to consist of a single recurring duration throughout an entire track, a characteristic that may result from the technical limitations of many older sequencers—those used in EDM's formative stages, and still favored by some producers today. This duration is usually a pure-duple number of measures. Eight- and sixteen-bar sequences seem to be particularly common: both Adam Jay and Neal Blue use sixteen-measure durations as the basis for all their tracks, whereas DJ Shiva notes that "in techno, especially, everything happens mostly on thirty-two counts. You'll have thirty-two beats, and

a. Using a single repeating sequence with certain parts muted
(parentheses indicate muted parts)

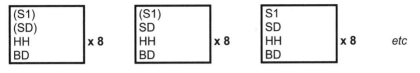

b. Using a variety of sequences in succession

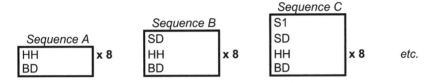

Example 6.1. Two possible approaches to sequencing.

then on the thirty-third beat [there'll be] like a cymbal hit and a new sound's introduced."

There are two main ways in which EDM producers use sequences to create a track. In the first possibility, shown in example 6.1a, they use only one or two sequences through the course of an entire track, creating textural variety by muting or unmuting selected parts in real time as the sequence repeats. In the second possibility, shown in example 6.1b, they form the track from a succession of many different sequences.

Adam Jay uses the first approach, as he explained in the following description of a track he composed:

> *Adam Jay:* Loaded in my sampler right now is just one sequence. Usually I only load one or two, because what I can do is mute parts. So what you'll hear is sounds coming in and out, and that'll be me unmuting parts and kind of bringing instruments in live. I do it in real time as I record. . . .
> *Mark Butler:* And when you say you have a sequence, basically you mean everything that could happen in a track is all there sort of as a chunk of potential?
> *Adam Jay:* Exactly. Exactly.
> *Mark Butler:* OK. So you sort of just set it going and you have some parts suppressed and some parts...
> *Adam Jay:* Right.

I subsequently asked a follow-up question to determine how widespread this approach is:

Mark Butler: But do you think most techno producers have a sequence like that that's repeating while they're recording?
Adam Jay: Absolutely. They're ... Uh, I'm trying to think who else ...
Mark Butler: [*interrupting*] Because a lot of times what you hear is it building up while you're listening.
Adam Jay: Right. And a lot of times, that wasn't recorded before it was ... that wasn't recorded, sequence-wise, before it was recorded into the CD player ... or into the CD recorder. You know what I'm saying? When I ... I'm recording in real-time, which means when I make that kick drum go out, my finger did that at that moment....

But I also know for a fact that a lot of people do things a really weird way. Like a lot of people will take ... they'll play the sequence all the way through, with a bunch of parts, and then they'll record that in their computer. And then they'll play a sequence—that same sequence with a different part, [and] record that in, and they'll have a bunch of little blocks. And they'll take that into a program called Pro Tools and assemble it; and they'll basically compose the song after the fact. They won't do it in real time; they'll do it all out so it's all out on the screen, so that they can just hit play and it all happens.

In the view of this producer, then, the two approaches just described are equally common. They differ, however, in several respects: not only in the number of sequences they use within a track but also in the extent to which they are planned out. Within the first approach, textural changes and the manipulation of effects are often improvised; within the second, every detail of a track's structure is carefully arranged. During our interview, Adam Jay explained the former way of working with a sequence as we listened to one of his tracks:

Adam Jay: If I want to bring, like, that kick drum out right there, I bring it out, and there's a synth that comes in here in a second. I can bring that in at certain times if I want. I've also got it set to loop for sixteen bars, so as it's playing I'm watching the time....
Mark Butler: So the sequence is set for sixteen bars?
Adam Jay: [*Agreeing*] Sixteen. So when sixteen is over I'll know that it's time for me to change it up.... So, I just took a ride [cymbal] out. But there's a break that's going to be coming up ... right here. [I] filter out the kick drum, and I'm bringing in the new synth line right now. Now, how the synth line varies [in pitch]—that was already recorded into a sequence.
Mark Butler: OK.
Adam Jay: Now I'm filtering out the synth a little more.... I can see when sixteen bars [comes around.] It's pretty much come to ... I know when ..., and,

as a DJ, you don't really count anymore, you feel it.[2] You know, like, "It's time for something new, *right now*." But that helps me.

Mark Butler: So it's sort of improvised, and you go by feel in terms of where you pull things in and out.

Adam Jay: Exactly. Exactly. Pretty much everything is written in real time, and I usually do it in one take.

For Adam Jay, the sequence seems to function much like a chord progression in the blues or jazz: as a recurring cycle that provides a framework in which improvisation can occur. He follows the sequence's progression as the track unfolds and structures his changes around his position within it. Yet the parameters involved in this improvisation are not harmonic, but textural and metrical.[3]

A sequence used in this way is very much like a loop, since both repeat at a certain fixed periodicity. The two concepts differ only in the level of structure with which they are associated and the number of parts they involve.[4] A loop can be any length, even a single sixteenth note, whereas a sequence is usually fairly substantial in duration (at least four measures); more importantly, a sequence controls a number of different loops. Although these patterns are mostly different in length, they are all synchronized at the level of the sequence. Example 6.2 shows how this type of patterning works in measures 9–16 of 808 State's "Cubik," given a hypothetical eight-bar sequence.[5] In order to better understand some of the distinctive characteristics of sequences and the ways in which they interact with multimeasure patterning and form, I will now consider their use in several complete tracks, beginning with James Ruskin's "Connected."

An eight-bar duration seems to be the most likely candidate for the basis of the sequence(s) in "Connected." The majority of textural and articulative changes take place at intervals that are multiples of eight; for instance, a change occurs after twenty-four bars in measure 73, after eight bars in measure 81, and after sixteen bars in measure 97 (see textural graph, pp. 296–97). Although these numbers are also multiples of two and four, a two-bar sequence is too short to be of use, and the music never expresses four-bar durations in any way. Mean-

---

2. In addition to production, Adam Jay frequently performs DJ sets and live PAs.

3. At the same time, as in many other forms of contemporary popular music, the involvement of recording technology does balance out some of these improvised aspects, since performers have a chance to revise, redo, or reject an improvisation if they find it unacceptable. In this respect, production differs from DJing and other arenas in which improvisation occurs during live performance.

4. Furthermore, as emphasized by the qualifying phrase "used in this way," the term "sequence" does not necessarily imply repetition, whereas "loop" always does.

5. Refer also to the sound palette and textural graph (pp. 287–93). Further discussion of the length of the sequence in "Cubik" will appear shortly.

Part	Length of Loop	Appears in	# of Iterations
Riff 1	4 measures	mm. 9–16	2
Hi-Hat 1	2 measures	mm. 9–16	4
Tom-Tom	1 measure	mm. 13–16	4
Snare Drum	1 measure	mm. 13–16	4
Bass Drum	1 quarter note	mm. 9–16	32
Sample 1	Not applicable: Articulative	upbeat to m. 9	1
Sample 2	Not applicable: Articulative	m. 9	1

Example 6.2. 808 State, "Cubik (Kings County Perspective)," loops in mm. 9–16 (0.16–0.32) with respect to an eight-bar sequence.
Courtesy of ZTT Music.

while, the length of the track as a whole helps to rule out the possibility of longer sequences: 184 measures is a multiple of eight (8 × 23), but not of sixteen or twenty-four.

Several questions remain regarding this analysis, however. First, the track is actually slightly longer than 184 measures (see p. 298). Although all sounds with definite rhythmic articulations cease at the end of measure 184, the short fadeout that follows causes the track to last a few seconds more. Nevertheless, as the termination of the last complete textural combination provides a very definite point of closure, one realizes that the track is structurally complete after the last F♯ in the bass line.

The interpretation of the beginning of the track is a more difficult matter. As discussed in chapter 3, the opening is quite ambiguous metrically; it is possible to hear a variety of different interpretations, shown in example 3.2 (p. 126), none of which correspond to the beat placement arising after the entrance of the bass drum. In interpretations *a* and *c,* the track begins on a downbeat, whereas interpretation *b* starts with an upbeat lasting for five sixteenth notes.[6] The textural graph, however, follows a producer-based approach to form, interpreting the entire track according to the meter that is eventually established. According to this reading, the track starts out with a dotted-quarter-note upbeat, as shown by the metrical placement of the bass line in the sound palette (p. 294). In accordance with my continuing emphases on interpretive multiplicity and diverse modes of musical interaction, I contend that the tension created by these differing perspectives need not be resolved. The listener, who is free to experiment among a variety of metrical interpretations, may not experience the opening as an upbeat. Producers, however, generally work with technology that expects the bar line and time signature to be fixed throughout a work—although they have clearly found many ingenious ways of enabling multiple metrical experiences within these constraints.

One might also question the status of the eight-bar sequence on the basis of the changes that occur in measures 119 and 149. In the first of these events, riffs 2 and 3 enter just six bars after the previous change (m. 113), and in measure 149, synth 1 comes in twenty bars after the removal of synth 2 in measure 129. In spite of these apparent irregularities, these changes can be situated within larger durations that *are* multiples of eight: after measure 119, the next change occurs ten bars later, suggesting a sixteen-bar span between measures 113 and 129; the change in measure 149 is followed by a twelve-bar duration, which suggests a larger thirty-two bar span.[7] The freeness with which the entrances in measures 119 and 149 are situated with respect to the work's generally uniform patterning might be taken to suggest an Adam-Jay-like tweaking of textural parameters based on intuition while a sequence of fixed length plays beneath. Other changes within the track, such as the bass drum removals in measures 112 and 160, also may have been improvised in this manner, of course, though this cannot be determined solely from listening. Furthermore, these other alterations, in contrast to those that create unusual divisions, do not stand out as interpretive issues.

Although an eight-bar sequence appears likely after analyzing and transcrib-

6. These interpretations also become relevant at the end of the track when the bass drum drops out in measure 177. At this point, interpretation *b* seems most likely: it involves displacement by just a single sixteenth note, and those who follow it will hear the track ending on a downbeat with the arrival of F♯ in the bass line.

7. Also relevant is the gradual fade-in of riffs 2 and 3, which makes it difficult to associate their entrance with any precise moment. Although the fade-in starts in measure 119, it does not create a definite point of articulation marking this measure for significance (in contrast, for example, to the entrance of the bass drum in m. 81).

ing "Connected," this sequence is not especially perceptible. Ruskin often allows as many as two or three uninterrupted repetitions of eight-bar durations,[8] a tendency that clearly has much to do with the underdetermination of multimeasure patterning in the work and also suggests one reason that listeners classify his work as "minimal techno." This underdetermination further highlights the gap between the perspectives of producer and listener. The sequence still affects the sounds that we hear in the track—for most of the textural and articulative changes are structured around it—but it is not immediately obvious as a particular sonic entity.

The opposite situation occurs in "How to Play Our Music" and "Cubik." In these works, multimeasure patterning and hypermeter are quite clear,[9] but the length of the sequence is ambiguous. "How to Play Our Music" is the more straightforward of the two (see textural graph, pp. 319–23). Given the prevalence of eight-measure spans, it seems to be based on an eight-bar sequence (note the regularity of eight-bar changes in the first fifty-six measures, for instance). However, because it relies almost exclusively on pure-duple multimeasure patterning, it could just as easily be based on a sequence of four, sixteen, or even thirty-two bars.

One detail crucial to these arguments is the interpretation of the last twenty-one seconds of the track (6:07–28). As in "Connected," a fadeout occurs during the final moments, though it lasts longer here. Once again I locate the structural close of the track prior to the fadeout, at the downbeat of measure 193; the rest of the track consists of two iterations of the sequence (assuming an eight-bar duration), one complete and one partial, as the track winds down. Under this reading, the "complete" portion of the track lasts 192 measures, a duration that preserves (up to the thirty-two-bar level) the pure-duple symmetry that is clearly so essential to the work. As in many rock and pop songs, the use of a fadeout following the end of "the song" suggests that the track as a whole is really one big groove (or cycle, loop, sequence, etc.) that could repeat infinitely if allowed.

Four- and eight-bar hypermeasures are clear throughout much of "Cubik" (see textural graph, pp. 290–93). However, a number of the track's features make the primary sequential duration difficult to determine (assuming that such a du-

---

8. Ruskin does bring about very gradual changes within some of these lengthy underdetermined passages, however. For instance, the fade-in of riffs 2 and 3 across the twenty-four-bar span of measures 49–72 creates a relatively dynamic effect within the passage in spite of its overall textural stasis. The process is comparable to the drawn-out timbral changes that slowly transform the rhythmically static sections of Plastikman's "Panikattack."

9. At the same time, the beginning of "How to Play Our Music," prior to the entrance of the bass drum, is characterized by the same sort of accentual ambiguity found in "Connected."

ration exists). First, the rate of change is much quicker than in the other tracks I have discussed; most of the alterations (which involve a large number of both textural and articulative changes) appear in increments of two, four, and eight bars. Second, a number of six-bar durations occur, as well as isolated instances of one-, three-, and twelve-bar spans. Third, the last audible sound happens in measure 183, but the track does not end for another seven seconds.

The one-, three-, and twelve-bar durations are not especially difficult to explain. The twelve-bar group (mm. 143–54) demarcated by the prominent textural change at measure 155 is balanced out by the four-bar group that follows, resulting in a larger span of sixteen measures. In measures 75–78, durations of one and three measures combine to form a four-measure group, albeit with unusual features such as typically anacrustic gestures leading to the second and fourth bars rather than the first and third. The six-bar spans of measures 89–94 and 105–110 also can be interpreted along these lines. However, the six measures of measures 57–62 are more problematic. This span—the first in the track whose duration is not a multiple of four or eight—does not combine with another to form a larger pure-duple duration. In relation to the regular patterns that precede and follow it (mm. 49–56 and 63–70 form clear eight-bar groups with strong pure-duple divisions), it can only be explained as either a deletion or insertion of two bars. For this reason, I have shifted the four-bar patterning used as the basis of the textural graph two bars to the right beginning in measure 63. This shift is supported by the location of most of the subsequent textural changes as well as by the point at which the track ends.[10]

Interpreting this alteration as the result of a deletion suggests that this particular mix of the track might originally have been two measures longer, and that the seven-second silence at the end is not gratuitous but the result of a sharp fadeout. According to this interpretation, the sounding duration of the track is actually 186 measures. When the two deleted measures are added, the total

10. A producer could make this sort of deletion or insertion with sequencing software such as Pro Tools, although in the case of this track the technology involved would be that available ca. 1990. An interesting phenomenon that is possibly related to this change involves riff 1: between measures 51 and 94, this pattern appears to be shifted with respect to the previously established four-bar hypermeter. In measures 51–52 and 55–56, the material previously found in the first and second measures of the loop now appears in the third and fourth bars of the hypermeasure. Further alterations appear beginning in measure 143.

It is also interesting to consider the perception of the six-bar unit in measures 57–62 with respect to the surrounding four-bar hypermeter. Does measure 63 sound like it comes early? Or do measures 57–62 seem like a four-bar hypermeasure with a two-bar extension? I favor the former hearing, which would support the use of deletion rather than insertion. The sense of reinterpretation is not very strong, however, since none of the loops used in this passage last for longer than two bars.

length becomes 188, which would work with a four-bar sequence, but not with an eight- or sixteen-bar one.

Because "How to Play Our Music" is so completely symmetrical, I speculate that its multimeasure delineations were probably planned out rather than improvised (with the possible exception of certain sporadic variations, such as those involving the bass drum in mm. 57–60 and 81–84; see p. 320). Although this is simply a hypothesis based on the characteristics of the track, the presence of such highly organized structure within a recorded track does point toward the use of a predetermined plan of sequences (method *b*) as the more likely production technique.

In contrast, the structure of "Cubik" (pp. 290–93) seems to be arranged much more freely. This characteristic does not make its form less interesting, of course, but it does undermine the clear determination of whether multimeasure delineations were planned out or improvised (method *a*). The large number of changes might be taken to suggest that the producers created the track by assembling a series of sequences (method *b*) rather than through live improvisation. Even if this is the case, however, no overarching formal plan is apparent; except for a general increase in the rate of change during the middle of the work (see esp. mm. 49–118), the prevailing aesthetic seems to be "let's change something now." To implement these changes solely through improvisation (method *a*) would probably require several run-throughs: perhaps one for changes within the sequence(s), then another to add the samples. One factor that supports this reading is the tendency of the samples to occur at different points within the measure. For instance, sample 2 appears *before* the downbeats in measures 21–24 and *after* the downbeats in measures 41–44 (see p. 290); this could indicate that the producers first established a relatively consistent sequential backdrop and then freely layered the samples on top of it. In any event, regardless of how various passes through the track might have functioned, it is clear that more than one stage of production was involved because this version of "Cubik" is a remix.

Other changes that may have been improvised during the production of "Cubik" include occasional anacrustic removals, either of all parts (as in m. 75) or of every part except one (as in m. 134).[11] Adam Jay describes how the latter type of cut might arise during the context of live production:

> *Adam Jay:* And then in the middle of the sequence, the same way I can bring certain tracks out, I can also hit this solo button and make it so it only plays this one sound. . . .

11. See textural graph, pp. 291–92; also refer back to example 5.2, ch. 5, p. 190.

Mark Butler: Tell me what you did again here?

Adam Jay: Basically, that bass line that's there, as, sort of like the middle of the track—the part where the DJ's not mixing; he's cueing up his next record—I just made it so only that bass line's playing.

Mark Butler: Oh, all right.

Adam Jay: So, right now that's all that's playing. And on the mixer I'm bringing out different frequencies there.

Mark Butler: Right, right.

Adam Jay: And then, I just hit that solo button again and it all comes back in.

The method of production also can have a significant impact on the length of a track. Although the duration of the sequence must be decided ahead of time, the number of times it repeats may depend upon judgments made in the moment, as I was surprised to discover during my conversation with Adam Jay:

Adam Jay: So this track finally did two sequences. But I probably had sixteen parts total that I'm bringing in and out.

Mark Butler: OK. So your two sequences were two sort of total combinations? And, how many ... So the whole track is a multiple of sixteen bars?

Adam Jay: Right.

Mark Butler: How many is it total?

Adam Jay: This track's about six and a half minutes long. It's probably around three hundred bars or so.

Mark Butler: OK. So it's sort of free in terms of how many times you want to repeat the sequence?

Adam Jay: Oh yeah. I mean, at the end of this track, I really liked how it sounded when I took out the drums to bring it all down; I really liked what the synths started doing, and then [I] messed with the effects, so I went an extra sixteen. You know? Just on the fly. It felt good at the time.

This approach has significant formal implications. First, the most important structural elements within electronic dance music are its repeating units—its loops and sequences. The use of these patterns within a track may suggest a predetermined compositional structure, but in many cases will not. This does not mean that quasi-improvised tracks are formless; as subsequent discussion will reveal, certain formal shapes recur. Producers' approaches to these shapes, however, are often quite free, and in many cases the form that is achieved is more a result of the ways in which those making the music interact with the loops and sequences than an end unto itself.

One attribute that the textural graphs make clear is the tendency of producers to keep sequences and loops intact. With the exception of upbeat removals, which are pervasive, most loops are heard in their entirety, and sounds are most often added or removed at the beginnings of sequences. Such characteristics may stem from technological limitations (with some equipment, it is impossible to cut off loops at a midpoint in real time) or from the habit of following the sequence's progression on-screen while recording (as suggested by Adam Jay's comment that "when sixteen is over I'll know that it's time for me to change it up").

Producers often circumvent this tendency toward wholeness with fade-ins and fade-outs. We have already encountered several tracks employing the latter technique in their final measures; in each case, a sequence fades away before reaching its end, thus providing a graceful way of ending the track within the context of a medium based on repetition rather than formal closure. Sometimes producers include fades within tracks as well, as in "Jerical" (pp. 300–303), where they help soften the track's otherwise relentlessly hard edges. After the abrupt entrances of the bass drum, hi-hat 1 and 2, snare drum, and handclap in measures 1–17 (and the razor-sharp removal of all parts in the second half of m. 24), Mills allows riff 1a and b to enter the texture very gradually. Fade-ins and -outs also can provide textural interest, even as they foster (hyper)metrical underdetermination. In measures 61–80, for example, Mills slowly brings in the bass line and toms while simultaneously decreasing the volume of riff 1a and b. No other textural changes occur in this passage: the fades are its most noticeable processes, yet they also make it difficult for the listener to associate the entrances of these instruments with any precise location. Measure 81, however, stands out very distinctly; Mills marks it for significance by abruptly cutting off what remains of the riff as well as the snare and bass drums. The preceding fade-ins and -outs make the suddenness of these textural changes all the more noticeable. Measure 97 also stands out through contrast: here, a number of parts previously associated with fades (the toms, bass line, and riff) now enter and exit the texture suddenly.

Thus far, I have emphasized the sequence as a repeating formal entity controlling a number of different loops. From the producer's standpoint, loops within the sequence must be aligned in a precisely defined way. However, from a perceptual standpoint (and, more specifically, from a metrical standpoint), they often seem to be nonaligned, generating metrical dissonance. How do metrical dissonances interact with sequence-based form in electronic dance music?

It is easy to envision how sequential production practices might create the effect of turning the beat around. Imagine, for instance, a producer building the first half of a track from a single sequence. Although this sequence might consist of a number of different parts—perhaps a hi-hat, a bass drum, two synths, and a sample—most of these instruments would be muted at the beginning. The sequence would proceed as normal, and the listener would make metrical interpretations based on the sounds that are not muted. If the track began with sounds that normally occur on the offbeats (such as hi-hats) and without the usual on-beat sounds (the bass drum), the offbeat sounds would seem referential. As the producer unmuted the bass drum and other on-beat sounds, however, the beat would seem to turn around. Hence, the listener's interpretations may be subject to change even when the sequence itself is not.[12]

Embedded grouping dissonances, however, are more problematic for sequential approaches to production. Sequences are usually based on pure-duple values, with which these dissonances will never align. How do producers overcome this difficulty? Although further research into specific production practices is necessary, two possible approaches seem likely. On the one hand, producers might create two or more sequences that operate independently. Although older, simpler technology would not allow this, more recent tools would, as one participant, Stanley, suggested. One possible example of this technique is James Ruskin's "Connected." In this track, no obvious relationship exists between the two dissonant layers and the eight-bar sequence governing the other instruments. Unfolding continuously throughout the majority of the track (from 1:26 to 3:07 and from 3:32 to the end), riffs 2 and 3 seem to have their own periodicity, one that will never be commensurate with the primary sequential duration.[13]

Another possibility is to integrate the dissonant layer into the rest of the track's sequences. This is the approach that Azzido Da Bass and Timo Maas employ in "Dooms Night." In this track, the producers foreground the relationship between the sequence and the embedded grouping dissonance through obvious manipulation of the dissonant layer. This manipulation becomes apparent during measures 49–88, the passage in which synth 3 emerges as a dissonant layer. Instead of allowing the dissonance to play out continuously in the manner of the Ruskin track, the producers keep "resetting" it: in measures 65 and 73, they move synth 3 back half a beat, so that its first note returns to the "and" of beat one, the metrical position with which it began the passage in measure 49 (see textural graph, p. 269). These changes, which are highlighted by articulative sounds, emphasize pure-duple multimeasure divisions within measures 49–88 (specifically, sixteen, eight, and sixteen). As a result, they make synth 3 seem even more dissonant against the very clear 4/4 meter, while also calling attention

12. When I spoke to Rick Smith of Underworld about "Cups," I described the TBA in terms of the synthesizer and hi-hat establishing a certain beat pattern, saying "and then the bass drum comes in on the eighth note off, basically, and shifts everything." Smith replied "Yes. ... yes. ... or *seems* to shift everything," thus making a clear distinction between producer- and perception-oriented ways of thinking about the track.

13. The recording does not provide enough information to determine the duration of any sequence(s) governing the dissonant layers, since there are no changes within these sounds that would indicate a pattern beginning anew.

to the relationship between this layer and the eight-bar sequence used in the track.

The reasons for claiming eight bars as the sequential duration of "Dooms Night" should be fairly obvious. As the textural graph and form chart (p. 273) show, every large section of the track lasts for a multiple of eight measures except for measures 89–116, which—as previously suggested (ch. 5, pp. 200–201)—can be understood as a forty-eight-bar section in which the tempo accelerates. Although the rate of textural change increases as the track progresses, to the extent that a four-bar sequence might appear more likely in passages such as measures 117–56, the most dramatic alterations tend to occur in multiples of eight throughout. The placement of atmospheric and articulative sounds within the first and third breakdowns (see mm. 25–48 and 157–80) provide especially strong evidence for an eight-measure sequence. There is no obvious perceptual reason for these changes; they occur within passages that are clearly meant to foreground synth 3 and are barely audible. Instead, they seem to function as almost subliminal reminders of the sequence's vestigial presence.

This reading suggests three different sequences involving the dissonant layer: one starting with beat 1.5, another with beat 1, and a third with beat 2. If they are allowed to occur unimpeded (that is, if they are not "reset"), they will occur in this order; I will therefore refer to them as A, B, and C, respectively. Example 6.3 shows these three sequences in order in a continuous twenty-four-bar succession.[14] The consonant layers are shown in a simplified format that includes the bass drum, snare drum, and bass line only.

Interpreting the track according to these sequences provides a cogent reading of all its formal sections.[15] Within the first forty-eight measures, before the dissonance has begun, recurring time spans prepare for its emergence. The twenty-four-bar duration articulated by measures 1–24 and 25–48 has special significance as the shortest length of time that will allow the dissonance to return to its starting point *and* line up with the eight-bar duration on which the se-

14. This example does not represent a specific passage in the piece, but rather an idealization of the three possible eight-bar sequences. In order to see how each passage can function as an independent sequence, it is important to keep in mind that a sequence consists of a combination of parts. Hence these three possibilities represent three distinct ways that all the parts can be combined within the context of an eight-bar duration.

15. During the following discussion, the reader may also refer to the textural graph and form chart (pp. 268–73). In the latter, the highest row of numbers above each box indicates the beat on which synth 3 begins within that formal section. The appearance of more than one number (as in the first Groove + S3 section) indicates a resetting to a particular beat; otherwise, synth 3 proceeds unimpeded. The number immediately above each box indicates the total number of synth 3 articulations during that section.

Example 6.3. Azzido Da Bass, "Dooms Night (Timo Maas Mix),"
hypothetical sequences involving the dissonant layer (synth 3).

quence is based. In other words, although the EGD can align with the predominantly four-bar hypermeter after only twelve measures, twenty-four bars are needed for it to return to a point of alignment with the sequential duration. When the soon-to-be-dissonant layer first appears in measures 25–48, therefore, we can imagine the passage to consist of sequences A, B, and C, in that order, with all parts muted except for synth 3 and certain atmospheric sounds.

After the first breakdown, the next section (mm. 49–88) uses the succession A B // A // A B. The double slashes indicate points at which the producers reset the track to sequence A (1.5), instead of allowing it to continue to sequence C (2). Because of this resetting process, measures 49–88 emphasize the sequence with which the dissonance began. Ending the passage with sequence B, however, leads naturally into sequence C, with which the next breakdown, as well as the next dissonant section (mm. 117–56), begins.

The second breakdown, measures 89–116, has already been explained as an accelerated forty-eight-bar span. Because it begins with and is also followed by sequence C, we can assume that it consists of two cycles of sequences C, A, and B. The following dissonant section, measures 117–56, continues in this vein, allowing the track to continue through sequences C, A, B, C, and A; unlike the first dissonant section, this passage does not reset the sequence. As a result, the next breakdown, measures 157–80, begins with a point of metrical, hypermetrical, and sequential alignment. It also ends on such a point: like the first breakdown, it cycles through an entire three-sequence succession (B C A) once within its twenty-four-bar duration. After this process is complete, the dissonant layer leaves the texture (m. 181).

To summarize, the treatment of metrical dissonance in "Dooms Night" suggests the following sequential process:

1. Mm. 25–48: Starts with sequence A (beat 1.5) and cycles through all the sequences once.
2. Mm. 49–88: The first dissonant section emphasizes the starting sequence (A) with the succession A B // A // A B, which leads into the sequence starting with beat 2 (sequence C).
3. Mm. 89–116: The second breakdown cycles two times through sequences C, A, and B, although the duration of the sequence becomes perceptually irrelevant due to the accelerando.
4. Mm. 117–56: The next section starts with the beat-2 sequence and cycles through all the sequences in order: C A B C A.
5. Mm. 157–80: The third breakdown begins with the beat-1 cycle (B). Continuing through sequences C and A to return to the point at which it began, it

aligns with the downbeat at its conclusion. After completing this cycle, the dissonant synth 3 part disappears.

FORMAL SHAPES IN COMPLETE TRACKS

Thus far, I have been cautious in my approach to form, prefacing my analyses with remarks on ways in which electronic dance music differs from the common-practice repertory. Because of these exceptions, one might imagine that form is not an important feature of EDM and that my concern with it is misguided—the result of a bias that stems from a background in classical-music analysis. However, my experiences in interviews made it clear that this is not the case at all. Participants clearly shared my interest in the formal attributes of EDM; although they did not as a rule use music-theory terms, they spoke about form frequently and spontaneously, often explaining its attributes in great detail.

Several participants described a prototypical formal structure found in many EDM tracks.[16] They based their descriptions primarily on textural changes, which they viewed as directly affecting the intensity or energy level of a track. Stanley explains this prototype in the following passage; as he spoke, he drew a form diagram, of which I provide a close replica in example 6.4.

> *Stanley:* I normally have an intro where I introduce the different melodies that I'm planning on working with, normally in more subdued forms than I will later on—also to get the listener sort of aware of the capabilities of the sounds that are going to be displayed. ... [*Starts sketching.*] I try to think of it like this is the energy level—I try to bring it up slowly, and then I'll have a section. ... And then I'll drop pretty abruptly. ... So it normally ends up looking something like this. . . . [*Returns to the beginning of the diagram.*] And so, I'll slowly bring in the different instruments, and I'll establish a groove. And then, normally in the second half of the song I'll bring in a new instrument—something a little harder, a little harsher, something that ... [is] a little higher in the mix, that either conflicts with or complements something from beforehand in an unexpected way. I'll always kind of get you ready for it. . . . This, to me, is the song [*pointing to first rectangle and drawing a large bracket over it*]—this part. That's what I consider "the song."
>
> *Mark Butler:* That's like the core?
>
> *Stanley:* That's the core of it, yeah. And then I either ... I lead into it, and I drop out, and bring in just a new element for a while—so this [*indicating the first breakdown*] is normally just the new element. And then I bring back in kind of like the song itself, kind of like a reprise, with the new instrument on top of it. So, that's kind of how I see it. And not every song goes by this formula. But I discover that, even listening to something, that's kind of what I want to hear. I like the groove, and I like it to be an established rhythmical

---

16. In each case, participants used the word "structure" before I did.

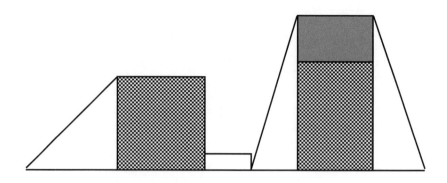

Example 6.4. Prototypical form of an EDM track, as drawn by Stanley.

thing. And this is not verse-chorus-verse-chorus-bridge-chorus-outro, that sort of thing. But it is a formula that I've found to work for me. And I don't really like to think of it as a formula; it's just kind of what naturally occurs when I'm making these tracks. It's like, OK, well, something more needs to happen here, because I've listened to this for however long and it's not doing it for me anymore.

Despite the primacy of texture in this model of form, rhythm and meter also play a role in delineating sections. The length of sections is measured according to rhythmic features such as beats and bars, and textural changes can have metrical consequences due to the close relationship of metrical and textural layers. In DJ Shiva's explanation of the characteristic structure of a techno track,[17] both texture and intensity loom large; however, Shiva also describes the sections within this structure in terms of the number of beats they contain and their relationship to the main beat:

> *Cornelia Fales:* And didn't you say last time that there's a whole sequence of kinds of phrases on each record?[18]
> *DJ Shiva:* Yeah.
> *Cornelia Fales:* Can you tell us what that sequence is again?
> *DJ Shiva:* Yeah, it's pretty much … you have the intro beats like I said for thirty-two or sixty-four beats; and then you usually have a little breakdown, for about sixteen beats, where they take the beat out, and you have maybe the introduction of the bass line or the introduction of the synth line. It's where they're introducing the meat of the song, basically, and also building up the

17. The following quotation comes from the second of two such explanations during our interview.
18. Here and in the following sentence, Fales is using "sequence" in a general sense, not in the technical sense described earlier in this chapter.

crowd. That's usually where you mix out or you cut the other record out and maybe cut back in. ... Then the beat drops again and you've got the thick part of the song, where you've got the main synth line, the main bass line. And they sort of play with that for a little bit—and that's pretty negotiable, how long they play with that. Then sometimes it just plays out, and they take the sounds out and just leave you with a sparse beat. [Or] sometimes there's another breakdown, maybe a longer one, usually more intense, like they really make the synth line—they tweak it out, they reverb the hell out of it, or whatever. ... They really make it dramatic, basically. And then the beat gets introduced back in, usually around sixteen or thirty-two on that. Then you have the sounds—like the bass lines and synth lines—usually kind of work their way out until you've just got the sparse beat of the song. So, you pretty much know what's going to happen, for the most part. So it is pretty structured.

Although DJ Shiva's and Stanley's descriptions are not identical, they are remarkably similar. Both describe a track that begins and ends with a thin texture. Within the track, there are several gradual buildups as well as sudden reductions in the number of instruments present. In addition, both participants refer to a section that seems to represent the track in its most essential form: Stanley calls this passage "the song," and also finds the term "core" acceptable, while Shiva refers to it as "the meat of the song."[19] I will refer to it subsequently as the "core." Stanley's model has a two-core structure, in which the second core is more intense: Intro-Buildup-Core/Breakdown-Buildup-Core/Outro.[20] DJ Shiva de-scribes two possible models, the first with one core and the second with two. Her description of the two-core model is as follows: Intro/Breakdown-Buildup-Core/Breakdown-Core/Outro.[21] Although she places the first breakdown after the intro, and she does not refer to a buildup preceding the second core, the overall shape she describes is the same as the one detailed by Stanley.

In addition, both participants refer to the same repertoire of formal sec-tions—intros, buildups (or "builds"), cores, breakdowns, and outros—which they associate with similar attributes and techniques. The intro is characterized by a thin texture, often starting out with just a bass drum, or "sparse beats." It not only begins the piece but also presents its main elements—as Stanley puts it

19. In the above quotation, DJ Shiva refers to "the meat" while describing how its material is introduced (she mentions a section where "they're introducing the meat of the song"). From the overall context of the interview, however, it was clear that she conceived of "the meat" as equivalent to the "core" or "the song" (and of the first part of the song as introducing this material). The "thick part of the song" referenced later is comparable to the meat plus one or more additional instruments, as seen in the peak of Stanley's graph.

20. Slashes divide the track into segments ending with cores.

21. In an earlier reference to the form of a techno track, which is not quoted here, DJ Shiva described the second of these two models only, thereby suggesting that it is the more common one.

quite elegantly, it makes the listener "aware of the capabilities of the sounds that are going to be displayed."

During the buildup, various instruments are added to the texture, usually one at a time. This process increases intensity—not only by thickening the texture but also by filling in various rhythmic positions within the measure. The buildup is not sharply delineated from its surrounding neighbors, the intro and the core; in this sense, it is more a technique than a distinct section.

In contrast, no single underlying textural process characterizes the core. In this section, the track has reached a degree of textural density typical for the genre; though changes may occur, the number of parts remains more or less the same. This passage best represents "the song" because it contains all or most of the track's characteristic sounds. In a well-made track, the combination of these sounds will be enough to create a sense of dynamism even though the texture of the passage remains relatively static. Within the track as a whole, however, producers often create additional intensity by repeating the core with a new, more intense element.

Unlike the buildup, the breakdown stands out very clearly from the section that precedes it, since it involves a sudden, dramatic drop to a thin texture. The bass drum is almost always removed, and usually most of the other instruments as well, so that a single instrument or small combination of instruments is featured. As the section unfolds, the producer and/or DJ will often "tweak out" these instruments by manipulating them timbrally with the EQs and (especially) the effects. Both audience and performers perceive tweaking as an intensifying technique; it usually culminates in the return of the bass drum. After a breakdown, the bass drum may reenter the texture abruptly or at the end of another buildup. If a buildup is used, it is usually shorter than the initial one, as shown in Stanley's diagram.

During the outro, instruments gradually drop out and the track returns to a thin texture. In this sense, the section is the mirror image of the intro and buildup. However, it is less important to the track as a whole: the sounds it contains have already been heard, and DJs have often begun another track by this point (in which case they may skip this section altogether). As a result, it is shorter than the opening, combining the functions of textural decrescendo and closing within a single section.

Although certain characteristics recur quite frequently in DJs' and producers' descriptions of the form of EDM tracks, it is clear that they treat this structure quite freely. In the quotations I have presented, Stanley takes care to note that this prototype is not a "formula," and DJ Shiva describes more than one possibility. Shiva also varies slightly in the number of beats she ascribes to certain sections, even though she is quite consistent in her description of the track as a whole. In the passage just cited, she describes the intro as lasting for thirty-two or sixty-four beats (eight or sixteen 4/4 measures), but earlier in the interview she gave this length as sixty-four or 128 beats (sixteen or thirty-two 4/4 measures). Thus, although pure-duple durations are most common, the length of sections may vary. This variation illustrates yet another dimension of flexibility in EDM's form. Like sequences, sections within tracks are relatively predictable structures that can be treated in a wide variety of ways. Although constraints do exist—for instance, certain unwritten rules seem to guide the order in which sections appear (one does not have a core followed by a buildup, or an intro followed immediately by a core), considerable freedom is nevertheless possible. Both the length of each section and the number of each section type are treated flexibly, and some freedom is allowed in terms of possible successions (e.g., a breakdown may be followed either by a buildup or by an immediate return to the core). Thus the prototypical form described here is best understood not so much as a distinct formal structure as a recurring shape that embodies certain fundamental principles of construction and growth in EDM.

Although these principles are simple and relatively few in number, their manifestations in individual compositions are quite diverse. Some tracks are quite similar to the prototype, while others utilize EDM's formal techniques in less obvious ways. Let us now consider two tracks in which the prototypical form is quite apparent. We will begin with Mario Più's "Communication" (refer to textural graph, pp. 312–17). This track starts out with an unusually long intro section featuring sixty-four measures of "sparse beats"; during this passage, the only sounds are a beat (the bass drum), a backbeat (riff 1), a decorative synth pattern (riff 2), and intermittent articulative sounds. The bass drum reaches full volume in measure 18, and the articulative sounds increase in frequency as the section unfolds. The removal of the bass drum in measure 65 signals the start of the first breakdown. Two features of DJ Shiva's comments on breakdowns are noticeable during this passage: first, the introduction of a new sound (SD2, m. 81), and second, a gradual increase in intensity. This intensification is enhanced greatly through the periodic doubling of rhythmic values in snare drum 3a (mm. 97–116), which leads to an increasingly fast surface rhythm. This rise in activity points to an overlap between the functions of "breakdown" and "buildup"; even as the absence of the bass drum marks measures 65–118 as a distinct section, techniques such as the rhythmic diminution build up anticipation for its return. These formal functions are conflated even further in measures 167–76, where the diminution is accompanied by a rise in pitch—a characteristic example of "tweaking"—within riff 2.

Between these two breakdown-plus-buildup sections is the first core, or "the song" (mm. 119–66), identifiable through the presence of the bass drum, riff 1, and three snare-drum sounds. The return of riff 2 near the end of this section (m. 159) creates a slight overlap with the following breakdown. The second core (mm. 177–200), just as Stanley described, is more intense because of the (re)introduction of this riff and its attendant rise in pitch. Both sections are more or less static texturally; in fact, the first is unusually so, lasting for forty-eight measures with very few changes. The removal of several parts in measures 201–208 (also note the fade-out of riff 3 beginning around m. 221) initiates the textural decrescendo associated with the outro (mm. 201–44); like the intro, this section is also quite long.

In "Communication," the prototypical form is strikingly obvious. In fact, such dramatically articulated formal features are a hallmark of its genre, which is trance.[22] Trance and related genres such as progressive house typically feature especially climactic builds, in which devices such as snare drum rolls (of which the diminution of snare drum 3a in this track is a rather regimented example) and crescendi create dramatic increases in intensity. In fact, the obviousness of these characteristics is a major point of criticism for those who do not like the genre—a group that includes many techno fans. I played "Communication" during my interview with DJ Shiva, with the intention of discussing the passages in which the beat turns around; however, the conversation quickly gravitated toward the formal features of the track and their aesthetic qualities. The following excerpt is representative of our discussion of the track, which Shiva described as "almost cheesy-Euro-trancey":

> Mark Butler: [as track plays; near end of core 1] This has that structure that you were talking about. So now we're in whatever is "the meat," and pretty soon we're going to get to the breakdown. But then this part [core 1] goes on for a really long time. [Breakdown/buildup 2 starts.] So we have another little buildup here.
> DJ Shiva: This is also [one of] those obvious builds … buildups—you know what I mean? Snare rolls …
> Cornelia Fales: Going up the …

22. When Frankie Bones plays this track on his DJ mix You Know My Name, he introduces changes that moderate its exaggerated formal features to a certain extent. He skips the entire intro, beginning instead during the first breakdown, around measure 72. Leading up to this point, in place of the intro, he substitutes about eight bars of another track's bass-drum beats. (Here I use the words "around" and "about" because fade-ins and -outs obscure exact entry points.) In measure 201 of "Communication" (the beginning of the outro), he starts to bring in the next record, and he cuts off "Communication" after measure 224 (thereby reducing the outro to twenty-four measures). Through these alterations he reduces the unusual length of certain sections and of the track as a whole, while still preserving the same overall shape.

DJ Shiva: Yeah, we're all about just bringing you up and smashing you down, and not making you think anywhere along the way.

Nevertheless, DJ Shiva associated a structure very much like that found in "Communication" with the typical techno track. How might that structure be manifested in a composition of that genre, and how does its appearance in techno differ from that of trance? In order to answer these questions, we will consider "Sighting," a track by techno producer Dave Angel (see textural graph, pp. 282–86). Like "Communication," "Sighting" is based on ordered successions of buildups, cores, and breakdowns, although its textural processes suggest three main segments instead of two. The number of patterns used, with articulative sounds omitted, is as follows: 2-3-4-5-6-7 / 1-4-5-6-7-6-7-5-6 / 1-2-4-6-7-8-7-8 / 3-5-6-7-6-4-5-1. The primary factor demarcating the beginning of a segment is the sharp textural reduction that accompanies the start of each breakdown. Within each segment, there is an overall process of textural growth (the obvious exception, of course, being the outro). The overall form, then, is as follows:

Intro: mm. 1–16 (duration: 16 mm.)
Buildup/Core 1: mm. 17–32 (duration: 16 mm.)
Alternate interpretation: mm. 1–32 = Intro (but with a clear division at m. 17)

Breakdown 1: mm. 33–40 (duration: 8 mm.)
Buildup/Core 2: mm. 41–88 (duration: 48 mm.)

Breakdown 2: mm. 89–100 (duration: 12 mm.)
Buildup/Core 3: mm. 101–36 (duration: 36 mm.)

Breakdown 3: mm. 137–40 (duration: 4 mm.)
Outro: mm. 141–204 (duration: 64 mm.)
Alternate interpretation: mm. 141–68 = Buildup/Core 4, and mm. 169–204 = Outro

Although certain textural processes—namely, building up, maintaining a relatively thick texture, dropping back to a thin texture, and gradually thinning out the texture—are evident, Angel applies them relatively freely, so that some passages can be interpreted in more than one way. For instance, although the beginning of measure 17 is strongly articulated due to the textural removal and articulative sound that precede it, it is possible to hear measures 1–32 as one large section, as the number of parts is steadily increasing until measure 33.[23]

23. If this section is described simply as an intro, then the form of the track matches the second model given by DJ Shiva exactly. The length of the section also corresponds to one of the durations she mentioned earlier in the interview (128 beats).

The final sixty-four measures also can be interpreted as either two sections or one. Furthermore, in contrast to "Communication," no clear point of division separates the end of each buildup from the beginning of the subsequent core; buildups occur after, rather than before, the return of the bass drum.

The ways in which Angel builds the energy level are also more subtle, relying on gradual textural changes (note that the number of instruments present rarely changes by more than two except at the beginnings of breakdowns) and processes of rhythmic intensification (e.g., increases in the variety of durations articulated by the loops) rather than rhythmic diminutions or rising pitch levels. He also maintains energy within the relatively static core sections by varying the texture considerably even after it has become fairly dense. Throughout measures 105–33, for instance, seven to eight instruments are present at any given time; however, two different seven-part and two different eight-part combinations are used (compare m. 105 with 121, and m. 113 with 129). The breakdowns are relatively short, often involving the characteristic presentation of a new synth part (in the first breakdown this part is also subtly tweaked), which is subsequently combined with the core to increase intensity further.

In short, both "Sighting" and "Communication" reveal a structure characteristic of many EDM tracks. In "Communication," the realization of this structure is very similar to the prototype, whereas "Sighting" exhibits the overall shape and growth procedures associated with the prototype without corresponding to it exactly. This difference is not surprising given the genres of the two tracks. Not only is form in trance typically expressed much more markedly, it is also much more commonly built into the record by the producer, whereas techno tracks are often considerably more static and generic prior to their manipulation by the DJ.

Although participants described these differences in a variety of ways, their accounts resonate strongly with each other. Stanley contrasts his first description of form (quoted earlier) with the more neutral approach found in many techno tracks:

> Stanley: And this is something I think a lot of techno looks like. [*Draws another diagram; see ex. 6.5.*] They'll be bringing things up and down in it, but it's all pretty much the same intensity level. And that makes a lot of sense for techno DJs, because techno is treated a lot more as a tool for the DJs. . . . Whereas with trance I think it's a lot more melodic and it relies more on a traditional structure.

Although Stanley does not limit his first description of form to trance alone, it is clear that he views trance, in contrast to techno, as involving many changes

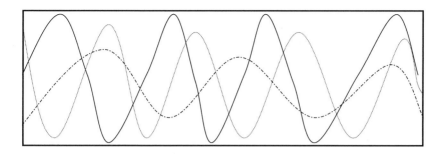

Example 6.5. Form in a techno track, as drawn by Stanley.

in intensity level. Furthermore, as these formal comparisons arose within an explanation of his own music, which is generally closer to trance than other genres, it is not surprising that the form he described earlier matches that of "Communication" so closely.

Stanley's discussion of form seems to be based on the structure of individual records prior to their manipulation by the DJ (hence his description of techno as "a tool for the DJs"), although he does not explicitly compare these two types of form. In my conversation with DJ Shiva, I did ask about the relationship between the two, and she provided an enlightening response:

> *Mark Butler:* And in terms of—you know, we were talking about the structure of tracks—they always have those breakdowns built into them, but it seems like a lot of DJing is making the breakdowns yourself, and finding your own places to put the bass in.
> *DJ Shiva:* To me that's the essence of techno. [In] a lot of DJ-based music that's built in for you. Drum 'n' bass: you have massive bass buildups and breakdowns. Trance: well that's pretty obvious—big wooshy synths and you know … just crap [*laughs*]. House: you've got your vocal breakdowns and stuff, so it's all kind of hook-y and kind of built into it. And so much techno is linear. It's super-linear.
> *Cornelia Fales:* How do you mean "linear"?
> *DJ Shiva:* Like, if you were looking at a drum 'n' bass track, it's kind of like here's the intro beats and here's that first break where the bass starts coming in, and then—*bam!*—here come the choppy beats and then—*bam!*—here comes the next breakdown—then *bam!*—[the beat] drops on you, and then you've got the outro. Techno is kind of like this: [*moves hand in straight horizontal line through air*] and it's like it's up to you to make this [*moves hand up and down*]. It's very loop-based, and very minimal[ly] loop-based. Even when there's a lot going on in a techno song, it's still very loopy and very—to a certain degree—repetitive. But that's kind of the essence of it. You take that repetitiveness and you mesh it with a totally different track which is also somewhat repetitive and then you just work the hell out of it. You can cut back and

forth; you can take the bass out and put the bass back in; you can tweak the mids; you can work the effects. ... I think it gives you a lot more freedom to actually make it your own, instead of just playing records.

Likewise, in a description of live PAs (the medium in which he performs), Neal Blue echoes DJ Shiva's description of the way in which performers interact with techno, as well as Stanley's characterization of trance as more traditional in design:

Mark Butler: I sort of have the impression that when some people do live PAs, a lot of times when they ... particularly when they're working with a computer, it seems less track-based. Like they have a lot of loops loaded into their computer and then they are sort of improvising with the loops. I don't know—do you think that's right, or do you think most people are working with sort of a track in mind?

Neal Blue: Well, it all depends on the type of music too. I think that with, say, trance, that you're definitely working with a song, but with techno, that's based more on tribal rhythms, it is more of an improv, because you can take out certain rhythm structures and put other ones in. And if there's no definition of a song there, and you're playing with those rhythms, then it's all up to improv. But there'll always be some sort of structure to how they're going to go about playing those.

Although both Stanley and Shiva describe techno's structure as linear, it is clear from their comments that this adjective applies primarily to the structure of the tools themselves—the records in isolation and the loops within them—before their manipulation. It is in the hands of a DJ that the peaks and valleys of the prototypical shape assume their most vivid form. In this sense, the markedness of this shape in "Sighting"—although less noticeable than the usual trance track—is nevertheless unusually pronounced; many other techno records are more generic in their unmixed forms. A good example of a track that is relatively linear is "How to Play Our Music" (pp. 319–23). One possible reading of the track's form is as follows:

Intro/Buildup 1: mm. 1–56 (duration: 56 mm.)
Breakdown 1: mm. 57–64 (duration: 8 mm.)[24]
Core 1: mm. 65–80 (duration: 16 mm.)
Breakdown 2: mm. 81–92 (duration: 12 mm.)
Core 2: mm. 93–108 (duration: 16 mm.)
Breakdown 3: mm. 109–12 (duration: 4 mm.)

24. Although the bass drum returns in measure 61, the energy level seems to remain at a lower level until the return of the bass line in measure 65.

Core 3: mm. 113–44 (duration: 32 mm.)
Outro: mm. 145–92 (duration: 48 mm.)
Fadeout: mm. 193-end (duration: ca. 11 mm.)

This interpretation is based primarily on analysis of the number of parts sounding; as a listener, I find it possible but not especially convincing.[25] First, textural density is relatively static, hovering around a level of approximately five instruments throughout the majority of the track. Although the behavior of the bass drum and bass line does suggest certain formal divisions, the absence of pronounced shifts often weakens the effects of the textural changes that do occur. Breakdown 1, for instance, has the same number of instruments as Core 1 (four and then five), the only significant differences being the absence of the bass line in measures 57–65 and of the bass drum in 57–61. Other changes suggest alternate interpretations: the first section might be heard to end at the downbeat of measure 49, where the texture drops back slightly, and it is also debatable whether measures 139–44 should be considered another breakdown (the bass drum drops out, but the change at m. 145 is more pronounced).[26] Thus, while the track contains a great deal of textural variety (the configuration of parts is constantly changing), it is difficult to hear distinct formal sections.

In Carl Craig's "Televised Green Smoke" (pp. 276–79), a distinct formal shape is evident, but it is simpler than the ones described by Stanley and Shiva. Textural patterning, which presents the sequence 2-3-5-6-7-7-8-8-11 / 9-8-6-5-6, creates a clear arch shape.[27] The entire first two-thirds of the track (through m. 136 or 4.29) is a very gradual buildup, followed by a slightly abbreviated reversal of the same process. There is no distinct intro or outro, nor are there any breakdowns.[28] At a very basic level, this type of form *is* similar to the prototype: both begin and end sparsely, gradually building up to a thicker texture

25. The number of instrumental parts used is as follows: 2-3-3-5-5-7-5 / 4-5 // 4-5 // 2-3-4 / 6-5-3-4 / 3 // 6-5-6-5-4-5-4-5 // 4-3-5-4-5-6-5-6 // 4. Two numbers of the same size appear twice in a row only when successive textural combinations consist of different instrumental configurations. Double slashes indicate stronger points of division.

26. If measures 139–44 were perceived as a breakdown, then it might also seem to follow that measures 145–92 are a core rather than an outro. In this track, however, the bass line's role in sustaining momentum seems to be nearly (or just) as important as that of the bass drum: the continuation of the bass line in measures 139–44 makes it difficult to hear this passage as a breakdown, while the removal of this part in measure 145 (along with the thinness of the texture) gives the impression that the track is beginning to wind down.

27. The slash indicates the shift in textural momentum only, not a division between sections.

28. The opening and closing sections in which the bass drum is absent (mm. 1–16 and 177–89, respectively) do stand out from their surrounding material, but each is clearly a part of a larger process. Nor do measures 145–68 have a breakdown effect, given the continuing presence of all the other parts.

in the middle of the track. In "Televised Green Smoke," however, the basic shape lies unformed, awaiting sculpting by the DJ.

Techno records work well as DJ tools because their design is relatively simple, allowing them to be combined in a variety of ways. Beyond this general principle, however, a number of specific formal features contribute to their effective use within DJ sets. Most obviously, the use of sparse beats during the intro and outro facilitates beat matching; as DJ Shiva explained, "when you're layering two records over each other, you layer the outro beats and the intro beats of the next song, and then the breaks all fall in the same spots." Adam Jay, a producer who is also a DJ, explained that he intentionally incorporates this feature into his records with the DJ in mind: "Normally my tracks will start with a lot of drums. That's for the DJ to mix." On a broader level, he notes that the overall thinness of these opening and closing sections has a specific purpose within DJ sets: "For the first minute and a half, two minutes, some stuff will happen, but half the elements aren't going to be in yet. And all the elements will be in [the track] in the middle, but as the track winds down, which is when he'll be—he or she—will be mixing in the next record, I'll bring those elements out, to make room in the mix for sounds from the next record that'll slowly be coming in." In other words, the sections in which the DJ is most likely to be moving from one record to another are intentionally made thinner so that the two records can be overlaid, while the thicker middle sections are more capable of standing on their own.

This tendency is quite evident in the techno tracks presented here. Each begins and ends with a thin texture and thickens during various internal passages. In this sense, each track is arch-like at a fundamental level of design. At the same time, although all tracks start out sparsely, not all begin with "sparse beats." In many cases, the bass drum does not enter until later in the track. Table 6.1 presents a summary of the openings of each track whose beginning I analyzed. Of thirteen tracks considered, only six present the bass drum at the very beginning.[29]

How do such compositions relate to participants' descriptions of the function of intros and outros? One possibility is that the participants think of the beginning of the track in more general terms. Thus the intros of tracks such as "Connected" and "Cubik," which only contain eight measures without beats, are still comprised largely of "sparse beats" and can be accurately described with that term. Another possibility is that some producers choose to avoid the most conventional

29. Tracks whose opening passages are not addressed in the text or appendix C are not included in the table.

Table 6.1. Openings of tracks analyzed.

Producer(s)	Track name	Point at which bass drum enters	Does BD turn beat around?
Dave Angel	"Bounce Back"	m. 1	N/A
Mario Più	"Communication"	m. 1	N/A
Azzido da Bass	"Dooms Night (Timo Maas Mix)"	m. 1	N/A
Jeff Mills	"Jerical"	m. 1	N/A
Plastikman	"Panikattack"	m. 1	N/A
Dave Angel	"Sighting"	m. 1	N/A
James Ruskin	"Connected"	m. 9 (0.15)	Yes
808 State & Frankie Bones	"Cubik (Kings County Perspective)"	m. 9 (0.16)	No
Reese & Santonio	"How to Play Our Music"	m. 17 (0.31)	Yes
Carl Craig	"Televised Green Smoke"	m. 17 (0.31)	Yes
Chemical Brothers	"Piku"	0.32 (m. 16)	No
Underworld	"Cups"	1.00 (m. 33)	Yes
Kenny Larkin	"Track"	2.18 (m. 81)	Yes

way of beginning a track in order to play with the listener's expectations. This seems likely in tracks that begin with fairly substantial beatless intros and culminate in prominent TBAs, such as "Televised Green Smoke" and "Cups."[30] A third possibility occurs in less dance-floor-oriented works, such as Kenny Larkin's "Track," in which approximately one-third of the track unfolds before the bass drum enters. Although the central portion of "Track" is clearly danceable according to techno conventions, the opening would stand out from the rest of a typical techno set.

One also might ask how DJs deal with beatless intros. In some cases, they may skip such sections altogether; this is the technique DJ Shiva described when I asked her about this issue in a follow-up e-mail:

Mark Butler: You talked about how it helps that a lot of techno tracks start and end with sparse beats, because that makes it a lot easier to beat-match them. However, I've also heard many tracks that start with no beats at all—just maybe a synth line and a cymbal or a snare. This makes them sparse still, but wouldn't it make it harder to match the beats? In other words, when you match beats, do you always choose a moment when the kick drum is going in both tracks?

30. Since turning the beat around typically occurs during the opening of a track or after a breakdown, in formal terms it is usually part of the intro and/or buildup.

DJ Shiva: I usually just spin forward until there are beats. Sometimes I'll use the no-beat sections for intros, but when mixing, I prefer to use the first kick-drum beat as my guide.

As DJ Shiva suggests, a second possibility is to use beatless sections as introductions. Here she refers to the intro of a complete set rather than an individual track. At the beginning of a set, a DJ may build up to the entrance of the beat gradually instead of bringing it in immediately, and intros in which the bass drum is absent work well for that purpose.

Third, a DJ might eliminate the effect of beatlessness by overlaying a beatless intro with the outro of another record that does contain beats (or vice versa). This technique could prove tricky: for mixing to be completely successful, the tempo and (hyper)metrical positions of the two records must be aligned exactly, and if one record lacks beats, the DJ must match the other with an internalized beat. A slightly imperfect match might not sound bad at first, but when the beat of the second record kicks in, any imprecision will be glaringly obvious. In theory, it seems that such mixes would work best when the meter of the beatless section is consistent with the rest of the track—that is, when the beat does not turn around. Thus, the beginning of "Cubik," in which the location of the bar line remains consistent, would be much easier to beat-match than that of "Televised Green Smoke."

If DJs tend to skip beatless sections of a track or combine them with other tracks in which beats are present, one might rightly ask whether the phenomenon of turning the beat around ever occurs within a DJ set, or if it is limited solely to unmixed tracks. In fact, I have heard DJs turn the beat around on a number of occasions, although it is true that this sort of shift occurs much more frequently in unmixed records. Interestingly, it occurs in the same sorts of formal locations in both musical contexts. Many DJs drop the beat in an unexpected location after a prolonged intro, which serves as an effective means of getting the crowd's attention. Less commonly, TBA may occur after a lengthy breakdown. My observations of DJs in performance suggest that both of these techniques are intentional: during the intro or breakdown, the DJ often watches the crowd closely to gauge their level of excitement and then drops the beat suddenly when they reach a fevered pitch. At the same time, certain TBAs may be unintentional—a by-product of EDM's layered structure and multiply interpretable rhythm patterns. In other words, a DJ may cut out the bass drum during a portion of a track without worrying about how the audience will interpret the remaining textural layers. Although the line between what is intentional and unintentional remains speculative unless the DJ can be asked about specific decisions, one can reasonably assume that very prominent events are usually intentional; the DJ's behavior, to the extent that it is observable, can provide additional clues.

The preceding paragraphs focus largely on the results of combining outros and intros. Records may be combined in many other ways, however, as long as the phrasing of each record is respected. The structure of EDM tracks facilitates this freedom of combination through a balance of predictability and irregularity. If every record had exactly the same form, the music would be overly predictable and dull. Instead, tracks present a relatively free mixture of a limited number of formal sections. These sections, along with other multimeasure patterns, tend to last for pure-duple quantities, but not every pure-duple division is articulated. As a result, if two or more tracks are combined at a point of alignment that is based on an appropriate pure-duple multiple, they will (1) never (or almost never) clash, (2) sometimes change at the same moment, and (3) sometimes change at different moments, thereby complementing each other.

Various potential combinations of James Ruskin's "Connected" and Jeff Mills's "Jerical" serve to illustrate the nature of this interaction.[31] Let us first consider example 6.6, which shows the result of starting both records at the same time (for more detailed illustrations of each record, see the textural graphs on pp. 295–98 and 300–303). In this case, the primary pure-duple value is four (measures), and changes almost always occur at the four-bar level within the two combined records. Sometimes one record changes and the other does not (m. 17, m. 33), while at other points the records change together (m. 9). When the records start together, however, the breakdowns do not occur at the same time. Examples 6.7 and 6.8 show two possible ways in which some of the eight-bar breakdowns found in both tracks could be aligned. In example 6.7, "Jerical" starts forty-eight bars earlier, so that it reaches measures 121–28 at the same time that "Connected" reaches measures 73–80. The largest pure-duple value of which forty-eight is a multiple is sixteen. In example 6.8, "Connected" starts ninety-six bars earlier, so that it arrives at its beatless outro (mm. 177–84) as "Jerical" begins its first breakdown. The largest pure-duple value involved in this combination is thirty-two. If "Jerical" starts at measure 12 of "Connected," however, the changes that occur in the two tracks will never align (see ex. 6.9).

One of the most important jobs of the DJ, then, is to determine a pure-duple value that works for the combination of records at hand. As with many types of musical performance, this process is often intuitive. Once an appropriate point of alignment has been discovered, however, the form is flexible enough for these principles to apply even when the records begin in different places (but not in

31. This particular combination is purely hypothetical; there are various reasons why it might not work, including clashes of pitch and/or timbre, an overly active surface rhythm, and the presence of EGD in the Ruskin. The point is to show how a flexible approach to pure-duple patterning facilitates track combination.

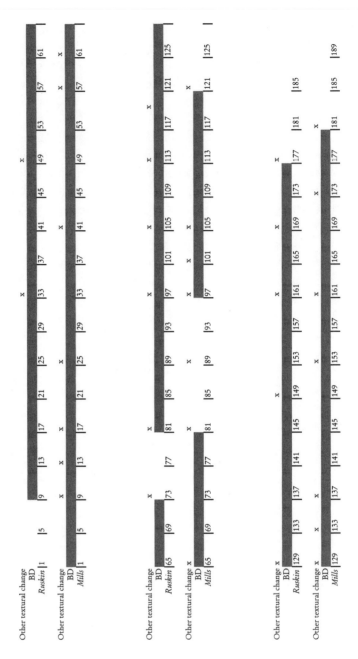

Example 6.6. Hypothetical combination of James Ruskin, "Connected," and Jeff Mills, "Jerical," with tracks beginning at same time. Courtesy of Tresor Records GmbH.

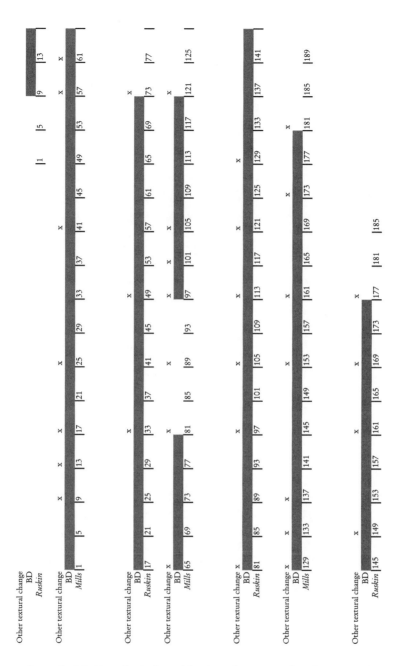

**Example 6.7. Hypothetical combination of James Ruskin, "Connected,"
and Jeff Mills, "Jerical," with "Jerical" beginning forty-eight bars earlier.**
Courtesy of Tresor Records GmbH.

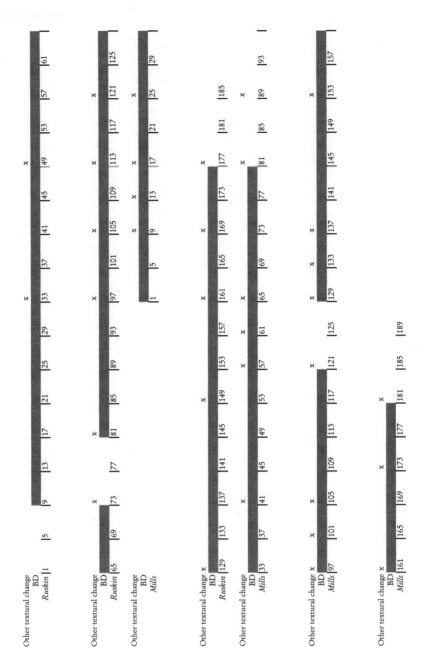

Example 6.8. Hypothetical combination of James Ruskin, "Connected,"
and Jeff Mills, "Jerical," with "Connected" starting ninety-six bars earlier.
Courtesy of Tresor Records GmbH.

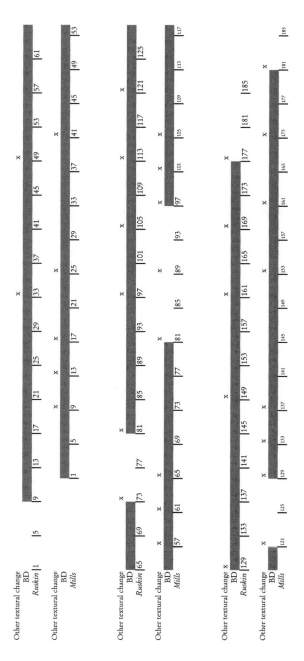

Example 6.9. Hypothetical combination of James Ruskin, "Connected," and Jeff Mills, "Jerical," with "Connected" beginning twelve bars earlier.
Courtesy of Tresor Records GmbH.

any place). The net result will be a mixture of reinforcing certain changes and balancing others out.

Creating and Shaping Sets

> What I think a lot of people miss about DJing is that it's not just records strung end-to-end; it's not single records; you're taking basically a bunch of blunt little tools and making an entire piece out of it. I think that's what missing in the understanding of it, is that it is an actual piece. I was talking to a friend who had a music teacher who said that dance music had nothing on symphonic music, and I said, "Actually, you're wrong. Because a well-done DJ set is ... kind of, at the essence of it, it's an entire piece of different movements." ... So, it's getting people to understand that it's a whole piece. The American understanding is you listen to song, by song, by song. Verse-chorus-verse-chorus-verse. Next: verse-chorus-verse-chorus-verse. And people are used to having it chopped up. And now, it's like they have to switch their heads back into that symphonic mentality where it's an entire piece. You're not listening to individual songs; you're listening to how all of them flow within the whole piece.
>
> —DJ Shiva, interview with the author, 3 December 2001

In these remarks, which grew out of a claim that good DJs need to have a sense of "composition," DJ Shiva argues that an effective DJ set must be a coherent musical entity, in which individual records stand not so much on their own but as contributors to a larger flow. As I conclude this chapter, I would like to consider how this coherence is defined and created as well as the role of record combination in producing it. From within the potentially vast topics of DJ practices and aesthetics, I will focus on several themes that emerged in participants' remarks: in particular, the nexus between planning and improvisation, sources and ideals of musical unity, principles and techniques of record combination, and the shaping and directing of entire sets.

The aesthetic ideals of EDM favor a flexible approach to live performance, in which choices regarding record selection and manipulation are made in the moment rather than beforehand. Too much emphasis on the "contingent" aspects of improvisation, however, risks giving the impression that these performances are completely open-ended situations in which anything can happen.[32] Particular criteria guide these improvisations, and specific musical attributes enable their

---

32. One might also ask whether some DJs might be prone to exaggerate the extent to which sets are improvised: to do so highlights their virtuosity, while also supporting a dominant EDM aesthetic.

flexibility. Moreover, prior planning may also be involved to varying degrees. Participants said that they were more likely to plan their sets in advance when performing in high-pressure situations—for instance, at a prestigious venue or before a very large audience—and they generally believed this to be true of other DJs as well. Advance preparation also can come into play through practicing at home. For DJ Shiva, this process involves informal experimentation, which leads to specific discoveries that can reappear in live contexts:

> Whenever I get new records, first thing I do is go home and play. Or sometimes I'll just be bored and playing. You kind of come up with little blocks of things that you know go together really well. You're just noodling around, and these two records just lock in like nothing else. And so that's always in my head if I need that, if a night's not going well, if technically things aren't going well, I can fall back on this and use it and I know it'll work.

For DJ Vixen Swift, planning involves developing a general outline of the program and its key tracks, in contrast to the more extensive predetermination that she associates with other DJs:

> Some people plan and plan and plan their sets. And I don't. . . . I just try to lay out kind of a general outline of the tracks that I want to go in kind of what order. But that night if everybody's feeling a certain … little more of a style, then I might try to stick with that a little more. If I'm not in the mood to hear this song tonight, then I'll just skip that. And then, as far as cutting it up or whatever goes, I just … whenever I feel like [I need to], I just [say], "Oh, I just need to cut this off right now." [*Makes cutting-off sound.*] There it goes. … I just kind of go and do what comes naturally. I have absolutely no methodology behind it. I just kind of wing it.

Like Vixen Swift, most participants emphasized flexibility over planning. They seemed to regard completely planned out sets as something of a crutch, to be relied on only in situations where complete perfection is required or when one lacks the skill to improvise successfully. DJ Shiva, for instance, associated the ability to "wing it" with experience: "But for the most part it's just like … I've been doing it so long; I know my records pretty well; and I can pretty much just wing it. I like to know the first couple of records I'll play, because I like to have an interesting intro of some sort. Past that I like to wing it."

The primary factor requiring a DJ to be flexible is the crowd. An EDM audience is not expected to be polite; if they do not like what the DJ is doing, they will leave the dance floor. Although DJing does not always involve pleasing the crowd in the most direct and simple way possible (as the teasing dynamic involved in withholding the beat illustrates), the DJ must be able to adjust quickly if a certain strategy fails to motivate. DJs often speak of having to "turn on a dime," to abandon their pre-planned sets, or even to omit their own best-loved tracks in favor of those to which the audience responds.

This flexibility does not preclude coherence, however. EDM DJs think of their sets as musical wholes, rather than as one song after another in a given time slot, in the manner of pop-radio DJs. In the quote that opened this section, DJ Shiva even described the experience as "symphonic." This comparison is obviously not strict, but rather an effective evocation of the epic scale and unified nature of these performances. At the same time, further consideration of form in these two realms can shed light on some of the qualities distinctive to sets. In a set, the emphasis is on logical flow—on making a continuous musical progression—rather than on unifying devices (themes, motives, keys) that persist throughout an entire work. Form is not based on an object-like model, in which coherence can be viewed within a complete musical structure just as one would perceive the unity of a sculpture (all at once), but, rather, on a sense of a continuous development through time. This approach to form is more perceptually than structurally based: it is like a journey on a train in which the destination is unknown to the rider, but one can see out the window the whole time. We end up in a completely different place than we started, but our route made sense; the coherence is that of the trip itself, not its components.[33]

On most journeys, the terrain changes very gradually, and the same quality applies to a well-shaped DJ set. A general goal of mixing is to move as smoothly as possible from one record to another; as Jimmi Journey notes, "It's about that *smoothness,* so they really think the music is just morphing." Another term used to describe this quality of smoothness is "flow," as in the following comments from DJ Shiva: "Most dancers are pretty instinctive, and they know where things are supposed to happen. . . . If you look up and you see people looking at the speakers like you're crazy you've probably just thrown them off. So you want to keep the flow going for them. That's how I like it as a dancer. I want to know that on that thirty-third beat—*bam!*—there's going to be a cymbal hit. It keeps the flow going better."

When EDM records are mixed properly, they should be integrated so thoroughly that something entirely new is created. In this way, DJs highlight their status as artists; rather than just playing other people's records, they have created something that never existed before. These emphases are apparent in Mystik's description of record combination:

33. The image of a train is also invoked in a negative sense by the term "train wreck" (cf. ch. 1, p. 56). One reason a train wreck (in the metaphorical sense) is so disturbing is that it disrupts the continuity of the beat.

We tend to have two records going simultaneously almost always. There's a lot of DJs out there that'll just beat-match the last couple of measures, and then they'll switch over to the next one. That's not our style at all. We like to create something totally different. And that way you're making a new song, in essence; it's not really the same.

DJs and fans of dance music often describe this new musical entity as "the third record." For DJ Impact, the creative essence of the third record lies in manipulating and reconfiguring elements of pre-existing sources to "make it your own":

When you're creating the music, say like a DJ, I can just transition from one record to the other by matching beats. But the real goal of the DJ, or a good DJ, would be to create what they call the "third record," and make it their own, by either scratching or manipulating the songs that they're using, or just basically sampling themselves [*i.e., sampling the music they are currently playing*]. DJing is nothing more than sampling, because unless you've written the tracks that you're playing, it's all somebody else's music that you're manipulating and changing to make your own or call your own.... Like in one of my mixes that I do, I create the third record by sampling some of the little lines of "King of Snake" by Underworld into Laurent Garnier's "Greed" track. So that when it ["Greed"] ends, it ["King of Snake"] comes in and you've heard it before, but you didn't know where it was from if you're not familiar with the song, and that makes it interesting to the person listening.... Now it's connected, where those sounds come from.

DJs realize this aesthetic of continuity and integration through techniques of effective record selection and combination. Although track selection can be shaped by the need to play crowd favorites or the desire to promote particular artists,[34] the musical construction of the individual records clearly plays a principal role. One of the most important factors involved is phrasing compatibility. Tracks must be similar enough to each other to allow their major formal sections to be aligned. As Mystik puts it, "You can't just put the other record in any old time. You'll end up having two records clash—the builds won't be the same. And that's bad." Alignment is particularly important for dynamic sections such as buildups, which stand out more prominently than the less active core sections. At the same time, tracks are designed so that they can still be combined with many different records in a variety of ways. The DJ also can use the EQs to make less suitable combinations work; for instance, s/he might cut out the bass drum

34. It is not uncommon for DJs to play records produced (and/or remixed) by themselves, by other artists on their label, or by their personal friends. An extreme example of this situation is the Timo Maas mix released as *Music for the Maases.* Every track on the two CDs is produced and/or remixed by Maas. This might not be immediately apparent, however, since his work sometimes appears under monikers such as "Kinetic A.T.O.M," "O," and "Orinoko."

in one record to match a breakdown occurring in the other record. Nevertheless, certain records will never be well-matched. A successful DJ must know records in their entirety in order to envision how they will combine with the formal sections of other tracks, and must know them well in order to be able to make such decisions quickly.

The individual patterns that constitute multimeasure groups and formal sections also must be compatible for records to combine effectively. In the excerpt below, Mystik invokes both positive and negative criteria—DJs "add" the elements of individual records together, while avoiding combinations that "clash":

> Like with vocals, you don't want to put two records that have predominant vocals in them together. I mean, obviously you're going to end up with something very muddled. So, you try to ... whether it be instrumental, whether one record has a hi-hat and the other one doesn't, you want to add that together, and ... put those two together. You don't take sounds that are going to clash, obviously, and put them together—it's not going to produce a pleasant sound for you or for anybody who's listening to you.

DJ Shiva spoke in similar terms, frequently mentioning records that "mesh" and discussing how records can "play off each other." These particular characterizations suggest that something more than simple addition is at work; rather, a successful mix places sounds in a particular kind of complementary relationship, in which each element supplies some feature or quality that is absent in the other. Furthermore, this dynamic may be realized within a variety of sonic realms. The following remarks, for instance, point toward the role of timbre:

> *Cornelia Fales:* And do things like reverb make a difference as to what you're going to mix with it?
> *DJ Shiva:* Yeah, to an extent, because certain songs ... or certain sounds play off each other better.
> *Cornelia Fales:* Now, you're not talking metrically now—or rhythmically now— you're talking about ...
> *DJ Shiva:* Like ... sound-wise.

Timbre, in relation to instrumentation, also factors into Mystik's previous remarks, which describe how creative mixing might fulfill the need for a hi-hat while avoiding an excess of prominent vocals.

At the same time, "playing sounds off each other" has a definite rhythmic dimension, as DJ Shiva made clear in a continuation of her comments:

> *DJ Shiva:* And sometimes I try and find songs where ... like maybe there's some weird metallic stabs, and I try and find one where there's another sound on the

offbeat, so it stabs and then there's a little vocal, like: [*imitates a clipped vocal sound*]—you know, whatever. … So I play them off of each other.

She references this phenomenon again in her description of the euphoria of spontaneously discovering a perfect record combination:

DJ Shiva: What's really fun is when it's completely off the cuff, just accidental. You were playing this song, and you're flipping through your crate, thinking, thinking, thinking, "What's gonna go? OK, that!" And you put it down on there, and you cue it in, and you're like, "Holy shit! I didn't know that!" Because it has a sound that's exactly the same as the sound in that record, only it's on another beat.

Clearly, these references to sounds that "play off each other" or "mesh" are not just loose synonyms for "blending nicely," but rather quite specific metaphors for ways in which tracks can combine. Within these combinations, both rhythm and timbre play a role. In timbral terms, DJs usually speak either of complementary sounds or of identical sounds found in two different sources; in either case, these sounds are usually described in rhythmic terms as occupying complementary positions within the measure. In this way, a characteristic of individual records— the tendency to combine one sound on the beats with another on the offbeats (most often a bass drum and hi-hat, respectively)—also appears in DJ sets. In broader terms, principles guiding the metrical construction of individual tracks also inform the combinations that DJs choose in mixes; the modularity of EDM's form extends to both realms.

In addition to the specific example of "meshing," several participants mentioned the overall level of rhythmic activity in each record as a potential criterion. If each of two or more records has a very active surface rhythm, the mix will sound cluttered when they are combined. DJs described this situation in negative terms, using adjectives such as "muddled" and "busy." As DJ Vixen Swift put it, "It needs to sound good together, and if it's too busy, I don't think it sounds good. And sometimes it's good if you can mix two really intricate parts together, but sometimes it just sounds like too much."

Related to the idea of avoiding a cluttered mix is a belief in respecting the prominence of certain sounds. If a particular element stands out within a track— whether because of its rhythm, its timbre, or some other factor—most DJs will keep the mix relatively free so that it can come to the fore. DJ Shiva explains the rationale behind this aesthetic principle:

DJ Shiva: But usually if there's something really overwhelmingly there, I don't like to clutter it.

Cornelia Fales: So when something's really overwhelmingly there ... what kind of thing would be overwhelmingly there?

DJ Shiva: Like I have this record: it's a pretty minimal record, but it's just a synth line; it's like "*dn dnn* [rest] *dn dnn* [rest] *dn dnn* [rest]," and they start bringing the reverb up, so it's like [*imitates the previous sound but adds distortion*]. And I wouldn't put anything over that song, except another song with a really sparse beat. Or a beat that goes on for a really long time, and then somewhere in the meat of the song, something else comes up. Because by then I could have mixed out. I wouldn't conflict with that synth line because it's so *good.* It's so *there.* It's so prevalent in the song that I want the attention to stay on that sound; I don't want to detract from it with something else.

Just as DJs must develop a sense of which record is right for a particular crowd at a particular moment, therefore, they must also learn to discover the most distinctive feature of a particular track and allow it to shine.

Although pitch is not usually a major consideration in techno, it can sometimes affect mixing when DJs avoid dissonant combinations:

Mark Butler: I was going to ask you about something you were saying a little while ago, when you were talking about synth lines that don't go together. When you were talking about that did you mean [lines] that actually clash in terms of pitch—that make dissonance?

DJ Shiva: Sometimes.

Mark Butler: Or is it more in terms of what you were talking about [with] them being really "present"—sort of dominant in the song?

DJ Shiva: I think either way. Sometimes it is pitch, because I do have a pretty good sense of that, so when I hear things like ... or bass lines that ... sometimes you can play bass lines off each other but sometimes they're just pitched differently. So I don't mess with it.

Analysts wishing to focus on aspects of pitch in electronic dance music might rightly ask why certain combinations are considered dissonant and others go by unnoticed. Although such matters would require investigation beyond the scope of this project, it seems likely that the textural prominence of the various parts involved and the metrical position and duration of any dissonant intervals would have significant effects upon the extent to which various lines seem to clash.

Another rhythmic factor that can affect both individual records and their combination is the bass drum's return after a section in which it was absent. DJs describe this return as "dropping the beat." The beat can drop after a breakdown that is built into the record (in which case timing is not really an issue unless the DJ wants to change it), after the DJ has withheld the beat for a while, or when a new record enters the mix. The second of these three possibilities is the most common. When the beat returns after a withholding, it is usually preceded by manipulation of the effects, which raises the intensity level and "builds" the crowd, and it almost always drops abruptly, as with turning the beat around. In the following passage, DJ Shiva references these aspects of the process in an effective evocation of its power and allure:

> What's really fun, on a Pioneer 500 [mixing board] . . . there's a reverb. You throw it on; you pull the bass out; and you just start turning up the reverb. Not the volume, but just the prevalence of it, basically. You just start turning it up— it starts sounding like the beat's just exploding, basically. *And then you turn it off and drop the beat* [*says this quickly, as if to suggest the abruptness of the act*], and it's clean. So it's just like … it's completely disturbing! [*laughs*] It's lovely—it's like nobody knows what's going on and then *bam*!

The dynamic that Shiva describes—disorientation followed by a clarification that is surprising in itself—resonates strongly with the qualitative dimensions associated with turning the beat around and other types of metrical dissonance.

DJs also emphasized the *timing* of the beat dropping. Mystik specifically mentioned two levels of pure-duple rhythms in which the withholding occurs as an upbeat, while also referencing the manipulation of effects and the beat's precise return:

> *Mystik:* One of my favorite things to do, and what really works well with the crowd: if you take the bass, and you just drop it out for a second or whatever, and then you bring it back, I mean *every time,* every time, the crowd just goes "[*imitates enthusiastic yell*]."
> *Mark Butler:* Everyone screams.
> *Mystik:* Yeah, they love that. Something as simple as that—just playing around with the bass, and combined with being able to turn up the mids and the highs, and arranging it just right so that when you do bring the bass back in it's like "Wow!" I mean, they love it; they totally love it.
> *Mark Butler:* When you're taking the bass out, how do you decide how long to keep it out?
> *Mystik:* A lot of times it goes … It depends on the song. It goes of course in fours. Sometimes I'll drop it out at … Well, there's four sets of four, and at the end of the last four I'll drop it out maybe for four beats, and you bring it back in—and that's perfect timing. It's all a timing thing—you can't just drop it out any time you want and have it sound right. It's got to be on beat.

Also noteworthy is Mystik's description of the joy this process brings to the audience. In many cases the interaction between DJ and audience takes on a quite sexual dynamic, as DJ Shiva explains in a striking passage that blends the technical and the qualitative as well as the DJ's perspective with that of the dancer:

Mark Butler: From what I've heard of DJs, it seems like a lot of times there's this sort of thing of making the audience wait for something, you know?
DJ Shiva: Oh yeah! Oh yeah—anticipation!
Mark Butler: And then—right then—then that's what makes them really excited.
DJ Shiva: Yeah. Well, you can take ... like, taking up the effects and doubling up a synth line or something ... you can pull the bass out, and then start not only doubling up the beat, but then tweaking the EQs too, and pulling maybe the midrange out into the room—like, if it's a really crazy synth line. I love to just pull the midrange up, and just let them suck on that for a while! [*laughs*] And if it's repeating itself, it's just like ... it's like sex. You're just toying with them right then—you'll get to them in a minute. And then it's like, you just get them to where they're freaking out and then you just pull it all out—*bam!*—drop the bass on them. I know what it does to me! Richie Hawtin's master of that—he'll take the bass out for like fucking five minutes and start tweaking with the effects, and you have no idea what the hell's going on, but you're liking it. ... And then you almost kind of forget that there was bass there, and you kind of start getting used to how it sounds, and all of sudden he drops the bass on you. "OH shit, forgot about that!" You're like, "Shit!" And then you just lose your mind. ... There's a lot of that—just toying with them.

The climactic effects of dropping the beat at just the right moment after a withholding highlight the ways in which DJs shape energy over time. Not only must they find effective ways of forming the "third record" and moving from one record to the next; they also must direct the set's development in a manner that creates effective growth across an expansive time frame. Listening to DJs and talking to them about their sets reveal a variety a ways in which they shape and direct them. I would first like to consider some of the ways in which DJs choose to *open* their sets.

In live-performance contexts, the beginning of sets can be affected significantly by the context in which they appear and by the stature of the DJ. In some cases, DJs are expected to match the start of their performance with the end of the previous DJ's set, so that the music will flow continuously in spite of the change of performers. This requirement is more likely to affect lesser-known DJs; those with "headliner" status have a better chance of starting from scratch, since in many cases the promoter or manager will stop the music and announce them before they play.

Certain approaches to beginning are particularly common. One technique might be termed the "ambient" intro. Here the DJ starts out with some sort of beatless track (which may not even be EDM), often featuring sustained sounds with soft timbres that "wash" through the stereo field, from which the beats eventually emerge. A recorded example of this technique occurs on the Stacey Pullen mix entitled *DJ Kicks: Stacey Pullen*. At the beginning of the set, as the first track ("Colora" by Jibaros) emerges, we hear samples from the movie *Blade Runner* (which, with its futuristic storyline, associates strongly with the thematic emphases of techno) as well as instrumental sounds clearly meant to evoke "Middle Eastern" music. I also have observed DJ Shiva begin with an ambient intro on several occasions; for instance, at a performance at the Indianapolis Arts Center on October 21, 2001, she began her set (a shared "tag-team" with Adam Jay) with one of the ambient tracks from James Ruskin's *Point 2* (either "Before the Calling" or "From Over the Edge"). The ambient intro provides a very gradual introduction, easing the listener into the world of hard and fast beats. It functions as a sort of buffer between the real world and the mechanistic music encountered within the set.

Another type of introduction, which I will describe as a "framing" intro, has a more specific function. It uses real-world sounds to establish a context for the DJ's performance; in fact, the sounds often refer specifically to the particular DJ who is performing. A clear example of this approach is the beginning of Frankie Bones's set *You Know My Name.* In addition to being a DJ, producer, and founder of the Sonic Groove record store in New York City, Frankie Bones is also known as one of the first people in the United States to start throwing raves (Reynolds 1999: 146–48). The beginning of the CD features the following interchange between a man and a woman:

Man: Hey girlie.
Woman: How much is it to get in?
Man: Twenty.
Woman: Is Frankie playing like the flyer says?
Man: He's here. He's coming on now.
Woman: Is it gonna get busted?
Man: Are you in or what?
Woman: Yeah, yeah.
Man: Twenty bucks. Come on in. Hurry up.

We are clearly supposed to understand the man as the person collecting money outside a rave and the woman as a patron trying to decide whether or not to enter. As they talk, we hear muffled beats that mimic the sound of a bass drum heard from outside the venue. After the woman decides to go in, we hear a creaky door shutting and the beats growing louder and more distorted as she walks down the passageway that leads inside. The snare drum from measure 81 of Mario Più's "Communication" then makes its dramatic entrance, and the set proper begins.[35]

35. The samples and door-shutting sound occur on the track "Play One Record" by Medicine Show. Later in the track, we hear a male voice with a Brooklyn accent (presumably Frankie Bones)

In this way, the intro guides the home listener from the "outside" world to the interior realm of the performance, highlights the specificity of the performance (it is Bones and not just any other DJ), and imbues the recording with a sense of liveness.

Misstress Barbara's mix *Relentless Beats Vol. 1* begins with an intro that is similar in function, though sonically rather different. The first track, entitled "My Prada Heels (Entrance Theme)," consists of the sounds of high heels clicking against the floor. The heels get louder and "closer" to the listener as the DJ (whose identity is implied by the title of the track) walks into the performance space. As with the Bones, this suggests a physical transition from the outside world into the realm of the musical event, while also referencing the DJ quite specifically (the heels point to her gender, and their brand could arguably be interpreted as a reference to her Italian ethnicity). This intro is also interesting from a musical perspective: the regularity of the heels creates a sense of metrical expectation—there are exactly thirty-two clicks before the next track begins, suggesting eight measures of 4/4—which is then subverted when the bass drum of the first "real" track (Umek's "Voltaren") enters the mix. Misstress Barbara drops the bass drum of "Voltaren" on what sounds like the offbeats of the "Heels" track, thereby abruptly turning the beat around. The fierceness of her musical entrance also turns around the implications of the opening's conventional symbol of gender, declaring that Misstress Barbara (who, as the liner notes indicate, puts an extra *s* in her name so that we will read it as Miss Stress) can be just as aggressive as any other techno DJ.

In some cases, EDM DJs begin their sets without any introduction at all, instead letting the beats flow from the beginning of the very first record. This strategy is especially common among hard techno DJs, who often prefer to "bang it" from the very start. Moving immediately from silence into hard and fast beats casts a sharp spotlight onto the performance's technological dimensions. This abruptness is more common at the end of sets than at the beginning, however. Many DJs kill the sound immediately when they decide that it is time to end, leaving the audience in stunned silence after an hour or more of very loud, almost constant beats. Kinder DJs might turn the sound down gradually, or use an outro that is similar (or even identical) to the intro. On the mix *Global Underground: London,* for example, Danny Tenaglia draws from the same material—a sample from the eighth track of CD1, Coca da Silva's "Saudade"—for the outro of both CDs and the intro of CD2. At the end of the first CD, where the music stops but

---

saying that the party has been shut down by the police and "I only got to play one record." However, this part of the track is not heard on the Bones mix CD; instead, he fades "Play One Record" out of the mix after its tenth measure and brings in "Communication."

the set is not yet completed, he presents the sample in its entirety. A resonant male voice says, "The enchantment is over, but the spell remains." At the beginning of the second CD, when the set resumes, we hear the phrase "the spell remains," while at the end of the complete set Tenaglia leaves us with the line "the enchantment is over."[36]

Within sets, DJs use a variety of techniques to create growth and climax. One possible approach is to build up gradually across the entire set, creating a single climax near the end. Obviously, this strategy is more easily accomplished within shorter sets, though it can occur within longer time spans as well. More commonly, however, DJs create several major climaxes within a set, with the last one usually being the most dramatic. DJ Shiva describes how this strategy informs her approach to mixing:

> *Mark Butler:* One thing I was interested in about when you're doing a whole set: do you try to make a climax at some particular point in the set? Do you think of it that way?
> *DJ Shiva:* Yeah. I like to do it kind of … like, peaks and valleys … like, bring it up slowly. So you'll kind of start out slow—sometimes … sometimes I just bang it—[and] kind of pick them up; let them down; pick them up higher; let them down. Yeah—I like to … midway through the set I just want them to be out of their minds.

Jimmi Journey also speaks of the importance of changing the energy level as the set unfolds:

> *Mark Butler:* [*to Jimmi Journey and Mystik*] And what about beats per minute? Do you all think about that?
> *Jimmi Journey:* That's something I don't get into as much as I had at one point, but I'm getting back into it, because *tempo* is a driving force. The tempo of music can take people up and it can take them down. And so I try to … the new set that I've actually put together, I start out low tempo, and I build them up, probably for the first ten minutes to a high tempo. But people are dancing: people are getting tired. If you keep it high tempo too long, they're just going to get tired and stop dancing. So you bring it up, you take them down. Bring them up; take them down. … That way they can endure it. You can't have them fatigued physically and be enjoying what they're hearing.

Journey's comments highlight the fact that this energy level is literally physical as well as metaphorical. In addition, clear linguistic parallels connect remarks about "bring[ing] them up" and "tak[ing] them down" to those of DJ Shiva.

When I asked about tempo, I expected to discover that speed increases

36. If one plays the second CD repeatedly, its end merges into its beginning, forming a continuous loop.

throughout sets. Participants' comments confirmed my expectations, but only to a certain extent: although several performers, like Jimmi Journey, said that they do raise the tempo intentionally, they also noted that tempo increases are generally slight. One reason that the range of variation is relatively small is the direct relationship between the tempo and the audience's physical response. As Mystik noted, "just a few beats per minute really makes a difference." Tempo variation is also constrained by genre (since BPM is a primary factor distinguishing certain genres) and by technology (turntables can only change the speed of a record by a certain amount, and this alteration also changes the pitch).[37] As a result, audiences often experience accelerations only subliminally.

One participant who does accelerate quite explicitly in his sets is Neal Blue. Although Blue performs a live PA of his own tracks rather than a DJ set, his approach shares many principles with DJ sets. It differs, however, in that it includes many different genres. In the following excerpt, he explains his treatment of genre and its aesthetic motivations:

> *Neal Blue:* Generally I put the trancier stuff all together, and then I put the harder, tribally techno at the end, and then ... the 505, like a turntable, can speed up BPM, but the pitch won't change. And so at the very end I speed up and play jungle. And so for me, that's the only problem with live PAs, is that they pigeonhole themselves. And so, if you're doing a live PA, and you're only playing techno, people will be there to see that you're playing techno, but all those trance kids, they don't want to hear techno, so they're bored for an hour. People that want to hear jungle, they're bored for an hour too. With me crossing genres I'm opening myself up to so many more people, and making my crowd bigger and my audience bigger.

One side effect of this cross-genrefication is an acceleration in tempo, as Blue indicates with his remarks about "speed[ing] up and play[ing] jungle." In the following continuation of our conversation, he provides more specific information about this process:

> *Mark Butler:* So there's almost an acceleration in beats per minute across the set ...
> *Neal Blue:* Definitely
> *Mark Butler:* and in terms of rhythmic layering?
> *Neal Blue:* I start off, generally, around 130 to 135. And my songs get more intense as my set goes on, and more thick. By the end I'm playing the hard stuff with just all tribal rhythms and hardly any melody at all, and usually that's

---

37. DJs sometimes alter their turntables so that they will be able to change tempo by much larger amounts. The pitch-shifting that occurs with changes in speed could be an asset, depending on the desired musical outcome.

at 145 BPM. And then [I] move from that to jungle, which is 180 BPM. ... And DJs do the same thing. They want to take someone on a journey in that hour that they have. It's no different than what a DJ does.

What *is* different about Neal Blue's sets, however, is the degree of acceleration and the extent to which it is explicit. Often, at the end of the techno portion of his set, he speeds up the beats to the point that they become almost a blur and then drops into a jungle track. The effect is very dramatic: at first the audience is unsure what is happening, and then they realize that the acceleration has led them to a new musical terrain.

Near the end of their sets, DJs often play tracks that are considered "classics." For example, Laurent Garnier plays "Beyond the Dance" by Detroit techno pioneers Rythim Is Rythim as the penultimate track of his *Laboratoire* mix, and DJ T-1000 chooses Morgan's "Flowerchild" to end his *Live Sabotage: Live in Belgium* performance. Using two copies of such a record can make the moment even more exciting, of course. A significant portion of this heightening is rhythmic in origin, as the double-copy effect produces a diminution of every part—the most important of these being the bass drum, which normally moves in quarter notes throughout almost all of a set. DJ Shiva draws a connection between playing a climactic track and using double copies in the following passage:

> *Cornelia Fales:* And what are you doing at a climax then?
> *DJ Shiva:* Just find the most absolutely floor-wrecking track I can find and just. ... Sometimes maybe even find that track and then do double copies. Start chopping between records.

Popularity and familiarity can clearly play a role in the ability of a track to "wreck" the floor, as can particular musical qualities. When I asked DJ Shiva about the relationship between tempo and climax, she placed herself in opposition to previously quoted participants, noting that she does *not* deliberately increase the tempo during her sets. In her remarks, she uses five adjectives— "hard," "wild," "crazy," "intense," and "driving" (as well as an equivocal endorsement of "loud")—to characterize the qualities of climactic moments:

> *Mark Butler:* So what about tempo? Is that a big influence on where the climax is? Do you try to speed up the tempo gradually?
> *DJ Shiva:* I think it kind of speeds up on its own, just as you're mixing through records. But I don't do it consciously. I try and keep it pretty uniform. . . . I like to keep them [the audience] going.
> *Mark Butler:* So it's more about what the intensity of the tracks is?
> *DJ Shiva:* Yeah. Exactly. It's totally the intensity of it. You can go from being really funky, to just sort of. ... And it's a really subtle build too. But you know, maybe you ... midway through the set you start getting harder. Or louder.

[*rethinking*] Not louder necessarily: the sounds start getting wilder, a little crazier, a little more intense, a little more driving. And then if you have effects you use, you can really start working the effects.

These comments resonate with those of Neal Blue, suggesting that factors such as thick textures, hard timbres, driving rhythms, and the increased use of effects by both producer and DJ play essential roles in the creation of climactic moments.

Despite the diversity of participants' remarks, all emphasized the importance of shaping *energy* or *intensity* within a set. Intensity, more than any individual musical factor, is the glue that holds a set together. Although the DJ must manipulate the intensity level in a way that makes sense within the conventions of electronic dance music, within the context of live performance, intensity remains contingent upon the audience's interaction.[38] In the absence of recurring motives, themes, and keys, this give-and-take is the primary source of coherence in a DJ set. It is the train that leads the audience through their journey. This does not mean that unity in live EDM performances is not musical in origin: after all, this unity stems from the DJ offering carefully selected musical morsels to the audience and their responding in kind. Ultimately, however, the sense of coherence associated with a well-done DJ set derives from an integrated mixture of "purely musical" compositional choices and on-site physical responses.

Throughout this exploration of the epic, we have seen the modular organization of electronic dance music extending to increasingly large levels. Although the size of the constructive elements has grown—the loops and layers of earlier chapters have become multimeasure patterns, sequences, sections, records, and sets—the guiding principles remain the same. Musicians continue to form structure from relatively simple, generic building blocks that are highly flexible. Just as individual rhythmic patterns offer multiple interpretive pathways, multimeasure patterning and formal shapes allow records to be combined in a variety of ways. And this interpretive flexibility continues to apply to the listener as well. From the looping sixteenth note to the revolving record, structure is less about the finished product and more about what we choose to do with it.

38. The DJ's shaping of intensity through interaction with the audience is also essential to Fikentscher's notion of "peaking the floor," a term he uses to describe the way in which DJs create climaxes by provoking "as strong as possible a response from the floor at least once during the evening" (Fikentscher 2000: 41).

Afterword:
Unlocking the Groove

In the introduction to this book, I noted that I would model my discussion on the structure of a well-formed DJ set, periodically revisiting certain unifying themes as well as building progressively across the discourse as a whole. With respect to the latter approach, the linear development of this voyage has been unified by a consistent emphasis on the ways in which time may be shaped. I began by looking at the properties of short rhythm patterns, then considered how they might be combined, and eventually came to address the increasingly lengthy entities of sequence, record, and set. At the same time, I situated this development within a cyclical motion from the broad to the specific and back again, beginning with a consideration of historical and theoretical frameworks, moving toward increasingly detailed analytical explorations, and gradually returning to the most expansive performative contexts in which this music is experienced.

Along the way, I have traced the paths of a number of recurring ideas through various smaller orbits, illustrating how many of the same principles of design—for instance, the diverse division of pure-duple time spans; a close interaction between rhythm, meter, and texture; underdetermination; and an emphasis on process—inform EDM's organization at both local and global levels. All of these levels are formed from a modest number of modular components that can be altered, interpreted, and recontextualized in many different ways. In the realm of musical creation, this modular disposition both reflects and encourages an open approach to form. For the producer, loops function as basic constructive elements that can be flexibly combined with other textural components, easily assume a variety of metrical functions, and form either side of the binary reversal seen in turning the beat around, while sequences serve as larger formal units to be interacted with in the creation of a complete track. In the hands of the DJ, the transformation and recombination of records leads to new formal designs that may differ dramatically from those inscribed onto their surfaces.

Musicians often highlight the modular nature of records by describing them as "tools for the DJ" rather than fixed "songs." In so doing, they call attention to *how they are used,* emphasizing the functionality of these musical entities as media to be interacted with rather than their status as self-sufficient objects. This "interactivity" operates in fundamental musical domains as well. As listeners' diverse reactions to "the meter" of electronic dance music illustrate, the rhythmic and metrical qualities of this repertory highlight the experiential possibilities afforded by its temporal phenomena. Although scholars wishing to emphasize "process" over "product" might say that all music is really about experience rather than structure, I contend that electronic dance music fosters this orientation toward experience in a particular way.[1] Specifically, I have claimed that sites of interpretive multiplicity involve listeners in a particular dynamic, one in which they must play an active role in shaping the direction of their musical experiences. Ambiguous structuring and divergent metrical paths encourage those who hear EDM to respond to it in a variety of ways; when the sounds transmitted to the listener do not suggest a decisive interpretation, he or she must play a more active role in forming one. These tendencies are deeply implicated in both the repetition of cyclical units as well as the processive development of music across time; the rates at which processes unfold, and the repetitions that they offer, invite listeners to seek out diverse ways of hearing and to experiment with these interpretations as a piece is going on.

This interaction occurs in minds and through bodies; it is both individual and social. On the dance floor, a communal space, each person responds to the music differently, while also reacting to the behavior of others. One person, the DJ, is largely responsible for shaping what is heard, but his or her choices are directed to a significant extent by the audience's responses. In the disorienting, decentralized environment of the club, a plethora of senses are stimulated simultaneously from multiple directions, requiring participants to seek out aspects of the experience on which they will focus. In the broadest sense, therefore, this interactivity both shapes and participates in the cultural traditions of electronic dance music.

In claiming that electronic dance music is characterized by a formal and interpretive openness, a releasing of temporal possibility that fosters diverse musical and social interactions, I have claimed that its groove is unlocked. Although

1. I would also object, as I have in the introduction, to arguments that attempt to freeze what music is "really about" in the interest of rhetorical authenticity.

I would never argue that there is any one "key" to its rhythmic essence—for this would stretch the metaphor much too thin—I have emphasized the qualitative aspects of "unlocking" at every turn. A sense of unlocking is evident in the intermingling of even, diatonic, and syncopated rhythms and in the presentation of rhythm patterns in ways that promote equanimity between the different modes of organization involved. It is apparent in rhythmic and metrical ambiguity, in the ways in which producers promote multiple interpretations. It is evident in the independence of textural and metrical layers—both in general terms and in the dissociative effects of metrical dissonance. It reveals itself in the fluidity with which the seemingly metrical turns into the antimetrical and the antimetrical into the metrical, and in the corollary to this phenomenon: the reversal of the roles of dissonance and consonance. For listeners, for producers, for dancers, for DJs, this unlocking of music's temporal qualities opens a door onto a realm of experiential and interpretive possibility.

Appendix A: Technical Issues
Related to Analysis and Transcription

Transcriptions appear in several different formats.[1] Two of these, the "sound palette" and the "textural graph," are used only in appendix C, and are explained in detail when they first enter the discussion (in ch. 5). In the main text, most examples employ conventional notation of rhythm and pitch. Typically, one staff per instrumental sound is used, although multiple sounds are sometimes placed on a single staff if the texture becomes quite thick. Sounds that do not have precise pitch, which are common, are mostly transcribed on single-line staves, sometimes with higher or lower notes to indicate approximate contour. In order to avoid cluttering the score, rests are not generally used in percussion parts when a series of attacks follows in close succession. In such cases, notes are shown as durations lasting until the next attack, even if they consist of a short attack followed by a rapid decay. However, rests do appear in certain circumstances: when a sound has an especially short attack (as with a closed hi-hat cymbal), when a gap of silence occurs between the end of a pattern and the beginning of its repetition, and when a repeating pattern is temporarily absent from the texture.

Various analytical notations also appear and are explained as they are introduced. In conjunction with my analytical strategies, many of the elements of "standard" notation are used (or not used) in ways that have interpretive significance. For instance, bar lines and time signatures have been carefully chosen and placed; their omission indicates that the transcribed passage is ambiguous with respect to metrical organization. The way in which patterns have been beamed also reflects certain claims I will make about rhythm and meter.

A recurring question facing analysts of any electronic music is what to call the sounds that occur. In a physical sense, the instruments of EDM are synthesizers, drum machines, and so on. All these machines, however, contain a diverse array of sounds, each of which might rightly be described as an "instrument" on its own terms. In discussions of examples, these "instruments" will be treated as individual sound sources with distinct names. The most commonly used names and their abbreviations are shown in table A.1.[2] Percussion instruments will usually be described by more or less standardized names such as bass drum, hi-hat, and snare drum, which are employed by EDM musicians and appear as sonic descriptors on a great deal of EDM equipment.[3] These are the names of acoustic instru-

---

1. See pp. 20–25 in the introduction for a broader, more conceptually oriented account of the use of analysis and transcription in this book.

2. The abbreviations shown are used for staff names beginning with the second system of an example, as well as the transcriptions that appear in appendix C. Instruments that appear only in individual works are named and abbreviated on an *ad hoc* basis.

3. The bass drum is also frequently described as the "kick drum" or "kick," but for the sake of consistency I will use "bass drum" only. In cases where a track presents multiple rhythm patterns

Table A.1. Instrumental names and their abbreviations.

Percussion instruments

Bass Drum	BD	Tom-Toms	T
Hi-Hat (Cymbal)	HH	Drum (of Unspecified Type)	D
Snare Drum	SD	Percussion (of Unspecified Type)	P
Handclaps	HC	Bells	B

Instruments with definite pitch

Bass Line	BL	Synth	S
Riff	R		

Other

Sample	SMP

ments as well, of course, but in this book all instruments should be assumed to be electronic unless otherwise noted. Other instruments that resemble acoustic instruments will be described in similar terms: "xylophone," "bells," "strings," and so on. Percussion sounds that do not seem to fall into one of the main categories will be described simply as "drums," or as "percussion" if the sound is not particularly drum-like.

Sounds with definite pitch that do not resemble a familiar instrument will be described either as "synths," "riffs," or "bass lines." The bass line is a category unto itself, distinguished by range, though at times the distinction between a riff and a bass line is not entirely clear.[4] "Riffs" are relatively short repeating sounds; although they have definite pitch, their function is more rhythmic than melodic, and they do not resemble an acoustic instrument or a bass line. The term "synth" denotes a pitched sound that is more melodic than rhythmic in function. "Synth" is also used to refer to sustained sounds that fill in the texture (a chord held for four bars, for example) and to pitched sounds that appear only intermittently. I follow dance music fans in using the abbreviated form of the word; when used repeatedly, "synthesizer" quickly becomes cumbersome. I also take care to restrict this term to certain types of sounds; otherwise, nearly every instrument used in EDM could be described as a "synth."

A similar restriction applies to the term "sample." Many EDM sound sources are sampled, but I use the term only for the "sound byte" type of sample: one in which the sound source is noticeably sampled, rather than created by the producer. Usually this type of sample involves a fragment of human speech or song, although instrumental samples also can stand out as sound bytes if they are drawn from recognizable external sources.

In order to enhance the focus of an analysis, and in some cases to make an example

---

using the same instrumental type, patterns are numbered in the order in which they appear within the complete track (e.g., "Snare Drum 1," "Snare Drum 2," etc.), regardless of the order in which they are discussed in the text.

4. I include the word "line" in this term in order to avoid ambiguity. Dance music fans often talk about "the bass," which, in its broadest sense, includes all very low sounds (namely, the bass drum and the bass line) considered (or felt) as a whole; however, they also use the term to refer to these sounds individually.

visually clearer as well, some transcriptions intentionally omit certain instrumental parts. For instance, if a pattern is faint or difficult to hear (e.g., if it can only be heard by listening closely through headphones), and if its presence or absence does not affect the analytical point being discussed, it may be more effective to exclude it; otherwise the reader will be confused by the presentation of sounds that s/he does not hear. I have generally made a note of such omissions, which occur more often in the main text; the transcriptions included in appendix C attempt to show every sound occurring in a track.

EDM also presents the transcriber with some uniquely ambiguous situations. First, as in other electronic music, it can be particularly difficult to identify sound sources, as many different sounds may come from a single piece of equipment. Moreover, it also can be difficult to tell whether a new pattern seeming to enter the mix is really a distinct "instrument" or simply an effect such as reverb or delay applied to an already sounding instrument. Furthermore, pitches fall "in the cracks" in some recordings, as both DJ mixing and the sampling of external sound sources allow the raising or lowering of pitch on a sliding scale. Such ambiguities are noted as they arise.

Appendix B: Technical Issues
Related to Field Research

As described in the introduction, field research for this study consisted primarily of interviewing DJ, producers, and fans of electronic dance music as well as attending and participating in a variety of EDM events. Having been involved in electronic dance music as a clubber for well over a decade, I was already an insider to "the field" to a certain extent. At the same time, I was initially an outsider with respect to my geographical location, since the demands of graduate study had kept me away from the Indiana EDM scene. At thirty, I also was considerably older than most field-research participants, who generally ranged in age from eighteen to twenty-three.

I met several participants by announcing my project at meetings of the Indiana University Disc Jockeys and Electronic Musicians Association and through an e-mail message sent to the lists iu-ravers@yahoogroups.com and indybassnet@yahoogroups.com. Other participants were introduced to me in various ways during the course of field research, or were known to me beforehand. I also created a Web page to allow prospective participants to find out about the project (although to my knowledge no one learned about the project solely through this site).

Most interviews took place in Indiana during fall 2001, although one occurred in spring 2002, and follow-up contacts took place throughout 2002. A detailed description of my field research plans was reviewed and approved by the Indiana University Human Subjects Committee before any interviews were conducted. A total of twelve people were "officially" interviewed, meaning that we arranged a specific time and place expressly for the purpose of having an interview and that the interview was recorded (with their written permission). I also spoke with many other people about EDM on numerous occasions. Most of the formal interviews lasted two or three hours, although some were closer to an hour, and one ran for over four hours; in most cases, we met in the participant's home, which allowed them to play music to illustrate points and to demonstrate the equipment they used. The majority of interviewees were musicians—either performers (DJs), producers, or both; two were producer-performers who play live PAs. Three participants interacted with EDM largely as fans, although two of these individuals also were professional classical musicians. In addition to these twelve interviews, originally conducted for my doctoral dissertation, I interviewed three internationally-known producers—Carl Craig, Graham Massey of 808 State, and Rick Smith of Underworld—via telephone during the summer of 2004.[1]

After they were recorded, most interviews were transcribed, either in part or *in totum*. Prior to recording, participants were asked to specify whether they wanted their names

---

1. In fact, I attempted to contact most of the producers whose work is analyzed in this study, but was only able to arrange interviews with these three.

used, and those who were quoted directly also were given the opportunity to comment upon the transcriptions of their remarks as well as my interpretations of them. As I explained to each participant, I have presented quotes verbatim, except that (a) repeated phrases are, in general, only shown once; (b) connecting words such as "um" or "like" are generally omitted, unless their omission affects the meaning of a statement; (c) statements that trail off without being completed are omitted, unless their inclusion seems to contribute to a larger point; and (d) grammatical errors, such as subject/verb disagreement, are corrected. The omissions described under points *a–c* are not indicated with ellipsis marks, but substantive omissions are shown by three periods . . . with spaces in between. Three dots *without* spaces ... are used to indicate pauses in conversation. Any words not actually spoken during the interview (such as omitted conjunctions or pronoun antecedents) are shown between square brackets in regular typeface. These changes are meant to enhance the readability of the text. In addition, italicized text between square brackets provides information about actions occurring during the interview (e.g., "No, I don't agree [*shakes head vigorously*]").

The questions asked in interviews involved general aesthetic aspects of electronic dance music as well as specialized knowledge related more directly to my topic. I generally began broadly and then moved to more specific questions tailored to the interviewee's expertise. I took a list of questions to most interviews, but used them as a point of departure rather than as a script. In most interviews, I also requested that musicians demonstrate their craft in various ways: DJs, for example, might have been asked to illustrate some of the techniques mentioned during the interview or to play a series of tracks from a recent set and explain why they chose that particular series, and producers were asked to show how their equipment works and how they use it in composition. I also asked fans to play some of their favorite tracks and talk about why they were appealing.

*Appendix C: Transcriptions of Tracks
Discussed in Chapters 5 and 6*

Sound Palette and Loop Lengths

Note: All written representations of this track (including those in the main text) are based on the first CD track of the Timo Maas DJ mix entitled Music for the Maases. *In comparison to the unmixed version of the track released by Edel (see discography), Maas introduces no alterations except for increasing the tempo by about 3 BPM and adding a second record (the beginning of which is also described below) near the end.*

Rhythmic sounds:

SOUND NAME	MOST CONCISE REPRESENTATION	LOOP LENGTH	OTHER COMMENTS
Bass Drum	*[notation]*	o	
Hi-Hat	*[notation]*	𝅗𝅥	Closed
Snare Drum	*[notation]*	𝅗𝅥	
Percussion 1	*[notation]*	2o	Metallic timbre. Pitch not precise but near F$^\sharp$/G
Maracas (M)	*[notation]*	o	
Synth 3	*[notation]*	𝅘𝅥𝅭	Very distorted/noisy; more percussive than pitched (but near E$^\flat$?)
Bass Line	*[notation]*	2o	
Record 2: Muse, "Sunburn (Timo Maas Breakz Again Mix)"			
Scratch (SCR)	*[notation]*	𝅗𝅥	Timbre like scratched record
Bells	*[notation]*	2o	

Articulative sounds:

SOUND NAME	MOST CONCISE REPRESENTATION	LOOP LENGTH	OTHER COMMENTS
Synth 1	*(approx. pitch; sharp)* *[notation]*	(𝅘𝅥𝅭)	Piano-like timbre. Faint volume; no exact cut-off point
Scratch (SCR)	𝅘𝅥𝅮𝅘𝅥𝅮𝅘𝅥𝅮𝅘𝅥𝅮 into downbeat (anacrustic)	N/A	Timbre like scratched record
Slowdown (SLW)	N/A	N/A	Imitates sound of DJ slowing record down. Accompanied by anacrustic BD variation

Atmospheric sounds:

SOUND NAME	DESCRIPTION
Wind	Obviously synthesized, but timbre resembles wind sound. Moves around stereo field. Rhythm of 8th-note triplets. Lasts ca. 6 mm.
Synth 2	Wash of sound. Pitch starts around D and rises in glissando
Synth 4	Bell-like timbre. Pitch starts around D and rises via filter sweep

Loops ordered according to length:

♩.	Synth 1 Synth 3
♩	Snare Drum Hi-Hat Scratch (Record 2)
o	Bass Drum Maracas
2o	Percussion 1 Bass Line Bells (Record 2)

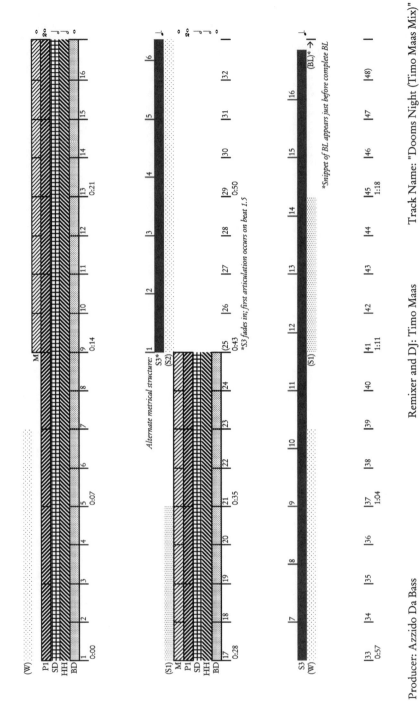

ca. 135 BPM

*S3 fades in; first articulation occurs on beat 1.5

Alternate metrical structure:

*Snippet of BL appears just before complete BL

Producer: Azzido Da Bass   Remixer and DJ: Timo Maas   Track Name: "Dooms Night (Timo Maas Mix)"

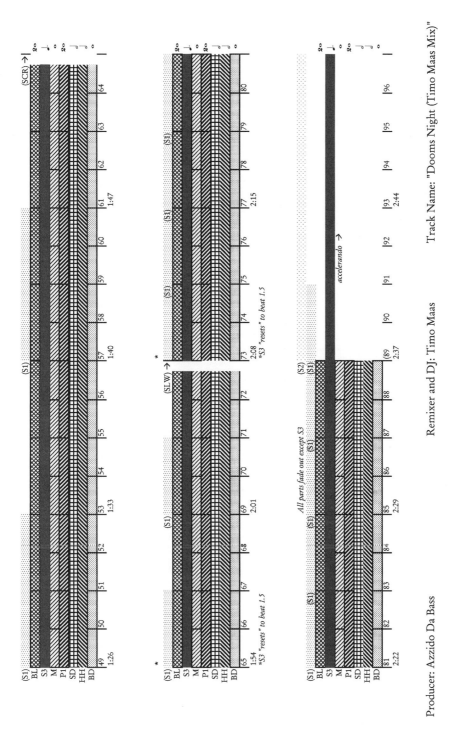

Producer: Azzido Da Bass

Remixer and DJ: Timo Maas

Track Name: "Dooms Night ('Timo Maas Mix')"

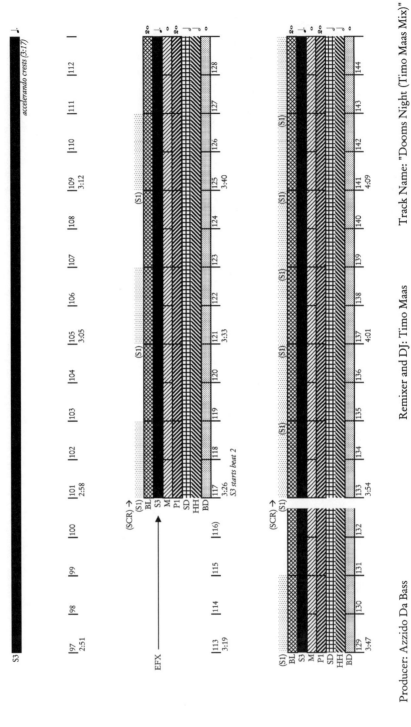

Producer: Azzido Da Bass   Remixer and DJ: Timo Maas   Track Name: "Dooms Night (Timo Maas Mix)"

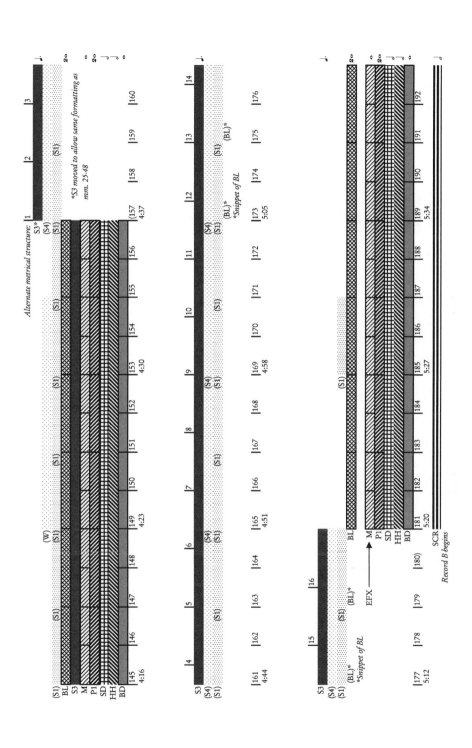

Producer: Azzido Da Bass

Remixer and DJ: Timo Maas

Track Name: "Dooms Night (Timo Maas Mix)"

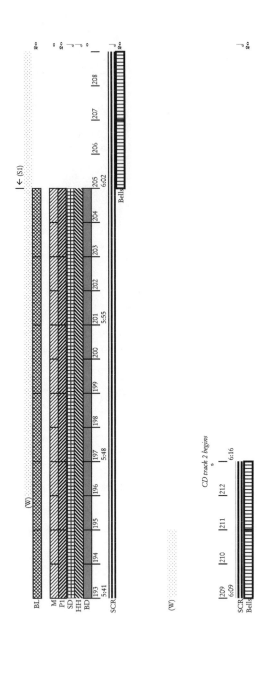

Producer: Azzido Da Bass   Remixer and DJ: Timo Maas   Track Name: "Dooms Night (Timo Maas Mix)"

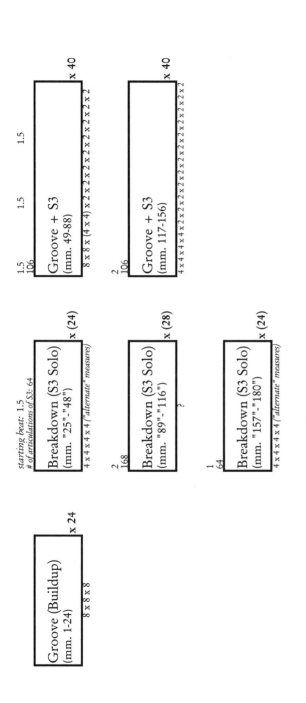

Form Chart

Producer: Azzido Da Bass   Remixer and DJ: Timo Maas   Track Name: "Dooms Night (Timo Maas Mix)"

Appendix C   273

Sound Palette and Loop Lengths

Rhythmic sounds:

SOUND NAME	MOST CONCISE REPRESENTATION	LOOP LENGTH	OTHER COMMENTS
Drum 1	*panned right* [musical notation]	𝅗𝅥	F$\sharp$ is approx. pitch. During opening, appears to begin at * and sounds like ♪♪ 𝄾 in 3/8
Drum 2	*panned center* [musical notation]	𝅗𝅥	During opening, sounds like either ♪𝄾 or 𝄾♪𝄾 in 3/8
Drum 3	*panned left* [musical notation]	𝅗𝅥	C$\sharp$ is approx. pitch. During opening, sounds like last ♪ of 3/8 measure
Bass Drum	[musical notation]	𝅗𝅥	
Hi-Hat	[musical notation]	N/A	No discernible pattern of recurrence. Mix of 8ths and quarters. Shown is a representative excerpt
Bells	[musical notation]	8o	
Riff 1	[musical notation]	o	Timbre: Roland TB-303. Rhythm occasionally varies v. slightly in last bar of 8-bar hypermeasure
Riff 2	Pitches: F4, C5 Rhythm: primarily 16ths	N/A	V. fast & irregular. Gives impression of highly active surface, but no clear rhythm to pitch changes

Snare Drum	A: [rhythmic notation] B: [rhythmic notation]	N/A	Only occurs once; lasts for 16 mm. Formed from mix of patterns A, B, & variants
Riff 3	Pitch pattern (each indicated pitch occupies 1 bar): B♭ B♭ G G F F E♭ E♭ B♭ B♭ G G F F E♭ F Rhythm pattern of each bar: [rhythmic notation]	16○	16-bar pitch pattern; 1-bar rhythm pattern

Atmospheric sounds:

SOUND NAME	MOST CONCISE REPRESENTATION	LOOP LENGTH	OTHER COMMENTS
Synth 1	[musical staff notation] Cm^{11} _____ Cm^{11} _____ Fm$^4_3$ Cm^{11} Rather than a clearly projected melody, the pitches transcribed above indicate notes within the harmony that are emphasized in order to bring out the 2-bar divisions.	16○	Cm^{11} chord is sustained and processed over 16 mm. Switches to Fm$^4_3$ chord in penultimate bar. Sound processing creates clear 2-bar divisions in the loop as well as overall 16-bar duration

Loops ordered according to length:

♩	Drum 1 Drum 2 Drum 3 Bass Drum
○	Riff 1
8○	Bells
16○	Riff 3 Synth 1

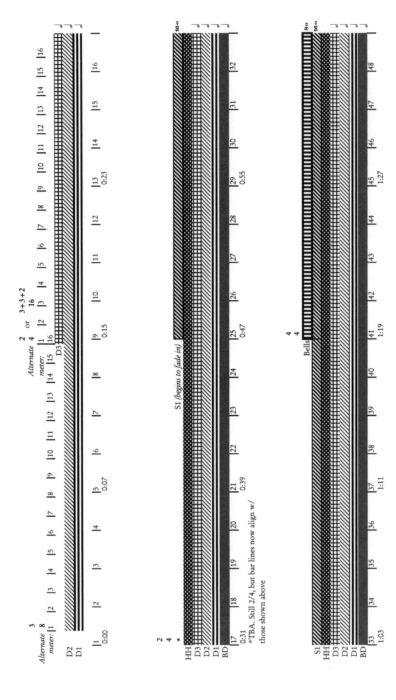

ca. 121 BPM

Track Name: "Televised Green Smoke"

Producer: Carl Craig

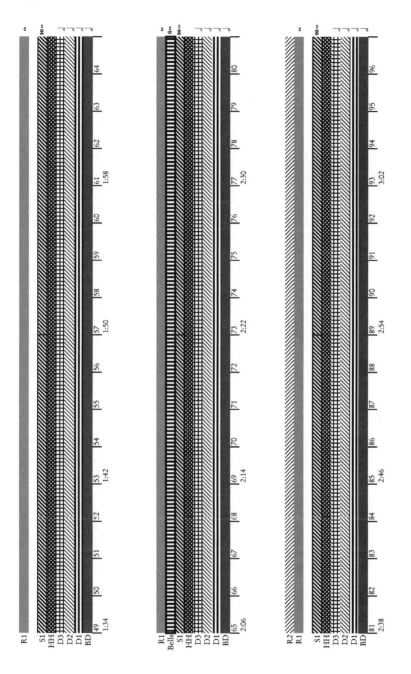

Track Name: "Televised Green Smoke"

Producer: Carl Craig

Appendix C   277

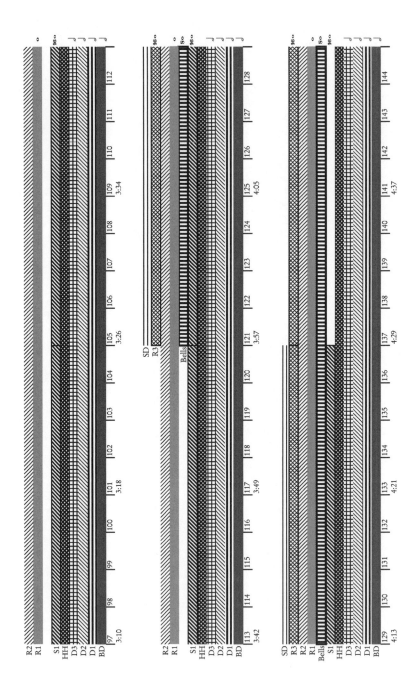

Track Name: "Televised Green Smoke"

Producer: Carl Craig

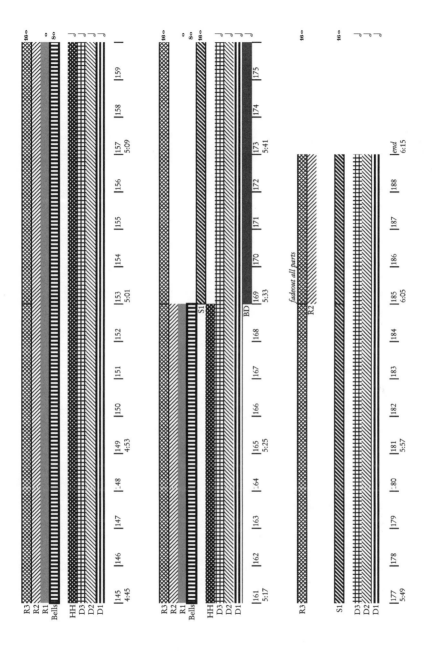

Track Name: "Televised Green Smoke"

Producer: Carl Craig

Sound Palette and Loop Lengths

Rhythmic sounds:

SOUND NAME	MOST CONCISE REPRESENTATION	LOOP LENGTH	OTHER COMMENTS
Bass Drum 1a		80	Bass Drum 1 is 1 instrument w/ 3 rhythmic variants
Bass Drum 1b		80	
Bass Drum 1c		80	
Bass Drum 2		𝅗𝅥	Possibly just reverb applied to BD1
Tom-Tom 1 & 2		𝅝	
Hi-Hat 1		20	Closed
Hand-clap		𝅗𝅥	
Hi-Hat 2		♩	Open
Riff 1		𝅝	
Riff 2a & b		𝅝	Upper line more prominent. Lower line very fast sequenced riff, 3+3+3+3+3+4 patterning.
Percus-sion 1		𝅝	Nonacoustic percussion sound
Synth 2		40	Overtones emphasized vary

Riff 3		40	

Articulative sounds:

SOUND NAME	MOST CONCISE REPRESENTATION	OTHER COMMENTS
Snare Drum	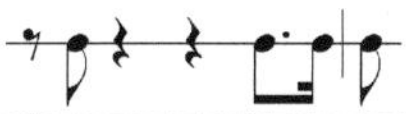	
Sample 1	"How does it feel to fly?"	Male voice; speaks on 4th bar of 4-bar hypermeasure. W/ panning & reverb.
Sample 2	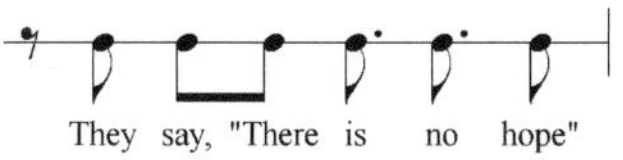They say, "There is no hope"	(Different) male voice. Sample from "No UFOs" by Model 500. W/ panning & distortion. In m. 134 only, presents next line of that track: "They say 'No UFOs.'"

Atmospheric sounds:

SOUND NAME	MOST CONCISE REPRESENTATION	OTHER COMMENTS
Synth 1	N/A	Rises and falls across ca. 8 mm. Hypermetrical position varies.

Loops ordered according to length:

♩	Hi-Hat 2
𝅗𝅥	Bass Drum 2 Handclap
𝅝	Tom-Tom 1 & 2 Riff 1 Riff 2a & b Percussion 1
20	Hi-Hat 1
40	Synth 2 Riff 3
80	Bass Drum 1

ca. 145 BPM

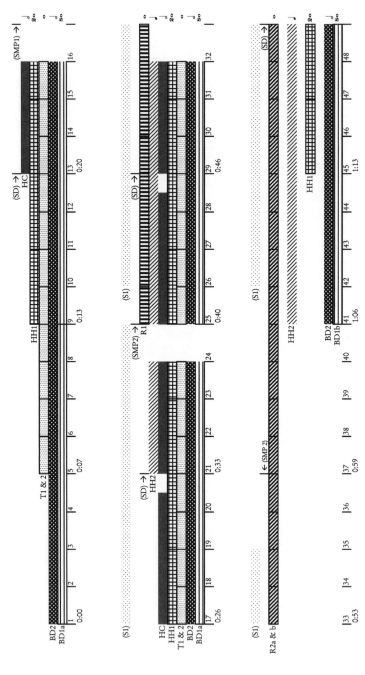

Producer: Dave Angel

Track Name: "Sighting"

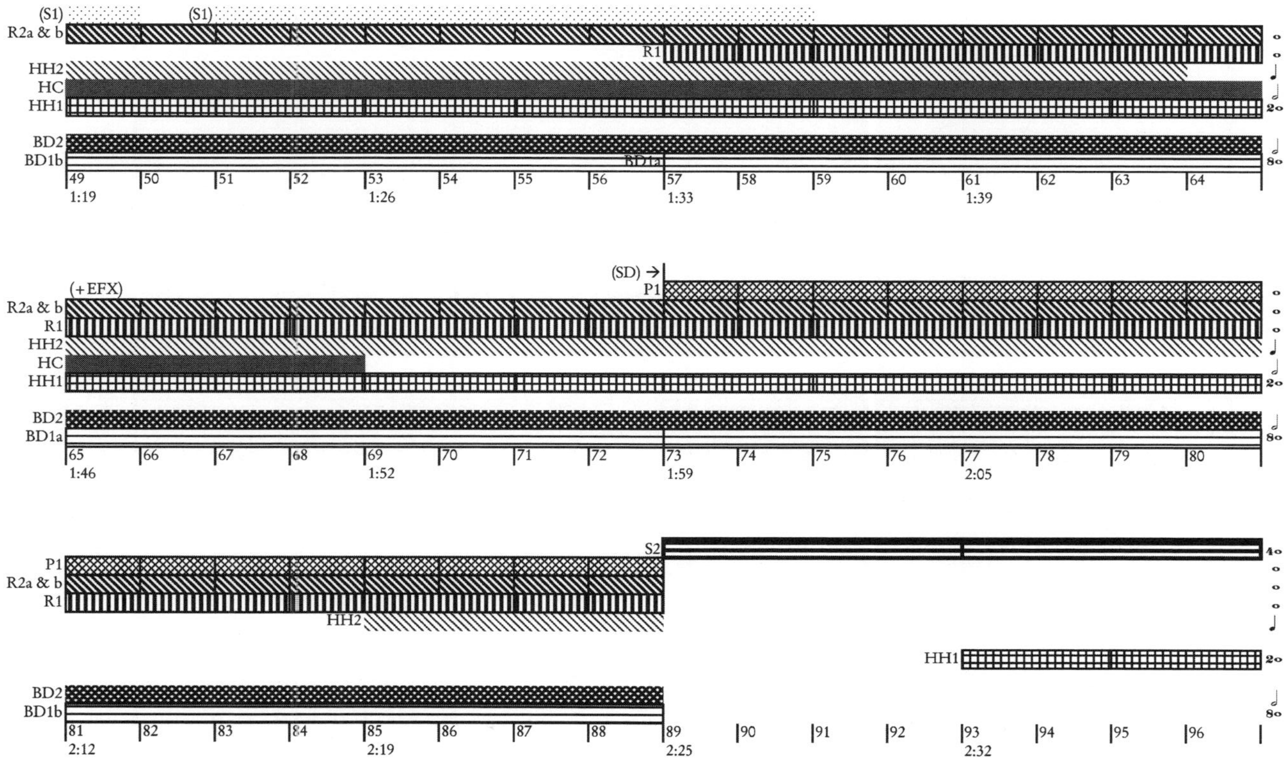

Track Name: "Sighting"

Producer: Dave Angel

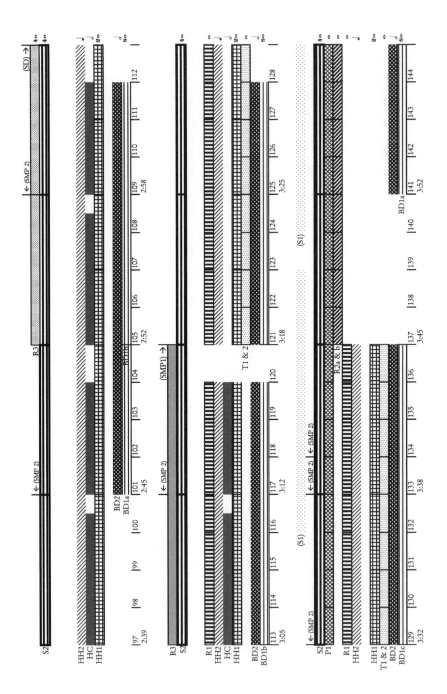

Track Name: "Sighting"

Producer: Dave Angel

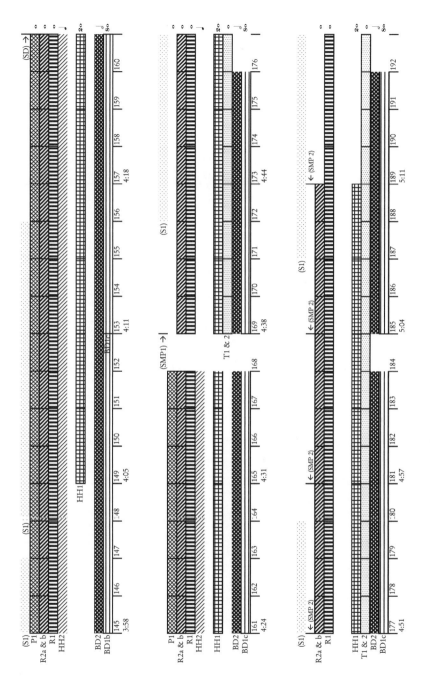

Track Name: "Sighting"

Producer: Dave Angel

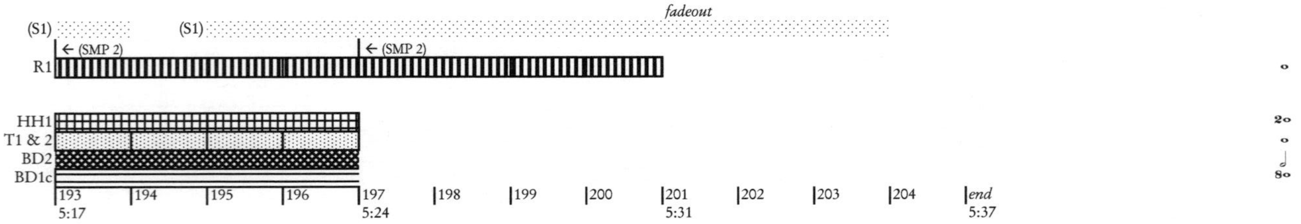

Track Name: "Sighting"

Producer: Dave Angel

fadeout

(S1)

(S1)

← (SMP 2)

← (SMP 2)

R1

HH1
T1 & 2
BD2
BD1c

|193 |194 |195 |196 |197 |198 |199 |200 |201 |202 |203 |204 |end
5:17   5:24   5:31   5:37

Sound Palette and Loop Lengths

Note: Because this track contains so many different elements, I have organized sounds according to "instrumental" categories rather than the usual rhythmic/articulative/atmospheric schema. All sounds are rhythmic except for the first three samples, which are articulative, and the three synth sounds, which are atmospheric.

Riffs:

SOUND NAME	MOST CONCISE REPRESENTATION	LOOP LENGTH	OTHER COMMENTS
Riff 1	*(musical notation, bass clef)*	4o	1-measure basic loop, w/ variation in 3rd measure
Riff 1'	*(musical notation, bass clef)*	o	
Riff 2	*(musical notation, treble clef)*	2o	
Riff 3	*(musical notation, treble clef)* *(panning back & forth)*	o	
Riff 4	*(musical notation, bass clef)*	2o	
Bass Line	*(musical notation, bass clef)*	o	

Percussion:

SOUND NAME	MOST CONCISE REPRESENTATION	LOOP LENGTH	OTHER COMMENTS
Hi-Hat 1	*(musical notation)*	2o	
Hi-Hat 2	*(musical notation)*	o	
Bass Drum	*(musical notation)*	♩	
Tom-Tom	*(musical notation)*	o	
Snare Drum	*(musical notation)*	o	

Xylophone 1		𝅗𝅥	"Xylophone" is an approximation of this sound's timbre
Xylophone 2		o	See above

Synths:

SOUND NAME	MOST CONCISE REPRESENTATION	LOOP LENGTH	OTHER COMMENTS
Synth 1		2o	
Synth 2		2o	Pitched, but distorted so much that effect is primarily timbral
Synth 2'		4o	See above. Timbral change creates 4-bar pattern; otherwise only 16th in duration

Other:

SOUND NAME	MOST CONCISE REPRESENTATION	LOOP LENGTH	OTHER COMMENTS
Guitar (G)	*(distorted)*	4o	
Sample 1	Rhythm:	N/A	Percussive sound + whispered voice (indeterminate text). Always anacrustic ("& 4")
Sample 2	Text: "Cubik" Rhythm:	N/A	Male voice. Either anacrustic (4-1) or on downbeat (1-2)
Sample 3	Text: "Hey!"	N/A	Female voice. Always anacrustic
Sample 4	*(freely)* Oh oh oh____	o	

Loops ordered according to length:

♩	Bass Drum
♩	Xylophone 1
o	Riff 1' Riff 3 Bass Line Hi-Hat 2 Tom-Tom Snare Drum Xylophone 2
2o	Synth 1 Synth 2 Riff 2 Riff 4 Hi-Hat 1
4o	Riff 1 Synth 2' Guitar

ca. 123 BPM

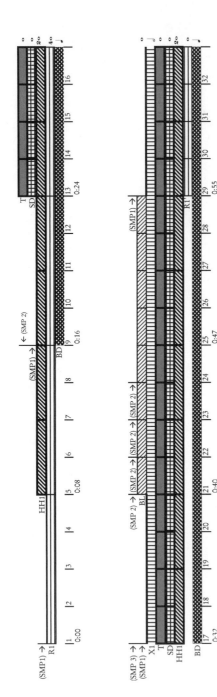

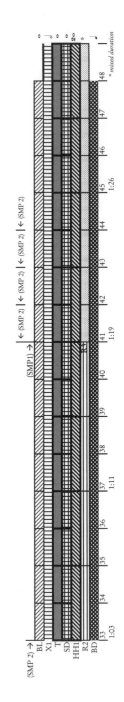

Producer: 808 State with Frankie Bones

Track Name: "Cubik (Kings County Perspective)"

Track Name: "Cubik (Kings County Perspective)"

Producer: 808 State with Frankie Bones

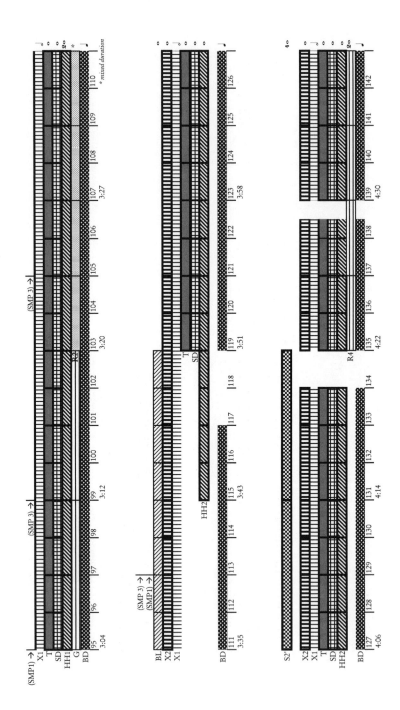

Track Name: "Cubik (Kings County Perspective)"

Producer: 808 State with Frankie Bones

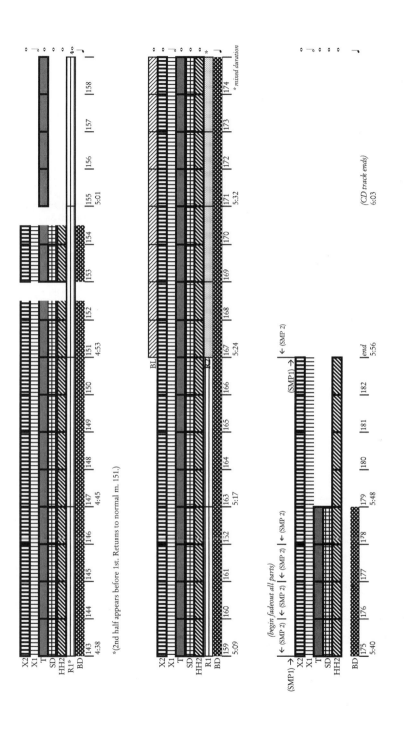

*(2nd half appears before 1st. Returns to normal m. 151.)

*mixed duration

begin fadeout all parts

Producer: 808 State with Frankie Bones

Track Name: "Cubik (Kings County Perspective)"

Sound Palette and Loop Lengths

Rhythmic sounds:

SOUND NAME	MOST CONCISE REPRESENTATION	LOOP LENGTH	OTHER COMMENTS
Bass Line	*(musical notation)*	o	
Snare Drum	*(musical notation)*	♩	
Hi-Hat	*(musical notation)*	♪	Very low in the mix; difficult to hear without headphones. Possibly an effect applied to the snare
Bass Drum	*(musical notation)*	♩	
Riff 2	*(musical notation)*	♩.	
Riff 3	*(musical notation)*	♩.	

Atmospheric sounds:

SOUND NAME	LOOP LENGTH	OTHER COMMENTS
Riff 1	o	Possibly an effect applied to bass line
Synth 2	8o	Extremely faint sustained synth
Synth 3	N/A	Only occurs once, at end of track. Sustained string-like timbre. Of indeterminate length

Articulative sounds:

SOUND NAME	COMMENTS
Synth 1	Single stab; indeterminate pitch

Loops ordered according to length:

♪	Hi-Hat	♩.	Riff 2 Riff 3	Synth 2
				8o
♩	Snare Drum Bass Drum	o	Bass Line Riff 1	

ca. 134 BPM

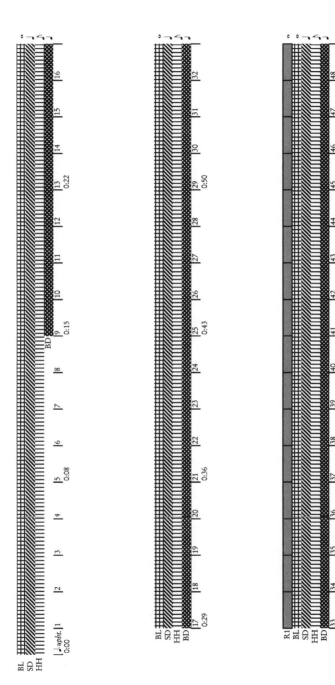

Producer: James Ruskin

Track Name: "Connected"

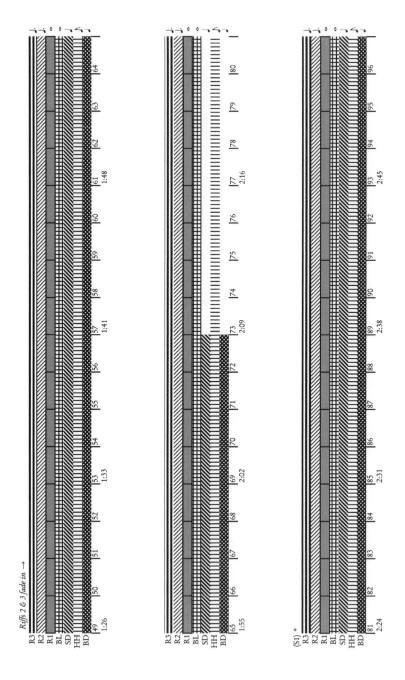

Track Name: "Connected"

Producer: James Ruskin

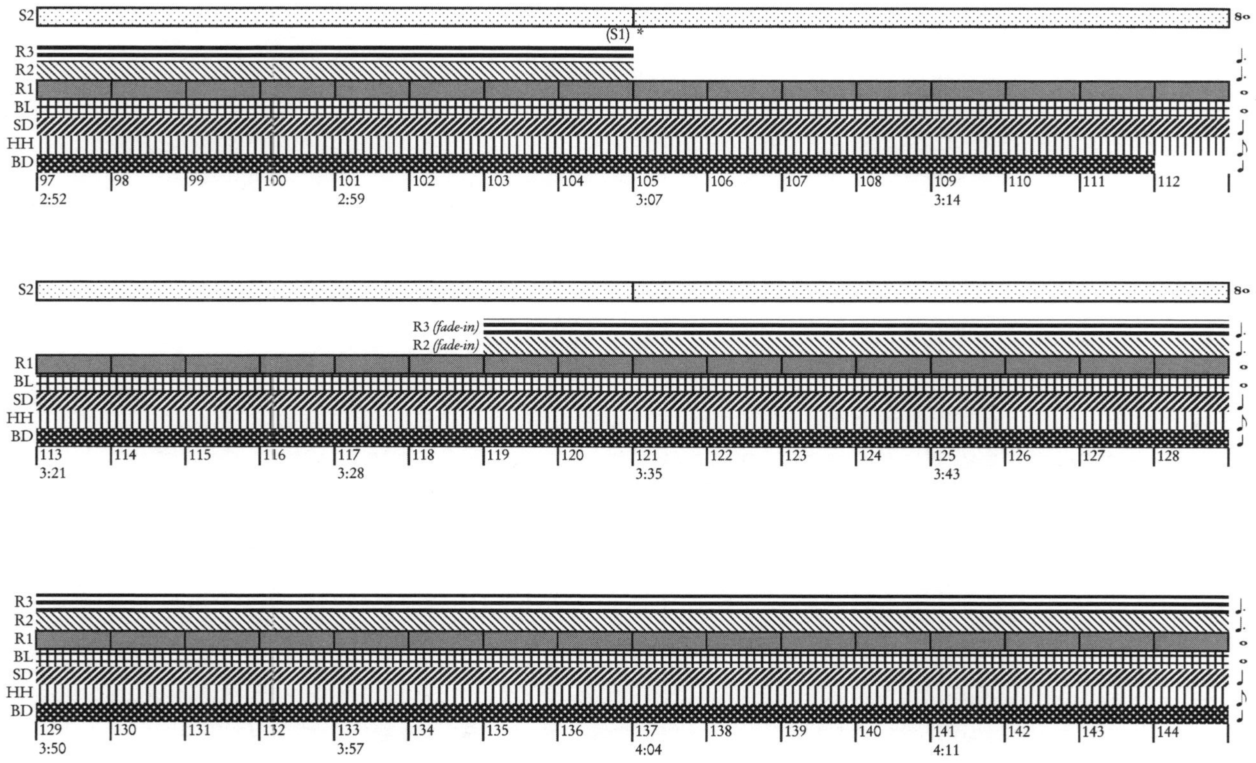

Producer: James Ruskin

Track Name: "Connected"

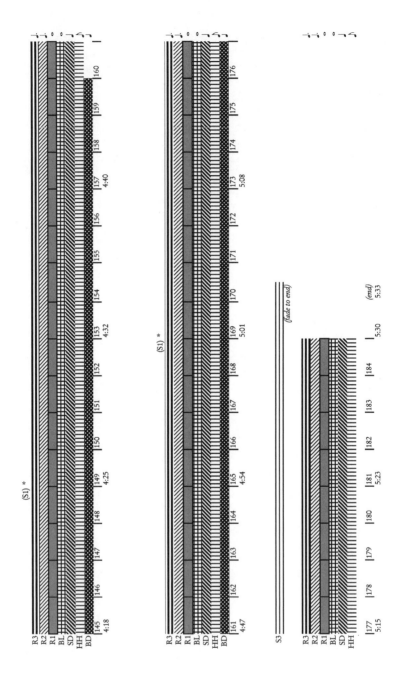

Track Name: "Connected"

Producer: James Ruskin

Sound Palette and Loop Lengths

Rhythmic sounds:

SOUND NAME	MOST CONCISE REPRESENTATION	LOOP LENGTH	OTHER COMMENTS
Bass Drum		♩	
Hi-Hat 1		♩	
Hi-Hat 2		♩	
Snare Drum		♪	
Handclaps		♩	
Riff 1a & b		o	
Bass Line		o	
Toms		♪	Timbre more resonant, less harsh than SD
Riff 1a & b'		o	

Loops ordered according to length:

♪	Snare Drum Toms
♩	Bass Drum Hi-Hat 1 Hi-Hat 2
♩	Handclaps
o	Riff 1a & b Bass Line Riff 1a & b'

Appendix C   299

ca. 139 BPM

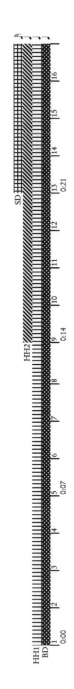

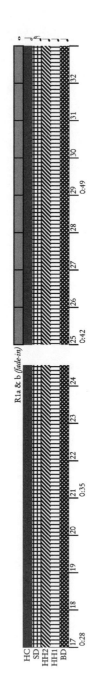

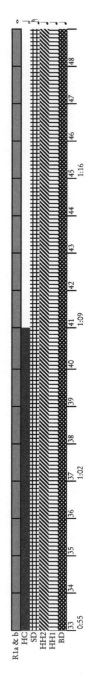

Track Name: "Jerical"

Producer: Jeff Mills

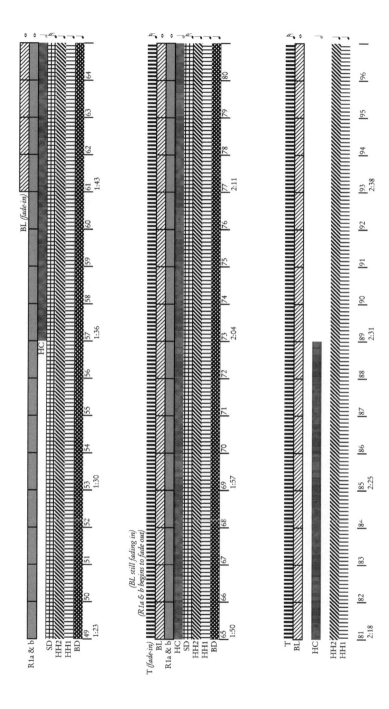

Track Name: "Jerical"

Producer: Jeff Mills

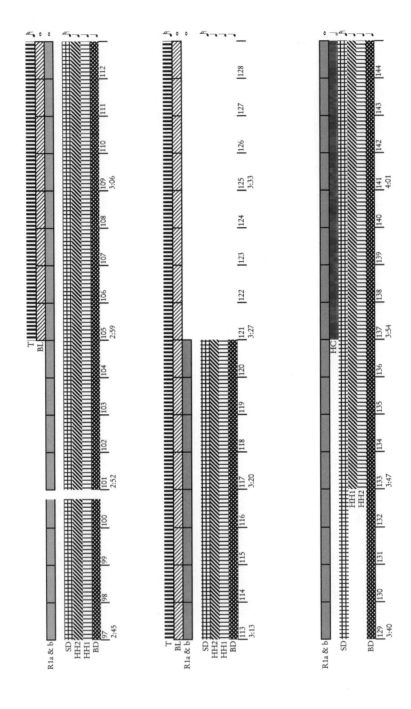

Track Name: "Jerical"

Producer: Jeff Mills

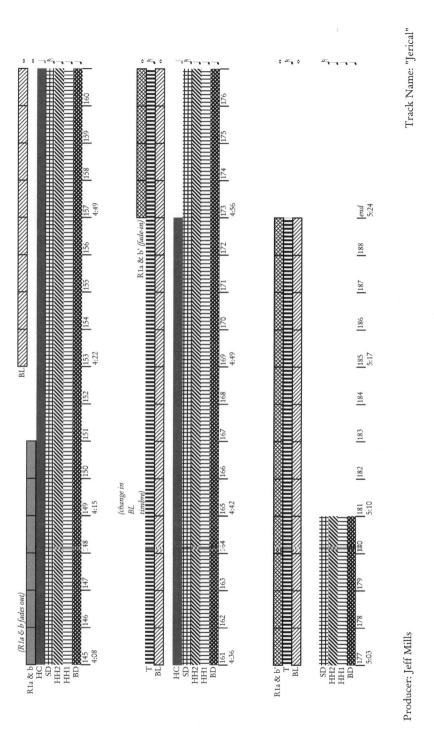

Track Name: "Jerical"

Producer: Jeff Mills

Sound Palette and Loop Lengths

Notes:

1. Because the loops in this track appear in a variety of metrical positions, they will be shown in their original, unshifted positions. Also, all parts that emerge within the initial 9/8 metrical context are shown with that time signature, even though 4/4 is eventually established as the primary meter. These choices allow for clearer, more concise notation.

2. Riff 3 is shown with a 9/8 time signature in order to indicate that the dotted quarter should be read within a 9/8 context. In 4/4, this note would be equivalent to the first duration of a half-note triplet (i.e., one-third of a measure).

Rhythmic sounds:

SOUND NAME	MOST CONCISE REPRESENTATION	LOOP LENGTH	OTHER COMMENTS
Riff 1	*[musical notation]*	o	
Riff 2	*[musical notation]*	o	
Riff 3	*[musical notation]*	1/3 o	Possibly an effect of reverb applied to R2. Varies timbrally throughout track
Riff 4	*[musical notation]*	♩	
Bass Drum	*[musical notation]*	♩	
Hi-Hat	*[musical notation]*	♩	Open
Snare Drum	*[musical notation]*	♩	
Riff 5	*[musical notation]*	o	Possibly an effect applied to R4

Articulative sounds:

SOUND NAME	DESCRIPTION
Synth 2	Continuous sound (ca. 7 seconds) like release of steam or gas. Indefinite pitch
Synth 3	Intermittent bursts of grace notes. Pitches vary freely and are too fast to be discerned individually

Atmospheric sounds:

SOUND NAME	DESCRIPTION
Synth 1	Loops continuously through stereo field. Rises & falls in pitch, in continuous (but reticulated) glissando

Loops ordered according to length:

♩	Bass Drum Hi-Hat
1/3 o	Riff 3
♩	Riff 4 Snare Drum
o	Riff 1 Riff 2 Riff 5

ca. 139 BPM

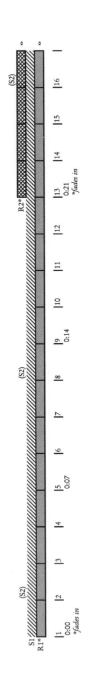

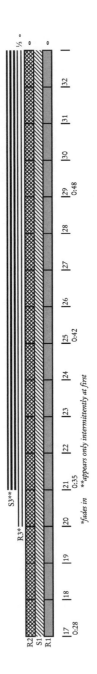

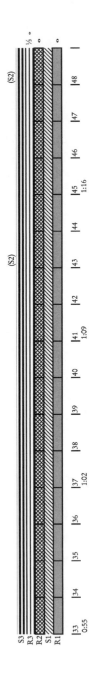

Producer: Kenny Larkin

Track Name: "Track"

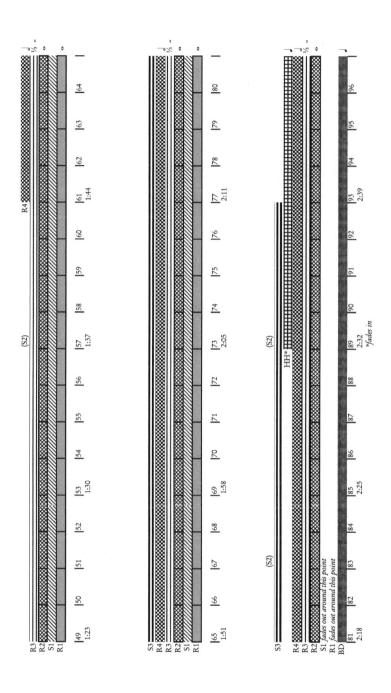

Track Name: "Track"

Producer: Kenny Larkin

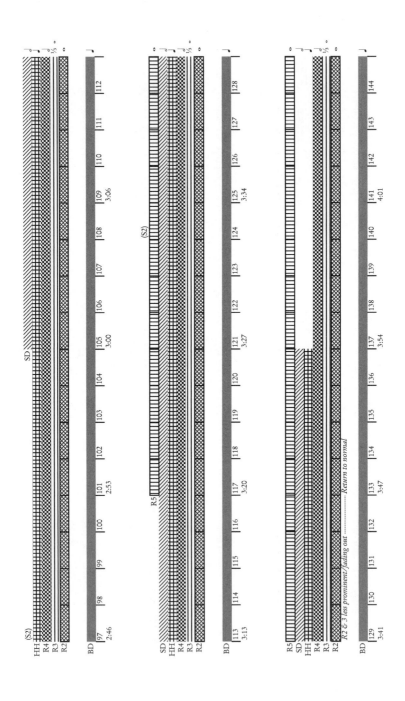

Producer: Kenny Larkin

Track Name: "Track"

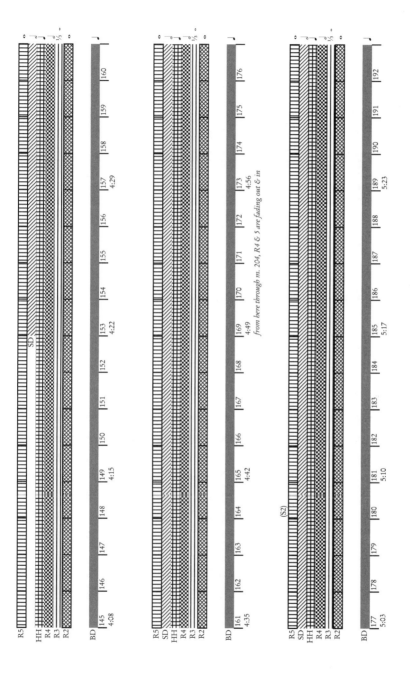

from here through m. 204, R4 & 5 are fading out & in

Producer: Kenny Larkin

Track Name: "Track"

Appendix C 309

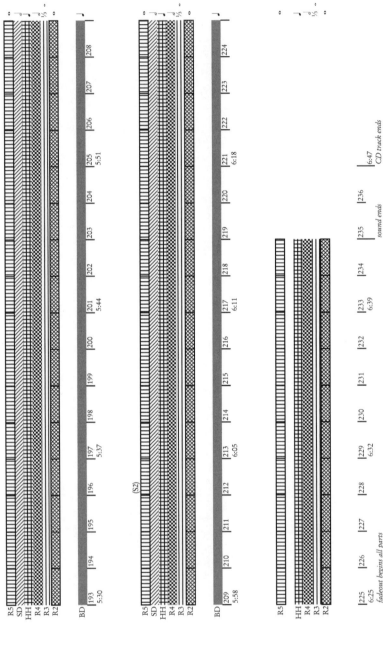

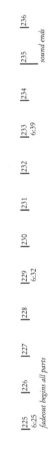

Track Name: "Track"

Producer: Kenny Larkin

Sound Palette and Loop Lengths

Rhythmic sounds:

SOUND NAME	MOST CONCISE REPRESENTATION	LOOP LENGTH	OTHER COMMENTS
Bass Drum	*[musical notation]*	♩	
Riff 1	*[musical notation]*	♩	Very distorted; effect is more timbral than pitch-oriented
Riff 2	*[musical notation]*	𝅝𝆹	At times, halved to produce either sustained or repeating C; also tweaked in various ways, some of which produce one-bar patterning.
Snare Drum 2	*[musical notation]*	𝅝𝆹	
Snare Drum 3a	Steady series of 8ths, diminuted to 16ths, then 32nds, then 64ths.	N/A	
Snare Drum 3b	*[musical notation]*	♩	Extracted from the fastest version of SD3a
Riff 3	*[musical notation]*	𝅝	

Articulative sounds:

SOUND NAME	MOST CONCISE REPRESENTATION	OTHER COMMENTS
Snare Drum 1a–c	SD1a: single snare hit on beat 4 SD1b: sixteenth note anacrusis + snare hit on downbeat SD1c: single snare hit on "and" of 4	

Loops ordered according to length:

♩	Bass Drum Riff 1 Snare Drum 3b
𝅝	Riff 2 variant Riff 3
𝅝𝆹	Riff 2 Snare Drum 2

Appendix C   311

ca. 135 BPM

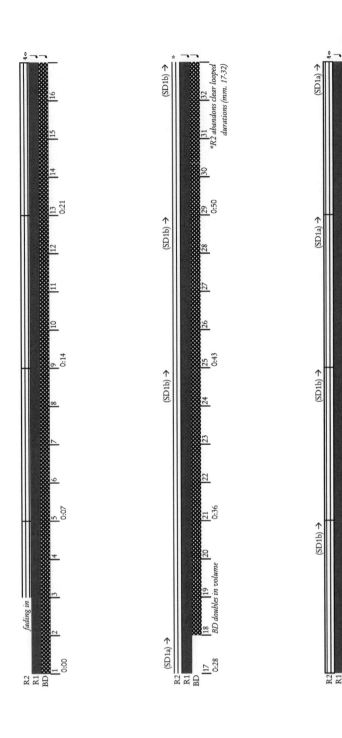

Producer: Mario Più

Track Name: "Communication (Mas Mix)"

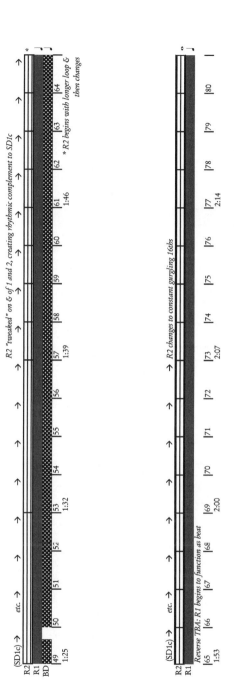

R2 "tweaked" on & of 1 and 2, creating rhythmic complement to SD1c

*R2 begins with longer loop & then changes

R2 changes to constant gurgling 16ths

Reverse TBA: R1 begins to function as beat

Track Name: "Communication (Mas Mix)"

Producer: Mario Più

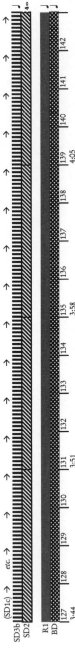

Producer: Mario Più

Track Name: "Communication (Más Mix)"

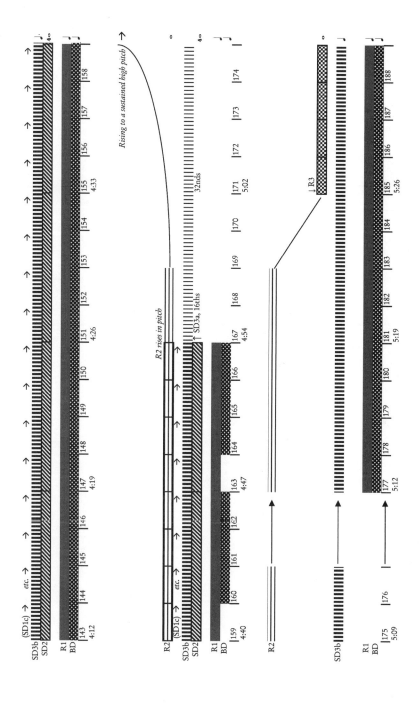

Track Name: "Communication (Mas Mix)"

Producer: Mario Più

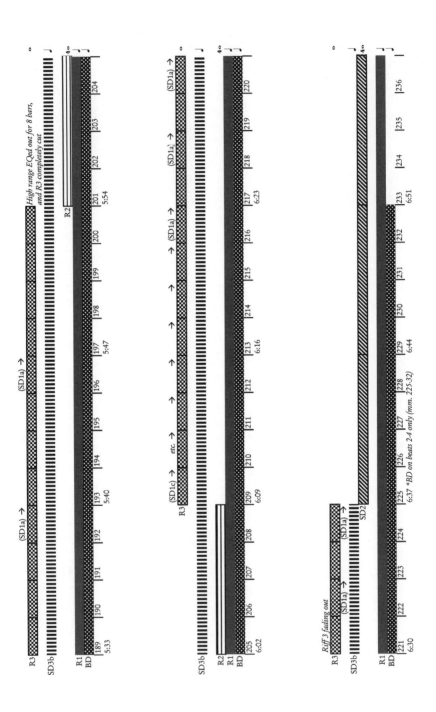

Producer: Mario Più

Track Name: "Communication (Mas Mix)"

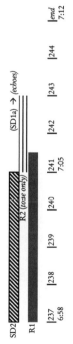

SD2

R1

R2 (tone only)

(SD1a) → (echoes)

|237 |238 |239 |240 |241 |242 |243 |244 |end
6:58   7:05   7:12

Track Name: "Communication (Mas Mix)"

Producer: Mario Più

Sound Palette and Loop Lengths

Rhythmic sounds:

SOUND NAME	MOST CONCISE REPRESENTATION	LOOP LENGTH	OTHER COMMENTS
Hi-Hat		o	Open, w/ distortion
Drum 1a & b		o	
Sample 1	You can't tell us how to play our mu-sic, oh no	2o	
Bass Drum		♩	
Bass Line		2o	
Snare Drum 1a & b		2o	
Snare Drum 2		o	
Sample 2		4o	
Riff 1a & b		𝅗𝅥	

Loops ordered according to length:

♩	Bass Drum
𝅗𝅥	Riff 1a & b
o	Hi-Hat Drum 1a & b Snare Drum 2
2o	Sample 1 Bass Line Snare Drum 1a & b
4o	Sample 2

318 Appendix C

ca. 124 BPM

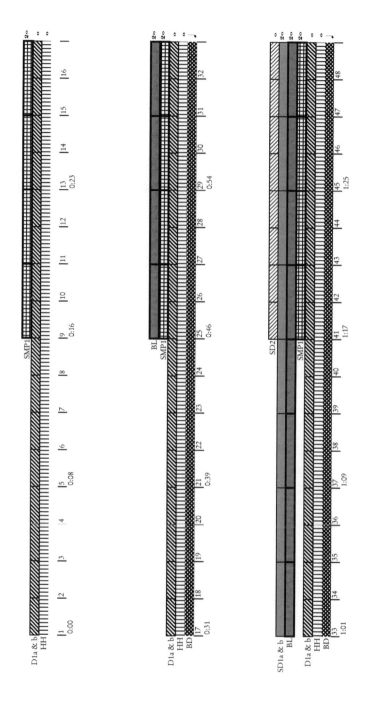

Producer: Reese and Santonio

Track Name: "How to Play Our Music"

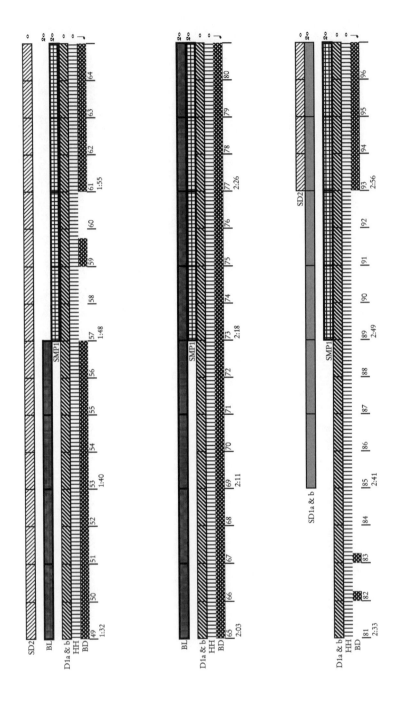

Track Name: "How to Play Our Music"

Producer: Reese and Santonio

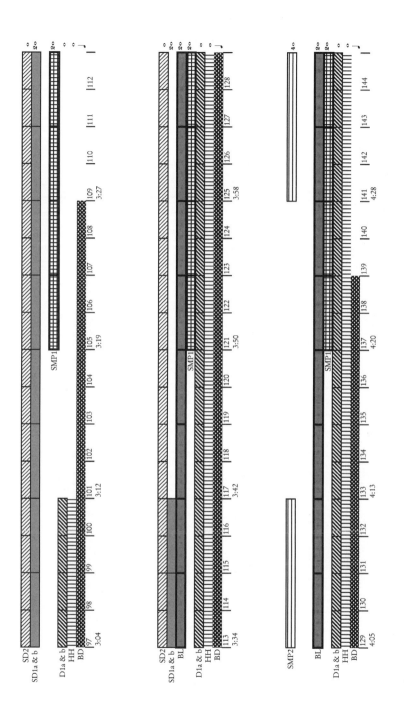

Track Name: "How to Play Our Music"

Producer: Reese and Santonio

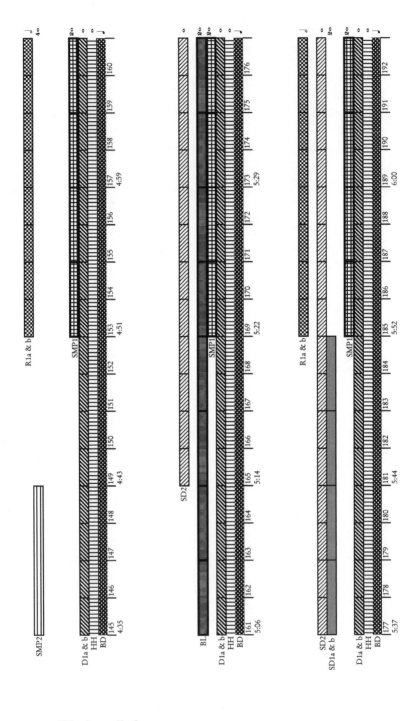

Track Name: "How to Play Our Music"

Producer: Reese and Santonio

Track Name: "How to Play Our Music"

(all parts begin fadeout)

R1a & b

SD2

D1a & b
HH

193	194	195	196	197	198	199	200	201	202	end
6:07				6:15				6:23		6:28

Producer: Reese and Santonio

Glossary of Terms
from Electronic Dance Music and Music Theory

backbeat In EDM and rock, a percussion pattern on the offbeats of a measure. The most common backbeat pattern, and the most common sense of the term, involves attacks on beats 2 and 4 of a 4/4 measure, but EDM also presents backbeats in which attacks fall on every eighth-note offbeat within the measure.

beat matching Process whereby a **DJ** maintains a constant tempo throughout a **set**. A fundamental skill of EDM mixing; less commonly known as "beat mixing." Involves minute adjustments (either positive or negative) to the speed of a record so as to match its tempo to that of the record currently being played. Records are not brought into the mix until they have been beat-matched; the process of adjustment is audible only to the DJ, who listens through headphones.

break 1. (n.) A percussion-only section of a record, particularly a funk or R&B record from the 1970s. 2. (n.) In EDM and hip hop, a sample taken from this type of break. *See also* **breakbeat**, sense 1. 3. (n.) In EDM, a section with a significantly thinner texture, usually marked by the removal of the bass drum. Also known as a **breakdown**. In this work, I always use "breakdown" to describe this type of section (though participants sometimes use "break" as well). 4. (v.) In EDM and hip hop, to dance acrobatically to a break (in the first sense) or music consisting of breaks. Synonym "break dance."

breakbeat 1. A **sample**, often accelerated in tempo, taken from the **break** of another record (most commonly a funk or R&B record from the 1970s). 2. A midtempo genre of EDM relying heavily on breakbeats.

breakdown In EDM, a section with a significantly thinner texture, usually marked by the removal of the bass drum. Cf. **break**, sense 3.

cardinality The number of **pulse-layer** attacks found in each pulse of an **interpretive layer.**

cycle The time span between points of alignment in a **grouping dissonance.**

diatonic rhythm A member of a class of rhythms that share certain special properties (such as **maximal evenness** and **maximal individuation**) with the diatonic scale. Diatonic rhythms are usually formed through the distribution of an odd number of attacks across an even-pulsed cycle, and most are asymmetrical. The most common diatonic rhythms in electronic dance music are 3+3+2 and 3+3+3+3+4.

displacement dissonance Type of metrical dissonance created through the nonalignment of two or more layers of motion with the same **cardinality.**

dissociation Effect of separation or disconnection that occurs when a dissonant layer of motion seems to function independently from a surrounding metrical context. Occurs most often with **embedded grouping dissonance** but also with **displacement dissonance** (especially **turning the beat around**).

DJ (disc jockey) 1. (n.) In EDM and hip hop, a person who puts together a continuous musical program by selecting, combining, and manipulating **tracks** (almost always in the form of vinyl records, though compact disc or .mp3 formats are occasionally used) with two or more turntables and a mixing board. This program generally unfolds through improvisational interaction with a dancing audience. Roles embodied by the DJ include musical connoisseur, performer, and composer; principal skills involved in EDM DJing are mixing and programming. 2. (v.) To perform as a DJ.

dropping the beat Term **DJs** use to describe the process of bringing in the bass drum after a **removal** or a **breakdown.** May occur within a **track** or at the moment when a new track enters the mix.

drum machine A **synthesizer** devoted exclusively to percussion sounds. Two drum machines made by Roland, the TR-808 and the TR-909, have been particularly central to the creation of EDM throughout its history.

embedded grouping dissonance (EGD) The simultaneous presentation of more than one **grouping dissonance** at multiple metrical levels. Arises when the **cycle** of a lower-level dissonance is incommensurate with the meter, thereby generating a higher-level grouping dissonance that unfolds at the same time as the lower-level dissonance.

groove 1. a short configuration of bass line and percussion that unfolds in continuously repeating cycles. 2. the way in which the rhythmic essence of a piece of music flows or unfolds.

grouping dissonance Type of metrical dissonance created through the nonalignment of two or more layers with noncongruent cardinalities. The layers involved in a grouping dissonance, unlike those found in a displacement dissonance, will align at periodic intervals. Cf. **cardinality; cycle; embedded grouping dissonance.**

interpretive layer A layer of motion moving more slowly than the **pulse layer** and grouping the pulse layer into larger units.

live PA A live performance in which a **producer** manipulates studio technology in real time to (re)create his or her own music. Fans and musicians almost always use the term in this abbreviated form; some claim that "PA" stands for "performance artist," whereas others give its meaning as "public appearance."

locked groove A short pattern, several beats to several measures in length, etched into a record in a way that allows it to repeat infinitely. Especially common in techno.

loop A repeating pattern, generally associated with a single instrumental sound, ranging in length from a sixteenth note to sixteen measures. The fundamental structural unit in electronic dance music.

maximal evenness A property that arises when a given number of elements (e.g., rhythmic attacks or pitch classes) are distributed as evenly as possible throughout a larger field or universe (such as a time span or a scale). Defined in Clough and Douthett 1991. A characteristic of **diatonic rhythms.**

maximal individuation A property of diatonic sets (including both **diatonic rhythms** and diatonic scales) in which each member of the set has a unique set of relationships with every other member of the set.

metrical dissonance Sense of conflicting patterns of accentuation created through the activity of noncongruent layers of motion or competing modes of metrical organization.

producer In EDM, the creator of the first recorded version(s) of a **track;** hence, the composer of this version. Also used in hip hop to refer to the creator of the instrumental portions of a track (as distinguished from the rapper, or "MC").

projection A perceptual process through which the duration of an event offers a basis for measuring the duration of an immediately successive event. The concept of projection is central to the model of meter proposed by Christopher Hasty (1997).

pulse layer The fastest regular layer of motion within a given musical passage.

remix 1. (n.) An alternate version of an EDM **track** based on studio manipulation of the track's master tapes. The extent to which the original recording is transformed varies widely, ranging from slight alteration to radical reconstruction. The person who creates the remix may be a **DJ**, a **producer**, or both. Though the term "remix" generally implies involvement from someone other than the creator of the original track, producers may also record several different versions of their own tracks. 2. (v.) To create a remix.

(bass-drum) removal The most common type of textural change in EDM, and the one with the most influence on metrical interpretations. May be initiated by the **DJ** or the **producer**. Lasts anywhere from one beat to several measures (e.g., sixteen). The removal of the bass drum may cause a formal section to be perceived as a **breakdown**. See also **withholding the beat**.

sample 1. A recording of any sound captured through the technique of digital **sampling**. 2. In general parlance, a sample in which the source of the captured sound is recognizable.

sampler Any device that performs the function of **sampling**. Samplers may be found within pieces of hardware devoted entirely or chiefly to sampling, within sampler-sequencers (in which sampling is one of two main functions), within types of hardware devoted primarily to other functions (such as synthesizers or mixers), or in software programs.

(digital) sampling A process in which analog sounds are converted to digital information (series of binary numbers) through periodic "snapshots" of the electrical signal of the source sound. The information recorded can then be used to generate new electrical signals, which—when presented in very rapid succession—collectively outline the shape of a waveform.

sequence A series of directions programmed by the **producer** that tells each instrument within a **track** when, how long, and how to play.

sequencer A hardware or software device that controls the instruments and events that occur in a **track**. Records and carries out a series of directions (a **sequence**) programmed by the **producer**.

set A single continuous **DJ** performance. Usually by one DJ, though sometimes involves two DJs alternating back and forth (a "tag team"). Sets typically last from one to four hours, but lengths up to twelve hours are not unheard of. DJs regard sets as wholes, which they unify by preserving a constant tempo and minimizing the distinctions between individual **tracks**.

synthesis The electronic generation of sound. Involves the generation of sound waves through hardware or software devices such as oscillators. Both analog and digital synthesis are used in the production of electronic dance music.

synthesizer A device that generates electronic sound through **synthesis**. Modern synthesizers also incorporate **sampling** and sound processing functions as well as varying degrees of sequencing capability. Most commonly a keyboard instrument, but also appears in a variety of other hardware and software manifestations.

track 1. A complete EDM composition, identified with a distinct title (and sometimes with a subtitle indicating a particular **remix**) and separate from other tracks on an unmixed record or compact disc. Connotes an instrumental, rhythmic emphasis, as opposed to the emphases on the voice and pitch found in a "song." 2. A single textural layer within a composition, as defined by a distinct instrumental sound; in particular, a single instrumental sound within a sequencing program. Cf. Krims 2000. This sense of "track" is not used in this work.

third record, the A hybrid musical entity created by the **DJ** through the combination and manipulation of two preexisting **tracks**; in effect, a "new" track created within the context of live performance.

turning the beat around (TBA) A process in which a metrical interpretation suggested by a previously established layer of motion is "turned around" through the sudden entrance of a new textural layer. Previously accented attacks are experienced as offbeats, and displacement dissonance results.

(metrical) underdetermination Metrical ambiguity resulting from the absence of one or more of the layers of motion needed to make a decisive metrical interpretation.

withholding the beat A type of bass-drum removal specific to live DJ **sets.** Involves a dynamic between **DJ** and audience in which the DJ teasingly takes away the bass-drum beat and the audience expectantly awaits its return (and then responds joyously when the DJ brings it back into the mix).

References

Agawu, Kofi. 1986. "Gi Dunu, Nyekpadudo and the Study of West African Rhythm." *Ethnomusicology* 30, no. 1: 64–83.

———. 1994. "Ambiguity in Tonal Music: A Preliminary Study." In *Theory, Analysis, and Meaning in Music,* ed. Anthony Pople, 86–107. Cambridge: Cambridge University Press.

———. 1995. *African Rhythm.* Cambridge: Cambridge University Press.

Amico, Stephen. 2001. " 'I Want Muscles: House Music, Homosexuality, and Masculine Signification." *Popular Music* 20, no. 3: 359–78.

———. 2003. Review of *"You Better Work!" Underground Dance Music in New York City,* by Kai Fikentscher. *Popular Music* 22, no. 2: 256–58.

Arom, Simha. 1989. "Time Structure in Music of Central Africa: Periodicity, Meter, Rhythm, and Polyrhythmics." *Leonardo* 22, no. 1: 91–100.

———. 1991. *African Polyphony and Polyrhythm: Musical Structure and Methodology.* Trans. Martin Thom, Barbara Tuckett, and Raymond Boyd. Cambridge: Cambridge University Press.

Austin, Brian Todd. 1994. "The Construction and Transformation of the American Disc Jockey Occupation, 1950–1993." Ph.D. diss., University of Texas at Austin.

Bader, Rolf. 1994. "Perception and Analysing Methods of Groove in Popular Music." *Systematische Musikwissenschaft* 2, no. 1: 145–54.

Barr, Tim. 2000. *Techno: The Rough Guide.* London: Rough Guides.

Barz, Gregory F., and Timothy J. Cooley, eds. 1997. *Shadows in the Field: New Perspectives for Fieldwork in Ethnomusicology.* Oxford: Oxford University Press.

Berry, Wallace. 1985. "Metric and Rhythmic Articulation in Music." *Music Theory Spectrum* 7: 7–33.

Bidder, Sean. 1999. *House: The Rough Guide.* London: Rough Guides.

Blacking, John. 1973. *How Musical Is Man?* Seattle: University of Washington Press.

Bourdieu, Pierre. 1984. *Distinction: A Social Critique of the Judgement of Taste.* Trans. Richard Nice. Cambridge, Mass.: Harvard University Press.

Bradby, Barbara. 1993. "Sampling Sexuality: Gender, Technology, and the Body in Dance Music." *Popular Music* 12, no. 2: 155–76.

Brewster, Bill, and Frank Broughton. 2000. *Last Night a DJ Saved My Life: The History of the Disc Jockey.* New York: Grove Press.

———. 2003. *How to DJ Right: The Art and Science of Playing Records.* New York: Grove Press.

Brownell, John. 1994. "Analytical Models of Jazz Improvisation." *jazzforschung/jazz research* 26: 9–30.

Buckland, Fiona. 2002. *Impossible Dance: Club Culture and Queer World-Making.* Middletown, Conn.: Wesleyan University Press.

Butler, Mark J. 2000. "Music as Action: Techno and the Perception of Agency." In *Semi-*

otics 1999: Proceedings of the Twenty-fourth Annual Meeting of the Semiotic Society of America, ed. Scott Simpkins, C. W. Spinks, and John Deely, 303–14. New York: Peter Lang.

———. 2001. "Turning the Beat Around: Reinterpretation, Metrical Dissonance, and Asymmetry in Electronic Dance Music." *Music Theory Online* 7, no. 6. Available from http://www.societymusictheory.org/mto/issues/mto.01.7.6/toc.7.6.html. Accessed 14 February 2004.

Cascone, Kim. 2000. "The Aesthetics of Failure: 'Post-Digital' Tendencies in Contemporary Computer Music." *Computer Music Journal* 24, no. 4: 12–18.

Chanan, Michael. 1995. *Repeated Takes: A Short History of Recording and Its Effects on Music.* New York: Verso.

Chernoff, John M. 1979. *African Rhythm and African Sensibility.* Chicago: University of Chicago Press.

Clough, John, and Jack Douthett. 1991. "Maximally Even Sets." *Journal of Music Theory* 35, no. 1: 93–173.

Cohn, Richard. 1992a. "The Dramatization of Hypermetric Conflicts in the Scherzo of Beethoven's Ninth Symphony." *19th Century Music* 15, no. 3: 188–206.

———. 1992b. "Metric and Hypermetric Dissonance in the *Menuetto* of Mozart's Symphony in G Minor, K. 550." *Intégral* 6: 1–33.

———. 2001. "Complex Hemiolas, Ski-Hill Graphs, and Metric Spaces." *Music Analysis* 20, no. 3: 295–326.

Collin, Matthew, with contributions by John Godfrey. 1997. *Altered State: The Story of Ecstasy Culture and Acid House.* London: Serpent's Tail.

Cone, Edward. 1968. *Musical Form and Musical Performance.* New York: W. W. Norton.

Cosgrove, Stuart. 1988. "Seventh City Techno." *The Face* 97: 86–89.

Covach, John. 1997a. "Progressive Rock, 'Close to the Edge,' and the Boundaries of Style." In *Understanding Rock: Essays in Musical Analysis,* ed. John Covach and Graeme M. Boone, 3–31. New York: Oxford University Press.

———. 1997b. "We Won't Get Fooled Again: Rock Music and Musical Analysis." In *Keeping Score: Music, Disciplinarity, Culture,* ed. David Schwarz, Anahid Kassabian, and Lawrence Siegel, 75–89. Charlottesville: University Press of Virginia.

Dyer, Richard. 1990 [1979]. "In Defense of Disco." In *On Record: Rock, Pop, and the Written Word,* ed. Simon Frith and Andrew Goodwin, 410–18. New York: Pantheon Books.

Eshun, Kodwo. 1999. *More Brilliant Than the Sun: Adventures in Sonic Fiction.* London: Quartet Books.

Evans-Pritchard, E. E. 1956. *Nuer Religion.* Oxford: Clarendon Press.

Fales, Cornelia. 2004. "Short-Circuiting Perceptual Circuits: Timbre in Ambient and Techno Music." In *Wired for Sound: Engineering and Technologies in Sonic Cultures,* ed. Paul Greene and Thomas Porcello. Middletown, Conn.: Wesleyan University Press.

———. Forthcoming. *Timbre, Techno, and Sonorous Bodies: Perceptual Revolutions in the Eighteenth and Twenty-First Centuries.* Middletown, Conn.: Wesleyan University Press.

Fikentscher, Kai. 1995. "Popular Music and Age Stratification: The Case of Underground Dance Music in the Post-Disco Period." In *Popular Music: Style and Identity,* ed. Will Straw, 89–94.

———. 2000. *"You Better Work!" Underground Dance Music in New York City.* Hanover, N.H.: Wesleyan University Press.

Fitzgerald, John L. 1998. "An Assemblage of Desire, Drugs, and Techno." *Angelaki: Journal of the Theoretical Humanities* 3, no. 2: 41–57.

Forte, Allen. 1981. "The Magical Kaleidoscope: Schoenberg's First Atonal Masterwork, Opus 11, No. 1." *Journal of the Arnold Schoenberg Institute* 5: 127–68.

Fritz, Jimi. 1999. *Rave Culture: An Insider's Overview.* Victoria, B.C.: Smallfry Enterprises.

Geertz, Clifford. 1973. *The Interpretation of Cultures: Selected Essays.* New York: Basic Books.

Gerard, Morgan, and Jack Sidnell. 2000. "Reaching Out to the Core: On the Interactional Work of the MC in Drum & Bass Performance." *Popular Music and Society* 24, no. 3: 21–39.

Gilbert, Jeremy, and Ewan Pearson. 1999. *Discographies: Dance Music, Culture, and the Politics of Sound.* New York: Routledge.

Goehr, Lydia. 1992. *The Imaginary Museum of Musical Works: An Essay in the Philosophy of Music.* Oxford: Clarendon Press.

Gore, Georgina. 1997. "The Beat Goes On: Trance, Dance, and Tribalism in Rave Culture." In *Dance in the City,* ed. Helen Thomas, 50–67. New York: St. Martin's Press.

Guck, Marion. 1994. "Analytical Fictions." *Music Theory Spectrum* 16, no. 2: 217–30.

Gwertzman, Mike. 2001. Review of DJ performances by Carl Cox and Danny Tenaglia, Twilo, New York City. *Urb: Future Music Culture,* May, 44.

Hadley, Daniel. 1993. " 'Ride the Rhythm': Two Approaches to DJ Practice." *Journal of Popular Music Studies* 5: 58–67.

Handel, Stephen. 1984. "Using Polyrhythms to Study Rhythm." *Music Perception* 1, no. 4: 465–84.

———. 1992. "The Differentiation of Rhythmic Structure." *Perception and Psychophysics* 52: 492–507.

———. 1998. "The Interplay between Metric and Figural Rhythmic Organization." *Journal of Experimental Psychology: Human Perception and Performance* 24, no. 5: 1546–61.

———, and James S. Oshinsky. 1981. "The Meter of Syncopated Auditory Polyrhythms." *Perception and Psychophysics* 30, no. 1: 1–9.

Haraway, Donna J. 1991. *Simians, Cyborgs, and Women: The Reinvention of Nature.* New York: Routledge.

Hasty, Christopher. 1997. *Meter as Rhythm.* Oxford: Oxford University Press.

Hatten, Robert. 2002. Review of *Fantasy-Pieces: Metrical Dissonance in the Music of Robert Schumann,* by Harald Krebs. *Music Theory Spectrum* 24, no. 2: 273–82.

Headlam, Dave. 1997. "Blues Transformations in the Music of Cream." In *Understanding Rock: Essays in Musical Analysis,* ed. John Covach and Graeme M. Boone, 59–92. New York: Oxford University Press.

Hesmondhalgh, David. 1995. "Technoprophecy: A Response to Tagg." *Popular Music* 14, no. 2: 261–63.

———. 2000. "International Times: Fusions, Exoticisms, and Antiracisms in Electronic Dance Music." In *Western Music and Its Others: Difference, Representation, and Appropriation in Music,* ed. Georgina Born and David Hesmondhalgh, 280–304. Berkeley and Los Angeles: University of California Press.

Hirata, Catherine. 1996. "The Sounds of the Sounds Themselves: Analyzing the Early Music of Morton Feldman." *Perspectives of New Music* 34, no. 1: 6–27.

Holleran, Andrew. 1978. *The Dancer from the Dance: A Novel.* New York: Bantam Books.

Hopkins, Susan. 1996. "Synthetic Ecstasy: The Youth Culture of Techno Music." *Youth Studies Australia* 15, no. 2: 12–17.

Horlacher, Gretchen. 1992. "The Rhythms of Reiteration: Formal Development in Stravinsky's Ostinati." *Music Theory Spectrum* 14: 171–87.

———. 1995. "Metric Irregularity in *Les Noces:* The Problem of Periodicity." *Journal of Music Theory* 39, no. 2: 285–309.

———. 1997. Review of *Meter as Rhythm,* by Christopher Hasty. *Intégral* 11: 181–90.

———. 2000. "Multiple Meters and Metrical Processes in the Music of Steve Reich." *Intégral* 14/15.

———. 2001. "Bartók's 'Change of Time': Coming Unfixed." *Music Theory Online* 7, no. 1. Available from http://www.societymusictheory.org/mto/issues/mto.01.7.1/toc.7.1.html. Accessed 14 February 2004.

Hughes, Tim. 2000. Review of *Understanding Rock: Essays in Musical Analysis,* ed. John Covach and Graeme M. Boone. *Indiana Theory Review* 21: 197–222.

———. 2003. "Groove and Flow: Six Analytical Essays on the Music of Stevie Wonder." Ph.D. diss., University of Washington.

Hughes, Walter. 1994. "In the Empire of the Beat: Discipline and Disco." In *Microphone Fiends: Youth Music and Youth Culture,* ed. Andrew Ross and Tricia Rose, 147–59. New York: Routledge.

Hutson, Scott R. 1999. "Technoshamanism: Spiritual Healing in the Rave Subculture." *Popular Music and Society* 23, no. 3: 53–78.

Imbrie, Andrew. 1973. " 'Extra' Measures and Metrical Ambiguity in Beethoven." In *Beethoven Studies,* ed. Alan Tyson, 45–66. New York: W. W. Norton.

Johnson, Hafiz Shabazz Farel, and John M. Chernoff. 1991. "Basic Conga Drum Rhythms in African-American Musical Styles." *Black Music Research Journal* 11, no. 1: 55–73.

Jones, Arthur M. 1959. *Studies in African Music.* London: Oxford University Press.

Jordan, Tim. 1995. "Collective Bodies: Raving and the Politics of Deleuze and Guattari." *Body and Society* 1, no. 1: 125–44.

Kaminsky, Peter. 1989. "Aspects of Harmony, Rhythm, and Form in Schumann's *Papillons, Carnaval,* and *Davidsbündlertänze.*" Ph.D. diss., University of Rochester.

Katz, Mark. 2004. *Capturing Sound: How Technology Has Changed Music.* Berkeley and Los Angeles: University of California Press.

Kauffman, Robert. 1980. "African Rhythm: A Reassessment." *Ethnomusicology* 24, no. 3: 393–415.

Keil, Charles, and Stephen Feld. 1994. *Music Grooves: Essays and Dialogues.* Chicago: University of Chicago Press.

Keller, Robert. 2003. "Mapping the Soundscape." M.M. thesis, Florida State University.

Kisliuk, Michelle. 1998. *Seize the Dance! BaAka Musical Life and the Ethnography of Performance.* Oxford: Oxford University Press.

Koetting, James. 1970. "Analysis and Notation of West African Drum Ensemble Music." *Selected Reports in Ethnomusicology* 1, no. 3: 115–46.

Korsyn, Kevin. 2003. *Decentering Music: A Critique of Contemporary Musical Research.* Oxford: Oxford University Press.

Kramer, Jonathan D. 1988. *The Time of Music.* New York: Schirmer.

Krebs, Harald. 1987. "Some Extensions of the Concepts of Metrical Consonance and Dissonance." *Journal of Music Theory* 31: 99–120.

———. 1997. "Robert Schumann's Metrical Revisions." *Music Theory Spectrum* 19: 35–54.

———. 1999. *Fantasy-Pieces: Metrical Dissonance in the Music of Robert Schumann.* New York: Oxford University Press.

Krims, Adam. 2000. *Rap Music and the Poetics of Identity.* Cambridge: Cambridge University Press.

Langlois, Tony. 1992. "Can You Feel It? DJs and House Music Culture in the UK." *Popular Music* 11, no. 2: 229–38.

Lerdahl, Fred, and Ray Jackendoff. 1983. *A Generative Theory of Tonal Music.* Cambridge, Mass.: MIT Press.

Lester, Joel. 1986. *The Rhythms of Tonal Music.* Carbondale: Southern Illinois University Press.

Levy, Janet M. 1995. "Beginning-Ending Ambiguity: Consequences of Performance Choices." In *The Practice of Performance: Studies in Musical Interpretation,* ed. John Rink, 150–69. Cambridge: Cambridge University Press.

Lewin, David. 1993. *Musical Form and Transformation: 4 Analytic Essays.* New Haven, Conn.: Yale University Press.

Littlefield, Richard. 1996. "The Silence of the Frames." *Music Theory Online* 2, no. 1. Available from http://www.societymusictheory.org/mto/issues/mto.96.2.1/mto.96.2.1.littlefield.html. Accessed 14 February 2004.

Locke, David. 1982. "Principles of Offbeat Timing and Cross-Rhythm in Southern Eve Dance Drumming." *Ethnomusicology* 27, no. 2: 217–46.

———. 1987. *Drum Gahu: The Rhythms of West African Drumming.* Crown Point, Ind.: White Cliffs Media Co.

Loubet, Emmanuelle. 2000. "Laptop Performers, Compact Disc Designers, and No-Beat Techno Artists in Japan: Music from Nowhere." *Computer Music Journal* 24, no. 4: 19–32.

Loza, Susana. 1996. "Techno Music and Sonic Communities: When Modern Markets and Postmodern Pleasures Collide." *Journal of Popular Music Studies* 8: 27–41.

———. 2001. "Sampling (Hetero)sexuality: Diva-Ness and Discipline in Electronic Dance Music." *Popular Music* 20, no. 3: 349–57.

Lysloff, René T. A., and Leslie C. Gay, Jr., eds. 2003. *Music and Technoculture.* Middletown, Conn.: Wesleyan University Press.

Maira, Sunaina. 2002. *Desis in the House: Indian American Youth Culture in New York City.* Philadelphia: Temple University Press.

———. 2003. "TranceGlobalNation: Orientalism, Cosmopolitanism, and Citizenship in Youth Culture." *Journal of Popular Music Studies* 15, no. 1: 3–33.

Malbon, Ben. 1999. *Clubbing: Dancing, Ecstasy, and Vitality.* New York: Routledge.

Maus, Fred Everett. 1993. "Masculine Discourse in Music Theory." *Perspectives of New Music* 31, no. 2: 264–93.

McLeod, Kembrew. 2001. "Genres, Subgenres, Sub-Subgenres, and More: Musical and Social Differentiation with Electronic/Dance Music Communities." *Journal of Popular Music Studies* 13, no. 1: 59–76.

McRobbie, Angela. 2002. "Clubs to Companies: Notes on the Decline of Political Culture in Speeded-Up Creative Worlds." *Cultural Studies* 16, no. 4: 516–31.

———. 1999. *In the Culture Society: Art, Fashion, and Popular Music.* New York: Routledge.

Middleton, Richard. 1990. *Studying Popular Music.* Philadelphia: Open University Press.

Miyakawa, Felicia M. 2003. "God Hop: The Music and Message of Five Percenter Rap." Ph.D. diss., Indiana University.

Moore, Allan F. 2001a. "Categorical Conventions in Music Discourse: Style and Genre." *Music & Letters* 82, no. 3: 432–42.

―――. 2001b. *Rock: The Primary Text: Developing a Musicology of Rock.* 2d ed. Burlington, Vt.: Ashgate.

Neal, Jocelyn. 1998. "The Metric Makings of a Country Hit." In *Reading Country Music,* ed. Cecilia Tichi, 322–37. Durham, N.C.: Duke University Press.

Nettl, Bruno. 1974. "Thoughts on Improvisation: A Comparative Approach." *Musical Quarterly* 60: 1–19.

Nketia, J. H. Kwabena. 1974. *The Music of Africa.* New York: W. W. Norton.

Noys, Benjamin. 1995. "Into the 'Jungle.' " *Popular Music* 14, no. 3: 321–32.

Pellman, Samuel. 1994. *An Introduction to the Creation of Electroacoustic Music.* Belmont, Calif.: Wadsworth Publishing.

Pini, Maria. 1997a. "Cyborgs, Nomads, and the Raving Feminine." In *Dance in the City,* ed. Helen Thomas, 111–29. New York: St. Martin's Press.

―――. 1997b. "Women and the Early British Rave Scene." In *Back to Reality? Social Experience and Cultural Studies,* ed. Angela McRobbie, 152–69. Manchester: Manchester University Press.

―――. 1998. " 'Peak Practices': The Production and Regulation of Ecstatic Bodies." In *The Virtual Embodied: Presence/Practice/Technology,* ed. John Wood, 168–80. New York: Routledge.

―――. 2001. *Club Cultures and Female Subjectivity: The Move from Home to House.* New York: Palgrave.

Poschardt, Ulf. 1995. *DJ Culture.* Translated by Shaun Whiteside. Hamburg: Rogner & Bernhard.

Prendergast, Mark. 2003. *The Ambient Century: From Mahler to Moby—The Evolution of Sound in the Electronic Age.* New York: Bloomsbury.

Pressing, Jeff. 1983. "Cognitive Isomorphisms between Pitch and Rhythm in World Musics: West Africa, the Balkans, and Western Tonality." *Studies in Music* 17: 38–61.

Rahn, Jay. 1987. "Asymmetrical Ostinatos in Sub-Saharan Music: Time, Pitch, and Cycles Reconsidered." *In Theory Only* 9, no. 7: 23–36.

―――. 1996. "Turning the Analysis Around: African-Derived Rhythms and Europe-Derived Music Theory." *Black Music Research Journal* 16, no. 1: 71–89.

Redhead, Steve, ed. 1993. *Rave Off: Politics and Deviance in Contemporary Youth Culture.* Avebury: Aldershot.

―――, and Derek Wynne, eds. 1997. *The Clubcultures Reader: Readings in Popular Cultural Studies.* Oxford: Blackwell.

Reich, Steve. 1988. "Non-Western Music and the Western Composer." *Analyse musicale* 11: 46–50.

Reighley, Kurt. 2000. *Looking for the Perfect Beat: The Art and Culture of the DJ.* New York: Simon and Schuster.

Reynolds, Simon. 1999. *Generation Ecstasy: Into the World of Techno and Rave Culture.* New York: Routledge.

Rietveld, Hillegonda. 1998. *This Is Our House: House Music, Cultural Spaces, and Technologies.* Brookfield, Vt.: Ashgate.

Rose, Tricia. 1994. *Black Noise: Rap Music and Black Culture in Contemporary America.* Hanover, N.H.: Wesleyan University Press.

Rothstein, William. 1989. *Phrase Rhythm in Tonal Music.* New York: Schirmer Books.

Rule, Greg. 1999. *Electro Shock! Groundbreakers of Synth Music.* San Francisco: Miller Freeman Books.

Rushkoff, Douglas. 1995. *Cyberia: Life in the Trenches of Hyperspace.* New York: HarperCollins Publishers.

Samarotto, Frank. 2000. "The Body That Beats." Review of *Fantasy-Pieces: Metrical Dissonance in the Music of Robert Schumann,* by Harald Krebs. *Music Theory Online* 6.4. Available from http://www.societymusictheory.org/mto/issues/mto.00.6.4/toc.6.4.html. Accessed 9 February 2003.

Savage, Jon. 1993. "Machine Soul: A History of Techno." *Village Voice* (Summer), Rock and Roll Quarterly insert.

Sawyer, R. Keith. 1996. "The Semiotics of Improvisation: The Pragmatics of Musical and Verbal Performance." *Semiotica* 108: 269–306.

Schachter, Carl. 1976. "Rhythm and Linear Analysis: A Preliminary Study." *The Music Forum* 4: 281–334.

———. 1980. "Rhythm and Linear Analysis: Durational Reduction." *The Music Forum* 5: 197–232.

———. 1987. "Rhythm and Linear Analysis: Aspects of Meter." *The Music Forum* 6: 1–59.

Scherzinger, Martin. 2001. "Negotiating the Music-Theory/African-Music Nexus: A Political Critique of Ethnomusicological Anti-Formalism and a Strategic Analysis of the Shona Mbira Song Nyamaropa." *Perspectives of New Music* 39, no. 1: 5–117.

Schloss, Joseph Glenn. 2004. *Making Beats: The Art of Sample-Based Hip Hop.* Middletown, Conn.: Wesleyan University Press.

Schwartz, Matt. 2001. "Are All-Night Dance Parties, or 'Raves,' Dens of Drugs—As Indianapolis' Mayor Says—or Just Fun Places to Socialize?" *The Indianapolis Star,* July 10.

Seeger, Charles. 1958. "Prescriptive and Descriptive Music Writing." *The Musical Quarterly* 44: 184–95.

Shapiro, Peter, ed. 2000. *Modulations: A History of Electronic Music—Throbbing Words on Sound.* New York: Distributed Art Publishers.

Sharma, Sanjay, John Hutnyk, and Ashwani Sharma, eds. 1996. *Dis-Orienting Rhythms: The Politics of the New Asian Dance Music.* London: Zed Books.

Shepherd, John. 1982. "A Theoretical Model for the Sociomusicological Analysis of Popular Musics." *Popular Music* 2: 145–77.

Sicko, Dan. 1999. *Techno Rebels: The Renegades of Electronic Funk.* New York: Billboard Books.

Silcott, Mireille. 1999. *Rave America: New School Dancescapes.* Toronto: ECW Press.

Small, Christopher. 1987. *Music of the Common Tongue: Survival and Celebration in Afro-American Music.* New York: Riverrun.

Stephenson, Ken. 2002. *What to Listen For in Rock: A Stylistic Analysis.* New Haven, Conn.: Yale University Press.

Stewart, Alexander. 2000. " 'Funky Drummer': New Orleans, James Brown, and the Rhythmic Transformation of American Popular Music." *Popular Music* 19, no. 3: 293–318.

Stone, Ruth M. 1985. "In Search of Time in African Music." *Music Theory Spectrum* 7: 139–48.

Tagg, Philip. 1982. "Analysing Popular Music: Theory, Method, and Practice." *Popular Music* 2: 37–67.

———. 1994. "From Refrain to Rave: The Decline of Figure and the Rise of Ground." *Popular Music* 13, no. 2: 209–22.

Taiwo, Olu. 1998. "The 'Return-Beat': 'Curved Perceptions' in Music and Dance.' " In *The*

Virtual Embodied: Presence/Practice/Technology, ed. John Wood, 157–67. New York: Routledge.

Taylor, Timothy. 2001. *Strange Sounds: Music, Technology, and Culture.* New York: Routledge.

Temperley, David. 1999. "Syncopation in Rock: A Perceptual Perspective." *Popular Music* 18, no. 1: 19–40.

———. 2000. "Meter and Grouping in African Music: A View from Music Theory." *Ethnomusicology* 44, no. 1: 65–96.

———. 2001. *The Cognition of Basic Musical Structures.* Cambridge, Mass.: MIT Press.

Théberge, Paul. 1997. *Any Sound You Can Imagine: Making Music/Consuming Technology.* Hanover, N.H.: Wesleyan University Press.

Thomson, William. 1983. "Functional Ambiguity in Musical Structures." *Music Perception* 1: 3–27.

Thornton, Sarah. 1994. "Moral Panic, The Media, and British Rave Culture." In *Microphone Fiends: Youth Music and Youth Culture,* ed. Andrew Ross and Tricia Rose, 176–92. New York: Routledge.

———. 1996. *Club Cultures: Music, Media, and Subcultural Capital.* Hanover, N.H.: Wesleyan University Press.

Tirro, Frank. 1974. "Constructive Elements in Jazz Improvisation." *Journal of the American Musicological Society* 27, no. 2: 285–305.

Toffler, Alvin. 1980. *The Third Wave.* New York: Morrow.

Walser, Robert. 1993. *Runnin' with the Devil: Power, Gender, and Madness in Heavy Metal Music.* Hanover, N.H.: Wesleyan University Press.

———. 1995. "Rhythm, Rhyme, and Rhetoric in the Music of Public Enemy." *Ethnomusicology* 39, no. 2: 193–217.

Yeston, Maury. 1976. *The Stratification of Musical Rhythm.* New Haven, Conn.: Yale University Press.

Zak, Albin J. 2001. *The Poetics of Rock: Cutting Tracks, Making Records.* Berkeley and Los Angeles: University of California Press.

Discography

Note: Only works shown in musical examples are included.

808 State. 1990. *Cubik.* Tommy Boy TBCD 959.

A Number of Names. 2001 [1981]. "Shari Vari." On *A Number of Names, "Shari Vari,"
Remixes.* Puzzlebox Recordings PBX-6.

Azzido Da Bass. 1999. *Dooms Night Remixes.* Edel 70962.

Carl Craig. 1997. *More Songs about Food and Revolutionary Art.* Planet E Records
PE65232.

Dave Angel. 1996. *Classics.* R & S Records 96089 CD.

Frankie Bones [DJ]. 2000. *You Know My Name.* Moonshine Records MM 80135–2.

James Brown. 1971. *In the Jungle Groove.* Polydor PD4054.

James Ruskin. 2000. *Point 2.* Tresor 145.

Jeff Mills. 1992. *Waveform Transmission Vol. 1.* Tresor 11.

Juan Atkins [DJ]. 1998. *WaxTrax! Mastermix Vol. 1.* WaxTrax! Records TVT 7254–2.

Kenny Larkin. 1994. *Azimuth.* WaxTrax! Records TVT 7219–2.

Mario Più. 1999. *Communication (Somebody Answer the Phone).* Avex AVTCDS–236.

Plastikman. 2000 [1997]. "Panikattack." On *Plus 8 Classics Vol. 3: 1995–1997.* Plus 8
Records 8075.

Reese & Santonio. 1997 [1987]. "How to Play Our Music." On *Faces and Phases: The
Kevin Saunderson Collection.* Planet E Records PE65235CD.

Stacey Pullen. 1996. *DJ Kicks.* Studio K7 7049cd.

The Chemical Brothers. 1996. *Dig Your Own Hole.* Astralwerks ASW 6180.

The Winstons. 1969. *Amen Brother/Color Him Father.* Metromedia 117.

Timo Maas [DJ]. 2000. *Music for the Maases.* Kinetic Records 2–54665.

Underworld. 1998. *Beaucoup Fish.* V2/JBO 63881–27042–2.

Walt J. 1997. "Reborn." Dow Records DW–005.

1. Example 2.4a. Jeff Mills, "Jerical" (0.00–0.14)
2. Example 2.4b. Jeff Mills, "Jerical" (0.14–0.21)
3. Example 2.4c. Jeff Mills, "Jerical" (0.21–0.28)
4. Example 2.4d. Jeff Mills, "Jerical" (0.28–0.42)
5. Example 2.4e. Jeff Mills, "Jerical" (0.42–1.06)
6. Example 2.8. 808 State, "Cubik (Kings County Perspective)," mm. 1–12 (0.01–0.24)
7. Example 2.15. Plastikman, "Panik-attack" (0.00–0.16)
8. Example 2.17. Plastikman, "Panik-attack" (0.16–1.54)
9. Example 3.1. Carl Craig, "Televised Green Smoke," mm. 1–15 (0.00–0.15)
10. Example 3.2. James Ruskin, "Connected," opening loops (0.00–0.15)
11. Example 3.3. James Ruskin, "Connected," second textural combination (0.15–0.58)
12. Example 3.6. Carl Craig, "Televised Green Smoke," mm. 16–31 (0.15–0.31)
13. Example 3.8. Kenny Larkin, "Track," opening
14. Example 3.9. Kenny Larkin, "Track" (0.20ff.)
15. Example 3.10. Kenny Larkin, "Track" (0.32ff.)
16. Example 3.11. Kenny Larkin, "Track" (1.00ff.)
17. Example 3.12. Kenny Larkin, "Track" (1.46ff.)
18. Example 4.4. Underworld, "Cups" (0.44–0.59)
19. Example 4.5. Underworld, "Cups," entrance of drumbeat (0.55–1.00)
20. Example 4.6. Underworld, "Cups" (0.59–1.13)
21. Example 4.7. Underworld, "Cups" (1.13–1.28)
22. Example 4.8. Mario Più, "Communication," mm. 93–118 (2.43–3.30)
23. Example 4.9. Mario Più, "Communication," mm. 117–30 (3.26–3.50)
24. Example 4.10. Carl Craig, "Televised Green Smoke," turning the beat around
25. Example 4.11. Kenny Larkin, "Track" (2.18ff.)
26. Example 4.17. James Ruskin, "Connected," embedded grouping dissonance
27. Example 4.19. James Ruskin, "Connected," displaced embedded grouping dissonance
28. Example 5.2. 808 State, "Cubik (Kings County Perspective)," mm. 131–38 (4.14–4.30)
29. Example 5.3. 808 State, "Cubik (Kings County Perspective)," mm. 17–24 (0.32–0.47)
30. Example 5.6. Underworld, "Cups" (0.44–1.06)
31. Carl Craig, "Televised Green Smoke," complete (6.19)
32. James Ruskin, "Connected," complete (5.42)
33. Kenny Larkin, "Track," complete (6.50)
34. Mario Più, "Communication (Mas Mix)," complete (7.17)
35. Plastikman, "Panikattack," complete (8.43)
36. Underworld, "Cups," complete (11.45)

Index

Page numbers in italics refer to illustrations.

gabber (EDM genre), 34n4
garage (EDM genre), 34n4; history of, 39–40
Garnier, Laurent, 243, 253
gay people, and EDM genres, 36, 46
Geertz, Clifford, 18n20
gender: in EDM production and perfor-mance, 50–51; in histories of EDM, 46; as research category, 6
genre: in electronic dance music, 25, 32, 77–78; in relation to "style," 25n27; as research category, 6–7
Gibbon, Walter, 38
Goehr, Lydia, 122, 203n1
gramophone, 35
groove, 5; locked groove, 5; "unlock-ing" the, 5–6, 137, 256–57
grouping dissonance. See under metrical dissonance
grouping structure, 98; in relation to meter, 99, 129, 183, 186–87

Hancock, Herbie, 39n19
happy hardcore (EDM genre), 80
Haraway, Donna, 17
Hasty, Christopher, 93, 100–103, 105, 110, 115, 129n11, 146n6, 187, 205
Hatten, Robert, 109n38
Hawtin, Richie. See Plastikman
headphones, 33, 51
hi-NRG (EDM genre), 39n20
hip-hop music, 7n2; rap, 34nn5,6
Horlacher, Gretchen, 108, 127n7, 196n16
house music, 8; history of, 40–41; styles of, 40–41; use of term, 33n2, 46
Hughes, Tim, 5n1, 23, 23n25
hypermeter, 30, 183, 185–201; interac-tion with metrical dissonance, 157, 194–201; music-theoretical ap-proaches to, 185–87, 194–96; role

in DJing, 55–56; ways of creating, 189–92
Hyper-On Experience, 9

Ibiza, 44
IDM (EDM genre), 80
Imbrie, Andrew, 126
improvisation: in DJ sets, 240–42; in EDM production, 208–209, 214; in relation to analysis, 204–206
Indianapolis, 28
intro (formal section), 185, 224, 248–50
Ives, Charles, 165n23

Jackendoff, Ray, 85n6, 91, 95n20, 98–100, 105, 110, 129, 165, 186, 195–96
Jay, Adam, 60n60, 65, 66n69, 67, 71n82, 138, 204, 206–209, 211, 214–16, 232, 249
Jefferson, Marshall, 45n36
Jibaros, 249
Jimmi Journey, 21, 193, 242, 251–52
Johnson, Charles, 41
jukebox, 35
jungle/drum 'n' bass (EDM genre), 32, 229, 252–53; history of, 46–47

Kano, 153
keyboard instruments, use in EDM pro-duction, 62
Koetting, James, 29n32
Korsyn, Kevin, 15n12, 17n14
Kraftwerk, 39n19, 42
Krebs, Harald, 100, 106–11, 134, 136, 139, 140, 149n9, 157, 162, *163,* 164–65, 167n25, 168–69, 197, 199n19. *See also* layers, of motion; metrical dissonance
Krims, Adam, 23n25, 27n30, 34n5

Larkin, Kenny, "Track," 133–35, *134, 135,* 140, *140,* 149–50, *150,* 151,

reinterpretation, metrical. *See* meter, reinterpretation of
remix, 20n21, 70–71
remixer, 47
repetition, 90, 127, 167, 180–81, 195, 256; as research category, 6
Reynolds, Simon, 9, 9n8, 29n31, 34n4, 35n10, 39n19, 69n77, 78, 80n2
rhythm, 4; individual patterns, 81–89; in relation to meter, 98–106, 183, 186–87; as research category, 22–23
Rietveld, Hillegonda, 7n3, 8n5, 10, 13, 16, 33n3, 46
riff, 260
Robinson, Vicki Sue, 141n2
Rogers, Lynne, 172n34
Rothstein, William, 141n2, 185–87, 187n5, 194n14, 195n15, 196, 197
Rushton, Neil, 45
Ruskin, James, 249; "Connected," 125–28, *126, 127, 128,* 139, *139,* 150, 160, *161,* 162n21, 165, 169, 171, *172,* 183, 198, 209–12, 217, 232, *233,* 235, *236, 237, 238, 239, 294, 295–98*
Rythim is Rythim, 43, 253. *See also* May, Derrick

Samarotto, Frank, 100n26
sampler, 33, 57, 65
sampling: in EDM production, 60, 260; as research category, 6–7
Saunders, Jesse, 40
Saunderson, Kevin, 12n10, 42–43. *See also* Belleville Three, the; Deep Space; Reese and Santonio, "How to Play Our Music"
Savile, Jimmy, 36
Sawyer, Keith, 204–205
Schenker, Heinrich, 196
Scherzinger, Martin, 15n13, 23–24
Seeger, Charles, 22n23
Sensorama, "Harz," 155–56, *156*

sequencer, 33, 61, 63, 65–67, 206
sequencing, 61–62, 255; duration of sequences, 209–13; interaction with metrical dissonance, 216–21; role of, in production, 206–16
sets (DJ performances), 21; beginnings of, 248–51; climaxes of, 251–54; coherence in, 242–43, 254; form of, 30, 240–54; length of, 178; tempo within, 251–53
Shapiro, Peter, 20, 39n19, 41n26, 69n77, 80n1
Shepherd, John, 14n11
Sicko, Dan, 7, 40n23, 45n36, 46, 69n77, 153
slip-cue, 37, 55
Small, Christopher, 85
sound palette, 179–80, 259
Stanley, 71, 204, 217, 221–22, *222,* 223, 224, 226, 228, *229,* 230, 231
step entry, 65
Stephenson, Ken, 23n25
Stewart, Alexander, 23n25
studio, recording, 20n21, 36, 38, 40, 48
subcultural capital, 24
Summer, Donna, 39n20
Sun Ra, 39
Sylvester, 39n20
syncopation, 23, 108n35, 109n38, 169n30; class of rhythms, 85–89, 105, 113, 115–16
synthesizer, 33, 42n28, 62–63; synthesis in EDM production, 33

tactus, 95
Tagg, Philip, 14n11
Takemura, Nobukaza, 71
techno (EDM genre), 25; form in, 227–32; history of, 41–43; use of term, 25, 45–46
technology: "creative perversion" of, 68, 166; in relation to meter, 113–14; in relation to metrical dissonance, 165–66, 174–75; as re-

technology (*continued*)
    search category, 6; use of obsolete
    technology, 68
Temperley, David, 23n25, 86–87, *86,*
    87n9, 88n10, 90, 98–100, 108n35,
    123n1
Tenaglia, Danny, 172, 250
textural graph, 179, 180–81, 215, 259
texture, 4, 10; in relation to meter, 90–
    97, 182. *See also* layers, textural
third record, the, 94, 243
Thomson, William, 124
Thornton, Sarah, 29n31, 33n3
timbre, 8, 53–54, 95n23, 244–45
time signature, 113, 259
Timeline Live, 71. *See also* Underground
    Resistance
Tirro, Frank, 204
Toffler, Alvin, 42, 45n38, 174
track, 9n7, 34n5; as individual entity
    (unmixed), 20–21, 202. *See also*
    form
"train wreck," 56
trance (EDM genre), 10; form in, 227–
    29
transcription, 259–61; as research strat-
    egy, 20, 22, 205. *See also* nota-
    tion, musical
turning the beat around (TBA), 19, 141,
    196; in DJing, 234; reverse of, 151–
    52, 171n33

turntables, 33, 51–52; design of, 55,
    56, 58
tweaking, 54, 211, 224, 247
twelve-inch. *See* records, twelve-inch vi-
    nyl

Umek, 250
underdetermination, metrical, 111–13,
    114, 115, 129–30, 167, 193, 255–
    56
Underground Resistance, 32, 71. *See*
    also Timeline Live
Underworld: "Cups," 141–44, *141, 142,*
    143, 147, 149, 169, 173, 197,
    197, 217n12, 233, *233,* 243; Rick
    Smith, 22n22, 26, 217n12, 263

vibe, 9, 72
Village People, 38n18, 39n19
Vixen Swift, 51, 214, 245

Walser, Robert, 170
Walt J, "Reborn," 130, *131,* 150–51,
    151
Warehouse, The, 39, 40
Western classical music, use of theoreti-
    cal models based in, 23–25
The Winstons, 78, *79*
withholding the beat, 91–94, 246–47

Yeston, Maury, 94n19, 106, 108, 110

MARK J. BUTLER received a Ph.D. in Music Theory at Indiana University in 2003. He is currently Assistant Professor of Music at the University of Pennsylvania.